REPORTING WAR

REPORTING
WAR

HOW FOREIGN CORRESPONDENTS RISKED CAPTURE, TORTURE AND DEATH TO COVER WORLD WAR II

RAY MOSELEY

YALE UNIVERSITY PRESS
NEW HAVEN AND LONDON

For information about this and other Yale University Press publications, please contact:
U.S. Office: sales.press@yale.edu   yalebooks.com
Europe Office: sales@yaleup.co.uk   yalebooks.co.uk

Typeset in Adobe Garamond Pro by IDSUK (DataConnection) Ltd
Printed in Great Britain by Gomer Press Ltd, Llandysul, Ceredigion, Wales

Library of Congress Cataloging-in-Publication Data

Names: Moseley, Ray, 1932- author.
Title: Reporting war : how foreign correspondents risked capture, torture, and death to cover World War II / Ray Moseley.
Other titles: How foreign correspondents risked capture, torture and death to cover World War II
Description: New Haven : Yale University Press, [2017] | Includes bibliographical references and index.
Identifiers: LCCN 2016036163 | ISBN 9780300224665 (alk. paper)
Subjects: LCSH: World War, 1939-1945—Press coverage. | World War, 1939-1945—Journalists. | War correspondents—History—20th century. | World War, 1939-1945—Radio broadcasting and the war. | World War, 1939-1945—Mass media and the war.
Classification: LCC D798 .M67 2017 | DDC 070.4/4994053—dc23
LC record available at https://lccn.loc.gov/2016036163

A catalogue record for this book is available from the British Library.

10 9 8 7 6 5 4 3 2 1

For Caspar, Hugo and Thomas
with love
Grandpa aka Gramps

CONTENTS

PREFACE

In 1815, as the British writer Brian Cathcart has noted, London had more than fifty newspapers. Not one of them sent a reporter to Belgium to cover the battle of Waterloo and an anxious public had to wait four days for a dispatch rider to arrive in leisurely fashion with the news of Wellington's victory. Then one of the century's great news stories finally saw print. All wars are different, and coverage of wars is different in each era. World War I was a newspaper war, World War II a newspaper and radio war, and Vietnam the first televised war. Censorship has varied from country to country, from one age to another. Problems for correspondents in reaching filing points, causing serious delays in the reporting of battles that had moved on, remained more or less constant until the time of the first Gulf War, when satellite phones appeared on the battlefronts. Correspondents in all wars have faced the threat of death, but the conflict in the former Yugoslavia marked the first time, in my own experience, that cars clearly marked with large PRESS or TV lettering were sometimes deliberately fired upon. Only since the rise of Islamic State have captured correspondents been beheaded. And only in the past few years have foreign correspondents constituted an endangered species, with many newspapers and broadcasters axing all or nearly all of their foreign staffs.

The years since World War II have witnessed a remarkable and recently escalating number of wars, some of which I covered as a wire-service and newspaper correspondent, but the 1939–45 conflict remains the one most firmly rooted in my consciousness. I was a child of 12 when that war ended and, like most American boys at the time, I was enthralled by the shifting fortunes of battle and remained glued to radio reports. But, as far as I can recall, I was little aware of newspaper dispatches. Soon after the war ended, I read *Brave Men*, a compilation of war reports by Ernie Pyle, the most famous American print journalist of the conflict, and that stimulated an enduring fascination with war history as well as a budding interest in a career in journalism.

The genesis of this book came in 2011 when I read *The End*, a brilliant analysis of the collapse of the Nazi regime in 1944–5 by the British historian Ian Kershaw. Midway through the book, I began to wonder how Western correspondents in Moscow, where I was once based, had managed to cover the fighting in Stalinist Russia. Had they been able to sift the truth from the Communist government's propaganda? Had the regime allowed them to visit battlefronts? How rigorously had their reporting been censored? These questions soon led to a broader curiosity about coverage throughout the world, then about the lives and personalities of those involved. Some of the correspondents were men and women whose names were familiar to me, but most of the characters who emerged from my research were not. By and large, I thought the American correspondents came off reasonably well, and some performed superbly. But the greatest surprise was discovering that some of the best reporting, and writing, of the war came from five Australians. Four of them hailed from one city, Melbourne.

I wanted the book to encompass as many nationalities as possible, with this exception: German and Japanese correspondents have been excluded because no independent reporting was possible in those countries. The same was true of French journalists working under Nazi occupation; the only French correspondent included in the book reported for an American newspaper. One correspondent from Fascist Italy is included; he was anti-fascist and, although something of a fantasist, produced some insightful reporting as he followed German troops into the Soviet Union.

Why write about them at all, some may ask? Because it provides a fascinating glimpse into an event of immense historical importance and, for those who care about such things, the history of journalism. Their reporting and personal experiences offer a perspective that does not often appear in conventional histories, and valuable insights into how people cope under extraordinarily hazardous circumstances.

My narrative has been arbitrarily limited to a select number of journalists from the United States, the United Kingdom, Canada, Australia, the Soviet Union, South Africa, Denmark, Sweden, Italy and France—just one each from the last five countries. Those interested in reading about the experiences of photographers and newsreel cameramen will have to look elsewhere—with two exceptions: Lee Miller and Carl Mydans were photographers, but also reporters and first-class writers, so they are included.

A final, personal note: in my own career as a foreign correspondent from 1961 to 2001, which encompassed several wars, I encountered fourteen of the World War II crowd and became friends with a few of them. Not one ever mentioned his or her wartime experience, nor did I ask. Perhaps this book will make some amends for that lack of curiosity on my part.

ACKNOWLEDGMENTS

The list of people whom I have to thank for their help in bringing this book to completion is not extensive but my gratitude to them is endless. I owe a special debt of thanks to Robert Baldock, my editor at Yale, who launched my career as an author with *Mussolini's Shadow* in 1999 and welcomed my latest offering with the kind of enthusiasm he previously showed for my work. His interest and encouragement have always bolstered my spirits. With consummate professional skill, Rachael Lonsdale at Yale played the principal role in putting this book together for publication, and working with her was always a pleasure. Sophie Richmond saved me from a number of errors with her careful editing.

My son John, a more talented writer than his dad, read early chapters and contributed important suggestions for improvement, as well as encouragement to keep going. A number of friends, all of them writers and some with their own experience of reporting from far-flung outposts including war fronts, generously undertook the chore of reading every word with critical eyes, much to my profit. They include James Burke, Robin Knight, Alex Frere, Gerry Loughran and Jimmy Barden. Pat McCarty helped supply research material. Charles Glass learned of the book at a late stage and became one of its most ardent champions. Thanks are also due to Roy Reed, Ernie Dumas and Richard Longworth for promoting my cause. My daughter Ann and son-in-law Clive Jones had other priorities during the birth of this book—the birth of my grandsons Caspar and Hugo. But they cheered me on, along with other family members and friends.

I would also like to thank Mike Pride, administrator of the Pulitzer Prizes, and Sean B. Murphy of his staff for making available the Louis P. Lochner entries that won him a Pulitzer in circumstances that are now subject to question (see Chapter 21).

My greatest debt of gratitude, as always, is owed to my wife Jennifer, who gave me the initial encouragement to embark on this venture, made her own valuable suggestions for improving it, and is my enduring love and inspiration in all matters large and small.

I have made significant use of excerpts from the following books by or about war correspondents, with permission granted by the following rights holders:

Eclipse by Alan Moorehead, excerpts reprinted by permission of Pollinger Limited (www.pollingerltd.com) on behalf of the Estate of Alan Moorehead;

Brave Men by Ernie Pyle, courtesy of the Scripps Howard Foundation on behalf of the Estate of Ernie Pyle;

Weller's War: A Legendary Foreign Correspondent's Saga of World War II on 5 Continents by George Weller, copyright © by Anthony Weller. Used by permission of Crown Books, an imprint of the Crown Publishing Group, a division of Penguin Random House LLC. All rights reserved;

A Writer at War: Vasily Grossman with the Red Army, 1941–1945 by Vasily Grossman, © 2005 by Ekaterina Vasilievna Korotkova-Grossman and Elena Fedorovna Kozhichkina. English translation, introduction and commentary © 2005 by Antony Beevor and Luba Vinogradova. Used by permission of Pantheon Books, an imprint of the Knopf Doubleday Publishing Group, a division of Penguin Random House LLC. All rights reserved;

Not So Wild a Dream by Eric Sevareid, reprinted by permission of Don Congdon Associates, Inc. © 1946, renewed 1974 by Eric Sevareid;

Lee Miller's War by Antony Penrose © courtesy Antony Penrose Estate, England 2015. The Penrose Collection. All rights reserved;

European Conquest by Osmar White, courtesy of Cambridge University Press;

Combat Correspondents by Joseph R. L. Sterne, courtesy of the Maryland Historical Society;

Forward Positions by Betsy Wade © 1992 by Betsy Wade. Reproduced with the permission of the University of Arkansas Press, www.uapress.com;

War Report by BBC (edited by Desmond Hawkins). Published by BBC Books. Reprinted by permission of the Random House Group Limited;

The Year of Stalingrad by Alexander Werth, courtesy of Cyrus Gabrysch and other Werth family members.

London, September 2016

INTRODUCTION

In the long history of human conflict, nothing approaches World War II in its scale of death, destruction and descent into industrial-scale barbarity. The military historian Max Hastings has justifiably termed it the largest event in human history. It took 60 million lives and resulted in the near-obliteration of historic and less-storied cities, mass starvation, an enormous dislocation of populations. One hundred million people were mobilized but two civilians died for every soldier killed.[1] It was the first truly global war, the first to involve serious use of air power, the first in which a rapid, mechanized form of battlefield warfare appeared. It saw the introduction of atomic weapons. For all these reasons, it was the greatest news story of all time, and one whose coverage differed markedly from later conflicts.

In modern wars, the presence of women correspondents is taken for granted. In World War II, they were a novelty and the Allied military did its best to bar them from combat coverage, while the more intrepid of them did their best to circumvent the military. In today's world, race and ethnicity among correspondents matters not at all. In World War II, just twenty-seven American correspondents, including one woman, were black journalists, representing the *Pittsburgh Courier, Chicago Defender*, Baltimore *Afro-American, Norfolk Journal and Guide*, the National Negro Publishers Association and the Associated Negro Press. Only two white-owned, mainstream publications, the New York newspaper *PM* and *Liberty* magazine, employed an African-American war correspondent (the same one). There were no black broadcasters.[2]

Today's correspondents file from satellite phones and other modern means of communication, so almost every spot on the globe is a filing point. The 1939–45 brigade faced huge, sometimes insurmountable, logistical difficulties, frequently having to travel great distances to a filing center and some dispatches went out over radio links that depended on people at the other end listening at the right moment, over telephones that often proved undependable or over cable or teletype links. During the Normandy invasion, some correspondents even used carrier pigeons—with mixed results—to ferry dispatches back to England. Not infrequently, important dispatches simply disappeared—one of the most soul-destroying things that can happen to a journalist, especially one who has put his or her life on the line to get the story.

Modern communications make it difficult, if not impossible, for governments to censor dispatches. In World War II, every story passed through the hands of censors, many of them untrained and often quixotic in their decisions. Correspondents fought endless, often losing, battles with men wielding a blue pencil, largely impervious to challenge.

They were encouraged to file "hero" stories about the fighting men, and on rare occasions censored themselves to avoid reporting something they feared might hamper the war effort. In no war since then has this been true.

Correspondents wore military uniforms—it was the last war in which American correspondents did so—and were given the honorary rank and privileges of officers. The uniforms carried a large C on the sleeve to distinguish them from fighting men (an initial suggestion of WC was sensibly rejected). The British military, with a penchant for abbreviation, referred to them as Warcos.

But some parallels can be found between war reporting now and seventy years ago. Since the Iraq War, which began in 2003, correspondents have been embedded with the military rather than operating on their own. In World War II, the same was true. Most of the time they traveled with military escorts, rode in military Jeeps, fed on army rations and often depended on the military to get dispatches to filing points.

Correspondents' reports, and their personal experiences, are an important part of the history of the war, contributing to the record from which professional histories were compiled. Yet there has been no serious attempt at a comprehensive history of the correspondents and their coverage since Richard Collier's *Warcos* in 1989. Surprisingly, much important material, some of it hidden away for decades, has only come to light since then. This book reports on-the-spot dispatches but also relies heavily on memoirs in which writers could report freely on matters censored during the war. Their stories are spiced with high drama, humor, frustration, fear and camaraderie. Occasionally reporters engaged in professional back-biting, not surprising among people who lived under constant tension and endless proximity to one another.

Those who covered the war represented a cross-section of societies from which they came: urban sophisticates who had graduated from leading universities, others from rural hinterlands who in some cases had never been outside their own countries, talented linguists and reporters with no knowledge of foreign languages, seasoned war correspondents and neophytes. The things that perhaps most of them shared were a sense of adventure and curiosity, a strong sense of patriotism and a willingness to undergo extreme hardship including the risk of death for extended periods. Some served for the entire length of the conflict, some only a few months or years.

The Associated Press (AP) correspondent Hal Boyle joked that war reporting was "the simplest job in journalism. All you need is a strong stomach, a weak mind and plenty of endurance." It was no harder than police reporting, the only difference being that "you're a little closer to the bullets."[3]

Of about 1,800 correspondents accredited to Allied forces at one time or another, sixty-nine met death on the battlefield, in accidents or as a result of disease. Three news agencies, the AP, United Press (UP) and Reuters, were hardest hit, each losing five men. No women were among the casualties.[4]

By the end of the war, 2.2 per cent of American reporters had been killed and 6.8 per cent wounded, compared with 2.5 per cent and 4.2 per cent for the American military. There is no overall figure for Soviet correspondents but sixteen working for just one newspaper, the army publication *Krasnaya Zvezda* (Red Star), died between June 1941 and spring 1944. Sixty Soviet photographers were killed in that period. A memorial to all the journalistic dead was unveiled at the Pentagon in September 1948. And on October 7, 1986, a tree was dedicated and a plaque unveiled at Arlington National Cemetery to honor more than 200 war correspondents killed in the last 100 years.[5]

Some correspondents were well known when the war started or, like Ernest Hemingway and John Steinbeck, renowned for something other than news reporting. Some like Edward R. Murrow and Walter Cronkite in the United States, Richard Dimbleby in the United Kingdom and Australia's Alan Moorehead rose from relative obscurity to national or world fame and brilliant postwar careers. Others enjoyed but a brief moment in the limelight. Twelve American correspondents won Pulitzer Prizes.[6]

Several American newspapers that had never employed foreign correspondents before the war, and never did so afterward, sent reporters abroad mainly to file stories about hometown boys involved in the fighting. Some correspondents worked for major newspapers, agencies or broadcast outlets that no longer exist; how many Americans below a certain age remember the *Chicago Daily News*, Mutual Broadcasting, *Collier's Weekly*, International News Service

(INS)? How many in Britain recall the *News Chronicle, Daily Herald* and the Kemsley newspapers, or a time when the *Daily Express* was an important world newspaper?

In writing about the enemy, correspondents routinely resorted to epithets that would hardly pass muster in journalism today. The Japanese were Japs or Nips, the Germans were Nazis (as though all of the population belonged to Hitler's Nazi Party), Jerries, Huns, Krauts or Heinies, the Italians were Eyeties. All this reflected usages of the time, and would not have offended many readers or listeners.

But one unforgiveable slur appeared in the memoir of Australian correspondent Noel Monks, referring to a black American soldier. Monks ridiculed him and called him "the coon."[7] And his British publisher let him get away with it. Readers offended by his racism may be pleased to know that, for wholly different reasons, Monks' American wife, Mary Welsh, left him, albeit for the self-aggrandizing boor Hemingway had become, and his publisher later went out of business.

Epithets aside, journalistic usage has changed in other ways. Some correspondents referred to American infantry troops as doughboys, a term popularized in World War I that sounds quaint now. It was never used in later wars. Likewise, French infantry troops were *poilus*, another term of World War I vintage now out of use.

Most correspondents wrote of Allied troops as "our" forces and referred to "our" missions, "our" victories. Allied forces didn't advance; "we" advanced. In a war unlike any other, a war in which the future of Western civilization was at stake, there was no pretense at even-handedness nor should there have been. That kind of usage has been absent from subsequent war reporting, but it remains a besetting journalistic sin in other contexts. Any journalist who has ever attended a U.S. State Department or White House briefing has heard reporters inquire as to what "our" policy is toward this or that country.

On the European front, a significant number of correspondents gained initial experience of battle in covering the Spanish Civil War or the Italian war against Ethiopia. Three American women—Martha Gellhorn, Virginia Cowles and Eleanor Packard—blazed a trail for their sex in Spain. In Asia, the Japanese invasion of China in 1937 afforded others a first taste of war coverage. But the vast majority were greenhorns at this aspect of journalism.

Hollywood and popular fiction present war correspondents as macho types, and there were some swashbucklers, such as Hemingway. But a fear of death or serious injury hung over many for years at a stretch and most did not resort to any pretense of bravado. "The war correspondents who really deserved the title, who earned their trench coats the hard way, were the ones who sought the action … Some were almost recklessly brave," Walter Cronkite, himself a fledgling UP correspondent during the war, wrote long afterward. "There were others whom I counted really as the most courageous. They were the ones who were scared to death, frequently admitted it, but went into action with the troops anyway because, well, dammit, they were reporters and that's where the story was."[8]

International law prohibited correspondents from carrying weapons or engaging in combat, but a few did and some either fired weapons or used them for the purpose of intimidation. The circumstances differed greatly. One correspondent shot down a German plane after gunners aboard the bomber on which he was flying were put out of action. A few others, unbidden by direct threats to their own lives, chose to take on the role of soldiers and killed enemy troops.

The Allied military employed correspondents of their own, to serve newspapers and magazines intended for the troops. Three from the army newspaper *Stars and Stripes* went on to major journalistic careers: Sgts. Andy Rooney (CBS), Jack Foisie (*Los Angeles Times*) and Herbert Mitgang (*New York Times*). A few correspondents quit the battlefronts for the army. A few others tried to do so but were told they were rendering a more valuable service as correspondents. Some reporters, sad to say, doubled as spies.

The correspondents faced bullets, bombs, mines, boobytraps, deadly tropical diseases, desert dust storms and months or years of separation from families. And, like all correspondents in all wars, none could know what was going on outside their immediate theater of operations, so depended for the wider picture on official communiqués. If things were going badly, communiqués often obscured the truth.

In the grim days that followed Pearl Harbor, the New York-based writer E. B. White quickly saw through this smokescreen. "Before Pearl Harbor the American press was doing the finest job imaginable," he wrote in early 1942. "Since Pearl Harbor it has been a touch on the wistful side." He cited a newspaper headline over a UP dispatch, ALLIES SINK JAP CRUISER. The coverage, he said, played down the fact the Japanese had seized in that battle the second largest naval and air base in the Dutch East Indies. The *New York Telegram* even carried a standing box headline called Good News "under which it collects each afternoon a few nosegays, favorable to us, ruinous to the enemy":

When, day after day, you are shaken by the detonations of American success and hear only small puffballs of the enemy's fire, a very definite feeling grows in you that Japan has really accomplished very little. The

facts show that the Empire of the Rising Sun is doing very well indeed . . .
If a man were to paper his den with headlines he would find himself living
in a hall of triumph.[9]

Ralph G. Martin of *Stars and Stripes* thought reporting was sometimes
circumscribed by public sentiment. "The tendency was to write what the
public wanted to hear," he wrote. "They felt that nobody wanted to hear
about the blood and the death. Most people wanted to hear about the successes
and the heroes. Most papers urged their correspondents to do that."[10]

Steinbeck, who filed mostly light war features for the *New York Herald-Tribune*, wrote after the war:

> There were no cowards in the American Army, and of all the brave men the
> private in the infantry was the bravest and noblest . . . We had no cruel or
> ambitious or ignorant commanders. If the disorganized insanity we were a
> part of came a cropper, it was not only foreseen but a part of a grander
> strategy out of which victory would emerge . . . We [correspondents] were
> all a part of the War Effort. We went along with it, and not only that, we
> abetted it . . . By this I don't mean the correspondents were liars. They
> were not . . . It is in the things not mentioned that the untruth lies.

Frustrated by his battles with censors, Steinbeck mentioned in one report
Herodotus' account of the battle of Salamis between Greeks and Persians in
480 B.C. Navy censors killed it. Their rulebook said place names could not be
mentioned and Steinbeck's dispatch referred to several classical place names.[11]
This book is replete with similar examples of censors going strictly by the
book—and worse. Only one correspondent of that era is on record as favoring
censorship; John Thompson of the *Chicago Tribune*, attending a 1988 dedication of a Normandy museum, told a military officer: "Obviously, some intelligent form of press censorship should have been in use in Vietnam."[12]

In his war memoir, Cyrus Sulzberger of the *New York Times* wrote: "The
jackal of our era is the war correspondent. His function is to describe in all its
horror how men kill each other, in what manner they die and for what cause
they imagine. His own and the censor's prejudice combine to see that this is
done in glowing terms."[13]

In this respect, nothing had changed since World War I. Wilbur Forrest of
UP wrote after that conflict: "The war correspondent of 1914–1918 was . . .
a sort of glorified disseminator of official military propaganda . . . The critical
correspondent was outflanked, decimated, routed."[14]

In World War II the Axis powers resorted to censorship but the Germans, while censoring broadcasts, allowed newspaper copy in the early stages of war to go out freely; they simply expelled those who wrote things they did not like, thus imposing a burden of self-censorship on the press. A steady procession of correspondents was expelled or left Berlin in disgust.

In his book *The First Casualty*, Phillip Knightley concluded that correspondents could have done a better job and suggested they identified too closely with the military, were guided too often by patriotic zeal and should have resisted censorship more vigorously. Correspondents' fierce battles with censors are on abundant record, but otherwise these are fair comments. Knightley quoted an unwarrantedly harsh judgment by Charles Lynch, a Canadian correspondent for Reuters, who wrote thirty years after the war:

> It's humiliating to look back at what we wrote during the war. It was crap
> . . . We were a propaganda arm of our governments. At the start the censors
> enforced that, but by the end we were our own censors. We were cheer-
> leaders. I suppose there wasn't an alternative at the time. It was total war.
> But, for God's sake, let's not glorify our role. It wasn't good journalism. It
> wasn't journalism at all.[15]

Fletcher Pratt, a writer on military affairs, said World War II, "instead of being the best reported war in history . . . was very nearly the worst reported." Most Americans, he said, remained ignorant of the larger issues, the way the war was fought and what actually happened. Robert S. Allen, a former Washington columnist who became a colonel on Gen. George Patton's staff, said the coverage was "stupid." Most correspondents "were scarcely more than police reporters" and were either "lazy or ignorant." The sage of Baltimore, H. L. Mencken, called the correspondents "a sorry lot," complaining that they turned out "dope stuff" or "maudlin stuff about the common soldier." He cited Ernie Pyle, the most famous American print correspondent, as a good example. "He did well what he set out to do, but that couldn't be called factual reporting of the war."[16]

A definitive judgment would require a reading of six years of war dispatches, and not just those collected in anthologies. But some great reporting came out of the war, reporting that even in a later, more critical era would have been regarded as such. There were correspondents content to stay close to command posts and report communiqués. But many others took enormous risks to tell what was happening upfront.

A more balanced appraisal, albeit one limited to comparing coverage with that of World War I, was offered by Joseph J. Matthews of the University of

Minnesota in his 1957 book, *Reporting the Wars*. "There were no news black-outs, no prolonged periods in which the public had little idea of what was taking place," he wrote:

> Nor, with a few exceptions, were major battles or campaigns misrepre-sented as to their military success or failure. To a greater degree than in World War I the tone of the news was realistic. Unfounded atrocity stories, fanciful heroics and victories without loss but with huge enemy tolls, appeared less often than in the earlier war.[17]

But there were significant failings. Battlefield defeats could not be hidden from the public, but critical analysis of the reasons for those defeats was largely missing, largely because of censors but to some extent, perhaps, because of restraints correspondents imposed upon themselves. Racism was rife in the American military, leading to riots between black and white GIs in England, and among the soldiers a minority became black marketeers, rapists or deserters. These were not stories most correspondents wanted to tell, and even sixty years later they were largely glossed over in Tom Brokaw's *The Greatest Generation*. The American myth of an almost unblemished generation of heroes was born in the newspaper pages and broadcasts of 1941–5 and is alive and well. The media outlets that the correspondents represented were some-times amiss in other ways, most glaringly in their reluctance to accept the veracity of the initial reports of concentration camp horrors their own corre-spondents revealed. A broader discussion of the successes and shortcomings of war reporting will be found in Chapter 21.

It is surprising that there was no demand from the media after the war for an inquiry into the censorship restrictions, their effect on the public's right to know and the implications for future wars. One possible conclusion is that newspapers and broadcast companies shared a belief that circumstances required a limitation on press freedom.

In 1943 the celebrated *Collier's* magazine correspondent and author Quentin Reynolds penned an unusual tribute to war correspondents. Describing himself as "a synthetic part-time war correspondent," he wrote: "War correspondents for the news services and the daily papers today are doing the greatest job any group of newspapermen ever did. The fabled 'old timers' who drank their way through past wars couldn't keep up with men like these." The average pay of correspondents was $100 a week, while "the highly paid radio commentators, writers of books and 'military experts' get the cash and the glory."[18]

Considering the stresses under which correspondents lived and worked, it is hardly surprising that some drank to excess when the opportunity arose and most smoked endlessly. In their memoirs, it is striking how often correspondents refer to their craving for cigarettes. Invariably, when given the chance, they gave cigarettes to dying soldiers. The addiction to tobacco may help explain why some had relatively brief lives. Joe James Custer of UP said correspondents relied heavily on beer and cigarettes and thus were hardly fit physically to cope with combat situations.

One especially odd fact: Cyrus Sulzberger, Ray Brock of the *New York Times*, Henry Gorrell of UP and Cedric Salter of London's *Daily Mail* went to war accompanied by pet dogs. Sulzberger's dog was slightly wounded in a bombing attack on Salonika, giving him the distinction of being one of two known journalistic canine casualties of the war. Another dog adopted by a correspondent in Normandy was later run over by a tank.

Some of the more harrowing accounts of battle came from correspondents who joined troops in seaborne landings—in North Africa, the Italian mainland and Normandy, to a lesser extent in Sicily, but above all in the Pacific. Every battle there involved going ashore on heavily defended islands under Japanese fire. While the invading troops could fire back, the correspondents had no defenses except to dig into the earth as rapidly as possible. That almost none died in the landings is one of the more remarkable aspects of the war. That great courage was required to take part is indisputable.

Editors routinely caution war correspondents not to take unnecessary risks, warning that no story is worth their losing their lives. It is a fairly meaningless mantra, for each correspondent in each battle situation must alone judge how far to go to get a story and such judgments can be notoriously fallible. In no conflict in history did so many correspondents face so many threats to life as in World War II. By any measure, they were a remarkable group of men and women and their exploits—not just their achievements but their failings as well—are largely but not entirely viewed through their own perceptive eyes in the account that follows.

CHAPTER 1

HITLER UNLEASHES THE WAR

At 4:40 a.m. on September 1, 1939, the German battleship Schleswig-Holstein, anchored in Danzig harbor, opened fire on a Polish fort at Westerplatte, a Baltic Sea peninsula. These were the opening shots of a European conflict that gradually would spread elsewhere. An hour later, the first of 1.5 million German soldiers began pouring into Poland, and German aircraft began raining bombs on Warsaw and other cities. Adolf Hitler and his great nemesis, the Soviet dictator Josef Stalin, had agreed a secret pact on August 23 to partition Poland between them. Stalin waited until September 17 to begin his offensive. Poland boasted the fourth largest army in Europe but few modern weapons. The main army contingents surrendered on September 29, and fighting ended on October 5.

Lynn Heinzerling of the AP and George Kidd of UP shared the distinction of being the first correspondents to hear the opening shots of World War II. A few hours before the shelling of Danzig began, Heinzerling overheard a German officer in his hotel place an urgent 3:15 a.m. wake-up call and understood the implications of that. Roused from sleep at 4:47 a.m. by the shelling of the Westerplatte, Heinzerling later wrote: "It came rolling up from the harbor like the rumble of doom. Men began to die here as Hitler stepped out on the road to ruin." Kidd also knew something was up and prowled the streets, then woke up the acting British consul, F. M. Shepherd, at 2:15 a.m. to tell him German correspondents were on the street, winding up movie cameras.[1]

In Katowice, in southwest Poland near the German frontier, 27-year-old Clare Hollingworth was jolted awake by the sound of explosions. Then aircraft roaring overhead. Looking out a window, she saw German bombers and the flash of artillery fire coming from the border, less than 20 miles away. Hollingworth became the first correspondent to report on the war within earshot of the border. (With the alteration of Polish territory after the war, Katowice is no longer close to the German frontier.) A less probable journalist in the role could hardly be imagined. She had never written a news story before London's *Daily Telegraph* hired her just seven days earlier to report on war from Poland, if it came. The fact she had previously worked for a refugee organization in Poland helped her land the job.

As shells and bombs exploded around her, Hollingworth telephoned Robin Hankey, a friend of hers at the British Embassy in Warsaw. "Robin, the war has begun!" she shouted. "Are you sure, old girl?" he responded. She held the phone out her bedroom window, and Hankey's doubts vanished. He advised her to get out of the city.

Three days earlier, Hollingworth had scooped the world press with a report on the first solid evidence that Germany intended to invade. She borrowed the car of John Anthony Thwaites, the British consul in Katowice, and drove into Germany. A gust of wind lifted up hessian sheets strung alongside the road, revealing hundreds of tanks, armored cars and field artillery. Her story appeared on the *Daily Telegraph*'s front page on August 29 under the headline: "1,000 Tanks Massed on Polish Border, 10 Divisions Reported Ready for Swift Strike." "The German military machine is now ready for instant action," she wrote.

Now with action under way, Hollingworth telephoned Hugh Carleton Greene, the *Daily Telegraph* correspondent in Warsaw, at 5:30 a.m. After she dictated a dispatch to him, he phoned the Foreign Ministry. An official told him: "Absolute nonsense. We are still negotiating." But as they spoke, air-raid sirens began wailing across Warsaw and bombs began to fall.

Hollingworth and Thwaites set out in his car for Krakow as German planes swooped down to rake the Katowice streets with bullets and bombs. The next day, determined to get to the front, she drove off in the car that Thwaites had generously put at her disposal. But the road was blocked with retreating Polish troops, dead and wounded soldiers, and horses. She turned back.

She and Thwaites set off for Lublin on Sunday, September 3, and heard on the radio that Britain and France had declared war on Germany. They were now enemy aliens, subject to arrest by the Germans. "It was the worst moment of the war for me and I felt slightly sick," she wrote. On September 6, they drove from Lublin to Warsaw, only to find that all British subjects had left. They headed back to Lublin. "I had been really scared and now I was exhausted and hungry as I had not eaten all day," Hollingworth wrote. But she had taken a bottle of champagne from Greene's flat and they drank that before arriving in Lublin at 2 a.m.

Hollingworth decided to return to Warsaw. "I was not being brave—I certainly did not feel courageous—ignorant, perhaps, and naive," she wrote in her memoirs. "My overriding feeling was enthusiasm for a good story, the story on the fall of Warsaw to the Nazi divisions. Who could resist that?" Her British colleague Cedric Salter wrote that she was "the most foolhardily brave journalist of all the Anglo-Americans in Poland." She traveled alone, over roads jammed with refugees, while German fighter planes poured down machine-gun fire. Then she ran into a German army detachment. Paralyzed with fright, she sat watching the troops before she recovered and "drove madly" across fields, back to Lublin.

Hollingworth crossed into Romania on September 14 and filed a story. After a brief return to Poland, she told Greene that Russia had invaded Poland. "Nonsense," he said. They went back to Poland but, seeing Russian tanks approaching, hastened back to Romania. She soon resigned from the *Telegraph* and joined the *Daily Express.*[2]

* * *

Hollingworth's report from inside Germany three days before the invasion of Poland may have provided the most solid evidence of coming war, but German belligerence toward its neighbor had kept Europe on edge for weeks beforehand. Yet some news organizations were slow to respond. In late August, the UP's Wallace Carroll approached British Minister of Health Walter Elliott after a Cabinet meeting and asked what the Cabinet had decided. "We decided that if Poland is invaded we will fight," Elliott replied. A few days later Frederick Kuh, also of UP London, reported the Germans had delivered what amounted to an ultimatum to the Poles. UP headquarters in New York warned both correspondents not to "get out on a limb" in suggesting war was imminent. The rival AP quoted a "trustworthy and authoritative informant" in Berlin as saying a German–Polish compromise was at hand and war averted. UP asked its Berlin bureau for a matching story but its correspondents, convinced that war was coming, declined to oblige.[3]

On the last day of August, 31-year-old Edward R. Murrow of CBS, then relatively unknown, told his audience the British government had announced an evacuation of children, mothers, blind persons and cripples from London and other cities. "Poland should conclude from this decision that war is being regarded as inevitable," he said. When the German attack came, he spoke of "a war which may spread over the world like a dark stain of death and destruction."[4]

Despite the warning signs, there had been no rush of correspondents to Poland. The handful of resident correspondents, some of them still in their twenties, was joined a few days before the outbreak of hostilities by 28-year-old Patrick Maitland of *The Times* of London, a member of a Scottish noble family, and Salter, a tall, handsome correspondent of London's *Daily Mail*. The *New York Times* was represented by a local stringer (part-time correspondent). It may have been just as well; after the invasion, Poland shut down communications with the outside world. When the government fled Warsaw, correspondents followed—desperate to reach Romania and file their dispatches. It became an exercise not in war coverage so much as in staying one step ahead of an army advancing at terrifying speed. In the absence of correspondents' reports, the world had to rely on Warsaw Radio and the German press and radio for news from the battlefronts.

It would be difficult to imagine coverage of a great war today beginning in such a shambolic fashion. The warning signs were plentiful enough, but newspapers, wire services and broadcast outlets—no doubt lulled by a false hope that war could be averted—did not rush correspondents to Poland, consider how to get around such possibilities as a shutdown of communications or plan on how to extricate those few correspondents on the scene once they could no longer function effectively and could even face arrest. The improvisations of the correspondents themselves could not be faulted.

* * *

After Hollingworth's call to Hugh Carleton Greene on September 1, he telephoned Maitland at 5:20 a.m. to tell him the war was on. "I was too bunged with sleep," Maitland wrote. "The news made no impression. It jumbled itself up with a dream." He went back to bed, then 10 minutes later woke with a start. "This time I bounded out of bed, ran to the phone, called up Greene to ask whether he had really spoken to me or not."

Soon he saw German bombers circle over Warsaw. Polish fighter planes engaged the bombers and several German planes plummeted to earth "with long, weird streamers of fiery smoke trailing behind like the tail of some ink-exuding fish." But the fighters soon disappeared and the Germans had the skies to themselves.

Hollingworth, according to Maitland, came through with a "splendid" story before she left Katowice. Local Nazis there had attempted a rising but had been quickly overwhelmed. "Clare had seen a score of them rounded up, herded into a lorry, driven outside the town, machine-gunned against a wall."

The first heavy bombing of Warsaw, including the ghetto, occurred that afternoon. "Here and there in the doorways already blown out sat huddled groups of homeless Jewish families, bewildered," Maitland wrote. "The men's long black coats, their greasy ringlets, their messy beards, only emphasized the horror."

Afterward Maitland remembered a dinner that night with Alex Small of the *Chicago Tribune* and the 29-year-old Greene, who had recently been expelled from Berlin. He described Small as a man who "takes a pride in being blunt, pretending to be tough." Greene was "fair, curly-haired, has a grin like a half moon, immense feet at the end of long legs and arms that dangle about." They had just experienced one of the most memorable days of their lives, but what did they talk about at dinner? The war? Oddly, no. "Greene had much to say that was intelligent, but both he and I were outclassed by Small, who held us fascinated for an hour with critical observations on Thucydides, Euripides, Aristophanes, Xenophon," Maitland wrote. Greene, the brother of novelist Graham Greene, soon abandoned journalism and became a Royal Air Force (RAF) interrogator of war prisoners. Before 1940 was out, he had joined the BBC, and would serve as its director-general from 1960 to 1969.[5]

Salter went to a Warsaw bar with two cameramen and they were arrested as German spies. But he talked police into releasing them. That afternoon, he and one of the cameramen visited the bomb-damaged Warsaw industrial district. A policeman, convinced they were spies, forced them into a taxi, pointing a pistol at them, and a crowd hurled stones as the taxi pulled away. They were released with profuse apologies 15 minutes later.

When the exodus from Warsaw began, Salter got away with the help of the *Mail*'s stringer, an Englishman named Sykes, who had lived in Poland for years. Sykes presented him with "an immense service revolver and a bottle of whisky." The revolver, he explained, was to repel attempts by panic-stricken people to commandeer his car. Salter joined forces with other correspondents, and described Maitland as: "young, in the Rudyard Kipling tradition. He is tall and thin, with horn-rimmed spectacles, and wears his hair long. He wore a loose bow tie, riding breeches and boots and a black trench coat upon which had been sewn two Union Jacks and, in Tory blue, 'The Times, London.'" This gear was surmounted by an Alaskan trapper's fur cap, "with ear pieces to protect him from the summer sun. His appearance in remote Polish villages . . . created something like a major panic, but served us well in maintaining the valuable Continental belief that all Englishmen are harmlessly insane." This cortege reached Romania on September 8, where correspondents were able to file their first dispatches since leaving Warsaw.[6]

* * *

Ed Beattie of UP watched the bombing from his hotel room and dictated a running account to UP in Amsterdam. Then calls to foreign countries were prohibited and no incoming calls permitted, so Beattie fell back on the use of a wireless service. Dispatches took up to 30 hours to reach western Europe or the United States. Then, like other correspondents, he was cut off.[7]

Elmer Peterson, the AP bureau chief, got a call through to the AP in Budapest, and he and Lloyd Lehrbas took turns dictating copy to Robert Parker Jr. While Parker was hard at work, 39-year-old Robert St. John walked into his bureau. Weeks earlier St. John, who had worked for the AP in the U.S. but quit to buy a farm in New Hampshire, realized war was approaching and tried to get a job as a war correspondent. Everywhere he went, he was told he was too old. So he and his wife Eda closed the farm, took their meager savings and sailed for Europe, hoping for better luck once they got there.

Born in Chicago, St. John was in a high school writing class with Ernest Hemingway and their teacher kept them after class one day to tell them: "Neither one of you will ever learn to write." At age 16, St. John lied about his age to enlist in the Navy toward the end of World War I. In 1923, he and his brother Archer founded the *Cicero* [Illinois] *Tribune* and he became, at 21, the youngest editor-publisher in the U.S. He ran a series of exposés about Al Capone's Cicero brothels and other operations. Four Capone gangsters accosted him in 1925 and beat him severely. Capone later bought his newspaper to silence him, and he joined the AP.

Bearded like an Old Testament prophet, St. John arrived with his wife in Budapest on the eve of war. At a restaurant they were having trouble understanding the menu, so he had the bright idea of going to the AP bureau and inviting a Hungarian speaker to join them and order for them. When he introduced himself, Parker looked up and told him the war had just started. Then, learning that St. John had worked for the AP, Parker told him to sit down and go to work. Eda was left at the restaurant to fend for herself.

Parker hit upon the idea of hiring jobless Poles to monitor Polish radio stations. Thus the AP managed to keep filing stories during the news blackout. Warsaw Mayor Stefan Starzynski frequently broadcast over Warsaw Radio, and St. John wrote that the AP staff in Budapest "took a fancy to him." "From his several broadcasts a day we were able to write dispatches giving as complete a picture of the situation in Warsaw as if we had had half a dozen reporters of our own up there." After the fall of Poland, Starzynski was never heard from again. Berlin announced he had committed suicide, but later said he was a prisoner at the Dachau concentration camp. Ten months later, a report reached London that he had been shot.

The Budapest office still had no word on what had happened to the AP's Warsaw correspondents, Peterson and Lehrbas, so Dan De Luce was sent into Poland to look for them. St. John described De Luce as a man in his twenties from Yuma, Arizona, blond, six-feet-plus in height and with a physique like a football player. He had been the AP's Hollywood reporter before his assignment to Budapest.

De Luce left on September 7. Three days later Peterson phoned from Romania, saying he and Lehrbas had followed the Polish government out of the country. (Lehrbas soon abandoned journalism and became an aide to Gen. Douglas MacArthur in Australia.) Three days later De Luce got his first call through to Budapest from Lvov (L'viv today, part of Ukraine). Back in Budapest the next day, "he came into the office as nonchalantly as if he had merely been down the street for a glass of beer," St. John wrote.

De Luce read the copy he had filed from Lvov and blew up at Parker for having rewritten some of it. He only calmed down when a congratulatory cable arrived from New York, signed by AP General Manager Kent Cooper. Cooper appended an editorial that H. L. Mencken had written in the *Baltimore Sun*: "One Daniel De Luce is worth all the gaudy journalistic wizards who sit in the safe hotels of unbombed capitals and tell us not what has happened but what to think."[8]

* * *

Denis Sefton Delmer of London's *Daily Express* left Warsaw five days after the war began, deeply ashamed not to be sharing the fate of the Polish people. Even after the city's outskirts were bombed, he wrote, Poles could not believe Warsaw was in danger. "People sat chatting on the café terraces. The horse cabs trotted gaily about the streets, carrying their usual freight of laughing lovers for a promenade on the banks of the Vistula."

Delmer, born in Berlin and the son of an Australian university lecturer, traveled to the Romanian border with Nathan Gurdus, a Polish Jew working for the *Express*. Police refused an exit visa even when Gurdus produced a medical certificate showing he was physically unfit for military service; he had been born with legs withered below the knees and could only move in a wheelchair. One doctor said: "You want to desert us, you Jewish pig? . . . Of course you can do military service. You can lie on your belly and fire a machine gun in a heroic last stand." Delmer had to go to five military physicians before one, prompted by a bribe from Delmer, would certify that Gurdus was incapable of military service. Later Gurdus and his wife Irka immigrated to Palestine.[9]

* * *

In Berlin, CBS correspondent William L. Shirer wrote in his diary that he hoped the French and British "bomb the hell out of this town without getting me. The ugly shrill of the sirens, the rushing to a cellar with your gas mask (if you have one), the utter darkness of the night—how will human nerves stand that for long?" Two days later, when Britain and France declared war, he noted: "Today, no excitement, no hurrahs, no cheering, no throwing of flowers, no war fever, no war hysteria."

Like Murrow, Shirer was a pioneer of broadcast news reporting. A veteran *Chicago Tribune* and wire-service correspondent who had worked in Germany, France, India and other places, he had been hired by Murrow in 1937, made his first CBS broadcast when Germany marched into Austria in 1938, then had been assigned to Berlin.[10]

Virginia Cowles, a 29-year-old Boston socialite and glamorous beauty who had previously covered the Spanish Civil War, arrived in Berlin just before the attack on Poland to report for the London *Sunday Times*. Like Shirer, she was intrigued by the passivity of Germans after Hitler announced the war to the Reichstag. "Although the avenue [Unter den Linden] was strung with loudspeakers and the words rang through the capital with vehemence, we were struck by the unenthusiastic response they drew. Even the storm troopers showed little enthusiasm."[11]

* * *

Salter went back to Poland on September 12. "I had left a people hard pressed, but still fighting, and even optimistic of ultimate victory. Now I found a terrified and broken country . . . The Polish retreat was now the Polish rout." Three times he had to dive into ditches as planes swept down and bullets smacked off the road. All along the route, purely Jewish settlements seemed to have been singled out for comprehensive destruction.

On September 17 he learned of the Russian invasion, went back across the border and saw Russian women soldiers. "They were strapping but not uncomely wenches, and they looked capable of knocking out any two ordinary men." Caught in an air-raid in Zaleszczyki, Salter ran into a butcher's shop as a bomb exploded 50 yards away. The ceiling came down and Salter was "neck deep" in the carcasses of sheep and cows. About 200 people in a nearby square were killed or injured. He hurried back to Romania.[12]

Richard Mowrer of the *Chicago Daily News* and the *News Chronicle*'s Willy Forrest were arrested and held for four hours in Zaleszczyki, suspected of being spies. Then Mowrer stripped to his underwear and waded across the Dniester River to Romania. The prematurely bald, 27-year-old Mowrer, described by Maitland as "a short, mousy-looking person of courage and resource," had told his colleagues before the war: "Well, chaps, frankly I'm scared. I don't *want* to get hurt." He was later described by CBS correspondent Cecil Brown as one of the most deceptive-looking men he had ever known: "He is the prototype of Caspar Milquetoast [a timid comic strip character], young, blond and balding, extremely slow spoken . . . But Dick is a fighter and, in his quiet way, could be pushed around with about the same ease as a mountain." Mowrer was the son of *Chicago Daily News* editor Paul Scott Mowrer. His uncle, Edgar Ansel Mowrer, was one of the newspaper's famed foreign correspondents.[13]

Otto Tolischus, a balding, Lithuanian-born Berlin correspondent for the *New York Times*, went into Poland and reported on September 11: "The Germans are today crushing Poland like a soft-boiled egg. After having broken through the shell of Polish border defenses, the Germans found inside . . . little more than a soft yolk."[14]

Joseph Grigg, a Berlin-based UP correspondent, flew and drove over battlefields after the German victory. "It was flesh and blood and sheer human courage pitted against tanks and Stukas [dive bombers] and a new technique of warfare." He was with the first group of foreign journalists to reach Warsaw on October 5, when Hitler staged a victory parade there. "The whole center of the city had been laid in ruins. Dead horses still lay rotting in the parks, their carcasses half hacked up by starving Polish troops during the siege. New graves bulged the grass alongside streetcar tracks . . . The brand new central railway station was scarcely recognizable."[15]

Tolischus reported from Berlin on November 25: "The Polish nation is . . . to be annihilated as a nation and whatever is left of it either denationalized or reduced to an inferior helot people without any national consciousness, without any intelligentsia and, therefore, without a chance or hope of rising again." The Germans, he wrote, had introduced labor duty for Polish Jewish men up to 70 years of age and for Jewish women up to 55. Such reporting and commentary were not to be tolerated for long in Hitler's Germany. In March 1940, after seven years in Berlin, Tolischus was expelled. That same year, he won the Pulitzer Prize.[16]

* * *

The British and French declarations of war produced an expectation in London of imminent German bomber attack. On the opening night of war, 29-year-old James Reston, a Scotsman who had joined the staff of the *New York Times* that day, wandered through London streets and sent his first dispatch. "I wasn't scared, I was terrified. I had read all the horror stories about the new German bombs that were supposed to pulverize concrete skyscrapers and toss battleships out of the water." He shipped his wife and infant son to the United States and wrote: "What was I doing here, waiting for the slaughter, frightened and ashamed of my fear?"[17]

Henry T. Gorrell, a veteran of Spanish Civil War coverage, arrived on September 1 to join the UP bureau. "London was teeming with excitement, but there was no panic." He emerged from an Underground station in Piccadilly and heard deafening explosions. The Irish Republican Army had planted time bombs outside shop windows and several bystanders were injured.[18]

Ed Murrow reported on September 9: "Motorists who claim in the future to have seen zebras in the forests should not be disbelieved. The New Forest Common Earth Defense Association advocated today that wild ponies should have white stripes painted on them so that they may be more easily seen by motorists in blackouts."[19]

Two days later, London morning papers printed a special edition with news that a British Expeditionary Force had landed in France. The report had been cleared by censors but the Ministry of Information changed its mind and Scotland Yard impounded the war extras. The news finally was allowed to appear in afternoon papers the next day. Angry correspondents descended on a government spokesman, who claimed news of the landings might have given "vital information to the enemy." That brought a roar of laughter; the French radio had broadcast news of the landings on the afternoon of September 11.

John Gunther of the *Chicago Daily News* asked for a copy of a leaflet the RAF had dropped over Germany but was told he could not have it because publication "might give the enemy vital information." Two million copies of the leaflet had been dropped on Germany.

In the months that followed, wrote Frank Gervasi of *Collier's* magazine, American readers were fed "a steady diet of half-truths, poisoned statistics, rumors and rumors of rumors . . . All fairy tales to fill space and justify expense accounts," he wrote, thus putting the blame on correspondents more than censors.[20]

Helen P. Kirkpatrick of the *Chicago Daily News* criticized British military intelligence for putting pressure on the Ministry of Information to clamp down on news reports. "The intelligence services . . . were unable to see that the public must have news if morale were to be kept high." Censorship was voluntary for the British press, compulsory for foreign correspondents. "It made little difference," she wrote. "There was no news in any case." American correspondents made themselves highly unpopular by fighting a vigorous battle against the "stupidity" of early censorship. "In the end the British may prove to have been wise. At this stage it seems madness from their point of view."

Kirkpatrick was one of the first women correspondents of the war and one of the brightest. A Smith College graduate, she had studied international law at the University of Geneva and worked for the Foreign Policy Association there. She joined the *Daily News* in 1939. Murrow wanted to hire her but CBS refused to take on more women. An opponent of Britain's appeasement of Hitler, she outlined her views in two prewar books, *This Terrible Peace* and *Under the British Umbrella.*[21]

Raymond Daniell, the *New York Times* bureau chief in London, shared her view of censorship. The typical British censor, he wrote, "often is a well-intentioned blunderer who either hopelessly slows things up or is so obtuse about differentiating between military information and harmless speculation that he drives correspondents to the verge of nervous breakdowns. The gray hairs now sprouting from my cranium weren't there when the war began."

At one stage later Daniell wrote of a dogfight over the Thames, but the censor rejected that: place names could not be mentioned. The censor asked if he wanted to substitute anything and Daniell airily replied: "Certainly, substitute Amazon for Thames." "Very good, sir," the censor replied. Daniell was confident his copy desk in New York would change that, but that's how it appeared in the next morning's *Times.*[22]

The war initially came to Britain on October 14, 1939, when a German submarine penetrated Scapa Flow, off northeast Scotland, and sank the battleship *Royal Oak*. Correspondents learned about it but censors killed their dispatches. "We complained about this since the enemy obviously knew all the facts, but we had to admit it would obviously depress the British people," Reston wrote.

A few days later, a submarine damaged the cruiser *Belfast* in the Firth of Forth, the censors again balked and Daniell decided to get the news out using a simple code a child could have deciphered. Sending his information in the form of messages instead of a news story, and using two different cable companies, he informed his head office that "it's the last word that counts."

If a reader put together the last word in each message, he would learn: "Submarine entered the [Firth of] Forth, attacked and damaged the Belfast and escaped." Near Christmas Daniell was visited by officers from MI5 and Scotland Yard. He admitted sending the messages, then went to the Ministry of Information and told the full story. Much later, he learned that Winston Churchill was amused by the affair, and that a certain admiral had fought for his criminal prosecution under the Defense Act. But he got off with a warning. Reston, later to become executive editor of the *New York Times*, concluded that Daniell's subterfuge was "a silly schoolboy exercise, which I approved and have regretted ever since."[23]

The British scored their first success when three cruisers clashed with the German battleship *Graf Spee* off the coast of Uruguay on December 13. The British ships were seriously damaged but so was the German vessel, which took refuge in Montevideo harbor. On December 17, her crew scuttled the ship rather than surrender, and the captain committed suicide. Talbot G. "Jimmy" Bowen of NBC was waiting to go on the air when the *Graf Spee* blew up, and moments later he broadcast a dramatic eyewitness account to New York. It was a rare instance, at that stage of the war, of a live news broadcast.[24]

The German tanker *Altmark*, carrying 299 British merchant sailors whose ships had been sunk by the *Graf Spee*, steamed into the waters of neutral Norway in February 1940, en route for Germany. The British destroyer HMS *Cossack* intercepted the tanker and it ran aground. The *Cossack* crew boarded the *Altmark* on February 15 and freed the prisoners after a fight in which six German sailors were killed and eight wounded.

Mary Marvin Breckenridge, an Amsterdam-based CBS broadcaster and American socialite (her great-grandfather had been vice-president of the United States), arrived on February 21 and broadcast a live interview with the *Altmark* captain. She reported:

> I saw a line of frozen blood and a lump of flesh which fell through the slats into the snow where a German sailor was fatally shot . . . So there lies the *Altmark* grounded in a lonely little Norwegian fjord, its rudder and screw broken, some of its men dead, the others confined to their ship, its captives

gone, its future uncertain and the ultimate effects of its adventure still unknown.

Breckenridge ended her brief, promising broadcast career in June 1940 when she went to Berlin to marry an American diplomat, Jefferson Patterson.[25]

* * *

A drama played out in Romania in 1939 and 1940 involved the partial dismemberment of the country, the forced abdication of the king and German occupation. The protagonists were King Carol II and his implacable enemies, the fascist and anti-Semite Iron Guard. On September 21, 1939, nine Iron Guardists assassinated Prime Minister Armand Calinescu, then forced their way into Bucharest Radio and announced they had "executed" him. Overpowered by police, they were driven to the scene of the assassination and shot dead. The Soviet Union and Germany plotted to undermine King Carol and Moscow forced Romania to evacuate Bessarabia, which had once been part of Russia, and adjoining Bukovina, which never had. Two months later, the Germans announced that part of Transylvania would be ceded to Hungary.

Rioting broke out across Romania, then fighting between the army and the Iron Guard. The king appointed Gen. Ion Antonescu to try to find a way out of the conflict. At Antonescu's behest, the king reluctantly abdicated in favor of his young son, Prince Michael, on September 6, 1940. German troops moved in but stood by while the army and Iron Guard continued battling. The Iron Guard launched a pogrom of Bucharest Jews and hundreds were killed. Afterward the Germans assumed full control.

Cedric Salter returned to Romania from Poland on the day of Calinescu's assassination, and he and Paul Bettany of Reuters witnessed the gunning down of the killers. "I turned away sickened, not at the sight of so much death but at the expressions of sadistic pleasure on the faces of men and women alike as they filed past to feed their eyes on the revolting sight," Salter wrote.

Censors refused to allow their dispatches to leave the country. So Salter and Jim Brown of INS agreed that Salter would stay in Bucharest, trying to book calls to various European capitals, while Brown would go to Bulgaria and file. Back in Bucharest, other correspondents belatedly hit on the same idea and two carloads of them set off for the border. At 7:30 p.m., censorship was lifted and Salter filed his and Brown's dispatches to Amsterdam, but Brown already had filed from Bulgaria. The other correspondents, refused permission to enter Bulgaria, returned to Bucharest and most managed to file in time for their newspapers' final editions. Gestapo agents posing as German businessmen soon flooded into Bucharest.[26]

Edmund Taylor of the *Chicago Tribune* speculated in one dispatch that a Russo-German attack on Romania might be imminent. His eccentric editor Robert R. McCormick fired off a blistering cable: "Suggest you join Foreign Legion or else take rest cure in sanitarium in neutral country until you regain control of your nerves."[27]

Leigh White now arrived in Bucharest. An ambulance driver for Spanish Republicans in 1937, he later worked for Reuters and several London newspapers, then for the Paris edition of the *New York Herald-Tribune*. Now he represented the Overseas News Agency, which had been established to report on Jews and other persecuted minorities. It was a front for the Jewish Telegraph Agency, which was not welcome in some countries. Finally, frustrated at his agency's sole focus on Jewish issues, White began broadcasting for CBS while continuing to represent the agency.[28]

In August 1940, after the Germans handed part of Transylvania to Hungary, the Gestapo provoked riots there to try to force Romanians to flee. Henry Gorrell of UP was in the thick of rioting in Cluj and the crowd got out of hand. Gorrell unleashed his bulldog, which he called Captain Jinks of the Horse Marines, and ran after him. "Who was going to shoot a guy out walking his dog?" Soon afterward he and Frank Stevens of UP learned that German troops had entered Romania, scooping their competitors by 12 hours with the news.[29]

In September, when rioting broke out, Robert St. John was in Bucharest for the AP. His reporting displeased the authorities and King Carol personally gave him 72 hours to leave the country. But the next day the army was fighting the Iron Guard and he continued reporting as Carol abdicated.

Clare Hollingworth was back in Romania. "She was young, as wiry as a tennis player in training, acted most of the time like a bundle of tightly wound springs, chain-smoked, asked no quarter because she was a woman and loved sensational newspaper stories," wrote St. John. Colleagues referred to her as "the female Scarlet Pimpernel of the Balkans."

"She carried a pearl-handled revolver in her handbag, laughed in the faces of Romanian policemen and Gestapo agents alike, was always trying to go to places where people told her she was not supposed to go," St. John wrote. "Clare Hollingworth was the only woman I ever met who was not worried by the sight of slit throats or pools of human blood."

On September 30, 1940, Hollingworth phoned to say he was wanted at her apartment. He arrived to find her in her dressing gown drinking coffee.

Two Iron Guardists stood in the doorway. She told St. John she had been awakened by pounding at her door, with the Guardists demanding she dress and come with them, as they had orders to escort her to the frontier. She asked them to wait outside. Then she took off her dressing gown and nightie, made coffee and phoned the British Legation to come and rescue her. Every time the Guardists threatened to break down the door, the naked Hollingworth opened it a crack and said: "Do you want me to come this way?"

After the Legation intervened, the authorities advised she had eight days to leave or be imprisoned. Eight days later St. John reminded her that it was the day she was supposed to leave. "By Jove, it is!" she said. She stayed on.[30] Leigh White wrote that Hollingworth worked openly for British intelligence, plotted sabotage, helped refugees escape to Turkey and maintained contact with British spies all over Romania.[31] St. John also suggested that she engaged in spying and "a bit of sabotage." Her great-nephew and biographer, Patrick Garrett, thought this "sounded a little far-fetched" but offered no definitive conclusion.[32]

The government had been expelling Britons since July and now others were arrested and beaten. Maitland and other correspondents were "scared out of our wits" and began moving only in groups and changing sleeping quarters from time to time. "Those who had not already done so obtained Webley automatics." Correspondents began to get anonymous phone calls, urging them to leave Romania.

"We knew that at any moment the hidden hand might descend and whisk us away to torture or near death. Most of us took a keener interest in the whisky bottle than hitherto." But Hollingworth was "courageous beyond description," while Henry Stokes of Reuters was "a hero" and Archie Gibson, Maitland's fellow *Times* colleague, was "maddeningly cool."

One morning, Maitland took a taxi to the airport, bribed police, soldiers and Customs officials and flew to Belgrade.[33] He had tried to persuade David Walker of the *Daily Mirror* to leave too, and so had the British Legation, but Walker and Stokes refused. "We began to receive anonymous phone calls informing us we were on the Death List," Walker wrote. He and Stokes finally agreed to leave in October. Walker paid farewell visits to Romanian friends, who said: "Do please come and bomb us—we deserve it."[34]

St. John left for Belgrade but days later Romania again cut communications with the outside world. Sensing he was missing a good story, he flew back to Bucharest. Antonescu had dropped three Iron Guard officials from his government and the Guards had gone on the attack. St. John saw Guardists douse one soldier with gasoline and set him on fire.

Then Iron Guards attacked the Jewish quarter. St. John found a synagogue on fire and Guardists forcing firemen away. Later that night, Guardists, after praying and drinking each other's blood—one of their rituals—put nearly 200 Jews on trucks and drove to an abattoir. The Jews were stripped, forced to get down on all fours, driven up the ramp of a slaughterhouse and put through a parody of the traditional Jewish methods of killing cattle. Their beheaded bodies were slung on hooks with notices labeling them as "kosher meat." Other Jews were taken to a forest and shot, or doused with gasoline and burned alive. Thirty Jewish bodies were fished out of the Dambovitsa River, some apparently suicides.[35]

Leigh White learned of the pogrom and went to the ghetto. Hardly a storefront along the main street had not been burned or wrecked and "the streets were filled with dirty, shivering people who stared at us dumbly as we passed." At the morgue, there was an overpowering stench from hundreds of bodies. White went outside, on the point of fainting.[36]

David Walker flew in from Athens. "One night, in a manner which cannot even now be disclosed," St. John wrote in 1960, "I discovered that Walker for years had been and still was a British secret service agent" with his own Balkan spy ring. Amid a security scandal in Britain after the war, Walker was publicly named as an agent of MI6, the foreign intelligence agency. In his memoir, Walker never mentioned his dual role but did pay an unusual tribute to American correspondents with whom he worked. "On the whole the Americans were both a pleasanter and a more efficient lot than we were. They also proved later that they had more guts."[37]

The revolution continued into February 1941, but the British Legation withdrew in protest at the German military presence, breaking relations with Romania. Hollingworth, Walker and St. John finally departed.[38]

Ten months later, INS correspondent Hugo Speck was in the Black Sea port of Otchav and saw a 14-year-old boy with a rifle. Speck asked what he was shooting at and the boy replied, "Jews. I get five lei for every one I kill." He carried a stick carved with thirty-four notches and said, "When I have 50, then I get an extra bonus." It was then 3 p.m. and he expressed hope he would reach his target by nightfall.[39]

CHAPTER 2

WAR IN FINLAND, NORWAY AND DENMARK

Two months after success in Poland, Stalin plunged the Soviet Union into war with Finland, which had a population of 3.6 million. Stalin's aim was to occupy the Karelian Isthmus and Finnish islands in the Baltic. To his great surprise, the heavily outnumbered Finns proved to be no pushover for Soviet troops ill-equipped for winter warfare. When the conflict ended on March 12, 1940, the Soviets had lost a quarter of a million men. But Stalin had acquired 10 per cent of Finnish territory.

Finland, of course, was not a natural base for foreign correspondents. When the Russians staged their surprise attack, Norman Deuel of UP's Moscow bureau happened to be passing through en route to the U.S. He was awakened by air-raid sirens; then a Russian bomb shattered a nearby building. Deuel picked himself off the floor and dictated to UP's Copenhagen bureau the first report of a new war.[1]

Correspondents poured in, and their reports of a heavily outnumbered Finnish military imposing punishment on the invaders rallied widespread sympathy for the Finnish cause. Afterward they were accused of having given a false impression that Finland was winning the war when it never had a chance. But Finnish censorship, which prevented some accounts of Finnish losses reaching the outside world, was at least partly responsible for this mistaken view.

Finland was in the grip of a harsh winter, temperatures dropping as low as 43° Fahrenheit below zero. Some correspondents traveled to battlefronts on skis. "The cold numbs the brain in this Arctic hell, snow sweeps over the darkened wastes, the winds howl [and] the Russians and Finns are battling in blinding snowstorms for possession of ice-covered forests," James Aldridge, a young Australian, reported for the North American Newspaper Alliance in a dispatch published on Christmas Day in the *New York Times*. He found frozen corpses locked together with bayonets penetrating each other's bodies. "Their bodies were like statues of men throwing all their muscles and strength into some work, but their faces recorded something between bewilderment and horror." He said the cold was taking as many Russian lives during the night as Finn patrols killed in daytime.[2]

Karl J. Eskelund, a 22-year-old Dane reporting for Copenhagen's *Politiken* and the *New York Times*, wrote: "Immediately after my arrival in Finland I ran into a beautiful story. I was on the first train to be machine-gunned by Soviet planes." He jumped out of a window into the snow. Six planes circled the train, firing machine guns. When the attack was over, four bodies lay on the track and five people were seriously wounded.[3]

Virginia Cowles saw farm girls stumbling through snow to reach cellars, bombs falling on villages with no anti-aircraft defenses, men standing in front of blazing buildings with no means of fighting fires. She traveled north and, at a field hospital from which the Russians had retreated, hundreds of wounded men had died in their beds. One had been left, half cut open, on an operating table. Before the retreat, Russian doctors had thrown the dead out of windows to make way for newcomers.[4]

Walter Kerr of the *New York Herald-Tribune* observed Finnish artillery batteries pounding Russian lines for 3 minutes to provide sound effects for a radio broadcast by Warren Irvin of NBC. The Russians, thinking an offensive was under way, fired back for 20 minutes. "There probably will be no more gunfire merely for radio sound effects here," Kerr wrote.[5]

Martha Gellhorn, the third wife of Ernest Hemingway and the best known of American women correspondents, interviewed louse-infested Russian prisoners, most of them wearing crude cotton trousers and coats despite the intense cold. "The sense of the insanity and wickedness of this war grew in me until, for purposes of mental hygiene, I gave up trying to think or judge . . . The way people stay sane in war, I imagine, is to suspend a large part of their reasoning minds, lose most of their sensitivity, laugh when they get the smallest chance, and get a bit, but increasingly, crazy."[6]

The seasoned correspondents were soon joined by a newcomer. On September 3, Richard Busvine had been director of a fashionable dressmaking business in London. Coming out of an air-raid shelter on Britain's first night of war, he decided he wanted to be a war correspondent. The next day, he was one. While living in New York earlier, he had written occasional pieces for the

Chicago Times and he cabled Gail Borden, managing editor of that paper, offering his services. Back came a cable appointing Busvine as the newspaper's European correspondent.

In Helsinki, he and Edward Ward of the BBC heard heavy explosions as they walked back to their hotel from lunch. They drove to the harbor where wooden buildings were ablaze. Ward grabbed a microphone from a Finnish Broadcasting mobile van nearby and interviewed firefighters against the background noise of flames, crashing buildings and cascading water. They dashed back to the hotel and filed exclusive reports. Expecting a congratulatory cable from Chicago, Busvine heard nothing. It was one of his first lessons in journalism: he had filed on a Saturday, when the *Chicago Times* did not publish, and, worse yet, had filed at the expensive urgent rate.

He encountered Webb Miller of UP, covering the seventh war of his legendary career. Staring at his typewriter, Miller exclaimed: "I can't write it again. I've written it all. Over and over again. Christ! I can't go on. I've got to get away from it before it drives me crazy!"

Later Busvine was aboard a train when an elderly woman with the stump of one arm bandaged was put aboard. "Four sons and one arm I have given to Finland, but one more son and one more arm I still have left to give," she told him. "Send that message to those who watch our struggle and fear to help." Busvine stumbled away, blinded by tears.[7]

Edmund Stevens also had his baptism as a war correspondent in Finland. In 1934, as an American Communist, he went to Moscow with a recommendation from Earl Browder, leader of the American Communist Party, and landed a job as a propagandist for the Communist International. By 1938, his enchantment with Communism gone, he had become a freelance correspondent for the *Manchester Guardian* and the *Christian Science Monitor*. He soon became a member of the *Monitor* staff, and on December 24, 1939, while in the Estonian capital of Tallinn, reported on the first Finnish victory. "The new 24,000-ton battleship *Kirov*, pride of the Soviet Baltic Fleet, limped into port here yesterday as a result of two direct hits by the Finnish Coast Artillery."

Stevens proceeded to the Karelia isthmus. He was told the Russians had crossed into Finland with bands playing, expecting a friendly reception because the Soviets had declared the establishment of a Finnish Communist republic. "But as soon as the Russians approached the first town, booby traps began going off, and in that first onslaught, they perished by the hundreds."

Stevens interviewed Soviet prisoners and found some were hastily conscripted farmers—ill-equipped, ill-clad and ill-armed. Nearly half of the 1,000-mile war front was above the Arctic Circle. (During the war, Geoffrey

Cox of London's *Daily Express* coined a memorable phrase: "It is reported in well-informed Arctic Circles . . ." Other correspondents made use of it.)

One division of 10,000 Russians was cut off by Finnish ski patrols and pinned down. "We were taken to view them, and I will never forget the sight," Stevens wrote. "All the men and equipment were clearly visible. The only thing wrong was that they were frozen fast by the thousands." Stevens reported that booty captured from the Soviets included thousands of pairs of new, unused skis and ski manuals. The Soviets learned a vital lesson that helped when they later had to engage the Germans on their own soil. Never again would Soviet soldiers go into winter battle ill-equipped, poorly trained and without warm clothing.

Stevens found a Russian lieutenant's unfinished letter. It read: "In this wilderness of lakes and forests the enemy seems everywhere and nowhere. Our information service is insufficient. Consequently, though we have good guns and plenty of ammunition, we don't know where to shoot. Then when the Finns start pounding us we can't come out above ground."

The United States had agreed to lend $30 million to Finland on condition it not be used to buy arms, prompting Stevens to observe: "So far as Finland is concerned this is like giving money to a starving man with the proviso that he cannot buy food with it."[8]

Leland Stowe went to Finland for the *Chicago Daily News*. Formerly with the *New York Herald-Tribune*, he had won a Pulitzer Prize in 1930. Three years later, after a visit to Nazi Germany, he wrote about Hitler's preparations for war in a series of articles that were not published because his editors found them too alarmist. He published them as a book, *Nazi Germany Means War*, but few people bought it. In 1939 the prematurely white-haired, pipe-smoking Stowe (he carried fifteen pipes with him everywhere) was told by his editor-in-chief, Wilbur Forrest, that he was too old at age 40 to cover a war. He resigned and went to work for the Chicago newspaper, which then had the nation's pre-eminent corps of foreign correspondents.

He quickly noted that the Finns were "tragically inferior in all war materials" and looking for aid from the democracies but likely to be disappointed—as proved to be the case. Having been labeled a "Red" by American right-wingers for his support of the Republican cause in Spain, he now found himself being denounced by Communists and fellow travelers as an enemy of "Soviet democracy." George Seldes purported to show in an article for *New Masses* that the Soviets had never bombed civilians in Finland. "I had lain in the snow and watched Russian bombs coming down at me when I was nearly one mile away from the only legitimate target anywhere around," Stowe wrote.

"I had talked with passengers whose train had been machine-gunned on the Turku-Helsinki line. I had been in bombed Finnish towns and villages."[9]

Ed Beattie of UP wrote of his bitter experience with Finnish censors. "The Finnish censorship was undoubtedly the most unreasonable, pig-headed, hidebound affair which any warring country ever set up."[10] Carl Mydans of *Life*, who had been a photographer for the Farm Security Administration in Washington before joining the magazine, reported that no foreign correspondent was allowed to witness a Finnish defeat. When he saw Finnish and Russian dead lying together on the battlefield, he was forbidden to photograph the Finns.[11]

Edward Ward had been a BBC news reader in London until he was asked to go to Finland. He was in Viipuri when twenty-five Russian planes bombed it. After going into an air-raid shelter, he wrote of the people there: "There they were talking and laughing away down in this shelter as though they were just taking cover from rather an annoying shower of rain which was lasting rather a long time."

A Finnish officer described how two captured Russian soldiers arrived with completely frozen hands and feet and could not see. After a while they became aware of the heat from a red-hot stove and put their hands flat on the iron. "They kept them there," Ward wrote. "They couldn't feel a thing. And there they stayed with their hands sizzling like rashers of bacon frying." The Finnish officer ordered his men to drag them away and shoot them. "It was the most merciful thing to do," he said. "They would have died anyway."

Ward went to Stockholm while Finnish–Russian peace negotiations were taking place, then decided to return to Helsinki. Before leaving, he rang the Finnish minister to Sweden, Eljas Erkko. Just in passing, and not expecting an answer, Ward asked: "Is it true that an agreement has been reached in Moscow?" Ward was astonished when he replied: "That is true. I cannot give you exact details of the terms but I can tell you that they are far worse than anything we had expected."

"I hung up the receiver, realizing that I had a world scoop in my pocket," Ward wrote. He had difficulty getting a call through to London and finally told Harold Callender of the *New York Times* he would give him a good story if he put a call through for him. Callender did and they filed to the BBC and the *Times*.[12]

Most Finnish people did not learn of their country's defeat until a Finnish minister announced it on the radio the next day. Stowe was in a room when a Finnish man took a phone call, put down the receiver and said: "The first of our friends has just committed suicide." The victim was a young woman writer.[13]

Gellhorn later pronounced her verdict on the war now spreading across Europe. Noting that the enemy was profoundly evil, she added:

> But there was also our side, and our record was not all shining and admirable, and one could not give one's undivided loyalty to our leaders, not by a long shot. We were guilty of the dishonest abandonment of Spain and the quick, cheap betrayal of Czechoslovakia. We niggled and refused asylum to doomed Jews; we inspected and rejected anti-Fascists fleeing for their lives from Hitler . . . In the immortal words of E. M. Forster: "Two cheers for democracy." Two cheers was all one could manage.[14]

Webb Miller returned to London, intending to report on the British Army in France. UP President Hugh Baillie, who was visiting London, wrote later:

> Few people hated war as Webb Miller did. Webb rarely talked about war; indeed, he rarely talked about anything. He was a very gloomy man, introspective by nature and a listener by choice. You could be with Webb Miller in a group and forget he was there, because he made no contribution to the conversation . . . He had a stony, handsome face with a pallid complexion and a pencil-thin mustache, and I don't think I ever heard him laugh. But . . . he had an ability to make people feel he was their friend: even Mussolini had thought Webb Miller was a friend of his.

Miller was born in 1891 on a tenant farm near the hamlet of Pokagon, Michigan, son of a part-time sawmill worker. In a memoir, he described himself as "totally unfitted by temperament and environment" for a career in journalism. "Abnormal shyness and hypersensitivity afflicted me throughout my youth and on into later life, strongly inclining me to become a nature-writing recluse. Any human violence . . . filled me with abhorrence." But he had been covering violence since the federal government staged a punitive expedition against Pancho Villa in Mexico in 1916, going on from there to World War I and later conflicts. By 1940 he was a legendary figure among fellow correspondents.

The British writer Richard Collier took a less charitable view of him than had Baillie. He wrote that Miller was a hard drinker and "a burnt-out case at 49, taciturn, pallid, unsmiling, a smalltown boy."

On the evening of May 8, 1940, Miller fell from a train in London and was killed. A coroner ruled the death was accidental and speculated that Miller had held the door of his railway coach open to relieve himself and was pitched out onto the track by the gathering speed of the train as it drew out of a station in blackout conditions. Collier thought Miller was "conceivably as far gone in drink as always," and Harrison Salisbury of UP's London bureau wrote: "I always thought it was suicide."

In Berlin, William Shirer wrote in his diary:

I have known him for 12 years, liked him, admired him . . . Webb was an inordinately modest man, despite as distinguished a journalistic career as any American has had in our time. His success never went to his head. I remember him on many a big story being as excited and nervous and . . . as shy, as the youngest and most inexperienced of us. His shyness was terrific and he never lost it.

Gordon Young of Reuters news agency recalled: "Chiefly I remember him on a score of occasions being tolerant and urbane and considerate to his colleagues, and flogging himself through a million experiences which he did not enjoy, for he was terribly hard on himself all through his life." He was the first war correspondent to die.[15]

* * *

Fighting soon broke out in neutral Norway, triggered by a British plan to sever Germany's winter link to Swedish iron-ore mines near the Norwegian frontier, among the richest in the world. In April 1940 Winston Churchill, First Lord of the Admiralty, persuaded government colleagues to authorize the mining of Norwegian waters. Four destroyers laid mines before dawn on April 8. A few hours later the Germans began air and naval landings, simultaneously occupying Denmark, where their forces met almost no resistance.

The Germans installed a puppet Norwegian government under Vidkun Quisling. A British and French landing force of just 26,000 men at Narvik was poorly trained and equipped. Soon facing an untenable situation, they re-embarked and Norway remained under German occupation throughout the war. The government and King Haakon VII sailed for Britain on June 7. Neville Chamberlain resigned as prime minister on May 10, to be replaced by Churchill.

Leland Stowe, Edmund Stevens and Indro Montanelli of Milan's *Corriere della Sera* arrived in Oslo on April 4, and met Otto Tolischus of the *New York Times*, who was leaving. He laughed and asked: "What are you guys doing here? There's no story."

Five days later there was one, a momentous one. Stevens was awakened by the Finnish ambassador, Urho Toivola, who jested that he wasn't much of a reporter—he was missing what was happening outside his window. Stevens looked out and there in brilliant sunshine were German paratroopers calmly directing traffic while a German military band played "Roll Out the Barrel". This song, written by a Czech and with lyrics in different languages, was popular with troops of several nations. Stevens awoke Stowe and Montanelli.[16]

Stowe saw five bombers flying in:

> They roared like hungry lions . . . "God help us if they let the bombs go now," I said. We twisted our necks and looked straight up, helplessly. A split second—no, we were safe . . . In a few minutes they were [back]; still swooping low, still roaring, still holding thousands of persons speechless and paralyzed on the streets or at their windows.[17]

Desmond Tighe of Reuters and W. F. Hartin of London's *Daily Mail* set out for Oslo by train from Stockholm that morning and, as they entered Norway, a low-flying Heinkel bomber flew past. More planes were bombing Oslo airport as their train passed. In Oslo, streets were deserted, offices and shops closed, bombers circling the city. "Tighe, old boy, we're sunk," Hartin told him. They decided to have a drink.

Then they walked into a column of marching Germans. "Oslo residents were standing bewildered and sullen on the pavement edge," Tighe wrote. "I noticed particularly how ill the German troops looked. Their faces were yellow and many of them wore glasses. They seemed to treat the whole thing as a joke."

Tighe and Hartin went to the Swiss Legation and hid in its cellar for eight hours. An express train for Stockholm was due to leave at 8 p.m. and they were determined to get on it. Fortified by a couple of stiff whiskies, they reached the station, guarded by German soldiers, who ignored them. Neither spoke until the train crossed into Sweden.[18]

* * *

Stowe and Stevens watched about 1,500 German troops march through the city center, escorted by six mounted Norwegian policemen. A few people along the streets gave the Hitler salute. At 4:30 p.m. Norwegian radio announced the formation of a "Quisling national government." Stowe tried to file a news story but was refused at the telegraph office and told to see Prime

Minister Vidkun Quisling at the Continental Hotel. "We happened to buttonhole Quisling in the corridor and he looked and acted as if he had as much authority as a woodchuck in a lion's den," Stowe wrote.

From a Norwegian sailor, Stowe and Stevens learned that, shortly before 1:30 a.m., a naval commander of three Norwegian ships lying in Oslo fjord was informed that German warships would soon be coming in, and he was not to resist. He obeyed. And someone in the naval base at Oskarsborg disconnected electric mines strewn in the narrows. Nonetheless, Norwegian sailors manning guns onshore opened fire when the Germans arrived and sank two cruisers. But in just 12 hours, every one of Norway's great seaports was captured.

Stowe was determined to get out of Oslo so he could file, but the Germans barred foreigners from leaving. On April 12 he checked out of his hotel and an American woman whom he had hired, Mrs. Day Adams Morgenstierne, picked him up in her car and deposited him at Fredrikstad, at the mouth of the Oslo fjord. Stowe left her, the wife of a Norwegian, and boarded a ferry for Sweden.

There he hired a car and drove all night down the coast to Goteborg. It was a Saturday afternoon and, as the *Chicago Daily News* syndicate served afternoon newspapers, he had to sit on his story until 6 p.m. Monday Swedish time. Despite the long delay, his report was still exclusive and made headlines across the U.S. One of his opening paragraphs said: "By bribery and extraordinary infiltration on the part of Nazi agents and by treason on the part of a few highly placed Norwegian civilian and defense officials, the German dictatorship built a Trojan horse inside of Norway." The new Norwegian government attacked the accuracy of journalistic reports and cited Stowe as "the most prominent of these writers."

Ed Stevens and Montanelli remained in Norway for a week and found further evidence of collusion or lack of courage. At Kongsberg officers had ordered 1,300 soldiers to surrender to 500 Germans. At Sarpsborg nearly 3,000 troops were instructed to hand over weapons to 300 Germans.

But they also learned of one major German setback. At 3:30 a.m. on April 9, a group assembled at Oslo harbor to await the arrival of the cruiser *Blücher*. When the ship hove into sight, Norwegian guns opened up and in less than five minutes the cruiser sank with huge loss of life.[19] It was this important nugget of information that prompted Stevens and Montanelli to leave Norway so they could file.

Before they departed, a German colonel told them: "What we feared most was a lightning reprisal by the British [at the start of the invasion]. If they had struck then, our whole expedition would have ended in disaster. Fortunately, one can always count upon the British to arrive too late."[20]

Betty Wason, an unknown, part-time young correspondent for CBS, scooped rival networks on April 12 with a first-hand report on the flight north of Oslo by the royal family and government officials, who came under German aerial attack. "Down the road ran King Haakon, Crown Prince Olaf, the British and Polish ministers and all the other government officials," she said. "They had to stand waist-deep in snow beneath fir trees while bombs crashed."[21]

* * *

In Sweden, Stowe set an example of dogged and courageous enterprise, reporting under difficult and dangerous circumstances. Driving to the mountainous north over treacherous, icy roads, past 15-foot-high snowdrifts, he crossed back into Norway. A panicky Swedish journalist in Formofoss told him the Germans were attacking nearby towns, machine-gunning everyone on the roads, and they must head back to Sweden. Stowe refused to leave and set out alone for Steinkjer, 50 miles away, over roads muddy and slushy with snow and ice. Steinkjer was at the head of a fjord that had been occupied by British troops. It had been heavily bombed by German planes two hours earlier, all of the survivors had fled and a German destroyer was shelling the town from the fjord. To Stowe, the young British Territorial soldiers looked like Boy Scouts.

A British lieutenant told him: "We've been massacred—simply massacred." Of 600 men in his battalion, 200 had been killed or wounded. Another British soldier said their forces had no anti-aircraft weapons, no field pieces, no proper clothes for mountain fighting. "Everything was very clear now," Stowe wrote. "It was not only a defeat; it was a rout, and behind the rout lay a colossal, almost unbelievable blunder. But these men were the victims." The next morning he listened to a BBC broadcast from London, saying British forces were pressing forward steadily.[22]

Peter C. Rhodes of UP and Giles Romilly of the *Daily Express* were in Narvik with British forces when the Germans arrived. Rhodes crossed into Sweden where he flashed the news, but Romilly, a nephew of Winston Churchill, was captured. He and two Dutch officers later escaped from a German prison and reached Allied lines. Romilly resumed his journalistic career after the war.[23]

Stowe hitchhiked back to Formofoss and encountered Betty Wason, who had come over the mountains alone. Barely five feet tall and fluent in no foreign language, she had come to Europe as a stringer for Transradio News.

Failing to earn enough to support herself, she returned home to work briefly for the New York newspaper *PM*, then went back to Europe, basing herself in Stockholm. CBS paid her $100 a week but there were complaints that she was too young and feminine and her voice lacked authority. She was asked to find a man to read her broadcast texts, and she hired another American, Winston Burdett. He soon became a contract employee of CBS, but she never was given a staff job.

She and Stowe set out for the Swedish frontier in a truck but it bogged down and they had to walk to the nearest village. A sheriff rescued them and delivered them to a frontier station. They hired a car, driving until 3:30 a.m. to reach the Swedish city of Östersund, where they could file. By then Stowe had had two meals in four days and less than seven hours' sleep in the past ninety-six. Within a week after they left Norway, the British forces embarked for home.

Stowe's dispatch, read on the BBC and published in London newspapers, gave the first report of the scope of the British disaster. It shocked the nation and was widely regarded as having hastened Prime Minister Chamberlain's downfall. When Stowe was back in Stockholm, he received a phone call from a British diplomat. Assuming he was about to face criticism, he went on the offensive.

"I imagine some of your folks in London are pretty riled over my story about Steinkjer," he said. "But, quite frankly, I believe I've done the British cause the greatest service I've ever had the opportunity of rendering." The diplomat replied: "Well, speaking with equal frankness, Mr. Stowe, I'm inclined to believe that you are entirely correct." Stowe was widely tipped for the Pulitzer Prize but did not receive it. That must rank as one of the biggest mistakes a prize jury ever made.[24]

* * *

The Allies made no attempt to intervene in Denmark, nor did its armed forces offer more than token resistance. The Germans marched in on April 9 and the occupation was a fait accompli within two hours. Karl Eskelund was awakened by the sound of German bombers sweeping low over Copenhagen. He phoned his uncle, chief of the government press bureau, who told him German soldiers had arrived two days earlier in coal boats. There was coal on the decks and troops in the hold. Eskelund and his Chinese wife later made it out of occupied Europe and went to Shanghai, where he began work for UP.[25]

The French and Polish embassies in Copenhagen enrolled their countries' correspondents as assistant press attachés, so they acquired diplomatic status and were allowed to leave for Britain and France. But the British ambassador in Copenhagen refused to do the same for four British correspondents. Selkirk Patton of the *Daily Express*, Anthony Mann of the *Daily Telegraph*, Stephen House of Kemsley Allied Newspapers and W. H. Kelland of the Extel agency were sent to a concentration camp for the duration of the war. In Berlin, four Danish correspondents and one Norwegian also were interned.[26]

Clinton Beach Conger of the UP bureau in Berlin witnessed the takeover of Denmark. He observed that "tourists" who had gone to bed in the luxury Hotel d'Angleterre the night before the invasion came to breakfast in the uniforms of German staff officers. Touring Copenhagen, he noticed that Danes ostentatiously left cafés when Germans entered. Later some Danes shaved the heads of girls who dated German soldiers.[27] Two days after the takeover, the AP's Berlin bureau chief Louis Lochner was among correspondents flown to Copenhagen on Foreign Minister Joachim von Ribbentrop's plane. Lochner saw the 68-year-old King Christian X take his usual morning horseback ride through city streets, unattended and unprotected. "It was not only an act calculated to instill confidence in the bewildered Danish people, but a slap at Nazi insistence that every person of importance have a retinue trailing behind him," he wrote.

He saw how, in just two days, German troops had descended "like locusts" on Danish stores and stripped the country of its merchandise—something that was to be repeated in other occupied countries, and which was a reflection of shortages on the German home front.[28]

CHAPTER 3

THE FALL OF FRANCE AND THE LOW COUNTRIES

More than seven months of inactivity on the German–French frontier followed the French and British declaration of war on Germany. The armies settled down for what became known as the Phoney War, the Bore War or the Sitzkrieg. At 4:35 a.m. on May 10, 1940, German forces began sweeping into the Netherlands, Belgium and France, quickly crushing Dutch and Belgian defenses. Belgium surrendered on May 28 as Britain began evacuating forces from Dunkirk. On June 10, Italy declared war on France, Paris fell without a fight on June 14 and France surrendered on June 17.

During the months of the Phony War, the scraps of news that were available were chewed into meaninglessness by France's rigid censorship. It was so strict that, even after hostilities began, many people abroad failed to realize that, for France, the German invasion would not be the start of a long war but the prelude to a swift surrender. The process of clearing dispatches took at least 48 hours, often rendering them virtually useless.[1]

Alexander Werth, a Leningrad-born Paris correspondent of the *Sunday Times* of London, wrote that French censorship left him with the feeling he had:

been cheating and swindling the British public . . . If you wrote a truthful story with all the pros and cons, the cons were blue-penciled and the pros alone remained. The result was nothing but undiluted panegyrics . . . The censorship has caused dreadful harm to France. It has cultivated a smug, complacent frame of mind, with victory taken for granted.[2]

French overconfidence was sometimes reflected in dispatches. The *Baltimore Sun*'s Paul Ward, after observing border preparations on September 22, 1939, wrote: "If the Germans choose to attack they will find the French prepared to receive them as no army in history has ever been prepared before."[3]

Martha Gellhorn, anticipating the fall of France, left Europe in the winter of 1939. "I didn't think there would be a battle; I thought there would be a massacre, and I could not bear to witness another, to watch helplessly while the innocent were destroyed . . . I wanted to see the Orient before I died . . . Journalism now turned into an escape route." She went to China.[4]

Clare Boothe, the novelist, playwright and wife of *Time* publisher Henry Luce, visited front lines in the spring of 1940 and was at first impressed by French defenses. "I saw that all this lovely, lovely part of budding France bristled with hidden death, like a beautiful woman with a dread disease. Woe, I thought, to the men who sought to embrace her!"

But when she questioned officers at the Maginot Line as to whether the Germans would come into France through the Netherlands and Belgium, not covered by this "impenetrable" bulwark, they laughed. The Germans would not want to take on 3 million Dutch and Belgian soldiers. "The Germans are stupid but not *that* stupid," the commandant told her. That erased Boothe's illusions. "I was very sad, that morning. I knew all of a sudden . . . that the Maginot would one day break their hearts, as it had almost bankrupted their exchequer."[5]

Drew Middleton of the AP described French soldiers he encountered before hostilities began as "slovenly, ill-disciplined and casual."[6] Louis Lochner, the AP chief in Berlin, visited the German front line and observed that soldiers were kept fit and taught offensive tactics. But the French settled down to card playing, reading and chatting. On May 7, William Shirer in Berlin wrote in his diary: "My guess: the war in the next few weeks will be on all over Europe."[7]

The Germans struck first in the Netherlands. David Woodward of London's *News Chronicle* and his new American wife Meg were awakened at 4:30 a.m. on May 10 by the crump of bombs hitting the nearby Schiphol Airport. They moved into the Carlton Hotel in central Amsterdam, and learned that the Dutch commander in chief, married to a German, was already negotiating his country's surrender.[8]

Richard Busvine of the *Chicago Times* saw fifth columnists shot by loyal Dutch on a roof opposite his hotel, while other traitors in the street were shot or attacked by housewives with kitchen knives. Later, over the sands of Harlem, he watched as German paratroopers were blown to bits in midair by anti-aircraft fire. At a suburban railway station, he witnessed the slaughter of a handful of Germans who had captured it. On May 12, all British correspondents and 700 other British nationals got aboard a small coastal steamer and, escorted by a British destroyer, reached the English port of Harwich.[9]

Nazi propagandists rushed Berlin-based correspondents to Rotterdam so they could let the world know of German military might. Frederick Oechsner, Berlin bureau chief of UP, found 28,000 buildings in an area of one and a half square miles destroyed (he didn't explain how he had time to count them).[10] The correspondents went on to Belgium, and were taken to meet British prisoners. Shirer wrote: "What impressed me most about them was their physique. They were hollow-chested and skinny and round-shouldered. About a third of them had bad eyes and wore glasses. Typical, I concluded, of the youth that England neglected so criminally in the 22 postwar years when Germany . . . was raising *its* youth in the open air and the sun."[11]

Bernard Gray of London's *Sunday Pictorial* managed to get into Brussels on May 15 with Harold "Kim" Philby of *The Times*, who would years later be revealed to have been a Soviet agent since 1934. They found people fleeing, with trains for France packed and cars that had run out of gas abandoned on the roads. A British officer said some farmers used scythes to cut arrows in the hay in their fields, pointing to British artillery positions for the benefit of German spotter planes. "Most of them were Germans anyhow," the officer said. "Planted here as far back as two or three years ago. Just to act as spies and Fifth Columnists."

The correspondents were ordered back to France and wound up at the port of Boulogne. German planes attacked and Gray found machine-gun bullets whistling past him. Eventually they were told on 45 minutes' notice to get on a ship. They stepped ashore at Dover on May 21.[12]

* * *

Eric Sevareid was a relatively new CBS correspondent in Paris. He had gone to Europe without a job in 1937 and met Ed Murrow in London, then moved to Paris and joined the staff of the Paris *Herald*. By 1939 he was working for the *Herald* by day and UP at night. Hugh Baillie, the UP president, came to Paris and offered him a full-time job; by coincidence Murrow phoned from London, also offering a job. Sevareid accepted the Murrow offer but a tryout broadcast to New York went badly; CBS authorities did not like his voice. Murrow told him he would fix it and advised him to quit his other jobs. He took the gamble, and Murrow got him on the staff.

On May 10 Sevareid was in Provence, planning to go to Algeria and Tunisia to line up correspondents in case Italy attacked. He quickly returned to Paris, then joined the Allied press headquarters at Cambrai, near the Belgian border. With the Germans advancing, he joined two other correspondents aboard a train for Paris that was jammed. An hour after they departed, German dive bombers killed fifty people waiting on the platform for the next train.

In Paris, censors refused to pass their stories, so Sevareid wrote a one-line telegram to New York in a prearranged code. The telegram lay on an editor's desk for hours before he remembered the code. Then CBS reported that, "according to a usually well-informed source," the Germans had made a major breach in French frontier defenses.[13]

French officers abandoned Cambrai on May 15, failing to inform three correspondents in their charge: Percy Philip, a Scots-born correspondent of the *New York Times*, Taylor Henry of the AP and Maurice Noel of Paris's *Le Figaro*. When they learned what had happened, they packed their bags and left them at the railway station while they went off to have a drink. The Germans bombed the station and on their return Philip found six dead bodies in the stationmaster's office, lying near his typewriter. He left it behind.

The three men bought bicycles and rode out of town, but became separated. With hysteria sweeping France amid rumors of German parachutists in their midst, French soldiers arrested Philip and, refusing to believe his papers were genuine, decided to shoot him. Philip, who had lived in France for fourteen years, pointed out he had the red ribbon of the Legion of Honor but the French thought that was extraordinary effrontery even for a German. They made him take off his riding boots while they searched him, then put him against a wall. Knowing police were on the way, Philip said: "Surely you will let a Scotsman put on his boots before you shoot him?" Grudgingly they consented, and soon police rescued him.

Maurice Noel bicycled into a village which had just been bombed and stopped to have a glass of wine. A crowd soon gathered and accused him of being a German. He made a long speech to prove he was French but his listeners were not convinced. Noel was mildly amused when an Arab soldier shouted: "I can tell by your accent that you are not a Frenchman." Police arrived and, in his boot, found a box of white powder he took for indigestion. The police and the crowd were convinced this was an explosive. When he tried to put a match to the powder to show that it wasn't, they flung themselves on him. The mayor arrived, realized his papers were in order and set him free.

Taylor Henry got away and joined forces with Gordon Waterfield of Reuters. He made contact with the French Air Command, whose officials were desperate for American help and stressed that they were outnumbered in planes ten to one by the Germans. But every time Waterfield put those figures in a story censors crossed them out. He and Henry persuaded a colonel to let them go on bombing missions. On one such flight, Waterfield was put in charge of a rear machine gun and "felt confident that I would be able to bring down any number of Messerschmitts." But his plane was not attacked.[14]

* * *

Robert J. Casey of the *Chicago Daily News*, an artillery officer in World War I, commented after arriving in France that obtaining a pass to visit advanced army zones required "evidence of character just about sufficient for canonization." He was in Nancy when the invasion began and was awakened by bombs falling nearby. Going out to survey the wreckage, he saw a mother who had been killed with her baby in her arms. The sight almost brought him to tears.

On May 12, French tanks led an assault on Longwy, a small rail center on the Luxembourg border, and routed its captors. Casey thought for a time that "maybe this contest with Hitler could be won quickly and easily." Then German tanks moved in and took possession once again. Unlike some correspondents, Casey thought the French had "a fine, brave army . . . The men were bettered by no other soldiers in the world; they were tireless and fearless and durable."

He fled south with Bill Bird of the New York *Sun* and Bird's wife Sally. They narrowly escaped bombing and machine-gunning by German planes, and a house in which they stayed briefly in Bordeaux was damaged in a bombing that killed 218 people. Finally they crossed into Spain and went on to Lisbon, where Casey boarded a plane for London.[15]

* * *

Quentin Reynolds, a boisterous Brooklyn Irishman and nationally famous feature writer for *Collier's*, arrived in Paris shortly before the invasion. Once a sports writer for the *Brooklyn Evening World*, he had become Berlin correspondent of INS before the war but had come now from New York. He met with Pierre Comert, chief of the Ministry of Information foreign press section, and found Comert unwilling to give him immediate accreditation. Reynolds went to a bar to think it over, then returned. "I am about to send President Roosevelt a cable asking him to facilitate my accreditation with Premier Reynaud," he said. "Naturally I do not wish to go over your head, and so I have brought the message to you for your approval."

A wide-eyed Comert read:

DEAR UNCLE FRANKLIN, AM HAVING DIFFICULTY GETTING ACCREDITED TO FRENCH ARMY. TIME IS IMPORTANT. WOULD YOU PHONE OR CABLE PREMIER REYNAUD AND ASK HIM TO HURRY THINGS UP? IT WAS GRAND OF YOU TO PHONE ME LAST NIGHT. PLEASE GIVE MY LOVE TO AUNT ELEANOR. QUINT.

Comert immediately insisted on sending the cable himself and assured Reynolds he would have his accreditation quickly. He was true to his word. Film actor Robert Montgomery, who had come to France to drive an ambulance for the American Field Service, offered to take Reynolds and his companions, Bob Cooper of the London *Times* and Ken Downs of INS, to Beauvais, 20 miles north of Paris. They arrived to find a third of the town in flames. Bombing attacks resumed at 5:30 the next morning. A French colonel ordered them out, as they had no authorization to be outside Paris.[16]

* * *

On June 9, Minister of Information Jean Provoust told correspondents to discount reports of the government leaving the capital. John Lloyd of the AP, president of the Anglo-American Press Association, took advantage of the occasion to invite Provoust to speak at the association's next luncheon. Provoust said he would be charmed, then hurried away. Minutes later, he and other government officials fled to Tours, south of Paris.[17]

The next day's London *Daily Telegraph* carried an unsigned dispatch from its Paris correspondent that began: "The French—true to the finest traditions of a nation that has never yet asked for quarter—have decided that they would prefer their city, with its finest art treasures, to be destroyed to any sort of capitulation to invaders. The German dead will be piled high in the suburbs before a single Nazi enters a great heap of ruins." Four days later the Germans occupied Paris without a fight and the correspondent was among those fleeing.[18]

Quentin Reynolds initially declined to join them, confident the Germans would want to trumpet their victory to the world. But Col. Horace Fuller, the American Embassy military attaché, told him he was on the German blacklist—presumably because of his reporting from Berlin before the war—and would be interned or sent to Spain. "I suggest you get out of here while you can," he said.

At a café, a waiter told Reynolds that another patron had a car for sale. She turned out to be an English woman married to a French neurosurgeon, and they were staying. Reynolds gave her all he had, $550. She handed over her tiny Austin. Over roads swarming with refugees, he reached Tours. Correspondents were required by censors to refer to their location as "somewhere in France." This despite the fact the German radio was ridiculing Tours as the "provisional, the very provisional, capital of France." The next day Reynolds moved on to Bordeaux, a city of 250,000 jammed with more than 2 million refugees, boarded a Dutch freighter and made it to England four days later.[19]

Alexander Werth left Paris just before the occupation, taking his Matisse but forced to leave his Derain behind. "When I think of Paris, of all these years in Paris and of all that Paris has represented to European civilization, I have an agonizing pang in my heart."[20]

A. J. Liebling of the *New Yorker* wrote: "The roads leading south from Paris were gorged with what was possibly the strangest assortment of vehicles in history . . . from fiacres of the Second Empire to a farm tractor hitched to a vast trailer displaying the American flag and a sign saying, 'This trailer is the property of an American citizen.' "[21]

Sevareid went to Bordeaux and heard French Radio announce that Prime Minister Paul Reynaud had resigned in favor of the elderly Marshal Philippe Petain, a hero of World War I. Sevareid's rival on another network reported that Petain had formed a war cabinet to carry on the battle. Sevareid went on the air to say in fact it was a cabinet of surrender. The next day, Petain announced the surrender.

Sevareid got aboard a crowded ship, afraid that Murrow would be angry with him for leaving. "There was something else: I knew, if I were honest with myself, that I was physically afraid of the violence of war . . . Others were too, but I had hoped I would be different." He phoned from Liverpool and found Murrow hugely relieved to learn he was safe. Referring to Edmond Taylor, another CBS correspondent in France, Murrow told Sevareid: "You and Taylor have pulled off one of the greatest broadcasting feats there ever was."[22]

* * *

Denis Sefton Delmer of the *Daily Express* learned at the last minute, on June 13, that Paris was not to be defended. He hurried to his hotel to pick up

Edward Ward of the BBC and Robert Cooper of *The Times* of London. "The astonishing thing was that Paris in this moment of humiliation was relaxed and gay," Delmer wrote. "Youths and girls were dancing, singing and kissing in the empty, trafficless streets."[23]

Gordon Waterfield of Reuters also was impressed, each time he returned from the battlefront, to "see the café crowds, the well-dressed women and the elegant young men thronging the Champs Élysées in the summer evenings as they had always done . . . It was not long before the boulevards resounded to the tread of German soldiers and those same well-dressed women were weeping behind closed shutters or fleeing southwards."[24]

Delmer and his fellow correspondents, plus his wife Isabel, were caught in a stream of refugees outside Paris. The 150-mile journey to Tours took 19 hours. Censors there killed their dispatches. A few months after his return to England, Delmer abandoned journalism for the British secret service.[25]

But censorship was lifted while Waterfield was in Tours, and he and Harold King of Reuters filed stories on the imminent French collapse that went to London without a word changed. Surprised British censors held up the dispatches while they tried to ascertain if indeed France was facing defeat.[26]

Noel Monks, an Australian-born correspondent of London's *Daily Mail*, had been covering the RAF in France at the time of the invasion. Monks went to Paris and joined his American wife, 32-year-old Mary Welsh, a former *Chicago Daily News* reporter whom he had married after she joined the *Daily Express* in London. They boarded one of the last trains out of Paris but Monks got off at Blois while Welsh went on to Biarritz. Monks and four colleagues moved to St. Nazaire, and watched a German plane bomb the troopship *Lancastria*. It sank with the loss of almost 3,000 men.

Monks and a colleague went on to Bordeaux, walking part way, and he rejoined Welsh. She reported that he "burst in wild-eyed, tattered, bewhiskered, dirty." They boarded a ship for England. Virginia Cowles, "with her mink jacket," was among the passengers. (The always-elegant Cowles had stood out in her high heels and heavy gold bracelets when she covered the Spanish Civil War.)[27]

Cowles had remained too long in England while France was collapsing, but once she realized what was happening she flew to Tours, then took a train to Paris and drove around for two hours in a taxi, trying to find a hotel, but all were closed. "I didn't want to remember Paris like this," she wrote. "It was like watching someone you loved dying; like seeing a face unrecognizable through illness. With only 24 more hours to live, the heartbeat of the capital had already grown so faint you could scarcely hear it."

She came across Henry Cassidy of the AP, who told her Tom Healy of London's *Daily Mirror* had just arrived in a Chrysler roadster. As the three of them left Paris, she suddenly felt indignation that America had not entered the war. "What was the matter with my country that it could remain so indifferent to the obliteration of the civilized world—her world?"

Outside Paris, cars that had broken down or run out of gas were pushed into fields. Old people lay on the ground under a merciless sun. When one woman's car broke down, some men pushed it into a ditch and broke its axle, leaving her there with her children. "In that world of terror, panic and confusion, it was difficult to believe that these were the citizens of Paris, citizens whose forefathers had fought for their freedom like tigers and stormed the Bastille with their bare hands," Cowles wrote. "For the first time, I began to understand what had happened to France . . . How could these people have faith in leaders who had abandoned them?"

Their own car swerved into a ditch and they had to wait for farmers to come with horses to pull them out the next morning. They finally reached Bordeaux and sailed for England. On June 29, Cowles broadcast over the BBC to the U.S.:

> Reports current in America that England will be forced to negotiate a compromise—which means surrender—are unfounded and untrue. Anyone who knows England knows just how untrue. The Anglo-Saxon character is *tough*. Englishmen are proud of being Englishmen. They have been the most powerful race in Europe for over three hundred years, and they believe in themselves with passionate conviction. Through English history the Guards regiments have fought to the death. When an Englishman says: "It is better to be dead than live under Hitler," heed his words. He means it.[28]

* * *

In Berlin, loudspeakers were set up in the Wilhelmsplatz, the center of government offices, on the day the Germans entered Paris, and they blared national and Nazi Party songs. But Joseph C. Harsch of the *Christian Science Monitor* counted just a hundred people in the vast square. "Not a sound of cheering. Not an exclamation of pleasure. They just walked off as though nothing of importance had happened."[29]

Shirer was among Berlin correspondents brought to Paris on June 17. "It was no fun for me," he wrote in his diary. "I had an ache in the pit of my stomach and I wished I had not come." On June 22, correspondents were taken to the forest of Compiègne to witness the French surrender. Shirer and NBC correspondent William Kerker broadcast the first news of the surrender, a world scoop that was ahead of even the German radio and press. They did not know until the next day that the official communiqué had to be approved by Hitler before it could be released in Berlin. But they went on the air 90 minutes after the armistice was signed.

"I saw an opportunity of taking advantage of the excitement of the Germans over the signing, and by much bludgeoning and with the cooperation of three Germans we dispensed with recording and went on the air direct to New York," Shirer wrote. He learned that Hitler, the High Command and Propaganda Minister Joseph Goebbels were furious. "Some of those who helped us get [the scoop] are catching hell."[30]

Eight American correspondents, representing the AP and UP, the *New York Herald-Tribune*, the *Chicago Tribune*, the *Saturday Evening Post* and *Time*, elected to stay in Paris, hoping the Germans would allow them to continue reporting. Soon all were requested to leave, but Sherry Mangan of *Time* remained until August, when he was expelled. The product of a well-to-do New England family, Mangan was a Trotskyist who doubled as an agent of the Trotsky-inspired Fourth International.[31]

Ralph Paine, chief European correspondent of *Life* and *Time*, wrote from Lisbon: "France was not conquered in 43 days. France collapsed in 43 days . . . The basic sin for which the French are now punished was their long tolerance of stupid, bureaucratic, corrupt, slothful, hopeless, inefficient leadership." He quoted a French soldier: "We've been led by men with the hearts of rabbits."[32]

Three weeks after the German conquest, Harsch visited Nancy. German soldiers had cleaned the town of coffee, tea, chocolate, soap, silk stockings and women's underwear—all items in short supply in Germany. "Up to the time of the conquest a pair of undarned silk stockings on the streets of Berlin was a remarkable rarity," he wrote. "I counted six darned runs on one pair of legs. Almost overnight after the fall of Paris the darns disappeared."[33]

Glen M. Stadler of UP visited Reims and learned that Luftwaffe fliers had visited the city and had taken away 2 million bottles of champagne. Then an aide to Foreign Minister von Ribbentrop arrived and requisitioned up to 12 million bottles. He paid 2 German marks per bottle, the price of two bottles of beer. In Berlin, champagne cost 100 marks, if it could be found.[34]

On Armistice Day 1940 in occupied Paris, students from the Sorbonne marched down the Champs-Élysées carrying fishing poles. The French word for a fishing pole is *gaule*, and the students chanted, "Vive de . . ." with a pause after the de, at which point they raised their fishing poles in unison. German troops broke up the demonstration.

Later Harsch offered this assessment of the early German war successes: "The Continent was lost because the German army which crashed through to the Channel coast was just about 20 years ahead of its opponents in almost every respect as a modern instrument of war." In Berlin before the invasion of France, he had listened to British and French radio commentators discussing with contempt German equipment and tactics. "I discovered even as late as spring of 1941 that to come out of Germany and try to tell people something about the German army was to lay oneself dangerously open to the charge of being pro-German," he wrote.[35]

* * *

In Berlin, foreign correspondents were at one stage coddled by the Germans. They were allowed to import coffee, butter and eggs—all items hard to find on the German market. Each was given a small identification card which helped in getting taxis and smoothed over infringements with police. Unlike Germans, they were permitted to listen to foreign broadcasts. And they were allowed to exchange money at a rate two or three times better than the official rate.

Propaganda Minister Goebbels built a palatial club for journalists. Not to be outdone, Foreign Minister von Ribbentrop established a Foreign Press Club.[36] But Berlin became increasingly oppressive, and American correspondents gradually began leaving—or were expelled. Ralph Barnes of the *New York Herald-Tribune* was given the boot in July 1940 and his colleague Russell Hill was expelled soon after. Max Corpening of the *Chicago Tribune* was thrown out after one day because he broke a story about Germany's peace terms for Britain.

"I ask myself why I stay on here," Shirer wrote in his diary on September 20, 1940. "For the first eight months of the war our censorship was fairly reasonable . . . But since the war became grim and serious . . . it has become increasingly worse . . . I haven't the slightest interest in remaining here unless I can continue to give a fairly accurate report."

The next day Shirer received a tip about a story he would never even have tried to report from Berlin. A man told him the Gestapo were systematically killing mentally disabled people. His informant said the Nazis called them "mercy deaths."

By mid-October he had decided to leave. He wrote in his diary: "I think my usefulness here is about over . . . You are reduced to re-broadcasting the official communiqués, which are lies, and which any automaton can do. Even the more intelligent and decent of my censors ask me, in confidence, why I stay."

On November 25 he wrote in his diary that he had got to the bottom of the so-called "mercy killings." A trustworthy German source told him 100,000 mentally deficient people had been put to death at three locations. Relatives were rushing to remove their kin from private asylums. While he could not file, the Vatican on December 6 made known the killings, denouncing them as "contrary to both natural and divine law."

Shirer concluded his diary on December 1, saying that a clash between Germany and America "is as inevitable as that of two planets hurtling inexorably through the heavens toward each other."

Six days later, Shirer arrived at Estoril, Portugal, and soon took a ship for home. Murrow came from London to see him off, but never forgave him for leaving his post in the midst of war. He also resented Shirer for later cashing in on the war with books and lectures, while earnings from his own books were given to charity. After the war, the two men traveled from New York to London together and, in a chauffeured car from Southampton, Murrow suddenly began cursing and punching Shirer. Taken aback, Shirer never understood the reason for the attack but said Murrow was drunk. Murrow apologized the next day.[37]

Reston left England after he fell ill with undulant fever and took a ship from Lisbon to New York, carrying the manuscript of what became Shirer's *Berlin Diary* which had been smuggled out of Germany. *Berlin Diary*, covering the period 1934–40, was published in 1941 and sold half a million copies. It was followed by *The Nightmare Years*. Shirer became an instant celebrity, given his own Sunday program on CBS and earning well from speaking engagements. He never returned to the war fronts.[38]

Sigrid Schultz, the *Chicago Tribune's* long-standing Berlin correspondent, also had had enough. Hermann Göring had once referred to the scrappy Schultz, who stood barely five feet tall, as "that dragon from Chicago," and Quentin Reynolds called her "Hitler's Greatest Enemy." She left in early 1941. Like Shirer, she had learned of the "mercy killings," involving not just crippled, handicapped and insane people but others who were ill. She did not want to risk carrying notes out of the country so memorized the details.

Shortly before her departure, she was hit in the knee by bomb shrapnel, and the wound still had not healed when she left. She came down with typhus in Spain. Back home, she underwent a three-year convalescence, then wrote a book about Germany and embarked on a nationwide lecture tour. Born in Chicago to parents of Norwegian origin, she had sometimes gone to Oslo or Copenhagen before the war to file dispatches under the name John Dickson, reporting government attacks on churches, persecution of the Jews and the existence of concentration camps. In July 1939, "Dickson" scored a major scoop by reporting the Germans and Soviets were on the verge of signing a non-aggression pact.

In 1944 she returned to Europe to cover the Normandy invasion and Allied march into Germany. She wrote several books after the war, was a founder of the Overseas Press Club and died in 1980 at age 87.[39]

In Berlin, Fred Oechsner was nominated as president of the Foreign Correspondents Association in December 1940, to the consternation of the German government. Italian and Japanese correspondents were instructed to prevent his election, and von Ribbentrop gave Oechsner a direct "order" to withdraw his candidacy. But he declined and was elected unanimously, winning even Japanese and Italian votes. "Even those who had compromised with the system paid this tribute to one whom they admired for his refusal to bow to it," wrote Joseph C. Harsch. The next year, when Oechsner was up for re-election, the government threatened to cancel all privileges enjoyed by foreign correspondents. Oechsner withdrew and a Swede was elected.[40]

The most ominous development concerning correspondents in Berlin occurred shortly before the German invasion of Russia. Howard K. Smith was working the overnight shift at UP when twenty Gestapo agents walked in and began searching the office. Smith was "plenty scared," then discovered the reason for the incursion: Richard Hottelet of UP had been arrested. Smith wrote that Hottelet had been too outspoken in his criticism of bureaucrats and had been warned by a tipster that his situation was becoming dangerous. "He was a little on the loud-mouthed side anyhow." The two men hated each other. Personal differences aside, Smith was politically liberal, Hottelet conservative.

Hottelet apparently was held in retaliation for the arrest in New York of Manfred Zapp, the American manager of the German Trans-Ocean News Service, and Guenther Tonn, one of his aides. A federal grand jury charged them with violating an act requiring agents of foreign powers to register with the State Department. Hottelet and Jay Allen of the North American Newspaper Alliance, who had been arrested in Paris, were released in exchange for the Germans held in the U.S. Hottelet remained in New York long enough to regain weight lost in prison, then returned to Europe.

Shortly afterward, eight Americans in Berlin were arrested, including Paul Dickson of Mutual Broadcasting, and seven were released the next day. Why didn't all Americans in Berlin leave after that? "In my own case, it was always the insidious urge to stay a little longer and see just a little bit more," Howard K. Smith wrote.

Goebbels eventually instituted censorship not just of broadcasts but of the written press, and invited captive nations to send compliant correspondents. "An amazing, motley crew of fake newspapermen began to show up in press conferences," Smith wrote. "They were noisy and exuded odors clearly indicative of their unaccustomedness to soap and water."

Both he and Hottelet left UP to join CBS, Smith while still working in Berlin. But he eventually decided to leave. "Reading over past scripts, I remarked how utterly vapid they were, and that they not only failed to give a fairly accurate picture of what was occurring inside Germany, but even gave a false impression," Smith wrote. "In the pressure of writing each script . . . I had not noticed how completely I had failed to report Berlin with any degree of fairness." Censorship of radio correspondents became "a veritable straitjacket" after the invasion of Russia. "I was actually *ordered* by the Nazis to use their propaganda material!" Finally, the Germans advised him, along with Alex Dreier of NBC and Paul Dickson, that they could no longer use German radio facilities.

Smith applied to leave but was refused for a month. When his exit permit came through, he boarded a train to Switzerland and crossed the border as Japanese bombs were falling on Pearl Harbor—just an hour before the border was closed. Of an original contingent of about fifty American correspondents in Berlin, eighteen remained. Their fate will be discussed in Chapter 7.

Smith, a native of Louisiana and a Rhodes scholar at Oxford before he joined UP in 1939, was confined to Switzerland, which had closed its borders, until after the liberation of France. Then he and his wife sneaked across the frontier and he returned to the war front. In 1946 he was named chief European correspondent of CBS. He left the network in 1962 to join ABC, later anchoring its evening news. He died in 2002 at age 87.[41]

CHAPTER 4

THE BATTLE OF BRITAIN AND THE AIR WAR ON GERMANY

In July 1940, after the defeat of France, the Germans began an aerial assault on Britain that went on for nearly a year. Britain hit back with raids on Berlin, something that Luftwaffe commander Hermann Göring had promised would never happen. On September 17, after heavy losses of aircraft, Hitler ordered the indefinite postponement of Operation Sealion, his plan for the invasion of Britain. The raids continued until in May 1941 Hitler began withdrawing aircraft for the coming invasion of the Soviet Union. The Blitz cost the lives of 43,000 British civilians and left 139,000 injured.

Aboard the ship that took her to England from France, the *Daily Express*'s Mary Welsh decided, as an American, she must find a job with an American publication. She joined *Time* magazine on July 10, the opening day of the Battle of Britain. "The opalescent summer air of London was aglow with staunch spirits," she wrote, "a kind of undaunted 'We'll muddle through.' "[1] The reporting of the Battle of Britain over the next months, by newspaper correspondents and broadcasters, represented one of the most significant achievements of the American media during the entire war. It helped galvanize sympathy for Britain throughout the United States and contributed to overcoming the mood of isolationism that until then had been widespread.

On July 28 the *New Yorker* published an article by Mollie Panter-Downes, a British novelist who had recently begun writing for the magazine; she would later become one of its legendary figures.

Although London may not be precisely comfortable, it is at the moment one of the most exhilarating cities in the world in which to find oneself . . .

Horror may glide down suddenly and noiselessly out of the summer sky
. . . but all the same it's stimulating to be here . . . because of a new vitality
which seems to have been injected into the staid British atmosphere.[2]

Many Britons anticipated an invasion, and the AP and INS began reporting
it was imminent. The UP office in Berlin was besieged with messages from
New York asking it to match the rival reports. "I guess this will finish me,"
Fred Oechsner, the UP bureau chief, told Shirer. "But I honestly couldn't say
they were set to invade when obviously they are not." Shirer agreed. Both were
aware the Germans had not massed landing craft on the French coast.[3]

Previously, British raids on Germany had been confined to areas within
reasonable range of RAF bases. But the British went for Berlin on the night of
August 25–6, a relatively light raid that caused little damage, but which, as
Joseph Grigg of UP Berlin noted, "destroyed the myth that Berlin was raid-
proof."[4] A few minutes before the raid occurred, a censor challenged Shirer as
to whether it was possible to bomb Berlin. "He laughed. It was impossible, he
said." Three days later, a larger British raid killed ten people and wounded
twenty-nine. "People here have not yet been told of the murderous bombings
of London by the Luftwaffe," Shirer wrote in his diary. "The papers decry the
'brutality' of the Brits."[5]

The raids continued. "Berliners, after being marooned for three and four
hours at a time in the middle of the night in their draughty, damp cellars,
showed up late for work in the mornings, pasty-faced and red-eyed and acting
snappish and bad tempered," Grigg wrote. As the raids increased, German
reporting restrictions did as well. Jack Fleischer of UP reported office windows
rattled from a flak barrage, and this was denounced at a German news conference as "intolerable sensationalism."[6]

On August 26, Ed Murrow broadcast about a visit to eleven air-raid
shelters. "In one a Scotsman was holding 25 people enthralled with the
story of the big fish that got away. Over near Wimpole Street . . . a man was
telling about the narrow escape he had when driving on the icy roads of
the Midlands last winter." It was one of the first in a series of broadcasts
in which Murrow expressed his admiration of the spirit of Britons under
attack. "How long these people will stand up to this sort of thing, I don't
know, but tonight they're magnificent," he said in the calm, measured tones
for which he would become famous. "I've seen them, talked with them and
I know."[7]

Born in Greensboro, North Carolina, in 1908 as Egbert Roscow, Murrow
was the son of a poor farmer who soon moved his family to Washington state.

Murrow first visited Europe in 1931 as part of a delegation of the National Student Federation of America, and in 1937 he went to London as European director of the 9-year-old CBS. At the time, no American network employed news correspondents abroad and his job involved arranging broadcasts of choirs and such things. The American Correspondents Association turned down his application for membership, not without reason.

But Murrow began recruiting young men and women to prepare for coverage of a war that seemed imminent. He became the most influential American broadcaster in Europe, his reports playing a significant role in swaying American public opinion in support of Britain. His opening line, "This . . . is London," delivered with a slight pause as suggested by his college speech instructor, Ida Lou Anderson, became a widely recognized trademark. In October 1940 the Overseas Press Club in New York singled him out as the "foreign correspondent who most contributed toward the information of the American people and the formulation of American national policy in international issues."[8]

On September 7, Murrow watched the first heavy German bombing of London from an airfield in the Thames estuary. With him were the novelist Vincent Sheean, reporting for the *New York Herald-Tribune*, and Ben Robertson of the New York newspaper *PM*. "The fires up the river had turned the moon blood red," Murrow reported. "The world was upside down. Vincent Sheean lay on one side of me and cursed in five languages . . . Ben Robertson of *PM* lay on the other side and kept saying over and over in that slow South Carolina drawl, 'London is burning, London is burning.' "[9]

Robertson reported: "We were horrified . . . It almost made us physically ill to see the enormity of the flames which lit the entire western sky. The London that we knew was burning—the London which had taken 30 genera-tions of men a thousand years to build—and the Nazis had done that in 30 seconds."

A correspondent whose writing often contained biblical references, Robertson described that night as like the Revelation of St. John. "It almost broke our hearts to think of what the world had to lose in that city . . . We were frightened and sick . . . it seemed to all of us like the end of civilization."[10]

John MacVane, newly evacuated from France where he had worked for INS, rushed to the Docklands, which took the brunt of the attack. Now with NBC, he broadcast the first report to an American audience of this raid, in which 430 Londoners died and 1,600 were seriously wounded. "The event was a baptism of warfare so horrible that nothing again could ever resemble it. I had been frightened to the point where fear itself had lost meaning and everything else . . . was an anti-climax."[11]

Robert J. Casey of the *Chicago Daily News* and Larry Rue of the *Chicago Tribune* went to the top of the *Daily Telegraph* building to survey damage. "Good God!" Rue exclaimed. "This looks awfully like the end of London." Casey agreed. "We were looking at the biggest spectacle of its kind that the world had seen since the previous Great Fire of London in 1666."

Casey went to the East End and noticed what had been a shelter for 200 people. It had taken a direct hit and no one survived. Through the night he helped in the search for survivors, then at dawn saw stacks of corpses being taken away. "Neither I nor anyone else in the world . . . could have foreseen the trend of the miracle that had begun that night, the triumph of the human spirit over torture, destruction and death. London was as strong as its people. And its people were indestructible."[12]

Before the bombing of London began, some correspondents covered the Blitz from Dover. "We lay in the grass among the red currants and the butterflies while the fate of the world was being decided about us," Ben Robertson wrote. He provided brief pen portraits of correspondents with whom he worked.

Helen Kirkpatrick, tall and beautiful, "had a first-class mind and she used it; already she had become one of the best American journalists, woman or man . . . Helen was a first-class professional journalist, Virginia Cowles a first-class amateur." Because of her social connections, Cowles knew practically everyone in London, including the king and queen and the Churchills. "She knew so many people so well and they told her so much that Virginia sometimes felt she was not justified in putting what she knew into next Sunday's print."

Hilde Marchant, a butcher's daughter from Hull, was a "brilliant" *Daily Express* correspondent, "the best woman journalist in England . . . Tiny, a sort of Spitfire attached to the ground, Hilde was passionate in her belief in the common people." She once refused to go with Baroness Moira Budberg to have supper with H. G. Wells on the ground she admired him so much he could not possibly live up to her mental picture. "She told Moira to ask her again 10 years from now."

The Grand Hotel in Dover was attacked in September and the manager blamed Marchant. He was convinced the Germans had read what she wrote about the hotel in her newspaper. Stanley Johnston of the *Chicago Tribune* was pouring Scotch for two naval officers and his *Tribune* colleague Guy Murchie in his fourth-floor room when the hotel was hit. Everyone plummeted to the ground. Murchie's back was injured, one of the naval officers was dead and Johnstone suffered torn trousers.

Murrow, according to Robertson, told correspondents he wished he had never gone to college. "If he had never worked for a half-baked education he would still be a lumberjack in the State of Washington; there was a satisfaction about that life; he said he had never known that kind of satisfaction since."

One American correspondent, whom Robertson did not name, told English soldiers and sailors that the English were a lousy people and he could take Dover himself in a couple of hours. "The English restrained themselves with good manners from knocking him on the jaw," Robertson wrote. The correspondent in question later told Sheean: "I wouldn't be allowed to talk to American officers like that—they'd knock the ——— out of me."

Robertson lost his sense of personal fear in Dover. "I understood Valley Forge and Gettysburg at Dover, and I found it lifted a tremendous weight off your spirit to find yourself willing to give up your life if you have to—I discovered Saint Matthew's meaning about losing a life to find it."

Benjamin Franklin Robertson Jr. went on to cover war in the Pacific and North Africa. Returning to Britain on February 22, 1943, to become London bureau chief for the *New York Herald-Tribune*, he was killed at age 40 when the Pan Am Yankee Clipper on which he traveled crashed into the Tagus River in Lisbon. Frank Cuhel, an Iowan, a Mutual Broadcasting correspondent, a former Olympic track star and veteran of war coverage on Java in 1942, also died in the crash at age 39. The singer Jane Froman was one of fourteen surviving passengers. After the war a film was made about her rescue and marriage to the pilot who saved her.[13]

Eric Sevareid, in one broadcast, referred to people on the streets the day after a bombing:

> People walk rapidly. They glance at their watches. If they stop to buy a paper, they stuff it in their pockets and hurry on. They run for darkened buses or stand in the middle of the street, impatiently whistling for taxis that go speeding by. Mothers are walking rapidly, pushing baby buggies, looking at the sky and thinking they're hearing a siren each time a car starts up in second gear.

The fear of death that Sevareid discovered in France got the better of him and he began spending time in air-raid shelters while Murrow and Larry LeSueur watched raids from rooftops. LeSueur, a former floorwalker at Macy's department store in New York, joked that Sevareid's problem was that he didn't drink enough. In October, sick and exhausted, Sevareid returned to America, after delivering a final, memorable broadcast:

Paris died like a beautiful woman, in a coma, without a struggle, without knowing or even asking why. One left Paris with a feeling almost of relief. London one leaves with regret. Of all the great cities of Europe, London alone behaves with pride and battered but stubborn dignity . . . Parting from London, you see clearly what she is and means. London may not be England, but she is Britain and she is the incubator of America and the West. Should she collapse, the explosion in history would never stop its echoing. Besieged, London is a city-state in the old Greek sense. Someone wrote the other day, "When this is all over, in years to come, men will speak of this war and say, 'I was a soldier,' 'I was a sailor,' or 'I was a pilot.' Others will say with equal pride, 'I was a citizen of London.'"

Later, Sevareid wrote of that broadcast: "I could not hold my voice quite steady and I felt ashamed of it; I felt that the broadcast was filled with bathos, mawkish and embarrassing to all who heard it." But when he reached home, a businessman told him he had listened to the broadcast while driving and had to stop his car for a moment, overcome with emotion. An American professor of English history heard it in his bedroom and had to bathe his eyes before he went down to dinner.[14]

On one occasion, LeSueur escaped death when bombs destroyed his apartment. Across London, correspondents were being bombed out of homes or offices. Fred Bate of NBC was in his office when a bomb struck. Flying debris gave him a serious head wound, and two women who worked for NBC found him wandering woozily about, covered in blood and hardly able to speak. He remained in hospital several weeks and returned to the U.S. on medical advice. The nearby apartment of James Reston of the *New York Times* was destroyed in the same raid. Murrow was bombed out of his London studio three times at three different locations. By mid-1941, he had lost 20 pounds and in a letter to his brother Lacey said he had "reached the point where my hands shake so much I can't even read my lines."[15]

Virginia Cowles was having tea with Lord and Lady O'Neill when the house opposite was hit, burying six people. Evidently someone thought her house had been bombed and phoned the Dorchester Hotel, where she was often found. A page went through the hotel, shouting, "Miss Virginia Cowles, her house is on fire." One bomb close to the apartment of Tania Long of the *New York Herald-Tribune* blew in shutters, smashed the windows and knocked pictures off the walls.[16]

Raymond Daniell, the *New York Times* bureau chief, became a victim of bombing on the second night of mass raids against London. All his windows came in at once and wooden shutters were blown off their hinges, but he wasn't hurt. He swept glass off his bed and went to sleep. Afterward he moved his staff into the Savoy Hotel at the *New York Times'* expense, but even the Savoy was not safe. One bomb struck while Daniell was entertaining guests and, four nights later, a former Belgian Cabinet member was killed in a raid. In a *New York Times* article, Daniell wrote of the British: "They are living through hell and behaving like angels."

He had left a wife and two children behind when he went to England, not only for their safety but because his marriage was a troubled one. In London, he met Tania Long and they soon became lovers. She was the daughter of a British journalist and Russian-born mother. On a trip back to New York in November 1941, Daniell divorced his wife and married Long, who already had joined the *New York Times* bureau.[17]

Ernie Pyle of the Scripps-Howard newspapers, arriving in England during the Blitz, approached the Savoy just before a raid and a doorman said to him: "They'll be here in five minutes." Pyle asked: "Who is 'they'?"[18]

In the early days of bombing, Mollie Panter-Downes complained that the American press appeared to be mesmerized by achievements of the Luftwaffe. The *New York Times* had claimed German planes "ripped apart English towns and farmsteads." "This read to people living in the supposedly ripped-apart towns like something the Hamburg radio commentator might have thought up," she wrote. After a raid on September 8 left 400 dead, she reported: "The calm behavior of the average individual continues to be amazing . . . For Londoners, there are no longer such things as good nights; there are only bad nights, worse nights and better nights. Hardly anyone has slept at all in the past week."[19]

Quentin Reynolds walked into the Savoy on September 9 and was handed a cable from his friend the comedian Joe E. Lewis in New York: "We are missing you here. We hope they are missing you there." Reynolds and Noël Coward went onto the terrace to watch the bombing. Coward was so entranced that Reynolds had to drag him back inside.

"Living in London became as exciting an ordeal as I imagine living in the Athens of Pericles must have been," he wrote. "The constant threat of death seemed to make people really alive. They would take their beatings, and in the morning shake the noise of the night from their heads and face the new day with a calm display of fortitude."

He went with Bob Low of *Liberty* magazine to a Chelsea dinner party given by a poet. Buildings on both sides had been destroyed but the poet's great concern was that black olives did not look right on his Oriental china.

He apologized for having been unable to serve green olives. Low concluded that such people could never be beaten.[20]

Late one night the apartment Reynolds shared with Low on Berkeley Square was struck by a bomb. They were away. On another night, when they were having a late-night drink with friends, a bomb fell on the square. The blast blew *Chicago Daily News* correspondent William Stoneman across the room and onto the chair where his future wife was sitting. He explained that he had crossed the room to save her. Reynolds and Low didn't like the romantic words to "A Nightingale Sang in Berkeley Square" and composed their own version:

The Abri [air-raid shelter] at the Ritz
Was full of shits
There were Heinkels aloft in the air
There were six miscarriages under Claridge's
When a screaming bomb fell in Berkeley Square . . .[21]

Reston wrote:

We were all unprepared for the terrors of aerial bombardment . . . When it finally started, however, the reaction of the people was surprisingly calm. Even those children who were left in London managed to pitch in. They were terrified of the hideous whoosh and ultimate crash of the bombs, and their screams in the night were almost unbearable, but during the firestorms they played an important part . . . When the little, slow-burning incendiary sticks landed on the roofs of nearby houses, some nimble little boy or girl would scramble up and toss them into the street.

Reston by now was fed up with British censorship. He complained that the Ministry of Information "put a shine on everything the Allies were doing," and advertised German atrocities while covering up "the hideous human destruction" of Allied bombers. In a letter to his wife Sally, he wrote:

The censorship is being tightened all the time and the only thing I can say to you is that we are not reporting what is happening over here . . . If the pride in one's work is destroyed by censorship, sometimes it doesn't seem worth the sacrifice. Anyone can grind out the communiqués and rewrite the official handouts, but we ought to be able to tell a little more of the truth of this beastly war without helping the Germans.[22]

Murrow reported on September 9: "This night bombing is serious and sensational. It makes headlines, kills people and smashes property; but it doesn't win wars."[23] That same shrewd observation was made by a more qualified observer. Carl A. Spaatz, an Army Air Force colonel, dined one night at a restaurant with Drew Middleton of the AP. They heard the scream of a dive bomber and Paddy, the waiter, volunteered that the Germans were "at it again."

"By God," Spaatz said, "that's good, that's fine. The British are winning." Middleton remarked it hadn't looked that way in the afternoon. "Of course they're winning," Spaatz said vehemently. "The Germans can't bomb at night—hell, I don't think they're very good in daylight—but they haven't been trained for night bombing. Nope, the British have got them now. They've forced them to bomb at night. The Krauts must be losing more than we know."

Middleton insisted that night bombing might beat the British to their knees. "Not in a million years," Spaatz said. "I tell you the Germans don't know how to go about it. And look at this bunch here. Do they look worried or scared? We're both a damned sight scareder than they are. The Germans won't beat them that way. Nope, the Germans have been licked in daylight." Four years later Spaatz was commanding general of the U.S. Eighth Air Force, and Middleton reminded him of the conversation. "Goes to show you that colonels are mighty smart fellows—sometimes," Spaatz said.

In one East End shelter Middleton visited, more than 200 people lay on its cold stone floor. There had been trouble on the first night when lascars (Indian laborers) from the docks raped a 14-year-old girl. "Now the older men had formed a vigilante society. The lascars were forbidden the place. The stink of sweat, dirty clothing, urine and excrement caught at your nose and throat." In Christ Church, people lay on dirty quilts in the chill of the crypt and some slept in great stone coffins.

"What distinguished the British experience was that at a time when almost every broadcast, every newspaper headline, told of reverses, defeats and defections, the people of London kept their heads and their hearts intact . . . The Londoners could do only one thing: take it and wait for the tide to change. They did it superbly."[24]

Ben Robertson commented after visiting a shelter:

Here they were, the people who had ruled a fourth of the globe . . . They had been imperialistic and had exploited, they had subjugated, but down in the Tubes of London they were demonstrating that they could take the same sort of punishment they had handed out. These were the people who for a thousand years also had fought for freedom of conscience and speech, for independence of organization . . . They were a tough generation of Englishmen . . . They had Elizabethan fire in their guts.[25]

Daniell reported that, until Buckingham Palace was bombed, the poor of the East End felt they had been singled out by the enemy and neglected by their government. Murrow did not share that sentiment. "It didn't require a bombing of Buckingham Palace to convince these people that they are all in this thing together," he said in a broadcast on September 15. "There is nothing exclusive about being bombed these days. When there are houses down in your street, when friends and relatives have been killed . . . there just isn't enough energy left to be outraged about the bombing of a palace."[26]

In October, while other correspondents were covering more dramatic stories, Robert Casey of the *Chicago Daily News* reported on F. G. Leighton-Morris of Jermyn Street in the heart of London. One night a bomb came through the roof of an adjoining building but did not explode. Leighton-Morris walked across the street, went up several flights and located the bomb in the attic. Rolling it across the floor, he carried it down a ladder, then rolled it gently down three flights of stairs. When he hailed a taxi, the driver asked what he was carrying and Leighton-Morris explained that it was a time bomb. The taxi sped off, as did two others. Leighton-Morris said later he thought the courage of London taxi drivers was considerably overrated.

He decided to walk to St. James's Park, but a policeman arrested him. He deposited the bomb under some shrubbery. When it exploded later, it knocked the front off a house. Leighton-Morris was charged with violating regulations on the handling of time bombs and fined a pound or so. But the press acclaimed him and his neighbors raised £25 to recompense him for a suit he ruined in his struggle with the bomb. Then they gave him an elaborate dinner. Casey later wrote:

The memories that one took out of London in 1940 were stirring and tragic—the wreckage that lay scattered along the broken pavements, the crunch of broken glass underfoot, the red skies by night, the blackened walls by day, the silence of deserted streets, the quiet, unassuming courage of the men and women who still went their ways through the terror . . . London may have been a nightmare in those days but it was certainly inhabited by nice people.

When he came back three years later, to a city crowded with returnees and American soldiers, "London was roaring and prosperous and bent on raising hell . . . Whoopee!"[27]

UP's Wallace Carroll reported that some of the London of Shakespeare, Oliver Goldsmith and Dr. Johnson "met death tonight in the flaming fury of a German fire raid."

> Beyond the fire we could see St. Paul's cathedral. I had never seen it looking so serenely beautiful. As the smoke and flames whirled around its dome it seemed to rise higher above them. So far as we could tell no military objective was destroyed, but what the Germans are destroying during the night can never be restored—beauty, serenity, grandeur, history in stone.[28]

Panter-Downes told of one lady who arrived at a railway station during an air-raid warning. A porter asked politely, "Air-raid shelter or taxi, madam?" And Gieves, a famous firm of tailors, ran an advertisement after its shop was gutted by bombing, saying it was necessary to inconvenience clients for a few days, "as though the fuss had been caused by a bit of spring redecorating."[29]

Ed Beattie of UP wrote: "During the Blitz London was steadfast . . . I suddenly realized . . . that London was home, as a foreign correspondent seldom finds it across the ocean; that it would always have a very special place in my memory; that it was part of me, or, humbly, I part of it. It was a very proud feeling to be a Londoner."

After the fall of France, though, he had thought some people in England wanted peace on any terms:

> It was said that powerful City influences wanted to protect their investments, that big landholders wanted to maintain their incomes, that there were "Munich men" everywhere who still preferred appeasement to a fight. The slow anger of the common Englishman, who had entered the war unwillingly, but with the intention of fighting it out, overrode whatever influences of that kind there were.

Beattie witnessed "the most terrifying spectacle in my experience" in Dover. As he walked toward Shakespeare cliff, a convoy of ships appeared in the Channel and suddenly eighteen Junkers 87s (Stuka dive bombers) were overhead. Two vessels were sunk. Eighteen more planes appeared but one was hit by anti-aircraft fire and exploded. "I was too terrified at what was happening to the convoy to follow the plane out to sea," he wrote.[30]

On December 30 Ernie Pyle looked out upon the Thames and saw something of beauty in a city on fire. "On that night this old, old city—even though I must bite my tongue in shame for saying it—was the most beautiful sight I have ever seen." He wrote of a London:

stabbed with great fires, shaken by explosions, its dark regions along the Thames sparkling with the pinpoints of white-hot bombs, all of it roofed over with a ceiling of pink that held bursting shells, balloons, flares and the grind of vicious engines . . . These things all went together to make the most hateful, most beautiful single scene I have ever known.[31]

The Blitz subsided during the winter but on April 16, 1941, London was hit by more than 450 bombers and more than a thousand people were killed. "London was exhausted after that raid," John MacVane reported. "You could see it in the faces of everyone you met."[32]

In May, Virginia Cowles wrote of one of the last raids:

On nights like this you wonder if future historians will be able to visualize the majesty of this mighty capital; to picture the strange beauty of the darkened buildings. In the moonlight; the rattle of the wind and the sigh of bombs; the long white fingers of the searchlights and the moan of shells traveling toward the stars. Will they understand how violently people died: how calmly people lived?[33]

Martha Gellhorn observed:

The English are an amazing nation and I think it is true that nothing becomes them like catastrophe. When they are really up against it, their negative qualities turn positive, in a glorious somersault. Slowness, understatement, complacency change into endurance, a refusal to panic, and pride, the begetter of self-discipline . . . And they are able to laugh, no matter what.

She visited badly scarred patients at an RAF burn center hospital and wrote of "the fear of these very young men that . . . they will never be able to compete with whole men and will not be able to provide properly for themselves or their families. So they make a joke of disaster and form a Beggars' Union."[34]

* * *

After the Blitz, Allied bombing of Germany continued intermittently, finally reaching its greatest intensity from 1943 to 1945 and obliging the Luftwaffe to concentrate its fighter aircraft on homeland defense. Only 11,228 Germans were killed by Allied bombing between 1940 and 1943, but in the next two years another 350,000 died. This contrasts with 60,595 British people killed by all forms of German bombardment. The British bombed by night, the Americans by day. More than half of RAF heavy bomber crews, 56,000 men, died. Of 100,000 Americans taking part, 26,000 died and 20,000 were taken prisoner.

Correspondents in North Africa had long been allowed to go on bombing missions, but not until 1943 were those in Britain granted that privilege. Stewart Sale of Reuters flew with the RAF over Berlin in January. Riding in the plexiglass nose of a Lancaster bomber, he looked down on "incendiaries which had just struck and looked like strings of gems, others were already an angry red. There were also dark crimson puffballs thrown up by the big bombs . . . The fires behind spread and brightened. Incendiaries streamed across the city in glittering laces."[35]

Flying to Germany in the early days was extremely dangerous. Long-range fighters that later protected bombers had not yet come into service, and casualty rates ran as high as 20 per cent. Harrison Salisbury of UP commented: "To fly in the Eighth Air Force in those days was to hold a ticket to a funeral. Your own."[36]

Sgt. Andy Rooney of *Stars and Stripes* was based in England and wrote:

American newsmen, without meaning to be propagandists, filed stories about hospitals, churches and schools in England that were bombed. Women, children and the sick were always killed in those stories. The stories were true if sometimes exaggerated, and they carried with them the implication that our bombers over Germany never hit a hospital, a church or a school and did not kill women, children or the sick.

Rooney, a celebrated CBS commentator after the war, once watched a crippled B-17 coming in to land. The pilot was unable to lower the wheels and had to make a belly landing. This was a death sentence for the ball turret gunner, trapped when the mechanism that rotated down to let him shoot became jammed. "We watched as this man's life ended, mashed between the concrete pavement of the runway and the belly of the bomber. I returned to London that night, shaken and unable to write the most dramatic, the most gruesome, the most heart-wrenching story I had ever witnessed. Some reporter."[37]

Walter Cronkite of UP and Homer Bigart of the *New York Herald-Tribune* also interviewed returning air crews. Bigart, a Pennsylvanian who began his career as a *Herald-Tribune* copyboy, had a profound stutter and Cronkite recalled one occasion when he tried to dictate a story from an airfield. Bigart turned to a sergeant and said: "Wo-wo-wo-would you mi-mind re-re-reading this to my off-off-office?" The sergeant replied: "Why can't you read it to them?" Bigart shot back: "Da-da-da-dammit. I'm de-de-de-deaf!" Bigart later won two Pulitzer Prizes. He told Harrison Salisbury: "I hate to write, but I love punctuation."[38]

Gen. Ira C. Eaker, commander of the Eighth Air Force, arranged a training session for eight American correspondents in February 1943 before allowing them to fly. Among other things, they were trained in how to fire .50-caliber machine guns. Despite the ban on correspondents taking part in combat, the Americans thought that, if a gunner were put out of action, the plane's survival might depend on someone taking his place. The journalists were to go on Flying Fortresses. But Capt. Henry Cody, public relations officer for the Second Bomb Wing, demanded that at least one should fly with his B-24 Liberators. "These guys deserve some recognition too," he said. The Flying Fortress was much more in the public eye, and most correspondents rebelled at the thought of going aboard a Liberator. But Bob Post of the *New York Times* volunteered.

This stunned William Laidlaw, public relations officer (PRO) for the First Bomb Wing. His fellow PRO, Hal Leyshon, had described Post as the "crankiest customer you ever met." A Harvard graduate and product of a socially prominent New York family, he had a reputation for arrogance but was also known for a good sense of humor.[39]

At the end of training, Cronkite recalled Post commenting that the odds were great one of them "will not be here after the first mission." Post turned to Bigart and said, "It will probably be you, Homer, you're . . . the silent amiable guy who always gets it in the end." Later Post confided to two women friends that he did not expect to come back alive. Yet he had been pleading for two years to go on a mission.[40]

An Air Force public relations man dubbed the correspondents "the Writing Sixty-ninth," a parody of World War I's Fighting Sixty-ninth. The correspondents themselves had considered the names "Legion of the Doomed" and "The Flying Typewriters." The mission in which they participated, on February 26, 1943, was to bomb Focke-Wulf aircraft factories in Bremen. If the weather was bad, the secondary target was the port of Wilhelmshaven. Each correspondent was assigned to a different plane.[41]

"I don't recall being so much afraid as introspective," Rooney wrote. "The chance of being shot down was estimated to be something like one in five or six. About as good as Russian roulette with a six-shooter—which isn't very good."

On the day of the mission, two of the eight correspondents decided they were not well enough to go. "Listen, it happens," Rooney wrote. "The thought crossed my mind that I didn't feel too well myself." The two were Paul Manning of CBS and Denton Scott of the Army magazine *Yank*, both of whom flew on later missions.

Heavy clouds over Bremen meant the target was switched to Wilhelmshaven. Rooney estimated the Luftwaffe had about a hundred planes in the air, and several B-17s were hit. He saw three of them go down. Ten parachutes emerged from one plane, three from another. The third plane exploded in the air. "I don't know what happens inside the brain but I was no longer nervous."

Then there was an explosion in the nose compartment. A shell or shrapnel had clipped off the tip of the nose, leaving a small hole. The bombardier tore off his gloves and tried to stuff them in the hole, cutting his fingers and leaving his hand frozen. The blast cut the oxygen mask supply line for navigator Bill Owens, who slumped over his desk, unconscious. Rooney rushed to the cabin with a bottle of oxygen and Owens recovered.[42]

Cronkite was in the nose of his plane and wrote: "I fired at every German fighter that came into the neighborhood. I don't think I hit any, but I'd like to think I scared a couple of those German pilots."[43]

Post's plane, *Maisie*, was at the back of the formation, and these were often the first planes attacked by fighters. The Liberators had more than one blind spot in their field of fire. Lt. Heinz Knoke, flying a Messerschmitt 109, concentrated on *Maisie*. Afterward he reported:

"My shots hit! . . . My Liberator is turning underneath . . . From behind and above, once again I attack. Strong defensive fire comes toward me. My high-explosive shells hit in the top side of the fuselage and the right wing." He watched the plane fall to earth with one wing torn off. "A crew member tries to climb out of the upper part of the fuselage. He gets free, but his parachute is burning. Poor fellow!"[44]

Before hitting the ground, the plane blew up. Bodies of crew members, and that of Post, were later found among the rubble. Post was 32 years old. Two crew members survived, suggesting Knoke failed to see them bail out. Final confirmation of Post's death only came after the war when his grave was found in Bad Zwischenahn, near Wilhelmshaven. His body was buried at a military cemetery at Neuville-en-Condroz, Belgium. Post had once covered the White House and was an old friend of President Roosevelt's as they were both Harvard graduates. While he was listed as missing, the president wrote on March 3, 1943, to his widow Margot: "I am deeply distressed about Bob. As you know, we were very old friends . . . And it was such a joy to have him covering the White House. There is, of course, always a chance and therefore, there is hope for us all."[45]

Salisbury speculated that Raymond Daniell of the *New York Times* was "clogged with guilt" at not having flown in Post's place. Daniell, he wrote, "feared people would say he pushed Post into it because he and Post didn't get along." Post had been acting bureau chief when Daniell was appointed in 1939. He then considered joining the army or navy, but the *New York Times* persuaded him to stay. Still, he could not have been satisfied with the status to which he was now relegated. Having hobnobbed with British government leaders and covered important stories, he suddenly had more routine assignments.[46]

Rooney wrote that, as good as Cronkite was as a reporter, he was never a great writer. He told Bigart he already had his lead sentence. "Wha . . . what . . . what is . . . is it?" Bigart asked. "I have just returned from a mission to hell!" Cronkite replied. Bigart looked at him for a moment, then said: "You . . . you . . . wou . . . wou . . . wouldn't!"[47]

The lead Cronkite actually wrote: "It was a hell 26,000 feet above the earth, a hell of burning tracer bullets and bursting flak, of crippled Flying Fortresses and flaming German fighter planes." Bigart's own lead: "Our target was Wilhelmshaven. We struck at Führer Adolf Hitler's North Sea base from the southwest after stoogeing around over a particularly hot corner of the Third Reich for what seemed like a small eternity."[48]

Years later, Bigart admitted to Salisbury he had taken part in firing on German fighters. "I just hope I didn't shoot down one of our planes," he said. "Wouldn't it be awful if it was one of us who shot down the B-24 with Bob Post in it?"[49]

Several days after the raid, Bigart wrote an article poking fun at Cronkite's account:

> True perspective is rather hard to maintain in the hours immediately after an assignment in which your own neck was directly involved. You are apt to feel you had a ringside seat at the most crucial engagement since Waterloo . . . This is known as the "I have just returned from a suburb of hell" reaction. To relieve this condition, it is necessary for the patient to hurl himself at the nearest typewriter, rap out a tingling yarn of a flak-filled heaven, of epic dog fights and derring-do.[50]

In another article, published on March 7, Bigart took a more serious tone:

> A mission to Germany is a nasty experience. Apart from the very real
> danger to life and limb, there is the acute discomfort of enduring sub-zero
> temperatures for hours at a stretch and taking air through an oxygen mask.
> The altitude can affect your sinews, your kidneys, even the fillings of your
> teeth. You are very tired when you return. If you are a delayed-reaction
> type, you are likely to feel slightly under par for a couple of days. I must be
> crazy, but I should like to go again.[51]

* * *

Richard Dimbleby became the first BBC correspondent to go on a European
bombing raid on January 6, 1943. He reported that incendiary bombs fell on
the German capital like "great incandescent flower beds." As the plane turned
for home, Dimbleby vomited. In a letter to a friend, he wrote: "I was paralyzed with fright, but it was an unforgettable experience." He flew on another
twenty RAF missions.[52]

Ed Murrow made his first flight over Germany aboard a Lancaster called
D-Dog on December 2, 1943. The plane was caught in searchlights and the
pilot swerved to maneuver out of it. "And then I was on my knees, flat on the
deck, for he had shipped the Dog back into a climbing turn," Murrow told his
listeners. "The knees should have been strong enough to support me, but they
weren't, and the stomach seemed in some danger of letting me down, too . . ."
He saw bombs bursting "like great sunflowers gone mad." The searchlights
continued to fix on the plane. "And the lights still held us. And I was very
frightened."

Looking down, Murrow saw fires spreading "just like butter does on a hot
plate." At the end of his broadcast, he commented:

> Berlin was a kind of orchestrated hell . . . In about 35 minutes it was hit
> with about three times the amount of stuff that ever came down on
> London in a night-long Blitz . . . The job isn't pleasant; it's terribly tiring.
> Men die in the sky while others are roasted alive in their cellars . . . This is
> a calculated, remorseless campaign of destruction . . .

Murrow flew on twenty-five combat missions before the war ended, over the
strong protests of his bosses, who could not afford to lose their most valuable
correspondent.[53]

On the raid reported by Murrow, three other correspondents were on planes that were shot down. Norman Stockton of the Australian Associated Newspapers and a Norwegian Army captain representing the Free Norwegian Press, not otherwise identified, were killed. Lowell Bennett, a 23-year-old INS correspondent, bailed out and was taken prisoner. He wrote later that he had "a strong, persistent premonition" that it would be a one-way trip. Bennett took with him a gun and 100 rounds of bullets. "The premonition that I would not *fly* back from Berlin had been strong enough that I wanted to ensure I had supplies to help ease the anticipated *walk* home."

As Bennett bailed out, he said aloud: "You wanted a big story. Well, here it is. Goddammit." He had a young, pregnant British wife, newly arrived in the U.S., and a 2-year-old son. He dropped into a lake and sank chest deep in mud. Two men in a rowboat pulled him out and carried him to a cottage where they gave him ersatz coffee, bread, liverwurst and cigarettes. Later two sergeants took him to a prison camp near Berlin. He was driven through the capital and saw a city "that had been killed, hammered and pulverized, burned out and blown up with a completeness defying description."

Bennett had been captured before, in France in 1940 when he worked as an ambulance driver. He escaped and enlisted in General de Gaulle's Free French Army before going on to a career with INS. After a failed escape attempt this time, he was taken to a camp near Frankfurt, where Lt. Joseph Borner, a Stuka pilot who had been a salesman in the U.S. and Britain before the war, befriended him. Borner offered to take him on an eight-day tour of Germany, with false papers identifying him as a French correspondent, to show "we are not so primitive a people as you think."

First stop was Hamburg, after the fire bombing that had destroyed most of the city. "This was a devastation unimaginable by previous experience," Bennett wrote. "It was deeply perturbing to witness what a terrible weapon man had invented in the air force and the incendiary bomb."

Everywhere he went he encountered a similar pattern—extreme destruction and death in the heart of cities, little or no damage to vital war installations surrounding them. He came away with a strong conviction that the destruction of cities had been a serious strategic mistake and the chief guilt lay with the RAF. American attacks, he wrote, were mostly directed against legitimate targets.

Back in a hotel near Frankfurt, Bennett snaked down a fire escape from his window, made it onto a freight train and arrived in Prague, where he hid out with a family for several weeks. A relative of the family, whose job took him to various European cities, carried out of Prague a letter Bennett wrote to his

wife and an article for INS. Dated December 11, 1943, the article reached the
INS bureau in London and was published in newspapers on January 22,
1944. In it Bennett revealed he was "hiding somewhere in Nazi Europe."

But his escape was short-lived. Trying to board another freight train, he
was captured, taken to Berlin, tried for espionage and sentenced to death. A
week later, told his sentence had been reduced to solitary confinement, he
was moved to a camp outside Berlin. He tried to escape again, was caught
and transferred to a small camp holding French prisoners. Bennett escaped
again but was caught and taken to a camp on the Baltic coast, where more
than 9,000 Allied fliers were held. On April 30, 1945, as Russian troops
approached, the guards fled, and prisoners accepted the surrender of nearby
towns. Bennett arrived in Paris on May 8, then flew home to see his second
son for the first time.[54]

CHAPTER 5

THE GERMAN CONQUEST OF GREECE AND YUGOSLAVIA

While the desert war in North Africa that began in earnest in the summer of 1940 was under way (see Chapter 10), Britain diverted 55,000 troops from the desert in March 1941 to deal with an unexpected invasion of Greece. Benito Mussolini sent an undermanned, ill-equipped army into Greece from occupied Albania on October 28, 1940, catching even Hitler by surprise. But the bigger surprise was to Mussolini himself. He assumed a country of 7 million people, generally lacking modern weapons, would be a pushover. By November, the Greeks had driven the Italians back into Albania. After Britain intervened, Hitler dispatched a superior German force on April 6. The British retreated in disorder, with 43,000 evacuated and 11,000 taken prisoner, and Germany controlled Greece. Then the Germans parachuted troops into Crete, leading to another British evacuation.

The Italians delivered an ultimatum to Greece just hours before they invaded. Patrick Maitland received hints that something was afoot and stayed awake through the night. At 4 a.m. on October 28, he phoned the Athens newspaper *Proia* and editors gave him full details of the ultimatum and Greece's rejection. It was too late to file to *The Times*, and international phone lines had been cut off, but the British Legation could still get calls through. Maitland went there to file to the *New York Times* for his friend A. C. "Shan" Sedgwick, fast asleep at that hour. His call came through at 6:45 a.m., 45 minutes after Italian troops streamed across the border from Albania—the first news to the outside world of the new war front.[1]

Foreign correspondents in Rome were barred from going to the battle-front. But Eleanor Packard of UP remembered that her husband, Reynolds

Packard, had an old Albanian pass signed by Foreign Minister Galeazzo Ciano that would have been good for another three weeks if all passes had not been canceled with the outbreak of war.

"If you doctor up that old permit you used on your last trip, you could make it look like new," she said. The UP office was equipped with official-looking stamps, and Reynolds Packard stamped his old permit "authorized" and "valid October 31, 1940." At Brindisi, a police officer told him his pass could not possibly be in order and he would be arrested. Packard shouted, "And wait until Count Ciano hears what little respect you have for his signature." The officer gave in and the next day Packard entered Greece. He passed through twelve villages, all of which had been evacuated except for the sick and elderly. A government press officer instructed Italian correspondents that their theme for the day was the warm welcome the Italians received from the Greek people. Packard refrained from sending anything.

Two days later, he was awakened when eight Greek planes bombed a nearby Italian-occupied airfield. An Italian press officer claimed four Greek planes had been shot down. Then Greek artillery opened up. The troops ran. Packard joined an Italian correspondent intent on driving to the front but machine-gun bullets struck the engine and they crawled and walked back to safety.

Packard wrote a series of articles and sent them to Eleanor with an Italian who was returning to Rome. When they appeared in U.S. newspapers, other American correspondents received angry messages from their home offices, asking why they had not been able to match the UP reports. They went to the Foreign Ministry to protest at their exclusion, as did German correspondents, even more furious. Packard was expelled and, in Rome, he was reprimanded by the authorities for violating military regulations. He refused to say how he got to Greece and the incident was closed. The Italians, he surmised, were reluctant to expel him and have him reveal more of their lack of preparedness for war.[2]

* * *

Leland Stowe, Ed Stevens and Russell Hill of the *New York Herald-Tribune* were in Romania when Italy invaded. Arriving in Greece when night had fallen, they drove into a stave protruding from a peasant cart, piercing the radiator. The Greek military provided another car and driver but he had to veer into a deep ditch to avoid a herd of horses. The car turned over but they were unhurt. Arriving in Salonika, they were lunching in a restaurant when bombs began falling. They dove into the cellar and, when they emerged, saw the blazing wreckage of two Italian planes. Two others had fallen into the bay.[3]

They went on to Athens and met up with Ralph Barnes of the *New York Herald-Tribune*, an old friend of Stowe's from his days at the same newspaper. On November 10, Stowe's 41st birthday, a waiter in their hotel marched in with a huge cake decorated with forty-one candles and a frosting that read: "Too young to cover a war." Barnes and Stevens had arranged that surprise. Barnes himself was then 42 and had become a legend in journalism, reporting in prewar years from Paris, Rome, Moscow and Berlin. Stowe described him as "a big, bear-like Oregonian who, after fourteen years in Europe, was as unmistakably American as Will Rogers or a Texas longhorn."

The next evening, Barnes went aboard an RAF plane that set out to bomb the Albanian port of Durazzo (now Durres). The next morning, the plane was reported missing. The RAF later confirmed it had run into gales, rain and fog and crashed in the mountains of Montenegro, far off course. Barnes left a wife and two young daughters. "He had been one of the few truly great reporters I had ever known," Stowe wrote. Earlier, Barnes had told the AP's Ed Kennedy in Cairo: "I've got a wife and children. Maybe I shouldn't take a risk like that [going on flights]. But just the same, as a reporter that's how I feel about it."

Recalling the dispatch from Berlin that got Barnes expelled, about fraying Nazi–Soviet relations, Stowe wrote that Barnes criticized himself afterward, saying he should have been more prudent and accused himself of having left his newspaper unprotected in Berlin. "Actually, he was blaming himself for having . . . filed one of the most significant and revealing dispatches that had been sent out of Berlin throughout the first 22 months of the war," Stowe wrote. In his article, Barnes referred to the Soviet occupation of the Baltic states, adding:

> It is not reasonable to think that anyone in the German High Command has any thought of an attack on Soviet Russia now, or even very soon. What is happening today in the Baltic may not have its sequel until next year or the year after . . . The very acts of Moscow today . . . might be used later by Berlin as a pretext for a settlement of accounts with the Soviet Union.

One year and two days later, when German troops were pouring into the Soviet Union, the *Herald-Tribune* reprinted that article.[4]

* * *

In late November, the Greek military authorized correspondents to visit the battlefront in the north. After viewing the action, Stevens wrote: "Despite the Italians' overwhelming numerical superiority the Greeks do not fear them, but despise them, especially as fighters, and are confident that they can cope with them." Russell Hill later summed up the feelings of many correspondents about the Greeks: "I had often cursed them . . . for their inefficiency, their deviousness, their obstructionism. But it was not this that stayed in the mind so much as the memory of a people that was loyal, brave and hospitable . . ."[5]

David Woodward of London's *News Chronicle* reported that the Greeks had few light machine guns, and their artillery and small arms dated from before World War I. Some carried rifles made in 1897. For Sam Pope Brewer of the *Chicago Tribune*, it was like watching an army going to fight in the American Civil War. "But the Greeks were possessed of a complete contempt for the Italians," according to Woodward.[6]

Cyrus Sulzberger of the *New York Times* wrote: "One ancient plane of the tiny air force, with a crew of two still riding in old-fashioned open cockpits, used to drop shoes, rocks and bottles on the Italians in low-level swoops once their bomb loads were gone."[7]

Woodward and Brewer wrote their frontline dispatches but couldn't get through by telephone to Athens. The telegraph office in Janina refused to accept their dispatches without a censor's stamp—and the nearest censor was in Athens. Driving through the mountains, the correspondents were confronted by Italian infantrymen marching toward them. They hid in bushes, then saw a Greek soldier carrying a rifle at the tail of the column. Two hundred prisoners were under the guard of three Greeks.

When they got back to Athens, angry cables from Woodward's head office were waiting, asking where he'd been. He filed the dispatches he had been unable to send earlier, later discovering that more than half of what he wrote had been deleted.[8]

* * *

The 28-year-old Betty Wason was based in Athens in 1940. CBS was still not happy to be represented by a woman and, once again, New York executives insisted she find a man to read her reports. So a diplomat at the American Embassy, using a pseudonym, introduced each broadcast with: "This is Phil Brown in Athens, speaking for Betty Wason." On her visit to the front, she witnessed a machine-gun battle in which the Italians surrendered after two hours. "I sat within a few yards of the cannon, holding my ears when it went off, wishing violently at that moment that I had never entered the profession of journalism." But Stowe, who was with her and Sulzberger, commented that she was the calmest of the three.

She was struck by the skill and determination of Greek fliers. "Aviators of the 45 plane Hellenic air force, in machines that resembled packing crates strung with wings, struck back at Italian airfields with a courage worthy of far better equipment. One pilot used to take off alone at dawn each day for a Fascist aerodrome, swoop low over the field on which stood 25 or 30 planes, and strafe them recklessly." He managed to harass the Italians for three months before he was killed. "He was a small man, extraordinarily quiet for a Greek, nothing of a hero in appearance."

Wason became romantically involved with a British counter-intelligence agent who was introduced as "Norman Smith." She called him "X." He had made contact because the British thought she was a spy but he soon became convinced she was not. The romance did not survive her exit from Greece.[9]

* * *

Henry "Hank" Gorrell of UP came upon Greek soldiers who had been virtu-ally without food for days and had little protection against snow, rain and sleet. "But still they pressed on, vaulting over the frozen corpses of men and mules, through an inferno of mortar and machine-gun fire."

Between visits to the front, Gorrell had an unusual problem. Before coming to Greece, he had had a romance with a Hungarian nightclub hostess in Sofia and she joined him in Salonika. But she was proving temperamental, and they quarreled often. He rented a cottage and various men were stopping by, asking for her. During one outburst, she told him they were Gestapo agents and she was working for them. "I detest you and all your friends, and should you try to interfere with me, I shall denounce you as an accomplice in espionage," she said. Gorrell went to Athens and persuaded a friendly official to send word to her that he had been expelled from Greece and had gone to Istanbul. The ruse worked and, once she had gone to Istanbul to join him, the Greeks barred her from returning.[10]

Richard Dimbleby of the BBC wrote that the Greeks had a bad reputation among the British:

But when Greece went to war our eyes were opened. I saw the Greek army fighting and dying in the snow, with its thin blankets and old guns. I saw the Greek air force fly away in its handful of old machines to meet the enemy, knowing it was flying to its death. I saw the men of the Greek navy, so proud of their middle-aged British destroyers . . . These men, in the Greece of 1940, were superb.

In one hamlet, shrapnel from Italian planes mowed down nearly a dozen mules. "I have seen many corners of battlefields where human beings had been torn apart by the weapons of modern war, but never since have I seen such a surfeit of carnage. These were only the remains of animals, but we felt sick."[11]

* * *

David Walker of the *Daily Mirror* wrote that Greek soldiers "had the utmost contempt for the Italian as a fighter, and the deepest pity for him as a man." He often saw Greek soldiers giving their slim rations to captured Italians.

Maitland described a steady procession of Italians marching into captivity. "Some came as we stood there, famished, demoralized, downcast. They had been driven by hunger, cold and wolves to forsake their cover." Some Italians pretended to surrender but held grenades as they threw their hands up, then lobbed them at their captors. The Greeks killed them.

Walker, Maitland and Sulzberger returned to Athens and found censors "had played hell with our material," in Walker's words. There were five censorships—the Greek military, Greek police, Greek press office, British Army and RAF. Five British cruisers arrived and the German news agency in Berlin reported their arrival that night, giving their names. But American and British correspondents were not allowed to report this until two weeks later. Censors also would not let correspondents report that the Greek army was suffering from frostbite—so 350,000 pairs of boots arrived from Britain too late to be of use. At Florina, a Greek doctor told Walker that 80 per cent of wounded men were frostbite victims, and 80 per cent of these were amputation cases.

Going back to the front at Christmas time, Walker found only two Greek planes and their pilots available for duty at Korytsa. After loading his aircraft with bombs, a captain added old boots, crockery and anything else insulting he could think of to drop on the Italians. A few days later, he was killed, shot down by nine Italian planes.[12]

* * *

In early December, Stowe and Stevens traveled to the southern Albanian town of Argyrokastron. While Stowe was in a hotel typing, Stevens went out to take photographs just as four Italian planes began bombing. "The next thing I knew I was thrown flat on my face in a doorway, which proved for me a lucky strike, as only a few feet away mangled corpses were strewn about," Stevens wrote.[13] Stowe found bits of window pane flying around him. "I am lying on the floor, trembling, flinching, gritting my teeth . . . I hate myself for it, but I am scared." He went outside and saw a man covered in blood and a horse writhing on the ground, its entrails strewn on cobblestones.

Later the correspondents saw a pilot parachuting from a stricken plane and they cheered, only to learn it was a British plane. The Greeks rescued the pilot, Sammy Cooper, whom the correspondents had known in Athens. His left leg had a long, wide gash going up to the hip. It took eight hours to get him to a field hospital, where doctors worked on him for three hours, but he died en route to a proper hospital.[14]

An Italian speaker, Stevens interviewed Italian prisoners and reported that privates were loud in their complaints about the weather and the lack of warm clothing and sufficient food. "They say nothing of the fact that the cold is just as hard on the Greek soldiers who also stand day and night in snow with only crusts of bread to eat and even worse equipment, so far as warm clothing is concerned, than their adversaries. Yet these Greeks go on fighting bravely and cheerfully."[15]

Stowe soon headed back to America. Walker observed that, on any story, there is nearly always one man who stands out, and in Greece that was undoubtedly Leland Stowe. "He had everything—an easy charm that made telephone girls put through his call before anyone else's, and a journalistic style that really got under the skin of the story." Walker thought Stowe's reports from Greece "were by far the best sent by any English-speaking journalist out of that country."[16]

Sulzberger and the AP's Wes Gallagher were in Salonika when Germans began bombing. Gallagher burst naked into Sulzberger's room just as a bomb hit the hotel and Sulzberger landed on the floor. Windows blew out, shutters and pieces of wall flew around the room and his bed was overturned. He and Gallagher found what they thought was a hot-water boiler that had been blown loose; it proved to be a 200-kilogram bomb that had failed to explode.[17]

George Weller of the *Chicago Daily News* arrived in Athens in April 1941. A Harvard graduate, he had studied acting in Vienna, partnering Hedy Lamarr as the only American member of Max Reinhardt's theater company. He was fluent in German, French, modern Greek and Italian, and conversant in Spanish and Portuguese. He had published two novels, numerous short stories and freelance articles, and had been on the *New York Times*'s Balkan reporting team. In 1940 he joined the *Daily News* and sailed for Europe in December, making his way across much of southern Europe before arriving in Greece.

Weller was in Salonika when it fell on April 14–15. He escaped on a tiny fishing boat, spending three days at sea, then went ashore in central Greece and came under German air attack:

> With your breath coming short and fast and the nape of your neck feeling exposed, you pick possible places ahead—trees, big or small ditches, stone walls, old foundations or simply deep grass . . . You run with your shoulders huddled low, ready to throw yourself to the ground as soon as the machine guns begin uttering their short epithetical bursts of hatred . . . The lightest movement may mean the hose of death which, like a gardener's watering can, is carefully pouring bullets upon every tree and shelter within reachable distance of the road.[18]

By late April, the only American correspondents remaining in Greece were Weller, Wes Gallagher and Betty Wason. Once the Germans were in charge, they kept refusing Wason's request to broadcast. Her pleas for an exit visa drew her to the attention of the Gestapo. She began receiving telephone calls but would find no one there when she picked up the phone. Secret police followed her on the streets.

In mid-May a Herr Plack, a German dealing with the American press, asked if she cared to broadcast to America. She made her first broadcast since the occupation on May 15, a carefully written script that satisfied German censors. Plack then suggested she visit a seaside prisoner-of-war camp. Loading her car with soccer balls, books and playing cards, she visited the camp where 16,000 men were interned. Wason was appalled by her interview with a British colonel.

"The conditions here are frightful, you know," he said. "Unspeakably awful. Thirty-five officers have got to sleep in the same room with the men. And that isn't good for the *men*, you know." Afterward she wrote: "Around a hundred British soldiers were lying in the sand with no cots, no blankets . . . And the colonel was worried because officers and men must share the same sleeping quarters!"

On June 20, the American Legation informed her that the Germans had granted permission to remaining American correspondents to leave. Three days later, she, Weller and Gallagher flew to Vienna but, arriving as unexpected visitors, they were held incommunicado by the Gestapo.

"The following 30 hours to me were more ludicrous than frightening," Wason wrote. They were jailed and questioned "by grim-faced men whose self-important severity made me want to laugh." Finally they were taken to a small hotel and given a sightseeing tour. Then they were put aboard a train for Berlin. Weller and Gallagher were released there but Wason was held for another week.[19]

Weller wrote of this experience:

Few of his fellow newspapermen, the writer may say without false modesty, have been kicked out of the Reich itself in such a magnificent and compli-cated fashion as he has been expelled from the *Lebensraum* [living space]. Until now the correspondent had been able to keep his professional record completely free of expulsions. Now he finds himself overnight excluded by Germany from no fewer than eight [Balkan] countries. This must be the jackpot of being undesirable.[20]

Wason returned to the U.S., never to work abroad again. She found herself inundated with requests for interviews and speaking engagements and wrote: "Everyone made a fuss over me but CBS." News director Paul White dismissed her by saying: "You were never one of our regular news staff."

"Then what, I wondered, had I been doing for CBS all that time in Greece?" she commented. She joined the Voice of America as women's editor, later working for magazines and NBC radio. "The tough struggle to make it as a woman correspondent, ending with the cruel rebuff by CBS, cooled my desire for more overseas war reporting." She turned to a long-time hobby, cooking, and at her death in 1998, at age 86, had written twenty-four books, most of them on cooking.[21]

* * *

After the German occupation, Berlin correspondents were brought to Greece. Louis Lochner of the AP found German officers indignant at orders to facili-tate the presence of Italian officers at a victory parade. "We are fixing those vain monkeys, all right," a lieutenant told him. "Those macaroni eaters won't reach Athens in time for the parade. We officers at the front have ways of 'interpreting' orders from GHQ."[22]

Richard Massock of the AP's Rome bureau visited Italian frontier positions after fighting ended, and a lieutenant implored him: "Whatever you write, don't say the Italian soldier is not brave. If you could have seen my men, in cotton breeches, some of them wearing canvas sandals, cold, hungry, without cigarettes, guarding their position, *poveri ragazzi* [poor boys]!" This special pleading conflicted with Lochner's observations that thousands of Greek soldiers, returning from the mountains, were in equally shabby clothing and often without shoes.[23]

Joe Grigg of UP's Berlin bureau was taken to a prison camp near Corinth. "It was not easy to explain what I, an American correspondent, was doing with the German Army. I explained that we were trying to do a distasteful but necessary job of telling the world what was happening. We quickly became good friends and I was later able to inform relatives of more than 100 of these prisoners that they were alive and well."[24]

* * *

Hitler's invasion of Greece coincided with a massive air-raid on Belgrade on April 6, 1941, in which 17,000 people were killed. German troops occupied Belgrade after six days and Yugoslavia fell in just 11 days. The crisis had been building for weeks. Prince Regent Paul had announced on March 25 his intention to sign the Tripartite Pact previously agreed between Germany, Italy and Japan. But two days later King Peter, who had just turned 17, overthrew Paul in a British-supported coup. That triggered Hitler's decision to invade.

In the spring of 1940, Patrick Maitland in Belgrade noticed trainloads of men arriving from Germany. He learned that some Germans had taken up residence at key railway junctions, others in important industrial cities. His articles prompted the Yugoslav government to expel Germans by the trainload. German and Italian ministers tried to have him expelled but, while the government resisted, it began complaining "about pretty well everything I wrote . . . I became conscious of being watched . . . The Gestapo were on my track."[25]

Ray Brock, 26, an adventurous Texan working for the *New York Times*, also found himself in trouble. He and his new, second wife Mary had sailed for Europe in 1939 on "nothing but a hunch that there would be a war" and the hope he would find a job. A former Texas A&M student, he had worked for INS and UP before going abroad. Settling in Paris, Brock and Mary found work with Paris-Mondial, a radio service for the French colonies. Later he joined Press Wireless, an agency based in Switzerland that transmitted correspondents' dispatches to their home offices. Then Cyrus Sulzberger offered Brock a job with the *New York Times* in Belgrade, and his career was launched.

Along with Winston Burdett of CBS, he broke a story, gleaned from Yugoslav sources, about German troops moving secretly into Italy. Italian and

German authorities demanded his expulsion and the withdrawal of broadcast privileges for Burdett. Later, a Serb official showed Brock confidential reports of anti-German rioting in Milan and Turin and unrest in Trieste. Brock shared this story with Burdett and, once again, the Italians were outraged. The next day, a Serb source told him that a kind of martial law had been imposed in Milan and Turin and Fascist Black Shirt demonstrations held in support of Germany. Brock telephoned the story to the *New York Times* office in Bern and was told that Herbert Matthews, the newspaper's correspondent in Rome, denied there was any truth in it. This time the Yugoslavs barred Brock and Burdett from making international phone calls and again suspended Burdett's broadcast privileges. Not long afterward, Burdett and his Italian wife Lea Schiavi, an anti-fascist journalist, left for Turkey, thus missing the German invasion. A year later, while Burdett was reporting from India, his wife was killed in Iran, aged 37. Reports differed on whether she was murdered by bandits or Russian soldiers.[26]

* * *

While the showdown between the king and prince regent was building, Brock learned of Paul's plan to sign the Tripartite Pact and, his filing privileges now restored, phoned a story to Bern. Later, he wrote of a possible army coup to put Peter on the throne. A colleague in Bern, Dan Brigham, told Brock: "That's enough to get you shot!"[27]

On the night of March 26, he found troops backed by tanks patrolling the streets. Military patrols stopped correspondents and confined them in a nearby hotel. Prime Minister Chetkovich passed by in a car, seated between two Air Force officers. An officer told the correspondents: "Did you see the late prime minister? He is our prisoner." According to David Walker of the *Daily Mirror*, Brock "let out a whoop like a Red Indian and flung his hat in the air." He dashed into the hotel lounge. "Coup d'état!" he shouted. "By God, they've done it."

Brock asked if he could go to the toilet. An officer said yes, and Brock made his way out the back door and returned to his own hotel. It was now 5:30 a.m. and, when he tried to file, he was forbidden to use the phone. Shortly afterward, the new king broadcast to his people, and there were wild demonstrations in his favor. The coup, of course, meant trouble with Germany and Brock persuaded a reluctant Mary to get aboard a train for Greece on April 4.[28]

Robert St. John of the AP attempted to file through Belgrade Radio but was told he must pay on the spot. He went back to his hotel, returned with the money and found the radio had shut down. Returning to his hotel, he discovered his wife Eda had obtained a phone line and was dictating a copy of his dispatch he had left with her.

Censors began threatening St. John with expulsion because his writing suggested war was inevitable. On April 5, the Ministry of Propaganda told him he would have to call on the minister the next day to be told when his expulsion would take effect. That night, German Foreign Minister von Ribbentrop went on air in Berlin, announcing the decision to attack Yugoslavia and Greece. He was still talking when air-raid sirens sounded in Belgrade.

As the Germans began bombing, Brock took cover in an air-raid shelter. Many people had run out into streets to curse the Germans and were killed. Others died when shelters took direct hits. A second wave of planes arrived and bombs began falling on and around the hotel where correspondents were staying. St. John wrote: "We could hear wagonloads of tiles falling into the street. No one screamed. No one spoke. We just stood riveted to the spots we had chosen." He had always imagined he would be "scared as hell" in an air-raid. "Well, I guess I was scared all right now, but I was madder than I was scared."

He looked up and saw that incendiaries had made a furnace inside the hotel. Accompanied by Russell Hill, he went upstairs knocking on doors. If no one answered, they broke down the door. The door of room 225 was locked and St. John asked Hill to help him break it down. Hill replied, "You damn fool, that's your own room."

St. John later described Hill—then just 22 years old—as one of the ablest reporters in Europe. He had graduated from Columbia University and received a fellowship to Cambridge. While waiting for the autumn term to open in 1939, he was taken on by the *Herald-Tribune*'s Berlin bureau to do odd jobs, then made a staff correspondent. When bureau manager Beach Conger was expelled, Hill was the only correspondent left. Ralph Barnes arrived as the new manager but, after several months, both were expelled for "false, hateful and sensational reporting."

Despite the fire upstairs, correspondents went to breakfast on the ground floor. Then a third wave of bombing began. St. John and Hill took cover under a grand piano and found Brock there with a cup of coffee. They left the hotel and went into a shelter, but it was so packed and hot they came out. Later, bombs hit the shelter and killed a hundred people. Streets were littered with dead and wounded, and many still lay there four days later.

"I kept saying to myself, I guess you aren't as tough and hard-boiled as you thought you were," St. John wrote. "Life had suddenly become nothing but blood . . . and pieces of sky that once upon a time had stars in them but now were full of black dots that made a noise like bees." He and Michael Chinigo of INS spotted a limousine in the street, with a young American diplomat inside. They asked for help in getting away but he slammed the door and told his chauffeur to drive on. In Terazia, a lively café and business district in the center of Belgrade, they counted more than 200 bodies.[29]

David Walker of the *Daily Mirror* saw John Segrue, a 60-year-old *News Chronicle* correspondent, sitting by a blown-out hotel window, calmly writing a dispatch with a pencil.[30]

Maitland watched the initial bombing and, strange to relate, enjoyed the spectacle. Then a German mine was dropped by parachute onto the War Ministry, setting it ablaze. "This brought me to my senses," he wrote. He found his car buried beneath a heap of rubble, then got hold of an old Chrysler and drove to a hotel where Walker and fellow British correspondent Lovett Edwards were staying. He invited them to join him in a caravan going out of Belgrade.[31]

Sam Brewer of the *Chicago Tribune* was arrested by Yugoslav irregulars who threatened him with death as a fifth columnist. A Yugoslav friend vouched for him and he escaped to Turkey. "I know what it is like to face a firing squad," he wrote.[32]

A group of American correspondents set out over icy roads for Bosnia. They arrived at Vrnjačka Banja, a summer resort where the government had fled, and sat up writing stories they could not file. Then they passed them around and read each other's dispatches. "They really were good stories," St. John wrote. "Thinking about them now, I'm sure they were the most graphic, the best-written newspaper stories that ever came from any of our typewriters." None ever saw print.

Hill, who had gone to a Belgrade wireless station to try to file, showed up the next morning. After he handed in his copy at the radio station, German bombers returned and he was forced at gunpoint into a basement shelter for two hours. He thought he had scooped the world but learned later his dispatch never left Belgrade.[33]

Maitland decided to abandon journalism until they were out of the country and offered his services to the British naval attaché, who took him on as chauffeur and interpreter. He turned over his car to Walker and Peter Brown of Reuters, who drove on to Sarajevo and set out aboard a tram to try to find a filing point. A Serb soldier put a revolver in Walker's stomach and boasted that he had already shot seven fifth columnists. Other passengers implored him to shoot the correspondents, but he held off when they produced British passports. He took them to a barracks and they were released, with apologies. "Our captor embraced us both heartily and took most of our cigarettes," Walker wrote.

They reached the government press department, handed in their stories and were assured afterward the cables had gone to London. But not a word had been sent. The next day Walker and Basil Davidson, a British spy like Walker who was using journalistic cover as a Reuters correspondent, set out for Croatia. But a pro-German coup in Croatia forced them to turn back. "We were nearly bayoneted in one village," Walker wrote.[34]

The British Legation advised correspondents to make for Cetinje in Montenegro, promising that a British destroyer was en route to pick up refugees, but Brock returned to Belgrade. *Opshtina*, a Serbian language newspaper, carried a dispatch by the Stefani news agency of Italy saying he had been captured in the Adriatic with Ronald Campbell, the British ambassador, madly rowing for Greece. "Now, this notorious American agent and journalist, Ray Brock, can do no more harm," Stefani reported. "He, like Campbell, is safely in our hands . . . and in our hands he will remain until our eventual victory."

The American Legation in Belgrade arranged to get Brock out of the country as a diplomatic courier carrying a pouch to Budapest. There he wrote an article predicting a long guerrilla war in Yugoslavia. Summoned to see the head of the Hungarian press department, he knew the Hungarians wanted to muzzle him so he was on his way to Bucharest at the appointed time. Cyrus Sulzberger contacted him and told him to join him in Turkey. Before he left Bucharest, an old Romanian tipster told him a German invasion of the Soviet Union was imminent. In Ankara, he wrote a story to that effect but Sulzberger was skeptical and suggested he tone it down. Subsequently, a Finnish military attaché and other sources also told him of the coming attack and he filed his dispatch. The next morning, June 22, he was awakened by Sulzberger, telling him the invasion was under way.

The redoubtable Mary, who had gone to Cairo, eventually joined Brock in Turkey and began broadcasting for NBC. But the marriage did not survive the war. In 1945, he wed Broadway actress Miriam Hopkins and that marriage lasted six years. Brock left the *New York Times* and devoted himself to writing books and freelance articles. He died of a heart attack in 1968 at age 54. The *New York Times's* obituary noted he had been married "several times," and all marriages ended in divorce.[35]

Of correspondents left at the coast, Lovett Edwards elected to stay. He had heard BBC broadcasts claiming Serb forces were advancing against the

Germans, and believed them. He was captured and interned in a Montenegrin concentration camp.[36]

Four correspondents escaped by boat in one of the most harrowing experiences of any journalists during the war. They were St. John, Hill, Leigh White of CBS and Terence Atherton of London's *Daily Mail*. They started out on a small sardine boat from the Montenegrin port of Budva, but ran into gale-force winds and the boat began to fall apart. They returned to shore and hired a carpenter to repair it. Then a Serb named Milan Francisikovicz, who called himself Mike Francisco, agreed to go with them in exchange for payment and the gift of the boat at the end of the trip. Setting off with little food, they expected to be at sea no more than ten days.

"In the days that followed, we were all in such a nasty mood that we kept at one another's throats night and day," St. John wrote. On April 20, they arrived on Corfu. A Greek naval commander arranged for them to go to mainland Greece on the *Spiradon Piraeus*, a three-masted schooner, but White feared the boat might attract Italian planes. He opted to take a sardine boat, the *Makedonka*, and Atherton and Mike agreed to go with him.[37]

They had guessed wrong. An Italian plane passed over the *Makedonka* several times, then came back and machine-gunned it, ripping holes in the sail. "It was just a single burst . . . It all happened too suddenly for us to experience any fear," White wrote. "Our only reaction was one of rage—tremendous, overpowering rage." Then they began to laugh.

They put in to shore and Greeks took them to a trawler preparing to sail to Ithaca and possibly Patras on the Gulf of Corinth after that. The next morning, the sky was suddenly full of enemy planes. Seven Stukas began circling and the captain ordered his passengers to go below. White and Atherton threw themselves on the floor of the cabin but Mike elected to lie on a bunk. The Stukas perforated the boat's wooden hull with hundreds of bullets then climbed for a second attack. "I looked up and heard Mike snuffling," White wrote. "His body was trembling as if in an epileptic fit. He continued to snuffle and then the snuffle changed and became a rattle." White examined him and said, "Mike's dead." He had been shot through the head. In a third attack by the Stukas, Atherton was wounded by shrapnel in his right knee. They got ashore with Mike's body, came under a strafing attack and eventually made it to Patras.[38]

Atherton limped into a café there where St. John and Hill were sitting. "Mike's dead," he said. They found that a train carrying Greek soldiers would leave at 5 a.m. for Corinth, near Athens, and boarded it. A German plane came over and began machine-gunning the train. "I've been shot! I've been shot!" White yelled. He had a deep wound in one leg, which was later found to be broken in four places. "It struck me with such terrific force that it set my femur vibrating like a bowstring . . . Someone stepped on me." The train stopped and, as the plane made a second strafing run, Atherton jumped out of a window, Hill ran toward the vestibule and St. John lay on the floor beside White. "They got me, boys," he said, then thought to himself it was a silly remark. St. John had been hit in the calf, but did not realize it until later.[39]

He and Hill carried White off the train and they continued their journey in an RAF truck they found on the highway. They took White to a hospital, where nurses poured iodine into his wound and give him a tetanus shot. The other correspondents went to a hotel. The Germans began bombing a train that had just pulled in carrying wounded Greek soldiers. Every car had a red cross painted on the roof; Stukas dropped incendiaries on the crosses.

"We could hear the screams of wounded men being killed and cremated inside those 20 or 30 cars," St. John wrote. The dead and dying were brought into the hospital courtyard. "The courtyard echoed with death rattles," St. John wrote. "All Corinth was permeated with the smell of burning human flesh."

The correspondents decided to go south to Argos, which had a hospital, and were caught up in the British evacuation. They carried White into the hospital, where his wound was dressed again and he was given morphine, then they slept on the floor of his ward. St. John was awakened by the whimpering of a child:

> She was about five years old. A pretty child with jet black hair. But there wasn't anything pretty about her right arm. It hung in black, tattered shreds. Just as if the hand had been chewed off by some animal . . . I shall never forget the arm of that little girl . . . And I'm afraid that her whimpering will always pound through my brain." A nurse told him the girl was crying for her mother. The whole family, except for the little girl, had been killed in the raid.[40]

White was moved to a private clinic but it was bombed and he was buried in rubble. A man was screaming in front of the building. His hands had been blown off, one leg was in shreds and shrapnel had ripped open his stomach. A doctor told White the clinic staff was going to Crete and he would be left behind. "It's a death sentence," White said. Outside, another bomb threw St. John against a parked car. "Atherton told me afterwards that I raved like a madman for an hour, completely off my head."[41]

White's colleagues were forced to leave him, escaping on a British destroyer to Crete, then taking ship to Alexandria when Crete was evacuated. St. John and Atherton had their injured legs X-rayed there and were found to have jagged pieces of steel buried against nerves and bone. Surgeons said it was best to leave them for the moment. St. John, joined by his wife Eda from Istanbul, soon flew back to the U.S.[42]

Atherton remained in Cairo as the *Daily Mail* correspondent but later, enrolled as a British Army major, joined two other men in going into Yugoslavia to contact partisans. They were never seen again, nor was a supply of gold and Italian money they carried. It was never established if they were killed by partisans, Germans or ordinary robbers.[43]

White was ignored by the Germans who occupied the Peloponnese. A Greek doctor and a dentist removed dead tissue from his wound but failed to find the bullet in his thigh. The next day his leg became swollen and turned the color of iodine. The doctor broke down and tearfully suggested that White prepare to die. But on May 3 he was taken to Athens, where another doctor operated on his leg. His Spanish wife Maricruz, still in Athens, rushed to his side when she learned he was there. His weight had dropped from 172 to 119 pounds and the wound was suppurating. His fever rose and a large chunk of decayed bone had to be removed. Then he underwent his fourth operation. It was not until September that he and Maricruz were able to leave for the United States. White underwent another 18 months of hospitalization and operations in New York.

They were penniless. The Overseas News Agency (ONA), his prime employer, had stopped paying his salary six months earlier. Its director, Jacob Landau, accused White of a breach of contract for having sent a report on the fall of Yugoslavia to CBS, his other employer, and not to ONA. But Landau asked for an exclusive series of articles about his experiences in Greece. "I was too sick to write as lengthily as the subject deserved, but I did write three articles that were syndicated by ONA in 20 or 30 newspapers," White wrote, adding that he never received a cent in payment. The ONA finally did pay part of his bills in Lisbon, but White became involved in "dreary litigation" to try to force the agency to pay his salary and expenses. In the end, CBS paid everything that ONA owed him, and his hospital and surgical expenses as well. As part of a legal agreement, ONA promised to repay part of its debt to CBS in installments.[44]

* * *

The correspondents left behind in Montenegro had their own problems. David Walker reached Kotor on the coast and a Sunderland flying boat came in but there was no place for him on the plane. He typed a dispatch on toilet paper, asking the pilot to pass it to Henry Stokes of Reuters when the plane reached Athens. Later he heard it broadcast by the BBC. Walker noted bitterly that foreign diplomats were taken aboard the flying boat but Serb pilots, who could have joined the RAF, were left behind to go into concentration camps. "It was an entirely disgusting performance."

Walker, other correspondents and British diplomats were captured on April 18 by the Italians. They were driven to Albania, then flown to Italy and transferred to the Tuscan spa of Chianciano Terme. There were 111 of them. Patrick Maitland, he of the outlandish garb in Poland, now wore a ghoulish, all-black outfit he had bought in Albania, and confided that it was his concentration camp uniform. "It included a black coat . . . and an evil black cap with a big brim, with flaps for the ears," Walker wrote. "He walked about clutching a sort of homemade rosary, a bootlace with knots in it, tied in a circle."

The prisoners were given two hours of exercise each morning and afternoon. They played baseball, soccer and cricket. "The Italians treated us quite extraordinarily well," according to Walker. "We lived in great comfort . . . The impression we got everywhere was that the Italian nation was sick of the war and hated the Germans more than ever . . . but they had still considerable faith in the Duce."

On the evening of June 11, after the American Embassy in Rome had negotiated a prisoner exchange, the diplomats were taken by train to Lisbon, where they were flown home. The others went to Gibraltar and were put on a ship for England.[45]

* * *

A final note on John Segrue, the *News Chronicle* correspondent whom Walker had seen during the bombing of Belgrade, calmly writing a news dispatch with a pencil in his hotel. Segrue and his wife escaped to Budapest but were later captured and sent to a German internment camp. He died there in September 1942, and his wife was interned for the duration of the war. "He was a great man—he was nobody's idea of an 'ace' war correspondent, but he saw more hard service than almost any other newspaperman," his colleague David Woodward wrote.

Woodward told of an incident in Vienna in 1938 when Segrue saw Jews forced to wash cars while SS troops shouted obscene jokes and kicked them. One SS man thrust a rag into Segrue's hand and shouted: "There, you damned

Jew; get to work and help your fellow swine." Segrue took the rag, went to the aid of an old woman, and finished the job for her. Then he returned the rag to the SS man and produced his passport.

"I am not a Jew, but a subject of his majesty, the king of England," he said. Then he turned to the SS commander: "I could scarcely believe that the stories about your brutality were true. I wanted to see for myself. I have seen. Good day."[46]

CHAPTER 6

GERMANY INVADES THE SOVIET UNION

The first of 3.6 million Axis troops began crossing into the Soviet Union at 3:30 a.m. on June 22, 1941. Soviet forces, caught unprepared as the enemy advanced on a 900-mile front from the Baltic to the Black Sea, surrendered in their hundreds of thousands. Hitler planned a victory parade in Moscow but rains in October slowed the advance and it ground to a halt at the end of November. The Soviets smashed into German positions in temperatures that dropped to 30 below zero. The Germans began a retreat but a Soviet counter-offensive bogged down with heavy losses. The Russians continued to suffer serious blows through most of 1942.

Joseph Newman of the *New York Herald-Tribune*, convinced from information he picked up in Tokyo that an invasion was imminent, wrote an article to that effect and heard nothing. Then he learned that it had been published on May 31 in the newspaper's business section. In London, AP bureau chief Robert Bunnelle also received tips of the invasion and told his colleague Drew Middleton: "The story should be written and written hard." The Soviet news agency TASS called Middleton's piece "a clumsy propaganda maneuver of the forces arrayed against the Soviet Union and Germany."[1]

In New York, Harrison Salisbury of UP started writing almost daily stories in mid-June emphasizing a possible attack. He based this on information from a variety of sources and words used or omitted by UP correspondents in censored dispatches. UP President Earl Johnson wondered if he might be going too far but, after checking the dispatches, was satisfied. In an article for Sunday newspapers of June 21, Salisbury broached the idea that an attack was imminent. On Saturday night, he told several friends: "Actually, I'm almost convinced the Germans will attack Russia this weekend. Hitler likes to start things on Sunday." On Sunday, his office phoned with news of the invasion.[2]

Weeks earlier, Howard K. Smith of UP noticed something unusual in a Berlin bookshop. A collection of Russian short stories by Michael Soistshenko was missing from the shop window for the first time in a year. A tipster told him Hitler had presented unspecified demands to Stalin. The next day Smith accepted a job with CBS. Censors removed all references to Russia from his broadcasts. At 5 a.m. on June 22, the Foreign Ministry announced the attack had begun.[3]

Joe Grigg of UP asked a Nazi why Hitler had attacked. The official replied that Hitler was convinced war with the United States was inevitable and needed to ensure a supply of Caucasus oil for his war machine and Ukrainian wheat to save all Europe from starvation. "It is an essential insurance policy for us against an Anglo-American blockade of Europe," he said.[4]

* * *

Only a handful of Western correspondents were based in Moscow—the *New York Times* had no one there—and they were straitjacketed in their reporting. Soviet authorities would not allow them to visit the front and they were dependent on often misleading official announcements and Soviet newspapers for scraps of information.[5]

Not so Curzio Malaparte of the Milan daily *Corriere della Sera*, who followed German troops into the Soviet Union. Born to an Italian mother and German father, Malaparte's original name was Kurt Erich Suckert, but he dropped that in 1925. He had been an early member of the Italian Fascist Party but later attacked Hitler and Mussolini and was imprisoned several times. Despite this, *Corriere della Sera* hired him in 1941 as a war correspondent. Before going into Russia, he covered the German occupation of Poland and wrote of the Warsaw ghetto: "The dead lay in the hallways, corridors, on the landings, the stairs or on beds in rooms crowded with pallid and silent people. Their beards were dirty with mud and sleet . . . They were as hard and rigid as Chagall's dead Jews . . ."[6]

After the capture of the Ukraine village of Cornolenca in July, he learned that a Soviet political commissar had been found strangled to death. A pencil-written note in his pocket said: "I have given my men the order to kill me." Presumably he preferred death to disgrace for failing to hold the town. On July 7, Malaparte wrote: "It is clear that the muzhik [peasant] of 1941 fights like a modern industrial worker rather than a muzhik . . . the major industrial creation of Communism is not the collective farms, the giant workshops of heavy industry, but the Red Army."[7]

On August 7, Malaparte encountered a stench of burned meat in Jampol. Hundreds of carbonized horses lay in the courtyard of a kolkhoz, or collective farm. In another kolkhoz, cows had been disemboweled by bombing and partly burned. Inside an overturned Soviet tank was the body of the driver, a woman in her thirties. He reported that the entire population of Jampol, 70 per cent of it Jewish, had fled into woods at the German approach. In a large ditch outside town, built for collecting manure, he found forty Jews crying out for bread. A German officer ordered troops to distribute bread to them.

Malaparte said German troops were amazed to find retreating Russians left the battlefields in good order, even taking away spent cartridge cases. "They leave only some dead, here and there; the last fallen, the last who remained to protect the retreat of their comrades . . . They lie on the green grass as if they had fallen from the sky."

The Germans told him the Russians were the best soldiers they had met. "They don't surrender. They fight to the last, with grave and calm stubbornness." In the autumn of 1941, he reported, Germans began killing prisoners who could no longer walk on blistered feet. They also set fire to villages unable to hand over a fixed quota of crops and livestock. "When only a few Jews remained, they began hanging the peasants . . . They hung them side by side with the rain-washed corpses of the Jews that had been dangling for days under the black sky."[8]

Author Phillip Knightley reported that the Germans complained to Italian authorities about Malaparte's writing and in September he was recalled to Milan and threatened with internal exile. Malaparte gave a different reason for his return. As a soldier in World War I, he had suffered lung damage from gas and said he found it difficult to breathe the dust in Russia.[9]

* * *

Censorship may have hamstrung correspondents in Moscow, but for a time UP had an advantage. Its London listening posts began picking up a special wireless phone transmission each evening to newspapers in Leningrad, sometimes as much as 24 hours before the dispatches reached London by cable. UP's competitors failed to discover the source until one of them offered a high salary to a member of the UP listening-post staff. Soon the Russians changed the transmission so it couldn't be picked up in London.[10]

Soviet correspondents, of course, covered the battlefronts. Vasily Grossman became a correspondent for the Red Army newspaper *Krasnaya Zvezda* (Red Star) at age 36 after he had been turned down for military service because he was bespectacled, overweight and leaning on a stick. As a correspondent, he was given the rank of private; officer ranks were reserved for Communist Party members. When he reached the front in Ukraine in August 1941, he was horrified by the army's lack of preparation and suspected Stalin was mainly responsible.[11]

Ilya Ehrenburg, a *Pravda* correspondent, had been based in Paris during the fall of France and was a friend of Picasso and other artists. He reported that German planes on July 20 dropped thousands of incendiary bombs on Smolensk, but almost all were rendered harmless by women, children and old men throwing water on them or covering them with sand. In Vitebsk, a brewery worked for a whole day filling thousands of bottles with inflammable liquid. "Then bold men crept up to the [German] tanks and destroyed 11 of them. They also threw incendiary bottles at motorcyclists."

The Germans found Vitebsk deserted. But seven men had waited two days near a mined bridge over the river Dvina for German tanks and artillery to appear. As they were crossing, they were blown up. Subsequently the seven men were killed. In one village, Ehrenburg wrote, German troops flogged children before their mothers' eyes to force the women to say where partisans were hidden. The women watched passively, saying nothing.[12]

German bombing of Moscow began on July 21 when more than 200 planes attacked. Seventeen were shot down and the next night the Germans lost fifteen. At the height of the raids, three-quarters of a million people were sleeping in subway stations and tunnels.

In those days, Soviet authorities put out propaganda claims of enormous German losses and relatively smaller ones for their own forces. The American novelist Erskine Caldwell (*God's Little Acre*), who had arrived in Moscow with his wife, *Life* photographer Margaret Bourke-White, to cover the fighting for the New York newspaper *PM*, seems to have bought these fantastic claims without question. But he also reported an unusual tactic adopted by Soviet fliers and used throughout the early stages of the war. When their ammunition was exhausted, they would slice off the tail of German planes with their wings. Their own planes did not always survive. Caldwell wrote that many bombs dropped on Moscow were duds. "And the pilots wouldn't earn merit badges for marksmanship at a Maryland clambake."[13]

* * *

Berlin-based correspondents were taken into the Soviet Union by the Germans to show off what they described as Russian brutality. At Lemberg (modern L'viv), they displayed several hundred corpses of Ukrainians and Poles who they said had been killed by Soviet agents when Russian troops withdrew. "Our reaction . . . wasn't horror. It was nausea," said UP's Jack Fleischer.

An SS lieutenant colonel then took them to a prison where he said the Russians executed all political prisoners before retreating. In the prison yard were rows of bodies of men, women and children, each shot in the back of the head. At another prison, about fifteen men were huddled in a corner and identified as Jews suspected of having aided the Russians in their executions. In a garage Fleischer saw another fifteen men in a room filled with steam. They were fully clothed, with sweat rolling down their faces, and a German officer explained this was to "soften up" the suspects to make them talk.[14]

* * *

By September 1941 Erskine Caldwell was nettled by Soviet censorship. "Almost without exception, what is sent out from the Soviet Union is favorable to the home side," he wrote. "Censorship of information and comment regarding civilian life is as rigid as that of military movements." But he contended that a controlled press had enabled the country to rally its people and halt the German advance. So much for his journalistic credentials.[15]

His wife, Bourke-White, once cabled *Life* in New York: MUST ASK FOR ANOTHER THOUSAND DOLLARS BECAUSE REGRET LIVING COSTS RISING ASTRONOMICALLY. Soviet censors changed that to: MUST ASK FOR ANOTHER THOUSAND DOLLARS BECAUSE REGRET LIVING.[16]

Foreign correspondents were taken on a six-day tour of the Smolensk area. Nine Junkers Ju-88s bombed Vyazma where correspondents were staying on September 27. Wallace Carroll of UP and Henry Cassidy of the AP were sharing a hotel room when the bombers struck. Carroll hit the floor but Cassidy just pulled the covers over his ears. Then a bomb blew out the windows. Cassidy dived over Carroll's bed and landed on top of him. More bombs came down and the hotel "trembled like a ship in a storm," Carroll wrote.

In nearby Ushakovo, the only habitation remaining was a wooden birdhouse in a birch tree. Another town, Yelnya, looked untouched but it was almost devoid of people. Russian officers told correspondents that, on the night of September 4, the Germans had locked inhabitants in a church and set fire to it before retreating. "This [Russian] army had seemed to us to be an excellent fighting machine," Carroll wrote. "The men were sturdy, well-clothed and well-equipped." But he thought the Russians seemed short of tanks and bombers.[17]

Philip Jordan, who arrived in Moscow for *The Times* of London but switched to the *News Chronicle*, was struck by how poorly equipped the Germans were for winter. "I have seen prisoners brought in on the Moscow front when the temperature was something like 25 degrees below zero Fahrenheit, dressed as I might be for a winter's day shopping in London." The prisoners lacked padded coats, woolen gloves and fur hats with ear flaps. "To protect ears, only flaps of forage caps, hardly more use than a pocket handkerchief would have been." Jordan believed the battle in the Smolensk area destroyed the myth of German invincibility. "It died precisely because the Russians never believed in it."[18]

* * *

The German drive on Moscow began on September 30. Grossman was in a forest southwest of Moscow. Some people looked up, saw what they believed were German bombers and ran, pursued by the shrill voice of a woman denouncing them as cowards. The "bombers" were a flock of cranes.[19]

Caldwell wrote that Americans in Moscow were doom mongers, predicting the Germans would soon march in. "The conduct of Americans in Moscow during those days frequently made me feel ashamed of being one myself. Of all the brave men in Moscow, the Americans were undoubtedly the lesser." He and Bourke-White ended their stay on October 1.[20]

* * *

The Russian-speaking Edmund Stevens broke off coverage in North Africa in August to fly to Russia as interpreter and technical adviser to members of Churchill's staff who had arrived to try to convince Stalin to meet Churchill and Roosevelt. After the visit, Stevens returned to North Africa.[21]

Likewise Quentin Reynolds failed to get a visa for Moscow so abandoned journalism briefly to become press officer for a mission to Moscow by Roosevelt's envoy Averell Harriman. After Harriman left, Reynolds visited Vyzama and a Russian major told him how the army had tried to convert a large warehouse into a hospital, but all the doctors and nurses had been killed when a time bomb left by the Germans exploded. "The smell of trapped bodies decaying in rubble hung nauseatingly in the air." Local people told Reynolds of shootings, hangings, torture, rape, starvation and epidemic sickness. He came to a "sobering realization" that he had often been guilty of glamorizing the war in his articles and books. When correspondents were ordered on October 15 to relocate to Kuibyshev, 600 miles east of Moscow on the Volga River, he went along. But a story he attempted to send was heavily censored, so he left for Cairo.[22]

* * *

Correspondents were soon pouring into the Soviet Union, some traveling in convoys of merchant ships on the dangerous route from northern Scotland to Arkhangelsk. Along the way the ships encountered mountainous waves, ice storms and the constant threat of attack by German planes and submarines. One British correspondent pulled out of such a trip after discovering his newspaper had not provided him with war-risk insurance.

"I wanted to see Russia more than I wanted to do anything else in my life," wrote Larry LeSueur of CBS. After the sea crossing, he and five colleagues spent seventeen days traveling by train to Kuibyshev. The city's population was swollen by half a million Moscow refugees and correspondents were plunged into despondency. The only news they received came from Moscow Radio, and Soviet newspapers arriving three days late. LeSueur had to walk more than a half mile over icy streets to reach the Kuibyshev radio station for broadcasts to New York. Because of a nine-hour time difference, he broadcast at 4 a.m. Russian time.[23]

After the attack on Pearl Harbor, one Japanese correspondent staying in the same hotel encountered Cyrus Sulzberger. Bowing and smiling, he said: "So sorry, we sank your fleet this morning. Supposing we are at war."[24]

Philip Jordan commented that he had never met a more competent, more patient or kinder body of colleagues than those in Kuibyshev. "We never quarreled. The only exceptions to this rule were the Japanese journalists, who could not hold their liquor, and were a thumping nuisance after midnight . . . In the days immediately after Pearl Harbor they used to celebrate all night, mainly by heaving the furniture about."[25]

On December 12 a communiqué from Moscow said German armies around the capital were in full retreat, and the correspondents—except for the Japanese—were allowed to fly to Moscow the next day. LeSueur made his first broadcast from the capital and received a cable from CBS: "Broadcast unheard in New York."

The next day, correspondents were taken to the front. Twenty-five miles north of Moscow were battered German tanks and artillery and burned-out villages. Women were picking through the wreckage, some weeping. In Solnechnogorsk, a pharmacist told how German soldiers had broken most of her medicine bottles until she complained and an officer made them stop. When the German retreat was ordered, two officers came into her house and began to cry. The Germans stole all her family's blankets and gave them no food.[26]

"For 25 miles stretched a graveyard of panzers, piles of frozen bodies, a jumble of personal effects," Henry Cassidy wrote. "I counted up to 1,000 wrecked tanks, armored cars, troop carriers, trucks, cars, motorcycles, then grew tired of counting."[27]

In the autumn, the German advance had been stalled not merely by stalwart defenders but by the weather. A short freeze and snowfall on October 6 was followed by a thaw that turned the terrain to mud. "The Germans must get stuck in our hellish autumn . . .," Grossman wrote. On December 17 he reported from a newly liberated village in which Germans had been camping just six hours earlier, their belongings still on the table of a log cottage. A woman told Grossman that Germans crowded into her house and "stood by the stove like sick dogs, their teeth chattering, shaking . . . As soon as they got warmer, they began to scratch themselves . . . Lice had started moving again on their bodies because of the warmth."[28]

Konstantin Simonov, a *Krasnaya Zvezda* correspondent, reported in November on captured Germans. "Back in July it was impossible to tell if a particular German POW was brave or chickenhearted. Like all conquerors, they were insolent and conceited . . . They are different now. Some of them shiver, whine and sing like canaries. Others just stare vacantly with the apathy of complete despair. A bully is always a coward." A month later he wrote: "The Germans will try to extricate themselves from our envelopments, but we shall force them to retreat through impassable forests and burned-down villages. Today they are freezing to death by the dozens; tomorrow frostbite will do them in by the hundreds."[29]

In January 1942 Grossman covered operations southeast of Kharkov. Roads were littered with German bodies, many killed by the cold. "Practical jokers put the frozen Germans on their feet, or on their hands and knees, making intricate, fanciful sculpture groups." The Germans wore torn boots, thin overcoats and had stuffed paper inside shirts to try to ward off cold. Three months later, Grossman took a break from reporting to write a novel about the fighting of 1941. Entitled *The People Immortal*, it was serialized over eighteen issues in *Kraznaya Zvezda.*[30]

* * *

Eve Curie, the daughter of Nobel Prize-winning physicist Marie Curie, arrived in Russia in January 1942 as part of what might be described as a Cook's tour of world battlefronts. She had written a best-selling biography of her mother that made her only slightly less famous, and she had a special war assignment from the *New York Herald-Tribune* that already had taken her to Egypt, Lebanon, Syria and Tehran. At all of her stops, her fame and that of her mother ensured she received privileged treatment. She quickly left Kuibyshev for Moscow and a visit to the front while other correspondents cooled their heels in the remote Volga city. "Mr. [Solomon] Lozovsky, the Vice-Commissar for Foreign Affairs, had decided that I should not be requested to follow the routine imposed on other correspondents and that my trip to Russia should have an independent program," she wrote with undisguised smugness. Lozovsky assigned a woman army officer, Lt. Liuba Mieston, to escort Curie and they set off for the front on January 15. At Istra, a town near Moscow where the writer Anton Chekov once lived, they discovered the Germans had blown up the famous Monastery of New Jerusalem.

Townspeople in Volokolamsk told them the Germans had burned alive 150 wounded Russian soldiers after locking them in a monastery. More dozens of prisoners were burned alive in the Children's Hospital, and the Germans were said to have machine-gunned children who laughed at them. Curie was uncertain whether to believe such horror stories, "but everyone in town gave the same story and swore it was true." At Mikhailova, Curie saw several hundred dead lying in the snow together with dead horses and disabled guns. The Germans had retreated too quickly to bury the men but had mined many of them.

On January 18 Curie traveled to Tula, 130 miles south of Moscow, and Yasnaya Polyana, the home of Lev Tolstoy that had become a museum. Tula, a city of 350,000 people, seemed less damaged than she had expected. But at Yasnaya Polyana, where she was accompanied by Tolstoy's grand-niece Sophia Andreyevna, windows were broken and there were large holes in the floors made by fires the Germans set before their retreat on December 14. Most of the author's books, documents, pictures and furniture had been evacuated to Siberia before the Germans arrived. They burned the local schoolhouse, a teacher's home and a hospital, then set fire to Tolstoy's home but the museum staff saved it.

Curie was given her third outing on January 23 to Mozhaysk, 80 miles southwest of Moscow. There the Germans had put 200 people inside the

Cathedral of the Holy Trinity and dynamited it. A Soviet commander told her Germans abandoned 300 wounded Russian prisoners without treatment for two days and some died from the cold. In Ouvarova, 15 miles west of Mozhaysk, sixty civilians had been shot and eight hanged. The Russians made three German prisoners available for Curie to interview. They told her that the German attack on Poland had been justified, but not the invasion of the USSR.[31]

* * *

Eddy Gilmore of the AP made his first visit to the front in January at Mozhaysk, apparently at the same time as Curie. The temperature was 52 below zero. While they controlled Mozhaysk, the Germans sawed in half statues of Lenin and Stalin. A Russian colonel told him more than 100,000 Germans had been killed in this area. He asked to see the bodies and the colonel said they had been buried. When he asked to see the graves and was refused, he became suspicious of the claim.[32]

Ehrenburg, also in Mozhaysk on January 24, wrote that the Germans blew up the Cathedral of St. Nicholas, the Church of the Ascension, the local cinema and the waterworks. "They had mined the hospital but failed to blow it up. They did, however, succeed in blowing up 100 of their own wounded." The Borodino museum, site of a pivotal battle between the Russian army and Napoleon's troops in 1812, was still burning.[33]

* * *

The correspondents in Moscow were sent back to Kuibyshev in March 1942. Philip Jordan had left Russia by then. An astute correspondent but also a believer in the Soviet system, he commented: "My greatest fear is that after the war [Russia] will make its peace with the capitalist countries of the world and thereby abandon to their own devices and to the malice of their enemies those of us who wish to see Socialism born into the world at large."

But life in Russia had opened his eyes, if only partially, to some aspects of the system. He found its social as opposed to its political philosophy abhorrent. The Communist Party, on the other hand, was incorruptible, "indeed almost monastic in many ways." But the same could not be said for Lavrenti Beria's NKVD (secret police). Still, he doubted that corruption "goes beyond normal limits." One can only assume he blushed in later years at that appraisal of one of history's greatest mass murderers. He observed that

Soviet censorship, when he arrived, was the most oppressive he had ever encountered. But later it became freer and "was always far more of a political censorship than a military censorship."[34]

LeSueur bridled at the return to Kuibyshev, "a correspondent's purgatory," he fumed. "The strain of the long winter is telling on me as well as on the other correspondents. The complete lack of fresh vegetables, the inertia of seven months' confinement in hotels because walking conditions are so bad in the snow and the frequent mild attacks of dysentery have made us all irritable and argumentative."[35]

* * *

Alexander Werth, the St. Petersburg-born *Sunday Times* correspondent, was asked by the British Foreign Office news department if he would be willing to go to Russia for Reuters. He agreed, after Reuters consented to his continuing to work for the newspaper. Presumably the Foreign Office paid his Reuters salary, or part of it, as it did for other Reuters correspondents. But Werth did not say. He arrived in June 1942 and found Moscow people looking haggard and pale, with scurvy fairly common. In dental clinics, teeth were now being pulled without anesthetic. Nearly half the population was still away and most shops were empty. He spoke to some German prisoners: "These fellows in the summer of 1942 were the most arrogant gang I had ever seen."

Like Curie, he visited Yasnaya Polyana. A vaulted room on the ground floor, where Tolstoy had written *War and Peace*, had been turned into a "casino," and the Germans staged drunken orgies there at night. There was no bathroom, so the Germans relieved themselves in one of the rooms.[36]

* * *

In June the correspondents exiled to Kuibyshev were back in Moscow, and on June 25 they returned to Solnetchnogorsk. An 8-year-old girl in hospital there, Natasha, had no feet. A nurse said the Germans forced her and others to walk across a field to see if it were mined. Natasha also lost her parents. Another girl, Tamara, had no hands. They were amputated because of frost-bite after she, her father and baby brother fled to the woods.

Censorship had been relaxed. Correspondents could now write about the hardships of Russian workers or defeats of the Red Army in Ukraine. They were all assigned rooms in the Metropole Hotel, just off Red Square, and given special treatment including food not available to most of the population. In the spring they were given strawberries and, although this brought on mild dysentery, "we who had not eaten any fresh fruit for seven months could not resist their red ripeness," LeSueur wrote.[37]

Japanese correspondents marched triumphantly into the hotel dining room, waving vodka bottles and singing patriotic songs every time their armies scored a success. The Metropole management finally moved them into a separate dining room.[38]

Walter Graebner of *Time*, on a brief visit, reported there were about twenty-five correspondents at the Metropole and every day they tried to scoop one another. But most of their news came from the four, four-page Moscow newspapers that were available to everyone at the same time. Competition was keenest among agency correspondents. Harold King of Reuters held an advantage because he had hired a motorcyclist to speed his copy to the telegraph office. The motorcyclist was christened the "King's Messenger." The AP and UP each had 14-year-old girl runners, Zena and Venus, who were "fast as fawns."

Graebner noted there were few women available for correspondents to meet—although Eddy Gilmore did meet and marry a Russian woman, Tamara Kolb-Chernashovaya—so most correspondents spent their evenings playing poker or chess. Walter Kerr of the *New York Herald-Tribune* was the champion at both, taking hundreds of rubles from his colleagues.

In June, reporters formed the Anglo-American Correspondents Association, and Graebner was amused by its proceedings. Henry Shapiro of UP, the president, opened one meeting by confessing he had made a mistake in requesting the Metropole manager to separate the correspondents' secretary-translators from them at lunch. The secretary-translators were moved to the main dining room, where they were given food of inferior quality. They complained, so Shapiro called the meeting to decide how to remedy his error.

A. T. Cholerton of the *Daily Telegraph*, who had never learned Russian in fifteen years in Moscow, "tried to make Shapiro's misery even worse by baiting him every time he opened his mouth." The argument went on for hours. Leland Stowe made a speech saying there was a larger issue involved than food: the Russian girls would now think the correspondents considered themselves superior to Russians and would draw the conclusion that the U.S. and Britain would be willing to let the Germans smash "inferior" Russians. The speech made no impression. Ralph Parker of the *New York Times* thought the girls would be happier to be away from their bosses at midday. Finally, the association voted to bring the secretaries into the same room but at separate tables, and to try to get the quality of their food restored. Thus, the kind of weighty issues burdening correspondents who couldn't often get to the front lines.[39]

* * *

Unlike most correspondents, Stowe found Russian censorship "extremely reasonable and fair." The *Chicago Tribune*, the *New York Daily News*, the Hearst press and some other newspapers, he wrote, "were consistently flouting [sic] an anti-Soviet bias and a thinly disguised aversion to fighting it out with Nazi Germany . . . The British press was less offensive than the American in tone, but some Britishers privately made up for that."

Through friendship with Ehrenburg, Stowe wangled a seven-day visit to the Rzhev war front in early October 1942. In a village near Rzhev, he went into a house and "found myself in a newspaper composing room." A Red Army newspaper, *Son of the Fatherland*, was being put together there, using a small press located on the floor of a truck behind the house. It was one of several score of army newspapers being published on the front lines.

Near Kalinin, Stowe interviewed a boy named Petya, who said the Germans came into the town looking for Jews and relatives of partisans. His father was fighting with the partisans, and the Germans took his mother, two younger brothers and two sisters, tied their hands with rope and led them to the biggest house in the village. All families of partisans and all Jews were crowded inside, then the house was set on fire. More than a hundred people died. "We heard them screaming and screaming when the fire began to blaze up high," Petya said. He and a brother escaped the roundup and found partisans, who told them their father had been killed in battle.

A young woman named Antonina told Stowe that Germans had stolen all the livestock and furniture from her family, smashing plates and shooting her father. They killed 128 civilians, 18 by hanging. She said they hanged one man six times; each time they cut him down before he was dead, then hanged him again. One 20-year-old woman partisan kept shouting "Long live Russia." Before shooting her, the Germans cut out her tongue. In another village, a boy of 8 had been hanged because he had a small knife in his pocket.

Stowe talked to prisoners and never found one "who betrayed the least concern over the barbarous crimes the Germans committed in Europe." Luftwaffe officers, he wrote, were the most unregenerate Nazis and some were also "the biggest liars." One told him he had been in the Luftwaffe since 1938

and, although he flew in a bomber, insisted he had never dropped a bomb—
had only flown reconnaissance missions.[40]

* * *

Scoops may have been hard to come by, but Henry Cassidy did get one, and
it was monumental. On September 28, he received a telegram from the AP in
New York. Stalin had received Churchill and Wendell Willkie, President
Roosevelt's special emissary, and the AP wanted Cassidy to arrange an interview with Stalin or, failing that, to submit written questions. Cassidy knew
that was an impossible assignment and he was annoyed.

"I had made many requests to Stalin for an interview or statement during
my two years in Moscow. I stuffed the telegram into my pocket and forgot
about it." A few days later, his conscience goaded him to write a letter to the
dictator, inviting him to comment on the possibility of a Second Front against
Hitler, on the effectiveness of Allied aid to the Soviet Union and on the Soviet
capacity for resistance. At 11:45 one night, a secretary of the Foreign
Commissariat press department phoned him and told him to come immediately. "It is very important," she said. Cassidy decided to go to bed; he had no
clue as to why he had been summoned and had no way of getting there except
on foot. But finally he agreed to go.

When he arrived, Nikolai Palgunov, head of the department, told him the
document he was waiting for was at hand—a letter from Stalin saying that a
Second Front occupied "a very important, one might say, a prime place." On
Allied aid: "Compared with the aid the Soviet Union is giving by drawing the
main forces of the German armies, the aid of the Allies to the Soviet Union
has so far been little effective . . . Only one thing is required: the full and
prompt fulfilment by the Allies of their obligations." On Soviet resistance: "I
think that the Soviet capacity of resisting the German brigands is in strength
not less, if not greater, than the capacity of Fascist Germany or of any other
aggressive power to secure for it world domination."

The letter was dated October 3, 1942. It was then 1 a.m. on a Sunday, too
late to write a dispatch, clear it with censors and transmit it for American
Sunday papers. Cassidy told Palgunov he wanted to hold the story for
Monday newspapers. When he returned to his hotel, he was so elated that
he told Walter Kerr and LeSueur of the letter. Later he showed the letter to
other correspondents, including his arch rival, Shapiro. Then he spent the
rest of the day in self-recrimination for not having written a more colorful

story and for having told others about it. There was an interruption in communications just as his story was about to be transmitted. When communications were restored, other dispatches went out ahead of his. After his article appeared, congratulations began pouring in from the AP and from Cassidy's colleagues around the world. "I became something of a celebrity to Russians."

Having succeeded once, Cassidy tried again on November 12, writing to Stalin after Allied landings in North Africa. Stalin replied the next night. He hailed the landings as opening the prospect of disintegration of the Italo-German coalition, took issue with skeptics claiming Anglo-American leaders were not capable of organizing a serious war campaign and described planning for the invasion and the fighting in the desert as "masterly." The campaign had turned the political and military situation in favor of the Allies, mobilized the anti-Hitler forces in France and created conditions for taking Italy out of the war.

Cassidy's latest scoop brought more kudos but it didn't have quite the impact of the first. He was, incidentally, so shy as a young man that his Harvard adviser had questioned whether he should go into journalism.[41]

CHAPTER 7

PEARL HARBOR

In the early hours of December 7, 1941, carrier-based Japanese warplanes and submarines attacked without warning the American Pacific fleet at Pearl Harbor in Hawaii, sinking four battleships and damaging four others. Also lost were three cruisers, three destroyers, a training ship and a minelayer. Further attacks destroyed 188 aircraft, most on the ground, and took the lives of 2,402 Americans, with 1,282 wounded. Germany and Italy declared war on the United States four days later. Tension between the U.S. and Japan had developed months earlier when Washington demanded that Japan get out of China, imposed an oil embargo and presented other demands. On November 27, Washington cabled all Pacific headquarters that an aggressive move by Japan was expected within days. Yet local commanders failed to act.

Helen Kirkpatrick spent the weekend of November 29–30, 1941, at the home of Ronald Tree, an American-born British journalist, investor and Conservative Member of Parliament, and his wife Nancy. In her diary, Kirkpatrick wrote: "Ronnie, who lunched at Chequers with the Churchills, says that FDR talked to the PM [prime minister] Friday night and said war with Japan within a week." Because of British censorship, of course, Kirkpatrick could not send this explosive information to her newspaper.[1]

In Shanghai, Clark Lee of the AP received a tip-off on November 14 from a friendly Japanese colonel that he should leave the city. "There is a possibility that after the next 10 days there may not be any way to get out," the colonel said. Lee's conviction that war was imminent grew stronger after a Japanese naval captain asked him and an American Marine officer to dinner. The captain said: "The Japanese Navy is invincible in the western and southwestern Pacific.

We will capture your bases. If you send your ships out to try to retake them, our dive bomber and torpedo plane pilots will crash their planes on your decks and sink your ships." Lee boarded a ship for Manila on November 15 and, en route, wrote several stories predicting war. He sensed that his Japanese contacts feared Tokyo could not win in the long run and hoped the U.S. would back down at the last moment.[2]

Oddly enough, Japanese press counselors at embassies in Rome, Berlin, Bern, Madrid and Lisbon gave parties for American and Japanese correspondents in early December. In Rome on December 4, a correspondent named Maida told Reynolds Packard: "In few days you have big new [sic]." Packard dismissed the comment as silly chatter of "just another Jap in his cups."[3]

For a week before Pearl Harbor, UP's Robert Bellaire in Tokyo had been filing strongly anti-American quotes from Japanese newspapers. Normally such material would be sent at the cheap press rate but Bellaire used the urgent rate. UP editors concluded he was trying to send a warning of imminent action. On Dec. 5, UP's William H. McDougall in Shanghai sent a coded message saying a Japanese friend had told him that Japanese diplomats in Washington, London and other capitals were getting orders to destroy code books and code machines in preparation for a crisis.[4]

There was a general assumption that, when war came, the Philippines—not the Hawaiian island group thousands of miles from Japan—would be a prime target. So in Hawaii, most people literally slept through the initial stages of the Japanese attack.

Frank Tremaine, the UP bureau chief, and his wife Kay had returned home late Saturday night from a black-tie dinner-dance. They had arrived in Honolulu in June 1940. The 26-year-old Tremaine had taken the assignment reluctantly, believing he was being sent to a backwater where nothing newsworthy happened. Kay was so tired she hung her evening gown on the bedroom door rather than in the closet. At dawn Tremaine was roused from sleep by anti-aircraft fire and heavier booms. He went nude to the front windows of their hillside home, 8 miles from Pearl Harbor. Black puffs of smoke were rising above the Navy Yard. It was 7:58 a.m. "Odd time for another drill," he thought. The noise grew louder, and smoke spiraled up from the Navy Yard. Tremaine rushed to the telephone, knocking Kay's dress onto the floor.

"Frank, why are you walking on my dress?" Kay demanded angrily. Tremaine got through to a Navy information officer, who told him "all hell's breaking loose" and his boss had gone to the navy yard to investigate. Returning to the window, Tremaine saw smoke above Pearl Harbor, and the air was full of anti-aircraft puffs. Rushing back to the phone, he called the G-2 (intelligence) office at Fort Shafter. Harry Albright, head of Army public relations, told him: "We're under attack but the planes aren't identified."

Tremaine replied with sarcasm: "You don't think they're German, do you?" He hung up and phoned the Commercial Cable Co., dictating an urgent one-line dispatch to UP offices in San Francisco, New York and Manila: "Flash Pearl Harbor under aerial attack. Tremaine." A "flash" is the highest priority wire-service dispatch, alerting head offices to interrupt any story running on the wires. Now Tremaine placed a call to UP in San Francisco. Knowing there would be a delay, he again phoned Albright, who said the attackers were Japanese. After dictating another urgent cable to the same three offices, Tremaine left for Fort Shafter after asking Kay to dictate his notes to San Francisco if his call came through.

UP correspondent Bill Tyree was then on his way to the UP bureau. And, fortunately, a third UP man was on hand. Francis McCarthy had been en route from New York to Manila but had been bumped off a Pan American flight to make room for what he called "a load of tires." McCarthy had partied all night, ending up uninvited at Tyree's home, and was returning to his hotel in Albright's car when they heard heavy gunfire and assumed it was firing practice. Smoke was also rising over Hickam Field and Albright, fearing that an ammunition dump had blown up accidentally, rushed to Fort Shafter.

Kay turned on the radio and heard Webley Edwards, manager of station KGMB, saying: "Take cover. This is an air raid. This is no drill." He conveyed instructions to all military, police, civil defense and Red Cross workers to report for duty immediately.

Back in his hotel, McCarthy provided this description: "A Japanese plane soared lazily overhead, down under 1,000 feet. It banked slowly, and the Rising Sun was plain on its wings. I watched it out of sight. In the street, servicemen, some dressing as they ran, rushed for transportation to their posts . . . Civilians seemed dazed, gathering in small clusters."

He and Tremaine arrived at Fort Shafter, where GIs were digging trenches and setting up machine-gun emplacements. Tremaine set off for Pearl Harbor but was caught in a traffic jam and stopped at Hickam Field. Turning in at the gate, he saw a wrecked barracks and many casualties lying about. The wreckage of dozens of planes littered Hickam Field. Tremaine phoned Tyree at the UP office to report this, then stepped outside and had to dive for cover as a Japanese plane swooped in, machine guns blazing. He called Tyree again and was told not to bother dictating further because the Navy had shut down communications. Later he learned his early cables had got through but arrived just after the White House announced the attack. His wife had given UP "a great eyewitness account" when the San Francisco call came through.

McCarthy phoned San Francisco from the G-2 office and, as it was an official line, got through immediately and started dictating. From time to time an operator interrupted to ask if he were on an official call. Each time he said, "I am phoning from G-2 at Fort Shafter." Eventually the operator cut him off.

When Tremaine's initial flash arrived in Manila, UP manager Frank Hewlett phoned the office of Adm. Thomas C. Hart, commander of the Asiatic Fleet. A duty officer told him: "Bunk. Tell your Pearl Harbor correspondent to go back to bed and sleep it off."[5]

* * *

Eugene Burns, the AP bureau chief, was having breakfast on his veranda over-looking Honolulu when he saw Japanese planes, then smoke rising from Pearl Harbor. Burns got a quick connection to San Francisco and dictated a bulletin: "At least five planes, their wings bearing the insignia of the rising sun, flew over Honolulu today and dropped bombs." Then the line went dead. His bulletin never made the AP wire—for reasons unknown, according to a later AP history.

Burns went to see the Japanese consul, Kagao Kita, and found him burning official papers. Kita denied the planes were Japanese and said the bombing was "just a mock maneuver" by the U.S. Army. Burns told him there were dead and wounded in the streets.

Tom Yarborough, an AP correspondent from London, was on a Dutch steamship that arrived off Honolulu during the attack. Most of those on board assumed it was a naval war game and crowded the decks, applauding the Navy for timing it during their arrival. A bomb hit the water about 100 yards away and a passenger said, "Boy, what if that had been a real one!" Yarborough, a veteran of the London Blitz, knew the bombs were for real. Then a shipping line agent told the passengers the bombers were Japanese and a state of war existed.[6]

Time magazine reported in its December 15 issue that pajama-clad citizens piled out of bed when the attacks started and many were nonchalant. One man dashed past an acquaintance and shouted: "The mainland papers will exaggerate this!"[7]

Joseph C. Harsch of the *Christian Science Monitor* had arrived in Honolulu just before the attack. Having completed an assignment in Berlin, he was en route to a new posting in Southeast Asia, and his wife Anne had agreed to accompany him as far as Hawaii. On December 6, they dined with Adm. Husband E. Kimmel, the Navy commander for the Pacific, who assured them there would be no war in the Pacific until after Germany defeated Russia. Awakened at their hotel on Waikiki Beach by the bombing, he asked if she wanted to know what an air-raid sounded like in Europe. This, he remarked, is a good imitation. Both went back to sleep, then proceeded to the beach for a morning swim. There, he saw a freighter offshore that seemed to list; still, he thought it was a practice turn to add realism to the maneuvers. Only when they returned to their hotel did they learn what had happened. Harsch wrote an eyewitness story but it did not reach the *Monitor*'s offices in Boston until five days later.[8]

One Hawaii resident was Edgar Rice Burroughs, author of the Tarzan books. At age 66, he applied to become a war correspondent and later traveled widely in the Pacific, interviewing GIs and sending stories to their hometown newspapers.[9]

* * *

In Washington, news agencies had their usual skeleton Sunday staffs on duty when a White House operator called and told them to stand by for a statement from spokesman Stephen Early. Once all three agencies—the AP, UP and INS—were on the line, Early said: "I have a statement from the president. The Japanese have attacked Pearl Harbor from the air."

AP Washington editor William Peacock shouted: "Flash!," then quickly typed a one-line flash and handed it to a teletype operator, his fingers shaking so much that he asked Ed Bomar to write a follow-up bulletin. "What do you want me to say?" said Bomar, who had just walked in. "We're at war, that's what," Peacock replied.[10]

* * *

Arthur F. DeGreve in the UP Washington bureau took Early's call and scribbled a news flash on a piece of paper. The UP wires had not yet been set up for the Sunday night report so DeGreve phoned UP in New York and told Phil Newsom: "This is DeGreve in Washington—Flash—White House announces Japanese bombing Oahu."

"Bombing what?" Newsom asked. "Oahu, dammit—Wahoo." Newsome persisted: "Spell it, for pete's sake." DeGreve replied: "O-A-H-U—Wahoo! We've got a war on our hands."[11]

Mutual Broadcasting's station WOR in New York interrupted the broadcast of a professional football game to read the UP flash. The networks remained on the air with news reports for thirty-four hours. At NBC in New York, editor Robert Eisenbach read the AP flash, then pressed a button telling the control room to interrupt network programs. He had never spoken on radio but now told 15 million listeners that the nation was at war. At 2:45 p.m. Eastern Standard Time, an NBC announcer read a bulletin from a member station in Hawaii: "We have witnessed this morning . . . the severe bombing of Pearl Harbor by army planes that are undoubtedly Japanese. The city of Honolulu has been attacked and considerable damage done. This battle has been going on for nearly three hours . . . It's no joke—it's real war . . . There has been severe fighting going on in the air and on the sea."[12]

Ed Murrow and his wife, in Washington on leave, dined with President Roosevelt on the evening of December 7. "Our planes were destroyed on the ground," the president kept saying. Beating on the table, he added: "On the ground, mind you, ON THE GROUND!"[13]

* * *

Karl Eskelund, the Danish correspondent who fled his country when the Germans occupied it, was in Shanghai with his Chinese wife Chi-yun and learned of Pearl Harbor after he and other UP staff saw a Japanese cruiser sink a British gunboat. The next evening two American correspondents, John B. Powell of the *Manchester Guardian* and Victor Keen of the *New York Herald-Tribune*, were arrested. (After the war, Powell came back crippled from confinement in freezing prisons and parts of both his feet had to be amputated to check the spread of gangrene. Aged 60, he died of a heart attack on February 28, 1947. Keen, released in 1942, returned to New York and in 1955 died of cancer at age 56.)

Eskelund and his pregnant wife escaped from Shanghai on a smugglers' boat and made their way to the Nationalist-held part of China. Later they were joined by "three dirty, bearded, flea-bitten Americans" who also had fled Shanghai—Bill McDougall and Pepper Martin of UP and Francis Lee, a former UP staff member in Tientsin. They had walked past a Japanese sentry at the door of their hotel, borrowed $500 from a Catholic priest and, pretending to be drunk, made their way through Japanese lines. For nearly three weeks they had walked through China, dodging Japanese patrols and living with peasants.[14]

* * *

Robert J. Casey of the *Chicago Daily News* arrived in Honolulu weeks after Pearl Harbor and in a postwar book was unsparing in criticism of the Americans for having been caught napping, saying they "looked like saps."

> This wreck of Pearl Harbor was startling, stupendous and disgraceful . . .
> The aura of desolation was over everything, along with the smell of burned oil and iron rust. The sense of an utter destruction was poignant and inescapable . . . The United States was right here in the ashes of Pearl Harbor, with its arrogance, its pride and its chances, if any, for salvation.

Casey saw a parallel "between the lazy nation that had allowed this thing to happen and the France whose errors it was repeating . . ." He admitted to a mounting sense of rage "against the Japs who could do it, and, perhaps more intensely, against the stupidity of another people who had eyes and ears and never knew what was going on." Japanese bombers, he reported, had been picked up by a detector device in Hawaii when they were 150 miles from the Japanese coast, but the operator couldn't get his superiors to believe what he had found.[15]

Keith Wheeler of the *Chicago Times*, arriving on December 26, characterized the sunken battleships as "sad and humbling wrecks of the country's pride." Honolulu was:

> a professional paradise out of work and suspected of vagrancy. The stores closed at 4 p.m. and an hour later the streets were deserted—utterly deserted . . . The sentries made the nights loud with quavering challenges to shadows and demands that alley cats halt . . . There wasn't much work for newspapermen. The war had come, struck like a hurricane, and passed on.[16]

* * *

Wake Island was bombed on December 7, and outnumbered Marines fought off invaders before they were forced to surrender on December 23. Joseph F. McDonald Jr., son of the editor of the *Nevada State Journal,* was the UP stringer on Wake and provided one of the first dispatches, putting it aboard a Pan Am Clipper that escaped to Honolulu. During the battle, the Pentagon reported that Maj. James Devereux, the commander, had cabled: "Send us more Japs!" At the end of the war, UP correspondent Murray Moler found Devereux in a Japanese camp. Moler asked why he had sent his message, and Devereux looked dumbfounded. "Hell, I never sent any message like that. We already had too damn many Japs."[17]

* * *

After Germany and Italy declared war on the United States, American correspondents in both countries faced months of internment, as did others in Tokyo, Manila, Shanghai, Hong Kong and Saigon.

In Rome, on the day of Pearl Harbor, the poet Ezra Pound, a Fascist sympathizer, paid Reynolds and Eleanor Packard—whom he had known earlier in Paris—an unexpected visit. He told them he intended to stay. Reynolds told him he would be a traitor if he did so, and now was the time to stop speaking about the glories of Fascism, as he often did on Italian radio. "But I believe in Fascism," Pound said, giving the Fascist salute. "And I want to defend it. I don't see why Fascism is contrary to American philosophy . . . I consider myself a hundred per cent American and a patriot. I am only against Roosevelt and the Jews who influence him."

The Packards thought Pound was embittered because his forty-one volumes of poetry, essays, stories and treatises had brought him no fame and little money. "He was regarded as a failure and an eccentric in his own country, and he knew it," Reynolds Packard wrote. "When war was declared a few days later, he continued his broadcasts and became a traitor."[18]

The Packards were undoubtedly the most colorful journalistic couple of their era. They had met in a Paris bar, where Reynolds got into a fight with six drunken Peruvians; Eleanor intervened and, by her future husband's account, hit all six where it hurt and they fled. After the Packards married they were posted to China. In Peiping (Beijing), Packard began a relationship with a Mongolian woman and, in a moment of passion, bit off her left nipple. Later the Packards covered the Spanish Civil War.[19]

They were in the U.S. Embassy in Rome when Italy declared war, and as they left two men approached, saying they had orders to take them to the Questura, police headquarters. The chief of police told them he had instructions to send Reynolds to the Regina Coeli prison. Eleanor could go home under police surveillance. Detectives asked Reynolds if he wanted to go by bus or taxi, explaining that he could travel free on the bus but would have to pay the fare if he went by taxi. He elected to take a taxi.

At the prison, he was placed in a cold cell with an Italian who had been arrested for safe-cracking. "Just because I was caught cracking a safe once, I am arrested now every time a safe is cracked," he explained. The next afternoon, two wardens ordered Packard to strip to the waist and drop his trousers. Livingstone Pomeroy of UP was brought in, and laughed. "I always wanted to catch my boss with his pants down," he said. In a corridor, Packard passed Herbert Matthews of the *New York Times* and Richard Massock of the AP. He and Pomeroy were put in a cell together and went to bed "with Pomeroy still chattering about a salary increase."

The next afternoon, the correspondents were taken to a third-rate boarding house and former brothel, the Pensione Suquet. There were six of them, including Camille Cianfarra of the *New York Times* and Robert Allen-Tuska, recently hired by Packard. Their wives won permission to bring them home-cooked meals. Soon they were joined by Louise Dudley "Teddy" Lynch, fifth wife of oilman J. Paul Getty. She had given up singing at the Stork Club in New York to study opera in Rome.

The group was told they would be interned in Siena pending the outcome of negotiations on exchange of Italian and American nationals. Arriving on December 22, they were put up in the city's leading hotel. Lynch remained in Rome temporarily. The correspondents hired one large room as a clubroom, which they christened "The Suquet Sporting and Debating Society."

"Here were seven of us who had never got along particularly well in Rome, suddenly isolated in an insular group," Packard wrote. "It was a psychological test of just how much the human mind could stand in the way of constant friction."

Later Teddy Lynch was brought to Siena. Then they were joined by David Colin, an NBC correspondent who had arrived just before the declaration of war and never made a broadcast. Packard wrote that he "contributed to a further disarrangement of neuron patterns by consistently winning at bridge."[20]

To help pass the time, Massock read all of the *Arabian Nights* and was well into *The Divine Comedy* when their internment ended. Matthews read Gibbon's *Decline and Fall of the Roman Empire* and was part way through the Bible. He also bicycled through the Tuscan hills and found it "fruitful and healthy, but very boring."[21]

The police complained that Teddy Lynch wore slacks in the hotel, forbidden by the regime, and some of them smoked pipes in the lobby in "an arrogant manner." Only Massock and Allen-Tuska were pipe smokers and Massock wanted to make a formal rebuttal but Packard, a non-smoker, objected and the two had "a stormy argument."[22]

The Italian authorities allowed the correspondents to go wherever they wanted in Siena, followed by detectives. They attended movies and a burlesque show that was "so bawdy that neither Teddy nor Eleanor went after the first visit," Packard wrote. In March 1942 he was allowed to go to Rome under police escort to discuss problems of the group with diplomats. Massock and Matthews also later visited Rome. Then the whole group was transferred to Rome and put on a train for Lisbon on May 13, 1942. Harold Denny, a *New York Times* man who had been captured in Libya (see Chapter 10), joined them in Rome. Packard wrote that Denny was white-haired and had a long beard, looking at least twenty years older than when he last saw him, two years before. Denny refused to discuss his internment. "I'm going to write it myself, and if you're really interested you can buy the book," he said.[23]

* * *

In Berlin on December 10, the day before Hitler declared war on the U.S., American correspondents were attending a news conference when Dr. Paul Schmidt, a German press official, burst in to say that German correspondents in the U.S. had been arrested. He asked the Americans to leave. As they started to file out, colleagues from various nations, even Japan, formed a line and insisted on shaking their hands, often murmuring their sympathies. Schmidt himself shook hands with each correspondent. That night Gestapo agents came to the various homes and took the fifteen correspondents to the main police station. They were transferred to a hotel annex in Gruenau, an eastern suburb of Berlin. The next evening an SS man told them they were free to return home but must be at the American Embassy at 9 a.m. the next day with their luggage.

Together with ninety-seven other Americans, including diplomats, they were put on a train and sent to the spa town of Bad Nauheim, near Frankfurt, where they would spend five months in a hotel that was normally only open in summer and was cold in winter. By contrast, Germans in the U.S. were interned in some luxury at White Sulphur Springs, Virginia.

Despite the cold, "we lived in relative comfort," the AP's Louis Lochner wrote. Two U.S. military attachés kept them busy with gymnastics and, in the spring, they were allowed to go to a stadium to play softball. Occasionally they were taken on long hikes under Gestapo surveillance and were allowed to write to people in Germany but denied the use of telephones and the telegraph. The AP's Ed Shanke had a tiny box radio, which the Germans mistook for a camera, and each evening they listened to BBC news broadcasts from London. To help fight boredom, they formed a chorus of twenty-four mixed voices. Finally, on May 12, they were told to start their journey to Lisbon.[24]

Robert H. Best, a South Carolinian and former stringer for UP and various newspapers, elected to stay behind with his fiancée, Erna Maurer, an Austrian reporter for the AP, whom he married on September 2, 1952. He was recruited as a commentator for German State Radio, broadcasting to the U.S. under the pseudonym "Mr. Guess Who" and denouncing Roosevelt, Churchill, the Jews and the Soviet Union. British forces captured him in Austria in 1946 and handed him over to U.S. authorities. He was convicted of treason in 1948 and sentenced to life in prison and a $10,000 fine. In 1952 he died in prison of a stroke, aged 56.[25]

UP bureau chief Frederick Oechsner abandoned journalism when he returned to the U.S. He joined the new Office of Strategic Services, forerunner of the CIA, as an assistant to director William J. Donovan, then later became director of psychological warfare under Eisenhower. After the war Oechsner joined the State Department, serving as deputy chief of mission in Warsaw. He retired in 1962 and died thirty years later, aged 89.[26]

Louis Lochner, then 55, spent two years after his release as a news analyst for NBC radio in the U.S., but returned to Europe to cover the last year of the war. Afterward, he wrote several books on Germany. He died in January 1975, aged 88.[27]

* * *

American, British and Dutch correspondents in Tokyo had a far more harrowing experience than their colleagues in Europe, perhaps none more so than Otto Tolischus. Expelled from Berlin in 1939, the *New York Times* man arrived in Japan in February 1941. When the Pearl Harbor attack occurred, he was awakened at 7 a.m. by a pounding on his bedroom door. He opened it and four plainclothes police surrounded him.

"I bet you don't know the big news," one of them said. They told him Japan was at war with the U.S., Britain and the Netherlands, and that Manila, Singapore and Hong Kong had been bombed. They made no mention of Pearl Harbor. He was told he had violated the National Defense Act and could spend ten years in prison. Then he was driven to the Tokyo Detention Prison. Tolischus believed his imprisonment was a mistake and he would soon be taken to some place of internment until the U.S. and Japan arranged an exchange of nationals. But when a heavy iron cot was brought in and nailed to the floor, his illusions were shattered.

"I was buried alive, and not knowing what was happening was the greatest mental torture," he wrote. Police accused him of having tried to discover their national secrets in his quest for scoops. His interrogators accused him of spying, and one said: "How would you like to be stood up before 10 rifles? That's what we do with spies in this country."

His captors turned to torture on January 8. First the interpreter, whom Tolischus privately dubbed the Snake, hit him over the head with the flat of his hand, demanded he confess to spying, pushed him into a corner and forced him down on his knees. Snake and another man began to slap his face, stamp on his knees and ankles and push his head against the wall, shouting over and over, "You are a spy!" After a half hour Tolischus's legs went numb and the pain abated.

The next day, a policeman (whom Tolischus named Rabbit) slapped his face. Another, Hyena, placed a fountain pen between the fingers of his left hand and started to break them over it. Snake seized his head in a ju-jitsu grip and began strangling him. After pushing Tolischus into a corner, he pounded his knees and ankles with his fists and feet. Snake then put the front legs of a chair on Tolischus's knees and sat on the chair. The pain was more than Tolischus could endure but he told his tormentors, "I'm not afraid to die."

From January 10 to the 14th, the police left him alone. But then, Snake and Hyena confronted him. Hyena knocked his feet from under him, and Snake told him he would spend twenty years in prison. "I have been beaten and spat upon in America," Snake said, thereupon hitting Tolischus and spitting in his face. The torture resumed on January 16. Tolischus wrote: "I knew now I could not stand much more of this, and did not want to. I tried to figure out a way of provoking them, so that they would kill me on the spot."

But on January 17 Snake greeted him affably, asked for his complete life history and said that if he answered correctly, "we shall continue treating you like a gentleman." When they asked him about a meeting with a Japanese contact, however, Rabbit twisted his right arm upward behind his back and threatened to break it. That was the last act of violence. On January 23, the police provided cigarettes, newspapers and even coffee from Tolischus's home. Later they brought stacks of books, tins of salmon, jam and fruit, even flowers. Once, when a policeman Tolischus called Fox escorted him back to his cell, Fox told him, "I feel very sorry for all the correspondents, and I am ashamed of my job."

Tolischus was tried on May 1 and sentenced to eighteen months but execution was suspended for three years. On the evening of May 20, he and Percy Whiteing of INS were released—Whiteing to return home to his family but Tolischus to a civilian internment camp set up in a Tokyo school. Most Americans there were missionaries but they included Robert Bellaire of UP, Joseph E. Dynan of the AP and Colvin "Tom" Crichton of Universal News Features. The prisoners said it was reputed to be the worst concentration camp in Japan, "but," Tolischus said, "I felt I was reveling in luxury."

On June 2 three other correspondents arrived—Max Hill of the AP, and Richard Tenelly and Raymond Crowley of the *Wall Street Journal*. They had received sentences identical to that of Tolischus but suffered no physical violence. The next day, the correspondents were taken to a lunch given by the Pacific War Relief Committee and told they could broadcast to America and explain how well they were treated. Hill told the Japanese it would be improper, but three correspondents recorded messages while the others, including Tolischus, declined. The committee chairman asked them to write articles to be sold to English-language newspapers to raise funds for relief of war prisoners. All declined to do so. Later the chairman came to Tolischus's hotel room and told him he would not be allowed to go home if he refused to write. "Well, if it's a matter of compulsion, I'll write," he said. One Japanese official choked Bellaire with his own necktie and threatened to hold him without food and water until he wrote. Dynan was punched in the jaw and suffered a broken dental bridge. After all had written articles, they were served beer and taken back to their camp.

On June 17, internees went aboard a ship in Yokohama, except for three men—not correspondents—who elected to stay. The ship later picked up more internees from Hong Kong and Saigon. When it reached the Mozambican port of Lourenço Marques in July, where the exchange with Japanese from the U.S. took place, Tolischus could not file to his newspaper because he had neither money nor collect facilities. He had to wait until the Swedish ship *Gripsholm* taking them back to America reached Rio de Janeiro on August 10. Fifteen days later, the ship entered New York harbor and passengers sang the national anthem as they passed the Statue of Liberty.[28]

* * *

Gwen Dew had taken leave from reporting for the *Detroit News* to make a documentary film when the Japanese attacked Hong Kong. On the night of December 18, the Japanese made their first large-scale landings and captured the Repulse Bay Hotel, where civilians and the British military were holding out. Two hundred people, including Dew, were marched to a looted paint factory on Christmas Eve. Hong Kong surrendered the next afternoon. The internees were then taken to a second-rate hotel, the Kowloon. Their Christmas dinner consisted of rice and water.

A nurse told Dew that when the Japanese came to her hospital she was gang-raped and two doctors were bayoneted. The Japanese ripped bandages from wounded British and Canadian soldiers, then bayoneted and killed fifty-two of them. They lined up all the nurses and took away three who were not seen again. The others were raped repeatedly all Christmas Day and night.

Dew was invited to tea by a Colonel Tada, head of Japanese military intelligence in Hong Kong, and she took advantage of the occasion to wolf down twelve sandwiches. On January 24, the prisoners were told they would be moved to an internment camp except for Dew, Richard Wilson of UP and two British civilians. Colonel Tada told Dew this group would never be sent to a camp, but he was reassigned and the day after he left they joined 3,000 prisoners at an internment camp.

Prisoners were given poor rations, including rice with worms and weevils that they refused to eat. Dew vowed never to forgive four Americans who smuggled in a large quantity of food supplies. While others were on the verge of starvation, the privileged group dined on ham, canned fruits, bread, butter, meat, eggs, shrimp and fresh lettuce. They held Sunday morning waffle breakfasts and champagne and whisky parties. Later, aboard a ship taking prisoners home, some Americans took revenge on the four and "several black eyes ensued," Dew wrote.

In the first two months, most prisoners lost between 20 and 100 pounds each, and a third developed beriberi, scurvy, pellagra and other vitamin-deficiency diseases. Correspondents in the camp included Vaughn Meisling of the AP, George Baxter and Richard Wilson of UP, and Joseph W. Alsop Jr., a syndicated columnist. Left behind in the camp hospital when they departed was Bill O'Neill of Reuters. Some Japanese newsmen gave Dew a bottle of Scotch whisky, which an American reporter stole from her, then refused to return when she confronted him.

The ship on which prisoners left on June 30, 1942, had picked up eight correspondents in Shanghai beforehand. Most of them, Dew wrote, had been kept in tiny, vermin-infested cells without heating or ventilation and with lights left on at all times. Relman Morin of the AP went aboard at Saigon. Dew smuggled out a list of 3,000 British and Dutch internees who remained prisoners, and when she got to New York she cabled it to Britain. She also hid, inside a pair of wooden Ming dolls whose heads came off, several hundred addresses of families and friends of prisoners. They had asked her to write to each of the addresses.

The exchange of prisoners took place at Goa. Correspondents based in India were allowed to meet the ships on the understanding they would not try to file dispatches until they had been censored by the Indian government. John Morris, UP manager for the Far East, tried to file from Goa but was caught out, and his attempt to evade censorship jeopardized his efforts to sell the UP service to Indian newspapers. Not long afterward Morris was back in New York and threw himself from a window of the twelfth-floor offices of UP. "He was extremely upset and frustrated about his difficulties in India," according to Harold Guard, who replaced him in India.

On her return home, Gwen Dew wrote a series of articles for the *Detroit News* and later expanded them into a book, *Prisoner of the Japs*. She left journalism and worked for the U.S. Office of Strategic Services, speaking at war bond drives. In 1948 she married Army Capt. James Buchanan, whom she had met in Japan. He died five years later. She died in Phoenix, Arizona, on June 17, 1993, one day short of her 90th birthday.[29]

CHAPTER 8

JAPAN INVADES: THE PHILIPPINES, SINGAPORE, BURMA

The raid on Pearl Harbor was quickly followed by attacks on the Philippines, Singapore, the Dutch East Indies, Hong Kong, Malaya and Burma, and lack of preparedness was on display on all fronts. American withdrawal from the Philippines began on December 22, and the islands fell on April 8. Thousands, including correspondents and their families, were interned, some until the end of the war.

En route from Shanghai to the Philippines just before the outbreak of war, Clark Lee of the AP told a friend that the Japanese "won't catch us napping as they did the Russian fleet at Port Arthur back in 1904 . . . The Japs will be the ones to be surprised this time." On December 5, New York instructed the Manila bureau to inform AP correspondents throughout the Far East that "Washington says situation critical." General MacArthur thought an attack would come after January 1.

On the day Pearl Harbor was attacked, Lee and the AP staff members in Manila, Ray Cronin and Russell Brines, discussed whether they should enlist, but decided they would be more useful in their current jobs. They phoned Guam and a cable company manager told them Japanese planes were attacking the island. "We have been in and out of our shelter since six o'clock," he said. "Our small forces are still fighting, but the Japanese have landed and are advancing. This can't last long."

They soon learned Hong Kong was under attack. Then the AP's Jimmy White in Shanghai reported Japanese capture of the International Settlement, the American and British sector of Shanghai, and the loss of two ships, one American, one British.

At mid-morning on December 8, an AP stringer phoned from the mountain resort of Baguio, 125 miles north of Manila, to report that the Japanese had bombed the American Camp John Hay. Clark Field, the main American air base 40 miles north of Manila, had also been heavily bombed, with many planes destroyed on the ground, and casualties were extensive.

Despite the failure to get planes in the air, and other signs of MacArthur's lack of preparation for war, Lee was extravagant in praise of the general in his memoir, describing him as "a man of culture, whom some men hated because he was both prophet and poet and a master of the English language; who could tell you the details of every great battle in history; whose incisive brain and great military knowledge should have been occupied in planning great battles . . ."[1]

Jack Percival, an Australian correspondent of London's *News Chronicle* and the *Sydney Morning Herald* and Melbourne *Age*, raced to Clark Field with Royal Arch Gunnison of *Collier's Weekly* and Mutual Broadcasting. A man in coveralls shouted: "Bombing attack, bombing attack." Nine Japanese planes appeared, bombing down the middle of the runway, then doubled back to strafe everything in sight. The attacks on American air bases destroyed 35 B-17s, 30 medium and 8 light bombers, 220 fighters and 23 other planes.[2] Gunnison, 34, had gone to the Far East after being expelled from Germany in 1934.

The U.S. military set up censorship on December 8, using naval reservists with no experience of dealing with news dispatches. "We had many a vituperative fight with them as to whether or not the people of the United States should be told the truth about what was happening in the Philippines," Lee wrote. Official communiqués stated that "our lines are holding" even after military leaders knew Manila was doomed. Battles with censors continued until the week before Manila fell; then news copy went through with few changes.

On December 22, U.S. forces spotted an enemy flotilla of eighty transports and warships. Lee, convinced the Japanese would be turned back on the beaches, ran into advancing Japanese troops near Manila and decided to flee to Baguio, making part of the trip on foot, past rice fields, up steep mountains and across rivers. Eventually he gave up and tried to get aboard a jammed train for Manila but had to climb onto the roof of a freight car. Twelve minutes after the train pulled out, the Japanese bombed the station, killing twenty-seven and wounding more than fifty.

On Christmas evening, the Navy blew up the naval base at Cavite, 9 miles southwest of Manila, as its fall was inevitable. Brines exclaimed: "Jesus! We've been building that place up for more than 40 years. Now we blow it up. That's the end of the U.S.A. in the Philippines for a while." According to Lee, Brines's story on the destruction of the base was "a masterpiece." Censors refused to pass it.

MacArthur proclaimed Manila an open city on December 24, meaning U.S. forces were withdrawing and asking the Japanese not to bomb it. "The hope of the populace rose, because the people loved MacArthur and believed no enemy on earth could defeat him," Lee wrote. The Japanese ignored MacArthur's proclamation and bombed Manila on December 27.[3]

Bert Silen of NBC, sheltering in an army dugout, provided this description:

Manila has just been bombed! In fact right now it is being bombed . . . The first we knew of the bombing, we heard terrible detonations and then saw huge flames from incendiary bombs coming out of Fort William McKinley and Nichols Air Field . . . turning the sky absolutely crimson. We saw the real fireworks display of blood-red anti-aircraft tracer bullets going after those Japanese bombers . . . and we thought we couldn't get this out because the bombers paid a visit to the transmitting stations through whose transmitter we are putting this broadcast . . . It looks as though the Japanese are coming back again . . .

Soon a U.S. Army demolition squad dynamited all radio transmitters and cut cable connections to avoid their falling into Japanese hands.[4]

Mel Jacoby of *Time* was in Manila with his bride, Analee Whitmore. A China scholar and a wealthy man, Jacoby was living in China when Henry Luce hired him to report for his magazine. On a visit to the U.S., he ran into Whitmore, a fellow Stanford University graduate and successful Hollywood screenwriter, who was anxious to cover the war between China and Japan. Jacoby secured her an appointment as Chungking representative of United China Relief, a charity, and in China the two fell in love. In November Jacoby cabled Whitmore, asking her to come to Manila and marry him. She quit her job and they were married just before the outbreak of war.[5]

On the west side of Manila Bay, Franz Weissblatt of UP was covering the U.S. 26th Cavalry Division and was later wounded and captured while throwing hand grenades at the Japanese. As a result, the Japanese treated him as a prisoner-of-war rather than a civilian internee.

Lee decided to take a freighter to Mariveles at the southern tip of Bataan peninsula. Carl Mydans of *Life* and his wife Shelley Smith thought this plan too risky and decided to stay and be interned. Ray Cronin and Brines agreed to do the same, feeling they could not desert their families. Analee Jacoby made up her husband's mind for him: "We're going, Mel." Frank Hewlett of UP and his wife Virginia decided he should go to Bataan while she remained in Manila, where she worked as a stenographer on the High Commissioner's staff and presumably would be part of a diplomatic exchange when fighting ended.[6]

Hewlett covered fighting on Bataan and Corregidor for three and a half months, not knowing if UP in New York was receiving his copy. Then a message from the UP accounting department came through: "What shall we do with your paycheck?" Hewlett sent a sarcastic reply: "Hell, why don't you buy Liberty bonds?" The next day UP carried a story about a reporter stranded on Bataan who asked his office to turn his salary into government bonds to help fight Japan. The story made front pages throughout the country. Another message arrived from foreign editor Joe Alex Morris: "Hewlett you getting excellent play descriptive stories Stop Your reporting been one of war's highlights . . . buying defense bonds with your salary as requested Stop Good luck."[7]

The freighter that Lee had located deposited him and the Jacobys at Corregidor Island, 30 miles west of Manila. MacArthur, who had moved his headquarters there, refused to allow correspondents to file anything on Japanese bombing of the island. Lee, Mel Jacoby, Hewlett and Nat Floyd of the *New York Times* got permission to take a PT boat to China and go overland to Chungking, but the plan was called off because boats were needed to take MacArthur out. Floyd concealed himself below deck on MacArthur's boat but his presence was discovered and he was left behind.

Correspondents came under fire after the Japanese put men ashore. After two weeks of fighting, the invaders were wiped out, and Lee visited a battlefield where 500 Japanese lay dead. "I wrote that I remained on the battlefield until the stench of death drove me away," he recalled. A New York editor substituted "horror of the scene" for "stench of death." Lee thought that was a serious mistake. "There was nothing horrible about the scene. Those Japs looked absolutely beautiful: they were so quiet and so perfectly harmless."

On February 22, Mel Jacoby told Lee that he and Analee were going out that night and he agreed to join them. They got aboard a freighter, the *Princesa de Cebu*, and reached Cebu city, where they boarded the *Doña Nati*. A Japanese cruiser was heading for Cebu and, as their ship pulled away, a Navy officer rushed to the dock and shouted: "Hey, you dopes, you better get off! The cruiser is only an hour away. If you stay aboard you'll be shark bait by this afternoon." It was too late to go ashore. The *Doña Nati* steamed out through the north channel, the cruiser came up the south channel. On March 30, after twenty-two days, they reached Brisbane, Australia. Soon Floyd arrived, followed by Frank Hewlett and Dean Schedler of the AP.

Mel Jacoby soon flew from Brisbane with Gen. Harold H. George, a World War I flying ace, planning to go to an expected battlefront on New Caledonia. They stopped en route at an airfield near Darwin and were standing by their parked plane when a P-40 fighter went out of control on takeoff, swerved across the field and crashed into the general's plane. Jacoby was killed instantly and George died hours later. Jacoby was 25 years old.[8]

* * *

The Australian correspondent Jack Percival remained on Bataan and, at the end of the battle, was lying under a wrecked weapons carrier with an American officer. A Japanese officer spotted them and Percival pushed across his passport. "No, no," the officer said. "You Austrian. No take." Percival and others got on a small boat, but a Japanese patrol boat "shot hell out of us." He paddled to shore, then spent three weeks on the run before surrendering. He joined his pregnant wife Joyce in a prison camp.[9]

Correspondents and their families who remained in Manila were taken on January 5 to internment at Santo Tomas University in Manila. They were part of a contingent of 3,500 mostly Americans and British and included Brines and his wife Barbara and 12-year-old daughter Coralie, Gunnison and his wife Marjorie Hathaway Gunnison of the North American Newspaper Alliance, Carl Mydans and Shelly Smith, Bert Covit of UP and Hewlett's wife Virginia.

Brines wrote that their daily food ration consisted of two small balls of dry rice, "about enough to fill the palm of the hand." Drinking water was scarce, washing facilities nonexistent, sanitary conditions primitive. The Japanese banned smoking, books and all forms of recreation except occasional exercise periods. They used the rack and lash to beat prisoners, and some were subjected to water-boarding.

On the third day of internment, many Filipinos appeared at the gate with food and clothing, and a doctor bicycled through the front gate each morning to attend patients in the camp hospital. One morning soldiers yanked him from his bicycle and beat him so badly he could hardly walk. The next day, he returned on a borrowed bicycle, grinning but visibly gaunt, and the Japanese let him in.[10]

On another occasion, guards pounced on a hapless Filipino who hadn't bowed low enough when he came through the gate. They trussed him on a bamboo scaffolding "after one of the most brutal beatings a human being could go through and still live," wrote Gunnison. With his body strung up by the wrists and neck, the guards began bayoneting him. The Filipino begged for help. "Your heart, your head, thumped with blind rage," Gunnison wrote. Some watching prisoners vomited.[11]

The internees did their best to fix up their dilapidated quarters, organized church services, established schools and formed a "government" to treat with the Japanese commandant. "We even had a police force . . . Once or twice a man who could not otherwise be persuaded to behave found himself in the back of the compound within a circle of men who walloped him into a community consciousness," Mydans wrote. Percival was more blunt: "We beat the shit out of them." One prisoner came upon some papers that another prisoner had written—personnel dossiers on internees, spelling out their anti-Japanese activities. When prisoners confronted the writer, he merely shrugged. They beat him to the point that the Japanese had to rush him to a hospital to save his life.[12]

The Japanese discovered that Mydans was a photographer and offered to free him and his wife if he would photograph their victory parade. Mydans refused. He wrote there were "endless rumors" and one man told him Carl Mydans had been killed in Australia in a plane crash. Mydans realized that Mel Jacoby was dead. As they had the same employer, people had sometimes been confused about their identities.[13]

In February 1942, four men escaped and one was never found. But two British merchant seamen and an Australian machinist were captured walking along a highway. Badly beaten by soldiers, they were taken to a cemetery and seated on the edge of an open grave. Then they were shot, and Filipino laborers were ordered to shovel dirt on them while the moans of one victim could still be heard. As secretary of the British committee in the camp, Percival was made to watch.[14]

In mid-August 1942, the Japanese informed some prisoners they would be eligible for removal to Shanghai if they wished. Only 113 agreed to go and they included the Gunnisons, the Mydans, Bert Covit and Brines. Jack Percival and his wife Joyce decided to stay. She had given birth three months earlier and they were assured fairly good food and medical care for their baby son. Gunnison thought they made a wise choice because nearly everyone who went to Shanghai fell ill and one man died. Prisoners were put in the hold of a ship, with cockroaches and rats running across their feet and faces during the night. Horses were carried at the bottom of the hold, and some died from the heat. "As the days passed the odor from the horses became more and more intense," Gunnison wrote. When the ship reached Shanghai, prisoners were told they could go to homes or hotels, but they had to wear red armbands when they went on the streets. Some went to the Palace Hotel but Brines was taken away on November 5, 1942, and held at a former Marine barracks.

On January 23, 1943, the Japanese advised all single men between the ages of 18 and 45 to report for internment. The Gunnisons and the Mydans were placed in a concentration camp on the outskirts of Shanghai. An exchange of prisoners between the U.S. and Japan took place in Goa, India, on October 19, 1943. Frank Hewlett was waiting when the ship arrived and rushed forward, shouting, "Where's Virginia?" His colleagues were reluctant to tell him the truth: Virginia had lost her mind in Santo Tomas and was too sick to travel. A doctor took Hewlett aside and broke the news to him.

Colleagues in Goa tried to file Gunnison's first article about the internment to *Collier's* but British censors refused to send it. The former internees arrived in New York on December 1, 1943.[15] The fate of prisoners left in Manila will be discussed in Chapter 20.

* * *

Singapore was Britain's "impregnable" island naval fortress at the tip of the Malay peninsula. Almost simultaneous with the attack on Pearl Harbor, Japanese bombers struck the island. Landing troops in Malaya, the Japanese steadily advanced toward Singapore, which fell on February 16, 1942. About 130,000 British troops were taken prisoner. Singapore's loss was almost as great a psychological blow to Britain as the bombing of Pearl Harbor was to Americans.

Cecil Brown was appalled. The CBS broadcaster arrived in late summer of 1941 and found Singapore's defenses were overrated, its military authorities overly confident. As war seemed increasingly likely, afternoon tea dances went on at the famed Raffles Hotel, attended by many officers. The British bluff about Singapore's strength, Brown wrote, had no effect in Tokyo. "The Japs have too good an espionage service here to be fooled by that propaganda."

John Young of NBC, equally disturbed, quoted the veteran *Chicago Daily News* correspondent Edgar Ansel Mowrer as saying Singapore's strength was the greatest hoax ever perpetrated on the American public. He might more pertinently have said the British public.

Then Leonard Mosley of London's *Daily Sketch* arrived and, after visiting several bases in Malaya, wrote: "Singapore . . . is sharpening her teeth. Giant guns [guard] the jungle-fringed shores . . . Australian, British and Indian troops in the hot, fly-infested forest are ready for anything, while clouds of planes daily patrol over neighboring islands."

Singapore correspondents were furious and Brown wrote: "I think that is as fine a piece of fake and dangerous writing as I have encountered." A British pilot told him that airfields Mosley mentioned in glowing terms were nothing but mud, grass and water, with few planes. Mosley wanted to get back to North Africa, and Brown suspected he had written a piece intended to lull his editors into complacency about Singapore.[16]

Brown became the censors' most persistent and hated critic. Harold Guard, the UP manager, also incurred government wrath when he toured military camps in the Malay jungle and wrote about defense deficiencies. The government called his story a canard. Guard had to consult a dictionary to learn the meaning of canard. But Adm. Sir Geoffrey Layton, who commanded naval forces in Singapore, confided to him that he shared his views about the island's vulnerability.

On December 2, the battleship *Prince of Wales*, the cruiser *Repulse* and six destroyers arrived. Layton told Guard privately that the two big ships would be vulnerable to aerial attack; smaller, more mobile craft, were required.[17]

The British commander Far East, Air Chief Marshal Sir Robert Brooke-Popham, held a news briefing and said there were no signs Japan was preparing to attack anyone. In fact, he said, Japan was withdrawing troops from French Indochina. Three days later the UP bureau in Manila reported that 100 Japanese transports, escorted by strong naval forces, had been sighted heading south. Censors refused to allow UP to relay this news to Singapore newspapers. A navy public relations officer laughed off the report as sensationalism and a censor accused UP of "yellow-sheet scare-mongering."[18]

That same day, Guard filed a report hinting that a Japanese attack on Malaya was near. A UP man in New York, Fred Fergusson, replied, saying the always hard-pressed UP was facing heavy expenditures. "We want nothing, repeat nothing, from your area." Any reporting would involve expensive cable tolls. New York later queried Guard about the reported landing of Japanese forces in Thailand. He was able to confirm the report but censors blocked his dispatch.

At 4 a.m. on December 8, his office assistant, a young man named Arshad, rang him at home and said: "Oh, sir! The teleprinter is broken, sir." An angry Guard replied, "How come broken?" Arshad said, "A bomb, sir! From the Japanese airplane." At that moment Guard heard a loud bang and looked out to see tracer bullets streaking into the sky.

At least three bombs fell in Singapore city that morning, one within 30 yards of the UP bureau. Guard learned that an RAF squadron leader had not been allowed to attack Japanese troops because war had not yet been declared. Every grounded British plane was hit by bombs and machine guns. Guard wrote in his diary of "officialdom's quacking platitudes and smug deception."[19]

On December 9, the British military—more friendly to Cecil Brown than the censors—asked if he would like to go on a four-day assignment whose purpose could not be revealed. Brown accepted. O'Dowd Gallagher, a South African-born correspondent for London's *Daily Express*, received the same call and learned they were to go on a mission with the *Prince of Wales*. But a captain told them they were to go on the *Repulse*. Both men reconsidered, thinking a voyage on the *Repulse* would not have the same resonance with readers as a trip on the big battleship. But Brown told Gallagher they might as well go ahead. "We'll have a sea trip for four days and when we get back we're going to get fired anyhow."[20]

Adm. Tom Phillips, commander of the *Prince of Wales*, phoned MacArthur and told him eighty Japanese ships were approaching Malaya and he was going to sink them.[21] After a few hours at sea, the ships sighted thirty enemy planes approaching. Capt. William Tennant, commander of *Repulse*, informed his men they were abandoning the operation and returning to Singapore. Brown wrote that the announcement was greeted with "cries of disappoint-ment and even bitterness in the wardroom."

At 11:15 next morning, Japanese planes approached. "The nine Japanese aircraft are stretched out across the bright blue, cloudless sky like star sapphires of a necklace," Brown wrote—his account entirely in the present tense. The ships' guns opened up, and Brown saw bombs coming down, "streaming toward us like ever-enlarging tear drops. There's a magnetic, hypnotic, limb-freezing fascination in that sight. It never occurs to me to try and duck or run." Most bombs landed in the sea but one scored a direct hit, killing fifty men and starting a fire. One bomber was shot down and the others flew away. Gallagher later commented: "I found emotional relief in shouting, stupidly perhaps, at the Japanese. I discovered depths of obscenity previously unknown to me."[22]

* * *

At 12:10 p.m., twelve planes were overhead, all concentrating on the *Prince of Wales*. A torpedo struck and the ship listed to port. A new wave of planes appeared and the *Wales* was out of control, its steering gear destroyed. Gallagher wrote that fifty to eighty planes "attacked the *Wales* like a pack of dogs on a wounded buck . . . I gazed at her turning slowly over on her port side, her stern going under, and dots of men jumping into the sea."

Nine low-flying bombers dropped torpedoes 300 yards from *Repulse*. Gallagher was thrown against a bulkhead as one hit the port side.[23] Brown was hurled across the deck. The planes machine-gunned the decks and, 10 feet from Brown, three gunners fell dead. Two planes were brought down. "Suddenly it occurs to me how wonderful it would be to be back in Ohio," Brown wrote. Two more torpedoes hit *Repulse* and it began listing to starboard. Tennant ordered his men to prepare to abandon ship, adding, "God be with you." It was 12:25 p.m.

"The coolness of everyone is incredible," Brown wrote. "There is no pushing, but no pausing either." He could not see Gallagher. "The *Repulse* is going down. The *Prince of Wales* is low in the water, half shrouded in smoke, a destroyer by her side. Jap bombers are still winging around like vultures, still attacking *Wales*."

Men on *Repulse* began throwing overboard anything that would float— rafts, lifebelts, benches, etc.—then jumped into the sea. One man hit the side of the ship and crumpled lifeless into the water. Twelve Royal Marines ran too far aft and, after they jumped, were sucked into the ship's propeller. Brown said out loud: "Cecil, you are never going to get out of this."

Tennant refused to leave his ship but his men pushed him over the side. Brown jumped 20 feet into warm, thick oil. His lifebelt absorbed oil and tightened the cords around his neck. "I'm going to choke to death, I'm going to choke to death," he said to himself. "This is the first moment of fear." He saw a life preserver and grabbed hold. Oil burned his eyes and he swallowed some, then began to feel sick.

"I see the bow of *Repulse* swing straight into the air like a church steeple. Some men closer to the ship are sucked back." A small table floated past and he scrambled on top. A Marine helped pull Brown aboard a raft as men on it were vomiting and glassy-eyed. "Two have just died and their bodies are being put over the side." Rafts converged on the destroyer *Electra,* and four men dragged Brown aboard. The deck was littered with a half-dozen bodies. The destroyer reached Singapore naval base at 12:30 a.m. on December 11.[24]

* * *

Gallagher, who could not swim, was slower to leave the ship. First he offered a cigarette to a sailor and took one for himself. They puffed once or twice, then Gallagher jumped. Coming to the surface in thick fuel oil, he got a last look as the ships went down. "I had a tremendous feeling of loneliness."

Two men were hanging on to a lifebelt, blackened with oil, and he told them they looked like a couple of Al Jolsons, referring to the American singer who wore blackface at his performances. One of them replied, "We must be an Al Jolson trio, because you're the same." A fourth man joined them on the lifebelt, then all lost their grip and Gallagher panicked until he saw a small boat with two sailors in it. One man dived overboard and put a life preserver over his head. Gallagher told the men he was a reporter. " 'Ere, give us a good writeup, won't yer?" one Englishman replied.

The men were rescued by the Australian destroyer *Vampire*. "My breath smelled of heavy engine oil for more than a week afterwards," Gallagher wrote. "I suffered from acute vertigo and had pains in the back of my head." He assumed Brown was dead until they met on shore. Brown wrote that the only man who did not congratulate him on his survival was the chief censor with whom he had frequently clashed. Once recovered, Gallagher flew to Rangoon.[25]

Censors allowed Brown to say the ships were sunk primarily due to lack of fighter aircraft protection. Later he was informed he could no longer broadcast from Singapore. A Colonel Field told him the local population could hear his broadcasts on short wave and regarded him as a fifth columnist. "I must say that I agree," Field added. He hadn't heard the broadcasts but said he had read them.[26]

George Weller arrived on December 26 and shared sleeping quarters with Brown and Martin Agronsky of NBC, following "their querulous battles [with censors] and listened for the snap as each nerve string parted." The two broadcasters, he wrote, got along well enough with the chief censors, but with subordinates "they were similar to caged animals trained by torture. Agronsky . . . looked like a distraught orangutan; Brown resembled . . . a Russian wolfhound." Not all correspondents rallied to Brown's defense when his broadcast privileges were removed. He departed for Batavia in the Dutch East Indies, but the Dutch authorities wouldn't allow him to broadcast. He flew on to Australia, then returned to the U.S.[27] Resigning from CBS to write his war memoir, he remained in the U.S., broadcasting for Mutual, and later worked for NBC and ABC. In 1967 he became a professor at Cal Poly Pomona in California, remaining there until his death in 1987.[28]

A year after the *Repulse* sinking, Brown wrote:

For the rest of my life, peace will be unnatural. Forever in my nostrils will be the smell of death. Always there will be in my ears the scream of Stukas and always in my eyes the crash of bombs . . . Forever there will be in my heart the lust to kill evil men, the consuming desire for vengeance against men who had sown misery in this world.[29]

On Christmas Day, the Japanese began dropping leaflets suggesting that Malay, Chinese and Indian residents mark the birthday of Christ by "burning all foreign devils in a holy flame." But this tactic failed. "They were saving foreign devils, not burning them," Weller wrote. The "natives," as he called them, were lining up to give blood as casualties mounted. "For the first time in Singapore's history, the blood banks did as big a job as the money banks."

The military blew up a causeway linking Singapore to the mainland, and the Japanese came within artillery range, but the chief censor would not allow correspondents to say Singapore was under siege. He agreed to accept "besieged." Correspondents wrote of the "besiegement" of Singapore, knowing their editors would change that. "It is difficult to mention the . . . censors temperately," Weller wrote. "They held the correspondents' noses fast to the grindstone of the communiqué, even when the communiqués were two or three days behind the facts." Some censors were "ferocious" and cut the first paragraph off dispatches before sending them "10,000 miles away to enter the newspaper office headless."

Thomas Fairhall, 30, of the *Sydney Daily Telegraph* was imprisoned on Christmas Eve because of observations based on discussions with Australian troops. The arrest took place despite the fact his article had been passed by censors. British intelligence officers tried to induce him to name his source, he refused and they released him.

Then the War Office in London ordered a public relations officer to disaccredit E. R. Noderer of the *Chicago Tribune*. The officer was embarrassed to have to tell Noderer of the decision, and even censors tried to persuade the War Office to rescind the order. But the War Office said that, on an earlier reporting trip to Egypt, he had not reported to Cairo authorities—not true, according to Weller—and his copy from Iran had been unfavorable to British interests.

Singapore was now being bombed day and night. "For several days the people of Singapore were dying faster than the people of London in the Blitz," Weller wrote. "More people died in the four heaviest raids than in two years of bombing of Malta." The Singapore radio kept playing dance music, and a waiter at Raffles Hotel kept trying to sell Teddy bears to British officers at tea dances. A shipload of RAF fighter pilots arrived but were never used, and they sustained considerable casualties through being bombed at the piers. Weller left in early February on a freighter that took him to Batavia (Jakarta).[30]

Harold Guard had been a Royal Navy submariner in World War I and, as a result of a naval accident, walked with a stiff right leg. But that did not stop him from heading upcountry to report on fighting in Malaya. He went into an almost totally deserted Kuala Lumpur, entered an empty office and was trapped there as a battle ensued outside. An Australian film unit rescued him. Back in Singapore, censors blocked his copy and said he was to be investigated by a military tribunal. He had referred to a leg of pork that he had tried to cook for dinner at the front line. Military officers thought Singapore Island was shaped like a leg of pork and accused him of using this means to try to evade censorship. But a Ministry of Information official told them Guard had written a harmless feature story and the case was dropped.

UP President Hugh Baillee cabled Guard to say he had become the most intrepid correspondent in the war and should use his discretion about staying or getting away. On February 11, 1942, he went aboard a tender carrying sixty people, three times its normal capacity. Singapore fell five days later and the tender reached Java on February 17.[31]

He and C. Yates McDaniel of the AP were the last correspondents representing American clients to leave Singapore. The son of Baptist missionaries, McDaniel had covered China since 1935. Even as smoke from blazing oil tanks rose in front of the Raffles Hotel on February 9, he wrote, cars were depositing patrons of the tea dance. Two days later he messaged the AP that he had "10 minutes to pack and get away [from] this land of the dying." He escaped on a coastal steamer, arriving at Sumatra and finally reaching Batavia on a British destroyer. As the Japanese closed in, he escaped to Australia.[32]

* * *

In Bandung, the press corps gathered at a makeshift military headquarters. One morning, nine Japanese bombers swooped low over the hotel where correspondents were staying, spraying machine-gun bullets. They dived into a shelter. On February 27, Guard and William McDougall of UP headed for Tjilatjap (Cilacap) but their driver got lost. They reached Jogjakarta and a colonel promised to try to get them aboard an American B-17 bomber plane to Australia. McDougall decided to stay in Java. The Japanese staged an air-raid over Jogjakarta and all five remaining B-17s were heavily damaged. The Americans salvaged some parts so two planes could fly, and Guard became one of twenty-nine passengers leaving as Japanese tanks rolled into town. He arrived in Australia and filed a story about his escape, then learned a censor had "torn the guts out of my story." New York headquarters cabled: "Your premature departure from Java left our coverage thinnest."[33]

* * *

Several correspondents boarded a ship for Australia but William Dunn of CBS and Frank Cuhel of Mutual Broadcasting decided to try to get away aboard a B-17 at the last minute. On March 1, Japanese began landing on Java but a Dutch censor refused to pass Dunn's copy reporting this. Later, the censor handed him a communiqué about the invasion and Dunn, after writing his story, rushed to a telephone. He received congratulations from CBS on a world beat. Now, he wrote, he was ready to start running.

Together with Weller and Cuhel he went to Tjilatjap, where Cuhel drove his car into the bay, jumping out at the last minute. Left behind were DeWitt Hancock of the AP, McDougall and Kenneth Selby-Walker of Reuters. Selby-Walker said he was going to the hills to join guerrillas. He was never heard from again. In his last message to Reuters, he wrote: "I am afraid it is too late now. Good luck!"

Dunn, Weller and Cuhel were put aboard a Dutch island steamer, the M.S. *Janssens*, along with American sailors who had been wounded when their cruiser, *Marblehead*, was sunk. There were 600 people on board, most of them Dutch navy personnel. The *Janssens* set out at midnight but at dawn was still close to the Java shore. Twenty-five Japanese bombers flew over en route to bomb Tjilatjap, then on their return machine-gunned and fired cannons at the steamer. Weller, sheltering in a passageway, found the right shoulder of his bush jacket drenched with blood. He was not wounded but three people who were lay in the corridor.

Eleven days later, the steamer arrived in Australia. Weller filed a dispatch about an American naval physician, Lt. Commander C. M. Wassell, 58, of Little Rock, who had looked after the wounded American sailors. He had taken them a hundred miles over mountain roads to reach the ship, and had tended to those wounded yet again in the Japanese aerial attack. President Roosevelt awarded him the Navy Cross.

"Despite his hillbilly accent, this Arkansas traveler speaks flawless Chinese and his war career, like MacArthur's, is just coming to public notice," Weller wrote. His story caught the public imagination and, a year later, Hollywood produced a movie, *The Story of Dr. Wassell*, starring Gary Cooper.[34]

DeWitt Hancock and William McDougall got aboard a ship in Java, the *Poelau Bras*, but it was attacked and sunk. McDougall jumped overboard and saw Hancock standing by the rail. He appeared to be smoking. McDougall yelled, "Jump, Hancock, jump!" But Hancock went down with the ship. Dunn wrote that Hancock never should have been sent to a battle zone because he was a diabetic on a strict insulin regime. McDougall spent several hours swimming alongside a crowded lifeboat until another one picked him up and took him to Sumatra, where he was put in a Japanese concentration camp. After the war, he became a priest in Salt Lake City.[35]

* * *

Burma came under Japanese aerial attack on December 23, 1941. In February and March of 1942, Japanese troops invaded and British defenses crumbled. Many Burmese welcomed the Japanese. Chiang Kai-shek offered two Chinese divisions, prompting the Japanese to send more troops. The Chinese were pushed back into China. The American General Joseph Stilwell, in command of the Chinese, retreated westward through jungle with a small group of men, finally reaching Imphal in British-ruled Assam on May 20. British forces retreated into India and the Burma Road remained closed for almost three years.

O'Dowd Gallagher was in Rangoon for the first Japanese bombing. "Bodies of people killed lay on pavements for three days. Rangoon presented scenes of disorder more ghastly than I had seen in war cities in Abyssinia, Spain, Shanghai in 1937, France in 1940 or the Middle East. Rangoon was permeated by a foul smell." Docks stacked with American supplies for China were burning.

With him was Leland Stowe of the *Chicago Daily News*. A second wave of thirty Japanese bombers came over and streets were "littered with bodies, guts, brains and blood," Stowe wrote. He and Gallagher rushed to Mingaladon airfield, 12 miles away, where the RAF had only one squadron of aging Brewster Buffalo planes and the American Volunteer Group—later known as the Flying Tigers—consisted of one squadron of old P-40 fighters. Pilots were jubilant and "fighting mad," according to Stowe. The two squadrons took on eighty Japanese planes and shot down at least fifteen.[36]

Gordon Young, who had left Reuters for the *Daily Express*, wrote that American pilots "tore into those 50 Japs like hungry wolves." When one American plane crash-landed, the pilot leaped out, sprinted to another plane and took off, accounting for two more enemy craft before the bombers turned away. In Rangoon, Young watched as Ronald Matthews of the *Daily Herald* "descended in a stately manner" into a slit trench, produced a copy of *The*

Pickwick Papers and told Young: "I have a nasty suspicion, old boy, that before this is all over we shall be suffering from acute gin starvation."[37]

By noon the next day, half of Rangoon's half-million population had fled, hotels were empty, shops shuttered. Japanese bombers came back on Christmas Day. This time British and American pilots accounted for twenty-eight kills, but only twenty-two planes were still in condition to fly.

Stowe noted that the Chinese had hundreds of anti-aircraft guns on the docks but refused to lend any to the British. That evening, at his partially wrecked hotel, two Englishmen, "immaculate in dress shirts and black ties," walked into the bar, escorting a woman in an evening gown. "They did not seem remotely aware that Rangoon's fires were still smoldering or that parts of the city were a shambles or its hospitals overcrowded with 2,000 wounded," Stowe wrote. "This was my introduction to the sleepwalkers among the bombs."[38]

Young flew to Sumatra. Here he reported on the story of the sole survivor of a crashed Japanese bomber who woke to find the jungle hut in which he had taken shelter surrounded. The Japanese fired on his would-be captors, hitting a Dutchman in the shoulder. "To our amazement, he then suddenly stood up in full view and, in reply to our demand for surrender, placed his revolver in his mouth and blew a hole in the top of his head."

When Young returned to Rangoon, he struck out on his own to try to get out of Burma with a captured Japanese rifle and hand grenades. Near Tharrawaddy, a tight wire cord had been stretched across the road between two trees. Four Indians, fleeing in a car at high speed, had hit the wire, beheading three occupants. The fourth, a woman, lay nearby, stripped and raped. Elsewhere, Burmese kept bonfires burning at night to guide Japanese bombers.

Young reached Magwe (still in Burma) and his dispatch was held up for three days. The governor's secretary told him it was an implied criticism of the British Civil Administration. The secretary was surprised when Young told him that was exactly what he had intended. The dispatch was then transmitted.[39]

Tom Treanor of the *Los Angeles Times* came under machine-gun fire:

I can tell you from this one experience what fear is like . . . Every damn thought and feeling is wrung out of your body, except a worn-out, tired, hopeless sensation in your stomach and your chest and up and down the backs of your legs. You feel . . . that you're going to be dead maybe in the next second. You feel as though somewhere you made a great mistake.[40]

Eve Curie, continuing her globe-trotting, met up with British troops at Kyaikto, 250 miles from Rangoon. To her surprise, officers with whom she lived changed for dinner. While some had whiskies and sodas, others slipped away and came back neatly shaved, wearing well-pressed tropical uniforms.[41]

Stowe and Gallagher left Rangoon on February 19 and reached Mandalay. Gallagher described this fabled city of kings in central Burma as an "arid, tin-shanty city with nothing to commend it save Kipling's ballad," and Stowe wrote: "Mandalay was the kind of place that made you wish Rudyard Kipling had had to eat his poem for breakfast every day of his life." The city was "just a sprawling monstrosity of shacks and shanties and miserable sheds of bamboo or other wood."[42]

They moved to the hill town of Maymyo, summer residence of the governor. Maymyo, Stowe wrote, was soon "saturated with confusion, defeatism and bitterness." He and Gallagher wrote of fifth-column activities but British censors suppressed all such reports. "The great make-believe policy held firm to the end." The correspondents took the first available plane for Calcutta so they could write as much as censors would allow about the reasons for Burma's fall.[43]

* * *

Wilfred Burchett, a 31-year-old Australian freelancer, was in Chungking (Chongqing), the Chinese Nationalist capital, when the Pacific war broke out. Foreign Minister Quo Tai-chi told him that, if Japan invaded Southeast Asia, China would send troops. He cabled a story to the *Daily Express*, which then hired him as its Chungking correspondent. He also interviewed Chou En-lai, the future prime minister of Communist China, and cabled that story to the Sydney *Daily Telegraph*, which replied: UNINTERESTED CHINESE COMM PRONOUNCEMENTS.

Born in Melbourne, Burchett grew up in poverty, was forced to drop out of school and held such jobs as vacuum cleaner salesman and farm laborer. In 1936 he went to London and worked in a travel agency that resettled Jews from Nazi Germany in Palestine. He would become a controversial figure after the war as a Communist sympathizer but, politics aside, he was a first-rate reporter. The *Express* ordered him to Burma and, after the fall of Rangoon, he and *Life* photographer George Rodger, who was British, retreated to northern Burma. They took Jeeps to India, through a jungle filled with Naga headhunters. Leeches dropped from trees and soon blood was streaming down their arms and legs.

Arriving in Calcutta, Burchett came down with malaria and found that many of his Rangoon dispatches had never left the censor's office. He later returned to Burma and was in a party aboard a sampan on the Mayu River that was attacked by six Zero fighters. Everyone in the group except a British major was wounded. Burchett's wounds were in his back, right arm and right leg. Gordon Waterfield of Reuters also was hurt. They were hospitalized in India.[44]

* * *

Two of the most intrepid reporters in Burma were Darrell Berrigan of UP and Jack Belden of *Time*. Berrigan, 28, a bespectacled Californian, had been in Thailand at the time of Pearl Harbor. Japanese planes were over Bangkok and he hurried to the American Legation, where two diplomats were spreading a huge American flag on the lawn. They said they were doing this to make sure the legation was not attacked by mistake. Berrigan told them: "They're at war with *us!*" The diplomats rolled up the flag.

Described by Gallagher as "the soul of good nature," Berrigan had done various jobs earlier, including that of hotel night porter. He had been a UP correspondent in Shanghai before going to Thailand. After Japanese troops landed, he was smuggled into a third-class rail car in Bangkok while the Japanese searched first-class compartments for foreigners. He traveled almost to the Burma border, then walked across. Later he drove a six-wheel truck on a 400-mile retreat from Rangoon to Maymyo, where he met Stilwell, who had just taken charge of Chinese forces.[45]

Belden, 32, a New Yorker and graduate of Colgate University, had worked as a merchant seaman during the Depression. Jumping ship at Shanghai, he became fluent in Chinese and went to work for UP, later joining *Time*. As Stilwell attempted to mount an operation to recapture Rangoon, Belden ran into a Japanese bomber attack on a Chinese motor supply column. Pyinmana was ablaze and, outside the town, Burmese rebels set the long grass on fire to try to spread the havoc caused by Japanese incendiary bombs. "I felt slipping into my bones a fear, the kind of fear that one feels in an unfamiliar country when suddenly confronted with the unknown," Belden wrote.

On April 4, 1942, Belden and Berrigan were in Mandalay when it was first bombed. Belden described housewives incinerated while preparing the noonday meal, shopkeepers and their customers burned to ashes. "The flames were so long they reached out and licked the clothes off these running figures and they staggered down the hot roadway, live moving exclamation points of fire, collapsing and dying where they collapsed." Mandalay burned for twenty-seven days and nights.

Belden wrote with sarcasm of "war" correspondents who stayed close to officials and communiqués and never went near the front. The only other correspondents who remained upfront were Daniel De Luce of the AP and Bill Munday of the *News Chronicle*.

In mid-April, Belden wrote, the Japanese attacked the Chinese "with the speed and force of a thunderbolt." Belden sensed a full-scale retreat was under way. "I seized a rifle and called goodbye to the headquarters staff. Berrigan and I planned to rush for Stilwell's advanced headquarters" at Shwebo, 70 miles north of Mandalay. Every town for a distance of 200 miles was burned to the ground. Mandalay was abandoned, "the most terrible and frightening spectacle of the Burma War."

A press hostel outside Shwebo was bombed, a cook was killed and Berrigan's local assistant was wounded in the leg. Several correspondents left for India. A plane arrived to evacuate Stilwell, but he declined to leave and Belden decided to stay with him. Berrigan joined De Luce and Munday in driving to India, following elephant tracks through mountains, and went to Calcutta.

Stilwell chose to move north through a trackless jungle, short of food, on May 2. "Here are the last days of Burma," Belden wrote in his final dispatch to reach London. "All about me there is nothing but utmost misery. Roads are lined with belongings abandoned by refugees." Belden went by Jeep until the road ran out. He sent another dispatch that was received in Chungking, but a censor refused to relay it because it didn't fit the Chinese propaganda line. Food supplies for Stilwell's force were almost exhausted and thousands died. "The retreat from Burma was one of the bitterest retreats in modern times," Belden wrote. Remnants of the Allied armies received some food supplies by plane, but men were slowly dying of malaria, exhaustion and starvation. Stilwell's plan to bring the army to India was countermanded by the government in Chungking. Thus troops were delayed for a week in a malaria district and many Chinese soldiers died.[46]

Frank Martin of the AP hiked for thirteen days from Ledo, India, to link up with Stilwell. His guide, a Naga tribesman, said the tribe "had stopped cutting off the heads of people over 15." Martin was startled by Nagas singing "Old MacDonald Had a Farm". They told him they had learned it from a missionary before cutting off his head.[47]

Fourteen days after the troops left Shwebo, they had only enough rice for three meals, and their bearers were threatening to leave. Pus-filled sores began appearing on men's legs and feet. They had to climb 7,000 feet into India. But finally they were met by a British officer who had brought bearers, food, cigarettes and rum. For five more days the men climbed through mountains and finally Stilwell could give his report. "The Japs ran us out of Burma," he said in typically straightforward style. "We were licked."[48]

* * *

Hard fighting lay ahead but Burma was regarded as something of a sideshow. In 1943 the British Brigadier Orde Wingate organized a guerrilla force of 3,000 troops to penetrate behind enemy lines. They accomplished little of military value, and 30 per cent of the force was lost. British General William Slim led the successful campaign to recapture Burma in the spring of 1945, which cost the Japanese 80,000 dead. Reporting on these campaigns was relatively sparse as few correspondents went into Burma after the 1942 defeat.

Stuart Emery of London's *News Chronicle* and Stanley Wills of the *Daily Herald* traveled into Burma with the eccentric and slightly mad Wingate in 1944. Returning to India on March 24, their Mitchell bomber crashed into the Assam hills in India, killing all ten men aboard, including Wingate.[49]

George H. Johnston of the Melbourne *Argus* was with American forces in north Burma in 1944–5. As he lay in elephant grass below the Naga Hills, he saw the death of an American tank. "The black smoke parted to reveal a sheet of bright blue flame and the tank gaped open, split like a tomato can, and began to smolder . . . It was my introduction to Burma—the Golden Land, the country of peace and happiness and temple bells singing in the wind . . ."

Soon the Japanese were in full retreat southward. "The [Burma] road was ours. Every inch of the 1,000 miles of it." Fighting was still going on farther south and Johnston was with a British force approaching Mandalay. A captain told him: "If this is the road to Mandalay, then I'll read T. S. Eliot in future. You can have Kipling!"

Johnston thought the scene seemed stupidly unreal:

The dead Japanese stretched grotesquely along the roadway with swollen bodies and distorted limbs were covered with white, chalky dust and looked like plaster casts left there for theatrical effect. Even the wounded . . . looked wrong, for their bandages were too red . . . It looked like a Cecil B. De Mille cast on location . . .

When he reached Mandalay, Johnston saw a British corporal smashing at a beautifully carved Buddha with his rifle butt. He had broken off the nose and one ear before military police arrested him. This was the only time Johnston saw a British soldier desecrating a temple, but it was a different story with the Americans:

> Temples and shrines were ravaged and looted and desecrated with a savage ruthlessness that often made me acutely embarrassed. Buddhas were lashed to the radiators of almost every truck and Jeep on the Ledo and Burma Roads. Buddhas were thrown into almost every river and creek . . . Splintered Buddhas and sculptured heads too heavy to carry were discarded along the roads and half buried in the undergrowth of every bivouac area. The Burmese used to look at the evidence of vandalism and thoughtlessness strewn all over their ravaged country, and their faces were just as expressionless as ever.[50]

* * *

China was a divided country throughout the war, its eastern part occupied by Japan from 1937, most of the rest of the nation ruled from Chungking (Chongqing) by the corrupt and incompetent Nationalist regime of Chiang Kai-shek, and a restricted territory governed by the Chinese Communists in Yenan (Yunnan) province. The American government supported Chiang but fretted about his reluctance to engage the Japanese.

Few Western correspondents were based in China, visitors rarely stayed long and none spent much time at battlefronts. Bombing raids on Chungking provided most of their experience of war, but the Nationalist capital was something of a backwater and living conditions for correspondents were fairly primitive. It was not the best of war postings. The correspondents, few of whom spoke Chinese, covered China's Byzantine politics, were severely limited by censors in what they could write and, in the case of *Time* correspondents, were restricted further by their publisher, the China-born Henry Luce, an admirer of Chiang and his American-educated wife, Soong May-ling. The China hands were almost uniformly critical of the regime.

Two correspondents who would later achieve renown as authors, Theodore White and John Hersey, arrived in 1939. The 23-year-old White had graduated *summa cum laude* from Harvard with a degree in Chinese history and studies, and went to China on a fellowship. He worked as supervisor of news-feature stories of the government-run China Information Committee. His clients were the foreign correspondents based in China and he tried "to deliver what shreds of information I could gouge out of the government for which I worked." He also freelanced for the *Boston Globe* and other newspapers.

Hersey, the 25-year-old China-born son of missionaries, represented *Time-Life*. He would later become a Pulitzer Prize-winning novelist but his fame would chiefly arise from a 1945 *New Yorker* article, then published as a best-selling book, on the effects of the atomic bombing of Hiroshima. Hersey hired White as a stringer, and White set out to cover combat to try to secure a staff job. He resigned from the Ministry of Information in December 1939, then set out on a swing through Southeast Asia during which *Time* made him a staff member. He was away from China from summer 1941 to summer 1942.[51]

Martha Gellhorn was an early visitor in 1940. "I wanted to see the Orient before I died." She wasn't long in China before she was longing to leave. "The notion that China was a democracy under the Generalissimo is the sort of joke politicians invent and journalists perpetuate . . . I do not believe that China ever was a democracy, nor will be, in our lifetime . . . I longed to escape away from what I had escaped into: the age-old misery, filth, hopelessness and my own claustrophobia inside that enormous country."

Before leaving, Gellhorn went to Communist headquarters in Kunming. When air-raid warnings sounded there, she wrote, people rushed out of town without even locking up behind them, watching from the hills as Japanese bombers further leveled their city. "Only the people who are too old or ill or disgusted to make the long daily trek stay behind, and get killed." Gellhorn was soon back in Europe.[52]

* * *

Leland Stowe arrived in October 1941 and was appalled by the living conditions of resident correspondents. He described the mud-walled press hostel as a version of an African kraal—"on the knob of a hill, a series of sheds facing a barren yard that turned to mud with rain." Residents had to go across an often-muddy courtyard to reach a community washroom and dining room. Two correspondents had wives sharing this "monotonous and trying existence."

> For my tastes, its most objectionable feature was provided by the armed soldiers or policemen who stood guard day and night . . . apparently under

orders to watch every move the correspondents made. Theirs is a tougher existence . . . than that of journalists I have known in any other wartime capital.

Stowe was equally appalled by the life of most Chinese. "I came to China . . . without any faint conception of the oppressive poverty and squalor which eats the flesh of China's 'one-fifth of humanity' . . ." But he was impressed by Chiang Kai-shek. "China's famous war leader gives an immediate impression of strength and tenacity and great reserves of will power . . . Here was a will, an exceptional will, rather than an intellectual force." But he detected "a hint of ruthlessness." Madame Chiang is "like a perfectly balanced and beautifully executed blade of Toledo steel. A dazzling array of sparks may fly from that slender flashing blade, but it is still steel."

Stowe wrote that a friend of China was supposed to ignore the presence of concentration camps holding 50,000 people. "Thousands of Chinese Communists are locked up in these camps. They also contain thousands of Chinese students and intellectuals . . . Most are confined for criticizing uncontrolled war profiteering and other abuses."

Chou En-lai, the Communist liaison with Chiang's government and later prime minister, told Stowe he believed Chiang would be forced to give freedom of action to opposition parties. "I thought General Chou was sadly mistaken."

Stowe left for Burma and there was deeply troubled by "the greatest racket in the Far East"—the Burma Road. Congress had voted nearly $500 million in aid to China, all of it intended to come across the 1,500-mile Burma Road from Rangoon to Chungking. Stowe reported that the Chiang government, in addition to requesting military supplies, had also asked for industrial equipment that could not contribute to the war effort for another one to three years. And the road couldn't handle that much traffic, so armaments worth an estimated $30 million were piling up in Rangoon.

Scores of American-built trucks stood idle, rusting in the rain, because spare parts had been stolen and sold in private shops in Kunming. Gasoline supplies found their way onto the black market. Crates that were supposed to include radios for Flying Tiger planes were stuffed with perfume and women's toilet articles.

He wrote seven articles describing a Burma Road "crippled by inefficiency, politics, lawlessness, racketeering and other abuses," placing the responsibility on "the Kuomintang dictatorship" and Chinese businessmen. In January 1942 he received a cable from his head office: BURMA ROADSTERS

CAUSING SENSATION. Shortly afterward, he got another cable saying publication of the remaining articles had been suspended "on urgent suggestion higher-ups." Apparently friends of China in U.S. government circles had protested to the *Daily News*.[53]

* * *

Eve Curie came to Chungking in 1942 and met Chou En-lai. "A highly intelligent political leader . . . a general who also had the smartness of a diplomat and could keenly analyze a situation without automatically sticking to the Party Line." Chou told her the Communists, while opposing Chiang, still saw him as an indispensable war leader and symbol of unity.

Madame Chiang invited Curie to tea, and Chiang joined them:

> The Generalissimo was like a subtle, indecipherable Chinese book full of complicated ideographs which made no sense to the foreigner. Madame Chiang was like a translation in English of the original text. She presented to the outside world a readable China . . . the China that any farmer in the American Middle West could understand and admire.

In Kunming, Gen. Claire Chennault, head of the Flying Tigers, told Curie: "I need more pursuit planes. I need bombers. I need men. Do they know it in Washington? . . . From China we must strike at Japan's heart, with American machines and American men."[54]

* * *

In the autumn of 1942 Theodore White reported on "the strangest battlefront of this war"—Chinese–Japanese clashes along the Salween River Gorge in Yenan Province. The Japanese held the 12,000-feet-high mountains on the west side of the gorge, listed as one of the three worst malaria regions in the world.

"This is a nightmarish, silent earth, where men who wake by day are dead by night without a shot being fired." White reported that Chiang had sent troops in without nets or quinine. In one night, seventy-eight men in one company died of malaria. An appeal for nets and quinine produced 500 tablets for 7,000 men. "The Japanese . . . have suffered badly, but they have the Burma Road to return their men to hospitals, plenty of food and unlimited quinine."[55]

Two years later the Flying Tigers played a decisive role in defeat of the Japanese at the Salween Gorge. Karl Eskelund of UP had a mixed view of Chennault's men. "I liked the Flying Tigers, but the glamor and romance which most Americans associated with them just wasn't there. They didn't love China . . . there were no blondes, no Cokes and no flush toilets, so it was no damned good. They . . . hated everything and everybody—except General Chennault."[56]

Jack Belden of *Time* was unstinting in praise of Chennault, "this wrinkled, scar-faced, half-deaf, 51-year-old ex-barnstorming pilot . . . the one genius that war on the Asiatic mainland has yet produced. His record is unequaled in the annals of combat aviation." Chennault was "an ever-victorious commander among a group of ever-defeated Allied generals."[57] Stowe also had a negative view of the Flying Tigers. "One of the first reactions of these young Americans was to bellyache about everything . . . Within the first month a half-dozen pilots asked to go home. Chennault wisely let them go . . . I heard many things which made me ashamed of them as Americans."

Chennault invited him to speak to "these thoughtless, over-cocky and intolerant young Americans." He knew they disparaged RAF pilots and told them he hoped they would prove as good as the RAF men he had seen in action in Greece. But, after Japan invaded Burma and the Flying Tigers performed brilliantly, Stowe had a different view. "Chennault took a bunch of unruly and hard-headed young American anarchists and made a truly great fighting team out of them . . . Chennault is one of the few outstanding military leaders that America possesses anywhere in this war." After observing the Tigers in action outside Rangoon, Stowe wrote: "This, in all truth, was one of the happiest moments I've ever had as a war correspondent . . . These American boys were still cocksure . . . But they were fighters."[58]

* * *

Theodore White met Stilwell in India in August 1942. Stilwell told him: "The trouble in China is simple: We are allied to an ignorant, illiterate, superstitious, peasant son of a bitch." Stilwell had had his first assignment in China 20 years before Pearl Harbor and was fluent in the language. "No American officer realized better than Stilwell the havoc that the years of corruption had wrought in the Chinese army," White wrote. "He believed a modern state could come only if American policy actively espoused democracy and efficiency . . . Stilwell was the greatest and most inspiring figure in the CBI [China–Burma–India] theater. His and Chiang's personalities clashed bitterly."

Stilwell was also in conflict with Chennault. He wanted to focus on reopening the Burma Road but Chennault thought all the supplies could be flown in.

In February 1943, White's convictions about the incompetence of the Chiang government were confirmed when he went with Harrison Forman of *The Times* of London to cover a famine in Honan (Henan) province, northeast of Chungking. They discovered it had claimed the lives of 2 to 3 million people and forced an equal number to flee. "The villages echoed with emptiness; streets were deserted . . . doors and windows boarded up. There were corpses on the road . . . A dog digging at a mound was exposing a human body."

In Chengcow (Zhengzhou), White and Forman found dead and dying people in the streets, people slicing bark from elm trees and grinding it to eat, refugees cramming soil into their mouths to fill their stomachs. Hospitals were filled with people suffering intestinal obstructions after eating filth. Two maddened parents had tied their six children to trees so they could not follow as they searched for food.

Missionaries told of cannibalism. One woman was caught boiling her baby and insisted it died before she started to cook it. Another woman fed on the legs of her dead husband. On mountain roads, refugees were killed for their flesh. Several young officer trainees at a military academy looted an abandoned village. They were buried alive in sand on orders of their commander.

White wrote that the government had bungled a relief program and continued to seize crops in lieu of taxes. He and Forman were invited to an official banquet where they were served chicken, beef and fish. "It was one of the finest and most sickening banquets I ever ate," White wrote. On their return to Chungking, they found no one believed their stories. White sent his direct to New York, evading censorship. *Time* published it on March 22, 1943, but omitted all criticism of the Chiang regime. Nevertheless, Madame Chiang was furious, demanding that Luce fire White. Luce refused. On other occasions White found that much of his copy was rewritten by *Time* editors to soft-pedal criticisms of the regime.

In August 1943 Hanson Baldwin, later of the *New York Times*, reported in *Reader's Digest* that China was losing battles, had no real army and its communiqués were almost worthless.[59]

* * *

Eric Sevareid was working for CBS in Washington in 1943. A friend of President Roosevelt, revealing that the administration was concerned over the reluctance of the Chinese to fight, asked Sevareid to go to China to assess the situation and, upon his return, broadcast what he learned. He set out from India on August 2 on a military aircraft but, an hour into the flight, the left engine died. Passengers and crew began bailing out. Sevareid was paralyzed with fear. As the plane was about to go into a dive, he leaped out of the door, then heard a loud voice saying, "My God, I'm going to live!" It was his own.

He landed near four crew members, two of them injured, including the radio operator with a broken leg. Within an hour, a Douglas transport was circling overhead, then dropped a bundle containing an ax, knives, blankets and other supplies. A note instructed the men to stay where they were until a rescue party arrived. As they waited, fifteen to twenty men appeared carrying spears and wearing only breechcloths. They were Naga headhunters but were not hostile. The aircraft returned and an army surgeon, Col. Don Flickinger, bailed out to tend the injured.

Eventually 100 British and American soldiers arrived to take them to safety. On August 22, troops helped Sevareid transmit a 400-word dispatch to Albert Ravenholt of UP so he could relay it to CBS. Later Ravenholt contacted him and said censors refused to pass his story with the word "headhunters" in it because that would indicate the general area in which he had come down. "I fear I lost my temper," Sevareid wrote.

Soon he arrived in Chungking and was quickly disenchanted with the regime. On his return to Washington, he produced an article critical of China's war effort and urging U.S. action to forge an alliance between Chiang and the Communists. It "was killed outright." The State Department had asked War Department censors to pass nothing on China without State's approval. Sevareid rewrote the article, toning it down slightly, but it was never published or broadcast.[60]

* * *

George H. Johnston of Melbourne's *Argus* arrived in Chungking in 1944. Authorities had built tunnels and caves extending deep under Chungking, housing hospitals, schools, factories and arsenals. "Here for years of suffering and hardship . . . the battered population lived like troglodytes." But, with a population swollen by refugees from cities under Japanese occupation, not all could be accommodated in the caves and many died in Japanese air attacks.

Johnston found Chinese censorship extremely strict:

Once I attempted to write a factual story of the medieval savagery and callousness and utter stupidity of a Chinese general who had sacrificed the lives of thousands of men in my presence. The censor refused to pass it. I altered the introduction and submitted it again to the same censor as a short story. He passed it. And it was published as fiction in . . . a leading magazine in New York. We newspapermen are often accused of writing fiction as fact; but only in China could one be forced, by the very incredibility of things, to write fact as fiction.[61]

* * *

Despite Luce's reluctance to publish criticism of Chiang, he did allow an article by White to appear in *Life* in May 1944 that described the regime as "a corrupt political clique that combines some of the worst features of Tammany Hall and the Spanish Inquisition."[62]

In the summer of 1944 the Japanese began a 500-mile drive in southeast China intended to wipe out forward bases of the U.S. 14th Air Force. By mid-November China's defenses had collapsed and White reported that Chungking was seized by panic. Cold weather, an extended supply line and U.S. reinforcements eventually stopped the Japanese advance, but not until they had captured eight provinces and a population of more than 100 million people.

Stilwell was pressing for the use of Communist armies against Japan but Chiang resisted, demanding Stilwell's removal. Roosevelt was reluctant but Stilwell left China on October 19, 1944. UP's Walter Rundle, in bed with malaria, received a visit from a Chinese friend who informed him that Washington had reluctantly agreed to Stilwell's dismissal. Rundle checked with other sources, who confirmed the story, but Chinese censors killed it. So Rundle wrote a message to UP in New York: "Informatively Berrigan's old sidekick been fired by home office. Suggest check with Lyle." In New York, UP editors recalled Darrell Berrigan's close association with Stilwell during the Burma campaign. "Lyle" was Lyle Wilson, the UP Washington bureau chief. UP broke the story the next day, well ahead of a White House announcement.[63]

A more detailed account of the feud appeared in the *New York Times* on October 31, 1944, and caused an uproar in Washington. Stilwell had told his story to Brooks Atkinson, Chungking correspondent of the *Times* and its drama critic both before and after the war. Atkinson left China and smuggled the story out from Cairo. Still, the *Times* had to take the issue to Roosevelt before an American censor would agree to publication.[64]

In 1944 White persuaded Luce to hire as his assistant Analee Jacoby, the widow of Mel Jacoby. At the end of the war they produced a book, *Thunder*

Out of China, which was critical of the regime and became a bestseller. Later White gained further fame with a series of groundbreaking books on American presidential campaigns. He died of a stroke in 1986. After the war Jacoby became a regular on the popular radio program *Information, Please!* She married the moderator, Clifton Fadiman. In February 2002, aged 85, she committed suicide after a long battle with breast cancer and Parkinson's disease.

White and Jacoby reported in their book that Roosevelt's ambassador in Chungking, Patrick J. Hurley, disapproved of criticism of Chiang, and blocked such reports by his own diplomats. He informed Washington of progress being made while in fact the country was moving toward civil war. "His fear of the working press became enormous," according to the two authors. "The corps of foreign correspondents could only fume in silence and frustration at a situation which they knew must some day erupt in disaster."

By the spring of 1945, according to *Thunder Out of China*, China had become of secondary concern to American strategy because of the military failures of the Chiang government.[65]

CHAPTER 9

PACIFIC ISLAND CAMPAIGNS

A small force of Japanese landed in March 1942 on Papua New Guinea, the world's largest island after Greenland. The Japanese wanted to seize Port Moresby in the southeast, the capital of the Australian-ruled island, and began trekking overland from the north coast through dense rainforest and the Owen Stanley mountain range. The Japanese pushed close to Port Moresby but U.S. bombing of the overextended Japanese supply line averted disaster and the Japanese began a retreat. Residual Japanese forces were mopped up in January 1943.

Osmar White, a 32-year-old correspondent of Melbourne's *Herald and Weekly Times*, arrived in Port Moresby on February 13, 1942, on the last civilian plane to cross from Australia. The Japanese soon began bombing but "their bombing was execrably bad." White was subjected, in a relatively mild way, to the harsh environmental conditions that would plague both soldiers and correspondents. "Every afternoon and every night it rained. Every night hordes of black, voracious mosquitoes came singing hungrily out of the grass. Every dawn hordes of black, voracious flies came buzzing in thirstily."[1]

Frank Legg of the Australian Broadcasting Commission (later the Australian Broadcasting Corp.) commented more extensively on these wretched conditions. "Malaria was rife, and along the swampy coastal plain dengue fever was particularly severe. Worst of all was the dreaded 'scrub-typhus,' caused by the bites of ticks. This frequently induced periods of apparent insanity, and could prove fatal." Of 298 casualties in one month, 291 were due to illness.[2]

The Australians had a limited number of anti-aircraft guns but no fighter defense, and George H. Johnston of Melbourne's *Argus* complained that correspondents could not mention this because "anything we write is censored into innocuous nonsense." Yet he recognized that, "if we write stories telling the truth about the defenses of Port Moresby, appealing for more men, more guns, fighter planes, the most interested people will be the Japanese. They'll come in like a shot and take the place by sneezing." So correspondents cabled: "Send *more* fighter planes."

Johnston, also on assignment for *Time*, wrote in his diary that Port Moresby was expected to fall and Australian soldiers had begun looting "and in some cases it's looting on a grand scale . . . carried into the realms of sheer vandalism." In one shop shelves had been torn from walls, women's clothing ripped apart and paint poured over it. But the priority was liquor.[3]

Japanese troops landed on March 8 and began the trek toward Port Moresby. White returned to Australia on May 6, convinced the garrison there would not last a week if attacked. When he returned in early June, he and Damien Parer, an Australian cameraman, went by boat to join an Australian guerrilla unit, the Kanga Force, at Wau, a gold-mining village near the north coast. They were put ashore at a point called Bulldog, and from there would have to walk more than 100 miles to Wau, part of the journey over mountains 9,000 feet high. In the wet and cold mountains, some bearers fell ill and had to return to Bulldog. At night the party was plagued by rats. "They came down from the bush . . . They ran over the blankets all night, sat on one's face . . . Generally played hell."

White and Parer (later killed in the Philippines) decided to return to Port Moresby in August but had to hike 60 miles to the nearest airfield. By the time they returned the Japanese had captured an airfield at Kokoda, and White and Chester Wilmot of the Australian Broadcasting Commission were refused permission to join an Australian force sent to attack the invaders. Wilmot, the son of a newspaperman, had worked for ABC before the war but had joined the army with the outbreak of hostilities. His military career ended when ABC recruited him, initially to report from the Middle East and Greece.

Thirty-five Japanese bombers with Zero escorts attacked Port Moresby airport on August 19, destroying or damaging twenty-eight aircraft. White and Wilmot were "depressed beyond words." But the next day, White, Parer and Wilmot received permission to go to the mountains. Without bearers, they had to carry rations for five days. Soon Parer came down with fever. The beefy Wilmot had trouble going up hills and White began to feel the recurrence of an earlier bout of fever.

"It is difficult to describe the abysmal depression that had me in its grip," he wrote. "The rain did not vary in intensity for as much as a minute . . . One's very bones seemed softened by the wetness." The correspondents caught up with Australian troops, who were soon under intense machine-gun fire from well-hidden Japanese. "The whole battle had become a blind groping in a tangle of growth," White wrote.

He and Wilmot reached a brigade position just as troops decided to evacuate. The Japanese broke through and a long line of stretcher cases was brought out under fire by native bearers. "My belly felt like lead," White noted. "I was deadly weary and deadly discouraged—appalled by the sense of being a partisan spectator to a disaster . . . My only job was to watch, and nobody cared the price of a matchbox in hell whether I watched or not." A brigade major ordered the correspondents out.

"All night I kept passing lines of wounded men," White continued. "At the tail of every string, men would drop off and lie face down in the mud . . . Some died there." He used a flashlight to lead wounded men at night. Then the battery gave out. "I started to cry. The tears rolled down my face, burning." The wounded struggled on and White found himself alone. "My breathing was getting painful. I didn't know it then, but I had pneumonia." Not having eaten in 48 hours, White paused in a village, Eora, where military surgeons were performing night-time amputations by flashlight. Leaving Eora, he passed a man, one of whose legs had been blown off below the knee. He had put a ligature on the stump, applied two dressings and wrapped it in old copra sacking. Crawling and hopping vigorously, he said he was quite strong enough to reach Eora. White and Wilmot returned to Port Moresby in September and White was invalided to Australia.[4]

Wilmot, 31, was described by Trevor Royle, a BBC executive, as a man who brought to his work "a good conceit of his own abilities . . . He could be overbearing and self-opinionated." He wrote that some people thought of Wilmot as bumptious or nakedly ambitious, but he also had an easy charm. In New Guinea, Wilmot continued a feud with Australian commander Gen. Sir Thomas Blamey that had begun in North Africa. In that campaign, Wilmot clashed with Blamey over the right of correspondents to make informed criticism of the direction of the war, and Blamey censored one dispatch in which Wilmot commented on the poor standard of reinforcements arriving from Australia.

Blamey now crossed swords with Wilmot again when he fired Lt. Gen. Sydney Rowell, whom Wilmot admired. Wilmot flew to Canberra to protest to Prime Minister John Curtin, who granted him a hearing, but Blamey's position was unassailable. When Wilmot returned to New Guinea, Blamey denied him access to his headquarters and ordered his staff to snub him. Later

Blamey removed his accreditation and ordered him back to Australia. Much later, when the BBC wanted Wilmot to help cover the invasion of Europe, Blamey asked the British War Office to deny him accreditation. The War Office declined to humor him.[5]

In his own reporting, White had referred to the inadequate training of Australian troops for jungle warfare. He, Wilmot and Parer campaigned to get the Australian army to adopt green uniforms for camouflage. The U.S. Army, acting on their advice, decided to dye its uniforms a mottled green, and the Australians soon adopted green as well.[6]

George Johnston, 30, reported that some Lutheran missionaries had been acting as guides for the Japanese. "It turns out that quite a little network of Nazi espionage and fifth-column activity existed on the north coast." The missionaries printed swastika flags and arm bands, kept airstrips in good repair for the Japanese and maintained a secret radio transmitter. Australian troops raided the area, seizing the emblems and photographs of Nazi leaders and finding the remains of the radio transmitter, which had been destroyed. One missionary, Johnston wrote, had been a German air ace in World War I and, at the outbreak of war in New Guinea, put on a Luftwaffe uniform and left by private plane. He also reported that a few Australian soldiers had been found to possess Nazi documents, photos of German leaders and aerial photographs of the Port Moresby garrison.[7]

* * *

On August 7, 1942, Vern Haughland, 34, of the AP had to bail out over New Guinea when his plane ran out of fuel. He and an army lieutenant spent forty-two days in hiding, only the first eight together, and living on grass and roots. Missionaries found him on September 19, exhausted and delirious. He became the AP's aviation writer after the war. A diary that Haughland kept tells of his ordeal:

Aug. 19—Second day lying on rocks, chewing grass and reeds, praying a great deal. Getting so weak. Hardly any hope now. Lost life preserver. Watched vainly all day for a plane. Only hope is a plane dropping food or ground aid arriving—both extremely unlikely. Looks like I shall die here soon.

Aug. 20—Worst rainy nite since Mike [the lieutenant] and I spent two terrible ones. I was just lying in the mud, soaked and stinking, all night. Somehow stronger today. Foot healing, too. If could get real food think could hike around mountain. Seems too bad to die when maybe could struggle to a village. If only the mountains didn't stretch on, sharper and sharper. If only knew shortest way to go to sea.

The diary referred to his once having gone two and a half weeks with nothing to eat. After Haughland was taken to a hospital, he received a visitor: MacArthur presented him with the Silver Star, the first time it had been awarded to a civilian.[8]

* * *

George Weller arrived in August. An officer told him the troops were "fighting the country 90 percent of the time and the Japs 10 percent." Weller referred to the inland country as "that steaming hell tied together with vines and creepers and infested by hundreds of wild animals and savages."[9]

Johnston agreed the Kokoda Trail provided some of the toughest fighting terrain in the world. Jungles were like an impenetrable green wall, rivers contained crocodiles and swamps teemed with leeches. There was an endless hum of malaria-carrying insects, and troops had to contend with "strange equatorial extremes" of heat and cold.[10]

In the Owen Stanley mountains the Japanese continued to push back Allied forces, outnumbering them three to one. Weller wrote that the atmosphere was "clammy-cold" and, for troops, "hands upon a rifle grow damp with the chill." Even at 14,000 feet, mountain peaks rarely got any sun. "No human beings, native or Australian, have ever attempted tropical fighting at such an altitude or under these rigorous circumstances," he wrote.[11]

General Blamey expressed confidence the Japanese would be defeated by the difficulties of maintaining supply lines the closer they came to Port Moresby. The setbacks prompted censors to clamp down on news dispatches. Johnston wrote that news was sometimes limited "to the bare terms of the official communiqués, which are often about as loquacious as a deaf mute with both arms cut off." But Blamey was right. The Japanese had covered the first 60 miles in five days, but the next 30 miles took fifty days. They came within 32 miles of Port Moresby, but their advance was stopped on September 16. Many dead Japanese were emaciated, and doctors who examined bodies said hunger had forced some to eat poisonous fruits and roots. "The stench of the dead and the rotting vegetation and the fetid mud is almost overpowering," Johnston wrote.

The Australians reconquered the Owen Stanley range and marched into the town of Kokoda, at the northern end of the trail, unopposed on November 2, 1942. But there was still heavy fighting along the beaches.[12]

* * *

In October, Byron "Barney" Darnton, 44, a *New York Times* correspondent, was killed when he set out to join the 128th Infantry Regiment of the U.S. 32nd Division, a unit with which he had served in World War I, in their attempt to dislodge the Japanese from Buna. From a grassy landing strip, Darnton joined fifty-seven men who rowed out to two old fishing boats—the *King John* and the *Timoshenko.*

At dawn on October 18, a twin-engine bomber appeared. Lt. Bruce Fahnestock ran to a machine gun while Darnton stood by the wheelhouse door, disdaining to wear a helmet. Coming in low, the plane dropped a 500-pound bomb that exploded on the water 500 yards away. On a second run, it dived on the *King John*, strafing the deck and dropping another bomb. A third bomb hit the port side of the bow. As Fahnestock slumped over his gun, wounded in the spine, a bomb fell near the stern and a fragment caught Darnton in the back of the neck. It was a "friendly fire" incident; the plane was American, whose crew assumed the boats were Japanese.

Eighteen men were wounded. Fahnestock died in the arms of a friend. Darnton was wrapped in an army blanket, bleeding profusely, and placed in a canoe, but when it reached shore he was dead. The bodies were later flown to a new American hospital outside Port Moresby, and Darnton's funeral was held two days later, with six correspondents acting as pallbearers. Darnton left a wife and two young sons. His younger son John, later a *New York Times* correspondent and Pulitzer Prize winner, wrote a book of startling frankness, *Almost a Family*, which was published in 2011, about his father's death and his own childhood with an alcoholic mother, Eleanor, who turned out not to be married to his father.

Weller had known Barney for nearly ten years, and paid tribute in his newspaper. "What this correspondent loved best in Barney . . . was his slow, dry wit which was completely untainted with Manhattan smartness but had, rather, a warm fatherly quality." Darnton had been "among the best-loved, as well as most respected, of war correspondents in the Pacific area." Weller penned a letter of condolence to Eleanor Darnton.

Harold Guard was aboard a landing craft not far from the scene of Darnton's death. He and Geoffrey Reading, an Australian correspondent, had to jump over the side and swim for shore when the air attack began. Darnton's death, he wrote, was "very upsetting for me, as I had spent much time with him . . . I kept his typewriter, an old Remington, as a memory of him and our time together in New Guinea for many years afterward."[13]

While Weller was in Australia, he ran across a story about medically untrained submariners performing a successful appendectomy on a crew member while deep under the sea. It won a Pulitzer Prize. Back in New Guinea in December, he was present for the capture of Gona and wrote that "the stench of dead bodies was so powerful that the Japs donned gas masks." There were more than 500 dead. "It is a Japanese Dunkirk, but there was no evacuation." The Buna area was marshy, steaming flatland and Weller wrote: "When the sun comes out you feel your body is an anvil being hammered. When it disappears . . . your whole torso bursts out with a thick black film of perspiration."

He told how *Life* photographer George Strock took a picture of a "dead" Japanese who came to life when Strock's back was turned. "He sat up and blinked, he did," said an Australian soldier, who shot the resurrected Japanese. After the battles there, Weller wrote that "everything you own including your body is partly broken, rusty, moss-covered, insect-infested, diarrhetic, fevered, dirty, diseased, wet and muddy, or smells of putrefying Japs."[14]

Johnston wrote that Australian troops were "almost overcome by the stench of rotting bodies," and he described jungles around Buna "that look like Gauguin paintings and sound like a good-sized earthquake and smell like a charnel house."

"Nowhere in the world today are American soldiers engaged in fighting so desperate, so merciless, so bitter, so bloody a battle," he wrote while it was still in progress. "The really staggering thing is the amount of punishment the Japanese have taken, and yet they still fought back as stubbornly as ever."[15]

Robert J. Doyle of the *Milwaukee Journal* penned a tribute on January 5, 1943, to the men who had captured Buna, and to victims of other Pacific battles: "You and the Aussies at Buna and Milne Bay and the Marines at Guadalcanal finally stopped the Japs. They caught us with our pants down, but you stopped them and started driving them back . . . Your comrades of the Red Arrow Division are thinking of you as they carry the battle forward at Saidor."[16]

Ian Morrison of *The Times* of London summed up the fight for New Guinea in a dispatch of April 7, 1943: "It was a war without chivalry, without honor. It was a bloody fight to the death, an elemental struggle with only one password—kill or be killed."[17]

Johnston wrote that, in the final stages of battle, Japanese soldiers swam into the sea, some fully dressed, others naked, and were found up to 2 miles offshore, where they were strafed by Allied planes. On January 23, 1943, he reported, the last Japanese soldiers in Papua New Guinea had been killed or captured; their total losses came to 16,000 men.[18]

By April 1943 Weller was down with malaria in a field hospital. Two months later, he left for Australia. After MacArthur's death in April 1964, he wrote a damning assessment of the general. "His censors, by suppressing almost everything political and meaningful from the Southwest Pacific, reduced the war to a series of banal hero stories costing the American people a generation of political education in Southeast Asia." Later he wrote: "He cowed the entire American press into suppressing the fact that his battle of malaria-ridden New Guinea was directed from the hotel apartment in Brisbane where he lived with his wife and son. Bataan it wasn't."[19]

Osmar White was equally contemptuous. "If you saw anything that flatly contradicted the communiqué it certainly didn't get past the censor." MacArthur press releases were often falsifications by omission or distortion. "They were crafted in many cases to build up the infernal man's ego."[20]

* * *

Lt. Col. James Doolittle led sixteen B-25s in an unconventional air strike on Tokyo on April 18, 1942. The two-engined bombers took off from the aircraft carrier Hornet *650 miles from Japan and caused relatively little damage but the raid demonstrated Japan's vulnerability. On May 7, planes from American and Japanese warships clashed in the Coral Sea in their first major battle. The next big naval battle, on June 3–4 off Midway Island, was a turning point of the war. The* Yorktown *was lost, but the Americans sank four Japanese carriers and a number of other vessels. A Japanese threat to the U.S. West Coast was now impossible.*

Richard Tregaskis of INS was aboard the *Hornet.* In a dispatch published on April 20, 1943, he wrote:

I witnessed the dramatic sight as 16 great, landlubbery planes—the celebrated Mitchell medium bomber—weighing 12 tons each took off from the pitching, rolling deck of the carrier while great waves crashed on the bow of the ship and washed over the flight deck . . . We were on tenterhooks lest the Japanese naval force should discover us before we could get all the planes, bound for Tokyo, into the air. We had been spotted already by one Jap patrol boat, which a cruiser in our task force blasted to atoms.

Joseph Dynan of the AP, now in a Japanese prison camp, saw one of the planes fly over as prisoners cheered. "The music of its motors was sweeter than Beethoven's Fifth Symphony, which our phonograph was playing at the time," he wrote after he was freed.[21]

Correspondents were now spread all over the Pacific, and over the next four years would report from Japanese-controlled islands, some mere pinpoints on the map, with names that meant little to most Western people—Guadalcanal, Taroa, Tarawa, Saipan, Tinian, Guam, Iwo Jima. One significant difference of the Pacific war was that MacArthur barred women reporters from his areas of operations. Thus there were not the romances and marital breakups that happened in Europe.

Stanley Johnston, 42, of the *Chicago Tribune* was the only American correspondent with the fleet in the Coral Sea battle. Australian-born, he had served in World War I and had become an American citizen after moving to the U.S. in 1936. While working for the telegraphic company Press Wireless during the German invasion of the Netherlands, he made his way to London and was hired by the *Tribune*.

Aircraft from the carrier *Lexington* spotted a Japanese fleet 180 miles away on May 7 and attacked. Johnston mistakenly reported that they sank a carrier (it was only heavily damaged) and a heavy cruiser, and shot down seventeen enemy aircraft with a loss of just three scout planes. The next day, the *Lexington* was sailing in bright sunlight while the Japanese fleet was under a curtain of rain. But scout planes located the Japanese ships, and another carrier was attacked by torpedo planes and dive bombers. As the planes headed back to the *Lexington*, twenty Zero fighters pounced and shot down all but one of them. Thirty-six Japanese torpedo planes and dive bombers converged on the *Lexington* and it was hit by five torpedoes. It began listing. Then a series of explosions sounded from deep within and, after a particularly violent one at 2:30 p.m., Johnston wrote in his notebook: "The end." At 5 p.m. the order to abandon ship was given.

A destroyer came alongside and took off 500 men. Others jumped into the sea and were not all picked up until two hours later. "There was calmness and order," Johnston wrote. Some sailors who had been below decks brought up large containers of ice cream and those still on deck, who had had no water for hours, gratefully had their fill.

The *Lexington*'s death throes occurred when bombs and torpedoes stored below decks ignited. The ship didn't sink but burned fiercely. "In the deepening twilight it was a sight of awful majesty, one that wrung the hearts of all who watched," Johnston wrote. With the blazing ship serving as a beacon to the Japanese, an American destroyer put four torpedoes into her to sink her. An officer standing beside Johnston murmured: "There she goes. She didn't turn over. She is going down with her head up. Dear old Lex. A lady to the last!"

Johnston's graphic description made him a celebrated figure in the U.S. He noted that the two fleets never saw each other but battled with their air arms, thus disclosing "how completely the carrier has displaced the battleship in importance in modern war."[22]

Harold Guard was in Australia and several of his colleagues were away from Melbourne when the navy issued a communiqué on the battle of the Coral Sea. Guard felt sorry for his absent colleagues and filed cables to all their newspapers, putting their names on dispatches he wrote.[23]

* * *

On June 4, 1942, a Japanese plan to capture Midway Island, at the northeastern tip of the Hawaiian archipelago, was uncovered when a Catalina flying boat spotted 145 warships led by 4 aircraft carriers steaming toward the island. American planes sent to attack suffered heavy losses but pilots who returned reported a number of hits on at least two carriers and a battleship. After the first attacks, Robert J. Casey of the *Chicago Daily News* thought there was a chance "to get this war well on its way to a finish in the next couple of hours." As more reports came in, he wrote: "It was still obvious that we had had something of a field day, still obvious that the bulk of Japan's attacking planes must presently be going into the drink for want of any place to land . . . We begin to realize that we have actually taken part in a decisive and important battle."[24]

Further raids resulted in the sinking or damaging of three Japanese carriers. Then, as planes began returning to the *Yorktown*, eighteen Japanese dive bombers appeared, giving correspondents aboard the cruiser *Astoria* their first view of this epic battle. Eleven bombers were shot down but the remaining seven peeled off over the carrier. "It seemed to take minutes for the planes to come down from first sighting to bomb-dropping distance," wrote Foster Hailey of the *New York Times*. A bomb struck the *Yorktown* flight deck. Another plane turned a somersault and a bomb broke loose, falling into the smokestack. "Thick black smoke poured out," Hailey wrote. Of the remaining Japanese planes, only one scored a hit—a bomb that penetrated the flight deck and exploded four decks down. The *Yorktown* signaled the *Astoria*: "Send small boat for admiral and staff."

"They came aboard looking like refugees from a chain gang, in smoke-begrimed coveralls," Hailey wrote. While crews fought fires on the *Yorktown*, two cruisers and two destroyers arrived to protect it. Meantime a scout plane located the undamaged Japanese carrier *Hiryu* and a strike force from the *Enterprise* was sent to attack it. Then more Japanese planes bore down on the *Yorktown*. The *Astoria* shot down one and another skidded into the sea.

"Two of the Japanese pilots were very brave men," Hailey wrote. "Right through the curtain of anti-aircraft fire they flew, straight for the *Yorktown*." They dropped torpedoes, the carrier began heeling to port and "abandon ship" flags went up. "The oil-covered sea was alive with bobbing heads . . . For over an hour the work of rescue went on."[25]

Casey described the scene toward sundown:

The horizon is a band of glowing orange. And against it the battered carrier stands in her glorious aloofness . . . You look at all of this with a catch in your throat . . . The carrier . . . stood majestically on the rim of the sea, the blazing sun behind her like the burst of light at the climax of a grand opera, her head up.[26]

On June 7, a Japanese submarine put two torpedoes into the *Yorktown* and she sank. In his dispatch, Hailey wrote:

The mighty "Y" is down. The aircraft carrier *Yorktown*, the fightingest ship in the United States Navy, was sunk this morning by a Japanese submarine as she lay helpless in the water miles north of Midway Atoll. I last saw her against the darkening western sky on June 4, as her cruiser guard steamed away from her, lying almost on her side in the water, a thin wisp of smoke curling up from her forepeak where a great fire had raged deep inside her hull that afternoon after a hit by an armor-piercing bomb.

Hailey, 43, who had served in the navy in World War I, wrote: "Midway was the most stunning and one-sided defeat ever suffered by a major fleet." In a month, he noted, Midway and other battles cost the Japanese six of their eleven major carriers, most of the air groups aboard them, five heavy cruisers, at least five destroyers, three or four big transports and perhaps 20,000 men.[27]

Casey wrote: "It turns out that we have fought a major engagement—one of the biggest naval battles of all time. And miracle of miracles, we have won

. . . We who a couple of months ago were shuddering at the sight of Pearl Harbor have taken control of the Pacific." A Japanese broadcast declared that its fleet had captured Midway and had attacked Pearl Harbor and Honolulu. Casey telephoned his managing editor, who told him it would do public morale no good "if we exaggerate the significance of a lot of minor battles."

"Good heavens, man!" Casey exclaimed. "Don't you know that the turning point has come and passed you by?" "No," the editor replied. "I hadn't heard of it."[28]

After Midway, Stanley Johnston was accused of disclosing information on Japanese strength that could have tipped the enemy the U.S. had broken the Japanese code. A federal grand jury investigated but no indictment was returned. Johnston had written from Chicago and testified that he based his article on his experience in covering the battle of the Coral Sea, on information contained in *Janes' Fighting Ships* and on discussions with naval officers.[29]

* * *

In May 1942 Keith Wheeler drew an assignment to a battlefront little remembered today, little noticed at the time. It was the Aleutian Islands off the southwest coast of Alaska. The Japanese had occupied Kiska and Attu on the western end of the chain when only a handful of Americans were there. Wheeler described the Aleutians as mountainous, barren and uninhabited, shrouded in fog throughout summer and lashed in winter by snow and gale-force winds.

He spent several months covering American attacks on the Aleutians while aboard ships or bombers. Then in November he went ashore on Attu. Twenty-six days later, when he left the island, "I still wore the same underwear, shirt, pants and socks in which I came ashore. During that time I had not shaved or bathed, and the special occasions on which I had washed my face or hands could be counted on one set of fingers. We were seldom warm, hardly ever dry, perpetually dirty, often hungry and always tired." In November he went ashore on Amchitka. "When the sun thawed ice around roots of evergreen trees, Amchitka became a morass. Every step was torture." When gas stoves inside tents were turned on, "what appeared to be firm ground became slimy swamps within an hour."

On May 11, 2,000 American soldiers landed on Attu without opposition. "My feet went from under me on a slippery slope and I rolled," Wheeler wrote. "When I got up again my right leg buckled and my knee flamed with pain . . . Using that knee thereafter was the distillation of hell . . . It was torture all day, every day, and all night it ached with the dull persistence of a rotten tooth."

Of 2,500 Japanese on the island, more than 1,000 were killed. "On the night of May 28 the Japs were beaten and knew it." Their commander ordered them to make one last attack and keep killing Americans until they themselves were killed. Japanese doctors were ordered to kill their wounded with morphine or hand grenades. "They killed 87, stacked the bodies in a hospital tent and burned them." The remainder set out in darkness, crept into American lines, killed the guards and stabbed a dozen sleeping men in foxholes. Then they began screaming: "Son of bitch Americans! We die—you die too! We kill American boys! We drink American blood like wine!"

Survivors ran shoeless and half-dressed. They formed a firing line to try to hold the Japanese back, but some enemy forces swept around it and, entering an aid station, bayoneted a dozen wounded men, two doctors and a chaplain. Completing their butchery in a second tent, the Japanese settled down to breakfast.

Some Japanese were armed only with bayonets lashed and nailed to sticks. The Americans killed hundreds and the others started killing themselves with grenades. The next morning, a hundred Japanese survivors came down a mountain and attacked the American line. Most were killed and the others committed suicide. Wheeler wrote:

I lived on this Attu for 26 days . . . I became accustomed to easy killing and simple dying. I was sniped at, machine-gunned and shelled by the Japs and bombed and strafed by the Americans. I accepted—without shock—the notion that I might be killed by an American who would rather kill me than wait to identify me—and nearly was. I heard the wounded in the tent hospital—when the shock and the morphine had worn away—screaming in the night and cursed their cries for keeping me awake . . . I slept with dead Japs beside me and ate heartily within a few feet of formless messes which shortly before had been living men presumably containing men's memories, loves, dreams, schemes and holiness . . . I ate what I could get . . . but I was always hungry. I was usually cold and forever wet.[30]

Robert Sherrod reported for *Time* on the final, furious Japanese banzai attack after he watched the burial of 125 American servicemen. "Many were obviously shot and killed, then stabbed time after time by the strange little yellow men who then proceeded to die, sometimes by their own hands, as violently as possible."[31]

The campaign cost the U.S. and Canadian forces 1,481 dead, the Japanese three times as many. It became known as "the Forgotten Battle." The mystery writer Dashiell Hammett spent part of the war as an army sergeant in the Aleutians and later co-authored a book about the battle.[32]

* * *

In 1942 the Japanese began building an airfield on Guadalcanal, one of six large islands in the Solomons group. This would have threatened supply lines between the U.S., Australia and New Zealand. The First Marine Division invaded on August 7 and seized the airfield. Then, in the early hours of August 9, a Japanese heavy cruiser squadron attacked Allied ships off Savo Island, sinking four and damaging three others. The battle went on for six months before Marines and Australian troops prevailed in January 1943. After Guadalcanal, the Japanese never held the initiative in the Pacific again.

Richard Tregaskis, the gangly, six-foot-seven, bespectacled correspondent of INS, went ashore with Marines two hours after a heavy naval and air bombardment on August 7. There were no enemy troops nearby. "Our debarkation was leisurely. It was hardly the hell-for-leather leap and dash through the surf, with the accompaniment of rattling machine guns, that I had expected."[33]

Clark Lee of the AP and Jack Singer of INS flew over the beachhead, the first correspondents to fly in Pacific combat. Their pilot was ordered to bomb troops hiding in woods near the runway. When they returned to an aircraft carrier, Lee looked in his notebook and saw that he had scribbled over and over again: "Hit 'em. Hit the bastards. Kill the lousy Japs."[34]

Following Marines, Tregaskis marched through miles of jungle, across streams and over steep hills. They came to a field and bedded down for the night "with bugs, mosquitoes and thirst," and macaws squawking in treetops. Near midnight, they were attacked by machine guns and rifles. Then the enemy withdrew. On August 8, Tregaskis passed two Marines bringing in three Japanese prisoners. "The prisoners were a measly lot. None of them was more than five feet tall, and they were puny."[35]

That evening, the Americans learned that an enemy force of heavy cruisers and destroyers was headed for Guadalcanal. Rear Adm. Richard K. Turner thought it unlikely they would attack at night with a relatively small force, and no extra precautions were taken. Just before 2 a.m., the Japanese struck near Savo Island, sinking four cruisers. According to Foster Hailey, "the response was near panic." Turner departed at speed.[36]

Joe James Custer of UP, aboard the *Astoria*, awoke on August 9 to find the ship under attack. By the time he got on deck, a fire was raging amidships. Going below for his lifebelt, he reached his cabin as a shell ripped through it. Another burst spun him around and his left eye was burning with pain. Blood streamed down his face. "Lean on me," someone said. He was helped off the sinking ship and onto a destroyer. But he lost sight in his left eye.[37]

Duncan Norton-Taylor of *Time* was aboard a destroyer ahead of the Australian cruiser *Canberra*. The destroyer was hit by shellfire, and "the *Canberra* was turned into an exploding holocaust of fire." The destroyer captain called to *Canberra* sailors to jump aboard his ship but they chose to stay with their wounded. "As our can got clear, the plucky Australian sailors stood along the rail of their doomed ship and gave our can a pathetic cheer."

They began burying the dead at sea. "Other casualties of the night battle died with less dignity," Norton-Taylor wrote: "the water was dotted with figures floating upright in life jackets. They were only heads and torso. The waters off Savo Island were thick with sharks . . ." News of this disastrous battle was withheld from the American public for some time.[38]

On August 23, Clark Lee got aboard a carrier-based torpedo plane that took him to Guadalcanal and, on landing, learned an enemy force spearheaded by three carriers had been sighted 200 miles to the northwest. He failed to get on one of the planes going out to meet the enemy, but Jack Singer of INS did and witnessed a battle in which American pilots, plus anti-aircraft guns, shot down 96 of 123 planes while losing 6. "Jack Singer had scooped me and had one of the best stories of the war," Lee wrote. "It was almost Jack's last story." On September 15, he was killed when Japanese submarines torpedoed the aircraft carrier *Wasp* and sank it with him on board. Singer, 27, had been a sports writer for the *New York Journal-American* before the war.[39]

Osmar White was on Guadalcanal when the Japanese launched their air attack. "I wonder what it's like when 123 pilots come into mess for breakfast, and only 20 come for dinner," he wrote. "Not even the Japs can take that for long."[40]

After the *Wasp* was sunk, "morale of the fleet was going down like an express elevator," according to Hailey. "The men wanted to fight. They wanted to give the Marines on Guadalcanal some support . . . Instead they were kept on a chain, sweltering in tropic heat, in waters fairly crawling with hostile submarines."[41]

Tregaskis remained in the Solomons until September 26, then flew to Honolulu and set out to turn a diary he had kept into a book. He had to go to Navy offices every morning, work under the noses of officers and hand over the diary to be locked in a safe overnight. He completed the book, passed it through censorship and sent it to a New York publisher. *Guadalcanal Diary* became an instant bestseller, then a movie, and made Tregaskis famous overnight.

In November, he headed back to Guadalcanal, where he found the First Marine Division "shot through with casualties, malaria and dysentery." But captured diaries showed the Japanese were short of food and riddled with tropical diseases. Still, they fought tenaciously.[42]

John Hersey, 28, a China-born *Life* correspondent, was with Marines caught in a trap at the Matnikau River west of Henderson Field, coming under heavy fire. "The mortar fire was what was terrifying . . . a visitation of death . . . We hit the ground. We were like earthy insects with some great foot being set down in our midst . . . And all the while snipers and machine gunners wrote in their nasty punctuation."

While the men lay pinned to the ground, one word was whispered along the line: "Withdraw." Marines began moving back slowly, then running. Capt. Charles Alfred Rigaud stood and shouted: "Who in Christ's name gave that order?" The men froze. "I am sure he was as terrified as I was," Hersey wrote. "Yet his rallying those men was as cool a performance as you can imagine. By a combination of blistering sarcasm, orders and cajolery, he not only got the men back into position; he got them in a mood to fight again." Rigaud understood that the position was untenable and he sent a runner to a command post with a request for permission to withdraw. Then he whispered an order for withdrawal.

Medical corpsmen started collecting the wounded. "I joined them because, I guess, I just thought that was the fastest way to get the hell out of there," Hersey wrote. "We slid, crept, walked, wallowed, waded and staggered, like drunken men."[43]

Ira Wolfert of the North American Newspaper Alliance came under intensive fire one day, and took it personally. He wrote:

> The Japanese tried very hard for about five hours today to get this reporter. They tried first with snipers, then machine guns and finally brought up mortars. The closest the Japs could come was to bedeck me with clipped-off leaves of the local vegetation and freshen my complexion with mud packs applied in clumps from rifle bullets that smacked into the earth around me.

Later Wolfert went aloft on a Flying Fortress and it became involved in a dogfight with a Japanese bomber:

Our plane shuddered under the impact of bullet after bullet and teetered and buckled under the blasts of its own guns . . . I could see the Japs clearly . . . small, shrunken-seeming figures huddled up over their guns. I could see a cannon firing at us, smoke blowing from its open mouth, and I could see our red tracer bullets pelt like darts into the Jap . . . This was kill or be killed all the way through . . .

The American bomber shot down the Japanese plane. Wolfert, who worked his way through Columbia University's School of Journalism by driving a taxi, won the Pulitzer Prize in 1943. After the war, he wrote a Hollywood screenplay, then became a novelist.[44]

In February 1943 Foster Hailey was aboard the destroyer *Nicholas* when it came under air attack. Eight bombs narrowly missed. Hailey saw the flash of an explosion between stacks of the destroyer *DeHaven*. One man was lying on a small platform. "It really was only a piece of a man. One arm and half the trunk seemed to be gone. Several men were lying on deck." Then the *DeHaven* sank. "One man had a finger hanging only by a piece of skin. He took out a pocket knife and casually cut it off and tossed it over the side."[45]

On February 9, 1943, correspondents were summoned to Marine headquarters and given a radio message that had been sent to Adm. William "Bull" Halsey, South Pacific commander: "Total and complete defeat of Japanese forces on Guadalcanal effected 1625 today." The long, costly battle, Tregaskis wrote, "broke the legend of Japanese invincibility, the first big step on the island-to-island ladder that led to victory."[46]

* * *

In mid-1943 the battlefront moved to New Georgia, west of Guadalcanal, in an attempt to isolate the Japanese stronghold on New Britain, which lay further west. Osmar White was on a destroyer sent to pick up Marines from a distant island on the night of June 21. As he and a crew of sailors set out in a boat for shore, they ran into rollers 15 feet high pounding the coral. There was no way to land, and no sign of the Marines. "I want to scream like a child, 'Take me aboard, I'm sick of it. If something doesn't happen, I'll go mad!' " White wrote.

They soon located the Marines, aboard a canoe carved like the head of a bird with ruffled neck feathers. They had been unable to get ashore because of the rollers. "They stank like goats."

On June 30, White joined three infantry regiments landing on New Georgia, where more than 10,000 Japanese were caught by surprise. They scrambled for their guns and, in White's words: "An officer pranced out of a shed, waving a sword. Bullets eviscerated him. His bowels ran out of his uniform like sawdust from a torn rag doll."

White joined troops at a command post and found the men's eyes hollow with sleeplessness. Many had knife wounds, inflicted by nervous comrades who had mistaken them in darkness for Japanese. The Japanese, hidden in dense undergrowth, came out boldly at night, sniped from trees, tossed grenades at foxholes, howled, cat-called and jibed.

White heard high-pitched Japanese voices sounding "like apes with human tongues." One tried to lure the Americans into firing on him and exposing their positions: "Aid, aid, doc! Give aid to me. I am wounded!" No one fired. White saw another Japanese soldier 15 yards away, inviting death for the same reason. Japanese soldiers with grenades were hidden behind him, ready to hurl them at the flash of a gun. American naval guns opened up to protect the command post, and the next morning thirty Japanese bodies lay around it. The man who had pretended to be wounded now cried: "Christ, he's got me in the guts! I'm stabbed! Water, water!"

The Marine attack now stretched to twenty-one days and might go on for weeks, so White decided to ship out. As he went aboard a vessel, the harbor was attacked by dive bombers. "Four men stood beside me in the wheelhouse. A 500-pound bomb struck the ship aft. It penetrated several decks and exploded. The four men are dead. I am now walking again. Why those four men should have died and I live and walk, I don't know." This wordage contains only a hint of the fact White was seriously wounded in both legs, spent months in hospital and only returned to war coverage fifteen months later.[47]

* * *

On July 6, 1943, an American task force went into the Kula Gulf, a funnel between Kolombangara and New Georgia. Unexpectedly, they encountered a Japanese task force bringing reinforcements. The Japanese destroyer *Amagiri* escaped and, on August 2, it rammed and cut in two PT boat 109, piloted by 26-year-old Lt. j.g. (junior grade) John F. Kennedy, in the Blackett Strait west of New Georgia. Two of the crew of twelve, the AP reported on August 19, were killed, and Kennedy saved one badly burned survivor by gripping a strap of the man's life preserver between his teeth and swimming for five hours to a small island 3 miles away. Kennedy, of course, was then known to the public, if at all, only as the son of Joseph Kennedy, millionaire businessman and former ambassador to Great Britain. Ten months after the AP story appeared,

John Hersey did a major article on the incident for the *New Yorker*, providing grist for Kennedy's presidential campaign in 1960.[48]

The battle for New Georgia ended in an American victory on August 5. On islands just west of there, it continued until October.

* * *

Some early American landings on Pacific islands were unopposed. Tarawa was different. In a battle that raged from November 20 to 23, 1943, nearly 6,000 Japanese and Americans died. Tarawa, a tiny atoll in the Gilbert Islands, was a stepping stone to the mid-Pacific Marianas Islands, where the Americans wanted to establish air bases. The battle proved to be one of the hardest of the war for Marines.

Robert Sherrod, 32, a Georgian working for *Time* and *Life*, was aboard the battleship *Tennessee* off Tarawa on the morning of November 20. At 5:05 a.m., a battleship fired the first shot at Betio, chief of the twenty-five islands in the atoll. "A wall of flame on Betio shot 500 feet into the air, and there was another terrifying explosion as the shell found its mark." It had hit a powder magazine. "The whole island seemed to erupt with bright fires" and was soon shrouded in flames and smoke. After the naval bombardment, about a hundred American planes launched bombing runs. "Surely, we all thought, no mortal men could live through such destroying power."

But that illusion was soon shattered, as a shell splashed into the water not 30 feet from Sherrod's landing craft. The naval bombardment resumed and finally the last big Japanese gun was silenced. Men started going ashore. "We shook and shivered because we were cold" and drenched by water coming into the boat. Sherrod noticed that boats carrying the first waves of Marines were not hitting the beach. The water was too shallow for the type of boats being used. Marines pinned down on the beach were being killed.

Sherrod was shaking with fear, convinced that Japanese machine guns would mow down men coming ashore by the hundreds. To his left, an amphibious tracked vehicle, known as an Alligator, took a direct hit from a mortar shell. The men with him were told their craft could not go all the way in and they would have to wade the last 700 yards. Sherrod and fourteen men began wading in neck-deep water:

No sooner did we hit the water than machine guns opened up on us. I was scared, as I had never been scared before. I do not know when it was that

I realized I wasn't frightened any longer . . . perhaps when I noticed bullets hitting six inches to the left or six inches to the right.

Sherrod called aloud: "You bastards, you certainly are lousy shots." He shouted to Marines to head for a log pier, and seven came with him.

They crawled beneath the pier and inched their way 400 yards forward up to the beach. A landing craft jammed with Marines, 600 yards out, was hit by a shell and parts of the craft flew in all directions. As a Marine walked past Sherrod, a bullet went through his helmet but missed him. "Then I saw the most gruesome sight I had seen in this war. Another Marine walked briskly along the beach. He grinned at a pal who was sitting next to me. Again there was a shot. The Marine spun all the way around and fell to the ground, dead." He had been shot through the temple.

Another Marine threw TNT into a pillbox 15 feet away. A Japanese ran out but a flamethrower stopped him. "As soon as it touched him, the Jap flared up like a piece of celluloid. He was dead instantly but the bullets in his cartridge belt exploded for a full 60 seconds after he had been charred almost to nothingness." Marine dead were piling up on the beach but many more were wounded. The dead included many naval medical corpsmen who were killed trying to recover the wounded.[49]

A Marine colonel told the AP's William Hipple: "I guess you got a story. It looks like the Japs want a scrap." Moments later the colonel was killed, but Hipple joined forces with Sherrod.[50]

Richard W. Johnston of UP and Frank Filan, an AP photographer, started ashore and ran into machine-gun and artillery fire. Marines on either side of them were killed. They reached the beach and collapsed behind a seawall. "Like the Marines I had to walk 500 yards shoreward through a machine-gun crossfire," Johnston wrote. "Throughout the last 60 hours, and probably through the next 60, Japanese snipers have been taking, and will take, a heavy toll."[51]

Toward evening, Sherrod and Hipple dug foxholes. "I was quite certain that this was my last night on earth," Sherrod wrote. "For the first time since morning, I was really scared . . . . the unknown was going to happen under cover of darkness." Sherrod turned to Hipple and said: "Well, Bill, it hasn't been such a bad life." Hipple replied: "Yeah, but I'm so damned young to die." Sherrod wrote that his knees shook and his whole body trembled like jelly.

The expected attack never came and Sherrod learned later that about 300 Japanese had committed suicide. But some swam out to landing craft during the night, firing at Marines still coming ashore. When morning came, Sherrod and Hipple found Johnston and Filan, whom they had feared were dead. After three days ashore, Johnston returned to his ship to file. A seaplane picked up correspondents' dispatches, and when they arrived at Pearl Harbor censors decided to pool Johnston's main report, as no other news agency man had filed. But he had written two other dispatches that went exclusively to UP clients.[52]

By the third day, defenses were crumbling as American tanks and armored half-tracks took their toll. The enemy staged a counterattack at dusk and 300 were killed. Betio was declared secured at 13:12 on the fourth day. "What I saw on Betio was, I am certain, one of the greatest works of devastation wrought by man," Sherrod wrote. Five thousand men died on Betio, of whom 685 were Marines. Another 2,100 were wounded and 169 missing.[53]

* * *

Further south, Marines landed on Cape Gloucester on New Britain Island, just east of Papua New Guinea, in December 1943 to help isolate and harass a major Japanese base at Rabaul. Brydon Taves, 29, the UP manager for Australia, had spent much of the war coordinating activities of correspondents and frequently protested that he wanted to see action too. Finally he persuaded New York to let him cover the Cape Gloucester landings but, en route, he was killed in the crash of a B-17 bomber at Port Moresby. Pendil A. Rayner, 34, of the Brisbane *Telegraph* also died. Two other correspondents were injured.[54]

CHAPTER 10

THE DESERT WAR

Britain began operations in the summer of 1940 against Italian units in Libya, with Gen. Sir Archibald Wavell throwing 36,000 men into battle against Marshal Rodolfo Graziani's 250,000. Wavell launched his biggest attack on December 6, sweeping into Libya and capturing thousands of Italians. By February 9, 1941, the British had advanced 500 miles, but four divisions were transferred to Greece to meet the German assault there, while Field Marshal Erwin Rommel's Afrika Korps was landing at Tripoli to bolster Italian defenses. The desert war stretched over four years.

Shortly before Wavell's offensive, Italian forces had been advancing in the Western desert. The British War Cabinet believed Egypt faced "mortal danger," but Richard Dimbleby, a young BBC broadcaster newly arrived in Cairo, reported there was no cause for anxiety. His controller in London was displeased with his coverage, judging him unreliable and overconfident. It was an inauspicious beginning for a correspondent who would later become the single most important voice of BBC news.[1]

Initially, there were only seven or eight correspondents covering the war in the desert. They faced baking heat in summer, freezing nights in winter, sandstorms, sand fleas, swarms of flies and scorpions. There was also the risk of becoming lost in the desert, without water, in which case they would go off their heads and die fairly quickly.

Many friendships were forged between correspondents during the war, none closer than that between Alan Moorehead, 30, an Australian working for the *Daily Express*, and Alexander Clifford, 31, of the *Daily Mail.* Drinking together in a Greek bar, they mused over how they could get a war assignment.

Deciding to take advantage of the fierce competition between their two news-papers, Moorehead cabled the *Express* that Clifford was on his way to Cairo, and Clifford sent a similar cable about Moorehead. Back came the hoped-for responses: "Follow Clifford." "Follow Moorehead." They followed each other until the end of the war.

"Young journalists thought very much about their careers at that time," Moorehead wrote after the war. "Should they enlist? Or was their work a suffi-cient excuse for them to continue in their jobs as most of them in their hearts wanted to do?"

The tall, bespectacled Clifford was a contrast to his shorter companion. "He was shy, precise and disillusioned," Moorehead later wrote. "I was aggres-sive, erratic and full of enthusiasm." But as time went by, he suggested, each may have absorbed something of the other's characteristics. Moorehead felt he had taken on a little of Clifford's precision, reticence and "quite extraordi-narily cerebral approach to life." He speculated that Clifford may have learned from him a sense of practical direction, the power to take decisions and a certain eagerness and gregariousness. But Clifford, he wrote, could be weak and indecisive, arrogant, overbearing and rude to officials.

His arrogance may have stemmed from impatience with men of lesser minds. Clifford's mother told Moorehead that her son was scarcely five when he first played Bach on the piano. She gave him an atlas at the same time and, within hours, he handed it back, saying he had read it—meaning he could now draw every map from memory. Before the war, he traveled over most of Europe, absorbing languages and cooking skills. "Most languages, dead and modern, came to him easily," Moorehead wrote.

While the two men worked together, they remained competitors. "It was a cross-current beneath our friendship, a kind of private, professional bitter-ness," Moorehead commented. "We never rejoiced in one another's successes."[2]

His remarks are illustrative of a seeming paradox: in all wars, correspon-dents who are nominally competitors in fact cooperate on many occasions to get the story. Partly this is because events are too wide ranging for one reporter to cover all of them. But it also happens because correspondents in dangerous situations find safety in numbers, and several of them may be forced to travel together in a single vehicle to reach battlefronts. In one instance, the AP's Ed Kennedy refused to ride in the same car with UP's Henry Gorrell to reach a filing point, and that rare breach provoked the scorn of other correspondents.

Moorehead drove out of Cairo and was at Sidi Barrani in August just after the Italians had been expelled. The staff had disappeared from an

Italian hospital, leaving injured patients, including an appendicitis patient cut open on the operating table. Surgical instruments were still sticking in the body.

Moorehead stumbled upon 7,000 Italians marching into captivity near Buq Buq in Egypt. In the town, thousands more had quit the fight, "a more broken collection of men than I had ever seen . . . The Italian egg had been cracked and it was rotten inside."[3]

For Ed Kennedy, the collapse was amazing. "In the first days of the campaign, some correspondents had amused themselves by rounding up willing prisoners in batches of 50 or 100," he wrote. "Now it was necessary to shoo them away to get any work done. Every Italian unit, every tank, seemed to carry a white flag as standard equipment."[4]

Clifford tried to rush to the front with several colleagues when the offensive began, but their vehicles broke down several times. Once they reached the front, they sent dispatches back to Cairo with anyone who happened to be returning. Clifford came down with sand-fly fever and jaundice and, while recovering, went on an RAF raid on Tobruk, the most important Libyan town in Italian hands. As the plane went in for its raid, Clifford froze. "Just for one second there was icy panic inside me and I wished I hadn't come. I wondered whether I was trembling from cold or fear. Then I grew far too excited to be afraid." The plane made three bombing runs. The town's 15,000 defenders surrendered shortly afterward.[5]

Walking through the wreckage of Tobruk, Moorehead "felt suddenly sickened at the destruction and the uselessness and the waste . . ." In the National Bank a British soldier was frying eggs on its mahogany counter. A storehouse caught fire and wine from vats next door spilled across the road. At night a ship burned in the bay and by its light the wounded were carried to the docks.

"The circumstances in which we wrote were strange," Moorehead explained. "We typed on the backs of trucks, on beaches, in deserted houses, in gun emplacements and tents. We hoisted our typewriters on kerosene cases, or just perched them on our knees. We wrote by candlelight or lamplight, or with an electric torch shining onto the paper. And in the end we could write anywhere at any hour of the day or night—anywhere, that is, except during a bombardment, for I tried it and failed miserably."[6]

Moorehead wrote that he and Clifford always went into the desert with a feeling of dread. "But once at the front Alex became the leader . . . I think he was less afraid than I was . . . Our main fear was that we should be taken prisoner, and after that we feared wounds, then death." Christopher Buckley of the *Daily Telegraph* gave no sign of fear and "took insane risks."[7]

En route to Benghazi, Moorehead and Clifford were with Capt. Geoffrey Keating, a War Office photographer, when they ran into an ambush. Their Welsh driver was hit in the arm and lay helpless in the road. The two correspondents cut off the sleeves of his greatcoat, sweater and shirt. Moorehead then took a bandage off his own sore knee and roughly bound the wound but it was quickly soaked with blood. Then the Italians "blew our truck to bits while we lay four yards away trying to stem the man's blood," Moorehead wrote. Keating put a first-aid pad on the driver's arm. Shrapnel struck Keating in the forearm and a bullet tore a hole in his leg. He fell on the driver, jerking convulsively.[8]

"Something struck me hard on the back of the thigh and I knew I was hit, and I lay and waited for the wave of pain to sweep over me," Clifford wrote. "But I felt nothing but a little dull ache and some wetness, and I knew it couldn't be bad." He had been grazed in his backside. A bullet passed through the sleeve of Moorehead's greatcoat. Like Clifford, he remembered "waiting frigidly for the pain to come."

Lifting the driver to his feet, Moorehead and Clifford dodged from bush to bush but were forced to stop and dress both their companions' wounds again. After walking 2 miles back toward British lines, they heard voices in the darkness. English voices. They hailed a Bren-gun carrier and rode to a dressing station located in a roadside cottage. A doctor patched up the wounded men and an ambulance took them away. Years later Moorehead wrote: "I do not think that I ever recovered from this incident."[9]

Clifford wrote: "We were beggars now, for we had no bedding, no typewriters, no clothes, no food, nothing." Other correspondents took them aboard their trucks and drove to Benghazi airport, where Italians had sabotaged the lighting, heating and water. Some Italians arrived, offering to surrender the city, the naval base and all other military establishments.

Six months earlier, in June 1940, Clifford barely escaped with his life aboard a flying boat from Malta that had been sent to photograph Augusta harbor in Sicily. It had begun bombing three ships when it was ambushed by Italian fighter planes. "Something seared hot and painfully through the seat of my shorts," Clifford wrote. "Only then did I realize that it was machine-gun fire." The pilot dived to sea level with smoke billowing through the plane and the co-pilot said, "Oh, Clifford, this thing's on fire. We've got to abandon her. Get ready, will you?" Clifford went aft and found other crew members battling the fire with extinguishers, water, lemonade and cold tea, finally managing to bring it under control.

Both midship gunners were wounded and Clifford used pencils to put tourniquets on their legs. The rear gunner slumped forward over his weapon, and the plane was now without gunners. Clifford and another crew member took over the midship guns and Clifford wrote that the other gunner shot down one of the planes. But Moorehead years later revealed that Clifford himself accounted for the enemy fighter. Clifford did not admit this because of the ban on correspondents using weapons. The crippled plane headed back to Malta but one engine began to seize up and the plane hit the water with a splintering crash. The men waded ashore as it sank.[10]

* * *

Frequently, correspondents would have to travel long distances to Cairo to file, only to become embroiled in battle with untrained, stubborn British censors. A Captain Berick, the chief censor, was especially despised because of his obtuseness. When one correspondent wrote that Gen. Annibale Berganzoli had taken asylum in Benghazi, Berick admonished him: "Now you know very well there is no asylum in Benghazi." Another correspondent who used the term "wells"—cablese for "as well as"—was rebuked for a prohibited reference to sources of water.[11] Ralph Barnes of the *New York Herald-Tribune* wrote a description of Egyptian territory over which the Italians had been advancing. Censors cut it out on the ground it was information of value to the enemy. Barnes showed them he got all his information from a *Baedeker Guide to Egypt*, but they were adamant.[12]

Frank Gervasi of *Collier's* magazine arrived in early 1941 when the British were refusing to accredit magazine correspondents. "A British defeat could not be reported unless it could be made to sound like 'a strategic withdrawal,' " he wrote. And a British victory would be withheld until the news had been made public in London. The word "sulphanilamide" was excised from one story because the censor thought it was a code word. Eventually a new press officer, Maj. Randolph Churchill, son of the prime minister, arrived to try to improve the dealings of correspondents with censors. Gervasi finally got his accreditation.[13]

Twelve Italian bombers attacked just after Richard Mowrer of the *Chicago Daily News* and Arthur Merton of London's *Daily Telegraph* arrived at Mersa Matruh on the Egyptian coast. Mowrer was partly buried in the collapse of a subterranean refuge in which he sought shelter. Two Egyptians were killed and a British military escort was wounded. Merton, a long-serving Cairo correspondent who had been the first journalist admitted to the tomb of King Tutankhamun when it was discovered in 1922, escaped injury but was killed two years later in an auto accident near Cairo in which Randolph Churchill was injured.[14]

In two months of fighting, the Italians lost half of their 250,000 troops, either killed or captured, plus two-thirds of their ships, aircraft and land weapons. Nineteen generals were taken prisoner. But, as Britain rushed troops to Greece, Rommel arrived in Libya in February 1941 with his Afrika Korps. Hard fighting lay ahead.[15]

* * *

Wavell launched an offensive against Axis forces on June 15, 1941, but, with his forces weakened after the Greek debacle, it foundered after two days. Gen. Sir Claude Auchinleck was put in command and began an offensive on November 18. The British relieved Tobruk and Rommel was forced to withdraw. But he launched his own offensive on January 21, 1942, and by the end of May the main force of the Eighth Army had retreated back into Egypt. On June 20, Rommel seized Tobruk and took 30,000 prisoners. Panic swept Egypt, many foreigners fled and the Mediterranean Fleet sailed away from Alexandria. Churchill arrived the following month and replaced Auchinleck with Gen. Bernard Montgomery. The stage was set for the decisive battle of the desert.

Eve Curie's tour of world battlefronts for the *New York Herald-Tribune* began in Cairo as the British offensive was getting under way. Moorehead described her as "dark, quiet, aloof, full of shrewd abstract deductions and completely cosmopolitan . . . very attractive." Women correspondents were unknown in the desert until then, but Randolph Churchill gave the famous author and daughter of Marie Curie special attention. Their first stop was an RAF airfield, where she and Quentin Reynolds interviewed pilots for a joint broadcast to London. "Reynolds was good as always, the pilots were marvelous and I spoiled everything by an embarrassed, idiotic laugh," Curie wrote.[16]

Dimbleby witnessed the initial successes of the Wavell offensive, recording "gutted tanks and armoured cars blistering in the sun, petrol and diesel lorries with burst tires and broken backs, exploded ammunition trucks standing like black skeletons in the pools of their debris. The Italians themselves lay tangled in the mess with the desert fleas crawling over them and the savage flies tormenting their swollen faces. The desert is an ugly place in which to die . . ."[17]

Harry Zinder of *Time* observed Italian and German prisoners keeping themselves strictly apart in their barbed-wire compound. The Italians "were the most dispirited and dejected specimens of mankind I have ever seen." The Germans "were a varied lot but all bore themselves proudly."[18]

Moorehead described the aim of the November offensive as "like penning a savage bull in a hen coop." The British were using American tanks called Honeys, no match for German tanks. Thirty were lost in one charge. At night, the Germans handed hot drinks to British wounded and threw blankets over some who would have died of exposure before morning.

Moorehead returned to Corps headquarters and, with the enemy threatening that position, hurriedly pulled out. "All day for nine hours we ran. It was the contagion of bewilderment and fear and ignorance . . . We did not know what to do."[19]

Edward Ward of the BBC was at Beda Fom in Libya after Italian forces were routed. A dashing Italian officer asked to be taken to the Eleventh Hussars mess, saying: "I know most of the officers intimately. I have often hunted with them in Leicestershire." He had several rounds of drinks with his friends before he was told he would have to join other prisoners of war.[20]

Ward hitchhiked with two Australian military policemen (MPs), who began treating him with suspicion. One told him he had a pistol in his back and they were taking him to headquarters in Tobruk. He was quickly released there, and was pleased to have an amusing incident to report. But a censor banned it because he said it ridiculed MPs who had made an honest mistake. Later the MPs told Chester Wilmot of the Australian Broadcasting Commission: "We knew he was on the level right from the jump, but we wanted an excuse to get into the town to look around, so we picked him up. As an excuse he was pretty good."[21]

On November 22, 1942, Ward was among nine correspondents covering operations south of Tobruk who were taken prisoner by the Germans. They included Harold Denny of the New York Times, Godfrey Anderson of the AP and a half-dozen South Africans. The correspondents had set out to visit units scheduled to take part in the relief of Tobruk. En route they were attacked by forty-five Stukas, swooping down and strafing almost at ground level. One bullet went through a fold in Denny's trouser leg without touching him. Three Stukas were brought down by machine guns.

"Ward and Anderson and I were hoarding the final three drinks in the bottom of our only whisky bottle," Denny wrote. They offered it to a South African sergeant who had shot down one plane, "one of the noblest acts of our lives." He drained it in one swig.

The next day Rommel arrived with eighty to a hundred tanks. German shelling went on much of the day, followed by machine-gun fire "like the bursting of a tropical rain," Denny wrote. Finally, the South Africans were out of artillery ammunition and German tanks advanced. A commander stood in the open turret of his tank with a machine gun pointing straight at Ward. He shouted in English: "Hands up! Surrender!" They surrendered. "I think I was too scared to be frightened—which might make sense to a psychiatrist, if to no one else," Denny wrote. "I know of no war experience so shattering as capture in battle. It does not strike one fully at first. It is too unbelievable a disaster." They were turned over to the Italians. "Because my brain was working badly, it did not occur to me that night that, as a neutral engaged in a recognized noncombatant profession, I was legally entitled to be released."

British tanks soon approached and the prisoners thought they were being rescued. Ward shouted: "What a story! What a story! We'll get the RAF to give us a plane and we'll fly back to Cairo to send it! Oh, what a story!" German guns opened fire on the British tanks, which did not return fire. Evidently they had run out of ammunition. Two were knocked out and four got away.

A burly, unshaven German officer in a dirty greatcoat drove up and began berating his soldiers. The correspondents recognized him as Rommel. Ward, who spoke German, related what he told his troops: "Why are you wasting your time gaping at this little lot of English? These are only a sample of what we will get. Go on! Get about your business! Get all the Schweinehunde!" Then he photographed the prisoners, afterward allowing his soldiers to photograph him. The prisoners were turned over to Italian soldiers. One took Denny's pocket knife, watch, fountain pen and a cigarette lighter. He suddenly exploded with anger, cursed the Italian and grabbed for his belongings, retrieving his pen and lighter.

The correspondents, along with an American army major, Michael Buckley, soon sailed to the Italian port of Taranto where civilians gave them cigarettes. Then they marched to the liner *Vittoria*, where, in Denny's words, "Italian waiters served us as attentively as if we had been de luxe passengers bulging with tips."

Buckley and Denny were soon transferred to Rome and treated well, but German secret police "borrowed" Denny for five weeks' solitary confinement at Gestapo headquarters in Berlin and interrogated him about his writings. Then he was returned to Rome. Just before the Japanese attack on Pearl Harbor, an Italian major told Denny he would be released in a day or two. It didn't happen and, on December 18, he was told he would be taken to Germany that night. "This was the most frightening news I have ever received," he wrote. He was imprisoned for another five weeks. The State Department had refused to discuss the release of thirteen Italians in the U.S. unless Italy gave up three American prisoners—Denny, Buckley and a priest from Rome. Denny was returned to Rome and, on February 15, 1942, interned in a prisoner-of-war camp in Tuscany. Two months later, he, Buckley and the priest were put on a train for Lisbon en route back to the U.S. An Iowa native and veteran of World War I, Denny died of a heart attack in Des Moines on July 3, 1945, aged 55.

Ward, Anderson and the South African prisoners moved to a camp outside Bologna, where they were joined by Patrick Crosse, 24, of Reuters, who had been captured in Libya. They were handed over to the SS, put aboard a train and taken to a camp at Moosburg, 50 miles outside Munich. It contained more than 20,000 prisoners, including many Russians. Ward wrote that the Germans turned police dogs loose in the Russian compound. The Russians killed the dogs and ate them. The correspondents were moved in 1945 to Lollar. When American artillery opened up near the camp, prisoners took shelter in a tunnel. The mayor tried to keep Russian girls from entering but Ward told him he would see to it the Americans shot him the moment they arrived. The mayor relented. Soon American tanks arrived and the prisoners were freed.[22]

* * *

Moorehead returned to the scene of fighting around Sidi Rezegh, southwest of Tobruk. A Messerschmitt came over, strafing 20 feet above ground, and Moorehead could see the pilot's "white taut face." A South African sergeant opened fire with a Lewis gun and the plane fell. "I had seen the pilot's face in the second of his death and it had showed no fear or hate or excitement—just intense concentration," Moorehead wrote.[23]

The British captured Tobruk on December 10, 1941. "The town was a giant rubbish heap," Clifford wrote. "There was not a wall that was not split or cracked or pitted with shot and shrapnel . . . It was and would remain an eerie city of the dead." In the harbor, a whole sunken merchant fleet lay in its depths. "Even now Tobruk was still being heavily bombed. It was difficult not to enjoy it, just as one cannot help enjoying the sight of a house burning even if one knows the owners."

A British major told Clifford he had become lost in the desert, had taken out a compass to get a bearing and found himself standing amid five Italian soldiers. "I suppose I lost my head," the major said. "I stuck my finger into the ribs of the nearest one and told him to put his hands up. Such an absurd thing to do. I mean, they could hardly get away with that in Hollywood nowadays, could they?" All five Italians put up their hands. The major marched them to British lines.[24]

Wilmot found Australian troops were setting fire to Italian paper money to light their cigarettes, or posting autographed notes back to Australia as

1. Edward R. Murrow preparing one of his famed wartime broadcasts from London.

2. Nazi propaganda chief Joseph Goebbels (left), interviewed by the AP's Louis Lochner, Berlin.

3. Publicity piece for Virginia Cowles's 1941 memoir, written after the fall of France.

4. George Weller (left) and Leland Stowe, *Chicago Daily News* colleagues, meet in Athens, 1941.

5. Alan Moorehead (left) and Alexander Clifford, inseparable rivals, in Egypt.

6. Clare Hollingworth interviews a British officer in Egypt.

7. John MacVane (left) of NBC on a North African battlefield.

8. Australian correspondent Osmar White in somber mood in Papua New Guinea, 1942.

9. Wilfred Burchett with two Chinese officers in Burma, on the first day Chinese troops set foot on foreign soil for nearly a century, 1942.

10. American correspondents training for flight over Germany, 1943. From left, Gladwin Hill, William Wade, Robert Post, Walter Cronkite, Homer Bigart and Paul Manning. Post was killed on the flight.

11. American women correspondents pose together in Europe, including Mary Welsh (far left), Helen Kirkpatrick (third right), Lee Miller (second right) and Kathleen Harriman (third left).

12. The AP's Ed Kennedy in Anzio, Italy, March 1, 1944.

13. AP correspondents Weston Haynes (left) and Don Whitehead with native people in Libya, December 26, 1942.

14. Ross Munro of the Canadian Press in the Italian countryside.

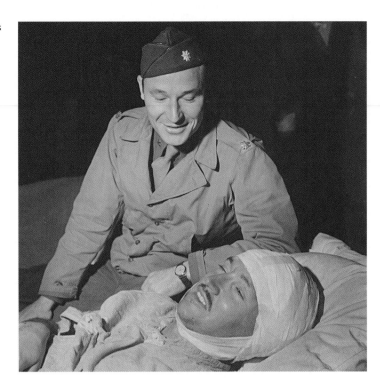

15. Richard Tregaskis recovering in Italy from a near-fatal head wound, 1943.

16. Martha Gellhorn talking to Indian soldiers in the British Army near Cassino, 1944.

17. Friendly rival columnists Hal Boyle (left) and Ernie Pyle on a hotel balcony after the Paris liberation, 1944.

18. Eric Sevareid (left), Gertrude Stein and Frank Gervasi at Stein's home in France, 1944.

19. Chester Wilmot broadcasting from a rooftop observation post in the Netherlands, 1944.

20. Ann Stringer of UP interviews GIs in Erpel, Germany, 1945.

21. Richard Dimbleby (right) and Stanley Maxted recording a BBC report aboard a glider tug over the Rhine on March 24, 1945.

22. Lee Miller in Hitler's bathtub in his Munich home, 1945.

23. Russian correspondent Vasily Grossman amid the ruins of war in Schwerin, Germany, 1945.

24. Ed Kennedy's controversial exclusive on the German surrender, under a *New York Times* banner headline.

25. Australian correspondent George Johnston in Papua New Guinea, 1942.

26. Homer Bigart after the liberation of the Philippines.

27. Robert Sherrod of *Time-Life* ready to board a landing craft off Okinawa, 1945.

28. Ernie Pyle, second from left, talking to Marines in Okinawa shortly before his death, 1945.

29. A memorial to Ernie Pyle fashioned by American soldiers on the spot where he was killed on Ie Shima, 1945.

AT THIS SPOT
THE 77ᵗʰ INFANTRY DIVISION
LOST A BUDDY
ERNIE PYLE
18 APRIL 1945

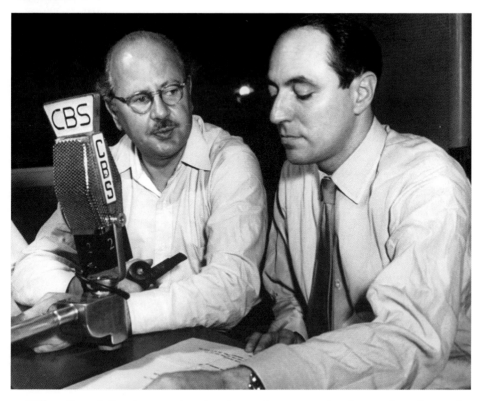

30. William Shirer (left) and Larry LeSueur broadcasting from New York with news of Japan's surrender.

31. The *Daily Express* headlines Wilfred Burchett's exclusive first-hand report from Hiroshima after the A-bomb strike—and mistakenly names him Peter.

32. Edward R. Murrow, lower left, presides over a postwar broadcast by the Murrow Boys from New York. From Murrow's left: Larry LeSueur, Bill Costello, Winston Burdett, David Schoenbrun, Bill Downs, Eric Sevareid and Howard K. Smith.

souvenirs. When they reached Benghazi later, they ruefully discovered the lira was still in circulation there.[25]

Russell Hill of the *New York Herald-Tribune* reported a grim joke making the rounds in Cairo: Rommel has not yet met the main British forces, because he has not been elected a member of the Gezira Sporting Club. "That is where the officers of GHQ spend much of their leisure time, lunching, drinking, watching the horse races, the cricket matches and the polo, swimming and playing squash, tennis, golf and bridge," he wrote.[26]

* * *

Larry Allen of the AP was aboard the British cruiser *Galatea* off North Africa when it was sunk by torpedoes on December 15, 1941. It was the first of eight ships that went down under Allen, who did not know how to swim. He fought off attempts by drowning sailors to rip a Mae West from his chest, and was picked up by a British destroyer. Massey Anderson of Reuters was on the ship and did not survive. Allen had experienced a near sinking when he was aboard the carrier *Illustrious* on January 10, 1941, off Malta, and won a Pulitzer Prize for his account of how German dive bombers almost sent the ship to the bottom.

On September 14, 1942, he was aboard the destroyer *Sikh* off Tobruk when it went down. Captured by Italians, he was turned over to the Germans and wasted no time asking for an interview with Rommel. The German staff told him Rommel was too busy. Allen was held prisoner in Italy for twenty months. Three times he managed to escape, the last time getting within 5 miles of the Swiss border, where peasants "sold" him to a German patrol for 2,000 lire. For eight months he was interned near Poznan, Poland, but was released on May 4, 1944. The Germans told him they were glad to be rid of him. Allen was the product of a Maryland family so poor he wore his older sister's outgrown shoes to school.[27]

* * *

Quentin Reynolds was with soldiers who were attacked by dive bombers:

Five planes dived at once, strafing and bombing. Bullets and hunks of steel tore into the sides of my trench. Until now I had never known the demeaning fear that makes the mouth dry and ties the stomach into knots. Although there were 5,000 men on the plateau, I had the feeling that I was being attacked personally.

Soon after, he returned to the U.S. and tried to enlist in the army. But he was 40 and a friend on the draft board told him to get lost. He returned to Europe as a correspondent.[28]

Richard McMillan of UP was in Tobruk after its capture and learned that some Italian officers were in a cavern waiting to surrender. The British commander was short of men, so McMillan and Robert Low of *Liberty* magazine volunteered to get them out. Going down steps hewn out of rock, they reached a couple of hundred Italians and ordered them to hand over their guns. They did so, and McMillan and Low marched them up the steps.[29]

* * *

Rommel staged his counterattack and Allied troops were soon retreating. A month after Rommel's capture of Tobruk in June 1942, the BBC ordered Dimbleby home and replaced him with Godfrey Talbot, who got a great sendoff from friends, officials, ambassadors and army commanders. "I was a journalist succeeding a personality," he wrote. "There were war correspondents and there was Richard Dimbleby." Dimbleby would remain in London until D-Day, organizing the BBC team that would cover Normandy and the battles to come.[30]

The British repelled two German attacks in June, but "what we saw thereafter was the disorganized retreat of a gallant but thoroughly beaten Eighth Army," Gervasi wrote. "We heard BBC broadcasts assuring us we were really winning, not losing, the war." The night of Tobruk's fall, the BBC said Allied forces were still resisting, and kept up that fiction for two more days. "It was almost too much to bear, the unctuous blather being broadcast from London."

Later Gervasi went on a B-24 bombing run over Tobruk. "It never occurred to me at the time that we were killing and maiming men. No, we were surgeons removing a cancerous growth, the enemy." He flew back to the U.S. and tried to enlist in America's new clandestine service, the Office of Strategic Services. But Gen. William Donovan, its commander, turned him down.[31]

Hill was with soldiers who came under artillery fire at a desert outpost labeled Knightsbridge, near the Libyan–Egyptian border. With him was F. G. H. Salusbury of London's *Daily Herald*, who had been an artillery officer in France in World War I. "His tall, thin, almost gaunt figure was invariably clothed in a perfectly tailored tunic even in the desert," Hill wrote.

The impression he made is best described by the word *distingué*. His bearing and tone deprecated these mortals and their folly . . . He was essentially an artist, and every news dispatch he wrote was primarily a piece of literature. He considered the war a frightful "bore," necessary perhaps, but fundamentally senseless and tedious.

During the artillery barrage, one shell landed near Salusbury, burying him in dirt. He was dug out, unhurt. Afterward Hill and Salusbury met other correspondents at El Adem, and one asked how things had been at Knightsbridge. "My dear fellow," Salusbury replied, "we had a very quiet night. I've seldom slept better. There was a little nastiness this morning. They shelled us a bit; but it was really nothing to get excited about."[32]

Less than a week after Tobruk fell, Rommel was nearing the Egyptian coastal city of Mersa Matruh, with the Germans broadcasting that they would be in Alexandria the next day. Moorehead set out for the front and found the road jammed with British troops fleeing to Cairo. For Clifford, the fall of Tobruk was "the bitterest moment I have known in the desert." Not long after that, he suddenly decided one morning he was "utterly sick of it all."

"I found myself hating the desert with a neurotic, tormenting hatred. I was obsessed by the waste of tears and blood and sweat that . . . I found I could no longer even write about it." He and Moorehead had been in the desert for the best part of two years. "The same mental chemistry had been at work in both of us," Clifford explained. He flew to England for a breather while Moorehead, his wife Lucy and newborn son went to the United States for a vacation.[33]

Allan Michie of *Time* and *Life* also departed, finding it impossible to work under a censorship "as repressive, stupid and blind as those in Franco Spain, Germany and Russia combined." He wrote that "one monocled Foreign Office prig" at the British Embassy said to an Egyptian family with whom Michie was friendly: "But really, you shouldn't have anything to do with the press socially. In England one just doesn't invite them into one's home." Michie commented: "This from a man whose specific job was to help us."[34]

Before Moorehead left, the *Daily Express* sent young James Cooper to Cairo as his assistant. In a letter to *Express* editor Arthur Christiansen, Moorehead wrote that Cooper was "as keen as mustard to be sunk in a battle-ship so that he can write one of the war's great stories." Cooper got his wish, survived the sinking of the ship he was on, but had to wait three weeks for censors to clear his copy. When his dispatch reached London, editors decided it was so out of date they declined to use it.[35]

* * *

On June 13, Hank Gorrell of UP went aboard a British cruiser, part of a convoy carrying supplies to Malta. "The entire Italian fleet was waiting for us. The Luftwaffe also was waiting." In three days, the convoy lost a cruiser, two destroyers and two merchant ships. But British naval guns brought down twenty-seven planes. "I would be kidding myself if I said that I wasn't scared, but I found myself joining the gunners in their songs between alerts."

An Italian E-boat (fast patrol boat) came within 800 yards of his cruiser and Gorrell watched it fire torpedoes. He was knocked flat by an explosion. The ship was damaged, but the only casualty was a pet parrot that had most of its feathers blown off. Squawking and cursing, it would occasionally screech: "Jolly good show! Jolly good show!"

Gorrell headed for Mersa Matruh just as Auchinleck prepared to attack the Germans. "I couldn't eat that evening because of my excitement, heightened by the realization that I probably would be the only war correspondent in the desert to witness this attack," he wrote. The next evening he turned on the BBC, confident his dispatch had been sent at least 24 hours ahead of any others. The announcer in London said: "The lull continues in the Western desert."[36]

* * *

Churchill arrived secretly in August 1942 to fire Auchinleck and replace him with Gen. Bernard Montgomery. He also toured the desert and an officer told Gorrell it was difficult to restrain him from walking into the firing line. Stukas dropped bombs 200 yards from where Churchill was sitting at lunch, but he scarcely looked up and continued flicking flies from his bully beef.

Later a British major took Gorrell into no man's land to show him German tanks his unit had knocked out. The presence of a German machine-gun emplacement a few hundred yards away unnerved Gorrell. Then a machine gunner opened up and bullets ricocheted from the side of the major's armored car as they hopped in. The major laughed and said: "Oh, don't mind that, Hank. He's only teasing you."

Gorrell traveled to Palestine and boarded an American B-24 bomber, *The Witch*, for a bombing mission over Greece. The planes attacked Navarino Bay and four of five German fighters that responded to the attack were shot down. "All our gun turrets were as busy as Singer sewing machines in a dress factory," Gorrell wrote.

German fighters riddled the plane with gunfire. A gunner told the pilot over the intercom, "I've been shot, sir." Gorrell joined other crew members in cutting off his trouser leg and applying a tourniquet. "My fingers were numb from the cold and the first-aid kit was flaked with frost." Two other men were hit and Gorrell helped bind the wounds of one of them. The plane limped back to Palestine after Gorrell stemmed a leak in a pipe that had been hit by cannon fire. President Roosevelt later decorated him with the Air Medal for gallantry.[37]

* * *

On October 23, 1942, a massive bombardment of German positions near El Alamein opened a battle that was to give the Allies their first important victory. Almost a week later, Rommel, returning from sick leave in Germany, began a retreat. Tripoli fell on January 23, 1943, and the Eighth Army reached Tunisia three days later. The Allies landed 63,000 men on the coasts of Algeria and Morocco on November 8, 1942, in an attempt to catch the Axis in a pincer. The Eighth Army, closing in from the east, easily repulsed a Rommel attack. A sick man, he left Africa and the Germans surrendered on May 13, 1943, with 238,000 becoming prisoners.

Tom Treanor, 34, a one-time society editor, Hollywood reporter and then columnist for the *Los Angeles Times*, arrived in Cairo just before Montgomery's big offensive. With characteristic whimsy, he described himself as The Only Correspondent Representing a Newspaper West of the Mississippi Ever to Visit the Middle East. Authorities in Cairo refused to accredit him, saying they had more correspondents than they could handle.

Later described by Damon Runyon as "one of the four best reporters developed in this war," Treanor was undaunted and set out to hitch rides to the front. A New Zealand soldier promised to take care of him when fighting started. "We pressed on in an absolutely terrifying thunder, and I'm frank to say I was shaken," Treanor wrote.

> It put the fear of God into me. I'd never heard more than an isolated gun go off before. I just didn't have the nerve to tell the soldier who had prom-ised to take care of me that I was dropping out. I slid along the line as though I were going to ask a question of the next man, and then I went to the next man and finally got out of sight. Then I began to lag and to wonder if our own men would bayonet me for slowing down. There was just nothing I could think of to say if I were challenged. I couldn't say: "I just let my life insurance lapse." I couldn't say: "Well, I'm a newspaperman." I couldn't say: "It's late for me to be out."

He climbed aboard a Bren-gun carrier that dropped him near the front line and remained there for four days before he was flown to Cairo "in disgrace" for lack of accreditation. Even so, authorities allowed his syndicated dispatches to go out, after a considerable delay. "It was a great satisfaction to me later to learn that . . . my story of the first night at El Alamein ran six columns across the top of page one of the *San Francisco Chronicle*. El Alamein was a great experience, and . . . I wallowed in it."[38]

Godfrey Talbot of the BBC watched "lamentable flocks of Mussolini's wretched soldiers begging to be captured . . . It was pathetic . . . Officers and men alike spoke bitterly of the Germans. The German captives were grim and sullen."[39]

Gorrell wrote: "The smell of death was everywhere, emphasized by swarms of flies buzzing over shallow, unmarked mounds in the sand, wetted down by the heavy rain. The German prisoners were the glummest folks I had ever seen, but the Italians were usually laughing." He reported that Italians had killed some Allied prisoners because they gave the V for victory sign. Others were chained to telegraph poles and lashed. South African blacks among the prisoners were forced to load bombs on planes.

George Lait of INS and A. C. Sedgwick of the *New York Times* were wounded by mortar and machine-gun fire. But, after the firing died down, twelve Germans approached correspondents with their hands up, while others attempting to surrender were cut down by their own troops.[40]

Russell Hill wrote: "Tight censorship had been clamped down on all dispatches . . . The Cairo communiqués were noncommittal." He came upon the litter of German defeat, including letters addressed to soldiers. In one packet were love letters from different girls to the same man, "apparently a very heartless Don Juan." With other correspondents he headed for the Egyptian coast and they spotted a machine-gun nest on a hilltop. The two Germans manning it walked down the hill and surrendered. They told Hill, a German speaker, they had thought the correspondents were Germans until they were told to put up their hands.[41]

Don Whitehead, a 34-year-old AP feature writer in New York who had grown up in rural Kentucky, chafed through the early war years with a burning desire to cover the fighting. "I knew I could never be happy until I had a chance to report this war from a sideline seat," he wrote in his diary. "There would have been a gnawing frustration that would have poisoned me for years." His pleading paid off when the AP sent him to cover fighting in Egypt. "Here was the opportunity I had been seeking. Those of us in the trade developed a snobbish pride in drawing a distinction between a 'war' correspondent and a 'combat' correspondent. We righteously considered our combat status a step higher in the correspondents' caste system."

He achieved that status after noticing that Jack Belden of *Time* disappeared from Cairo from time to time. Whitehead asked where he had been and Belden said he had been up front with the troops. Whitehead realized he "had not been covering the war as it should have been covered . . . From that time on, I decided I would use the Belden approach to reporting and get as close as I possibly could to the fighting."

Whitehead was present at the January 1943 liberation of Tripoli. The night before Allied troops entered the city Arab policemen massacred many Jewish merchants. Whitehead went into the ghetto:

> Never have I had such an experience—it was embarrassing and shocking. As soon as the Jews learned we were Americans and English, they mobbed us. Men threw their arms around us and kissed our faces. Women patted us. Children clung to our legs and kissed our shoes . . . They gave us wine, nuts, candy. We were given a royal welcome as though we personally had liberated them. They told us the Italians had treated them worse than the Germans.[42]

Edmund Stevens and other correspondents were greeted by a cheering crowd in Derna, east of Benghazi. They were put inside "Derna's sole surviving hansom cab, which served as a victory chariot for our triumphant tour of the town." Then the correspondents came upon heavily armed Ghurkas crouching in battle formation as they advanced. "We informed them Derna was ours," Stevens wrote.

Stevens told of the capture of Tripoli in a January 26, 1943, dispatch. Capt. Geoffrey Keating, Montgomery's top press aide, loaded a few guns and cameras into a Jeep and asked Stevens and two soldiers to accompany him. They found the town center deserted. When Montgomery arrived, wearing a fatigue jacket covered with dust, he met the Italian governor and his aides decked out in full-dress uniforms with gold braid. "Who are these fairies?" he asked. Stevens, an Italian speaker, acted as his interpreter.[43]

An AP man, Harry Crockett Jr., was killed on February 5, 1943, when the destroyer *Welchman* was torpedoed and sank. He had earlier covered the Rommel offensive from the front lines, "where only a man with real courage would want to stand," wrote Ed Kennedy.[44]

Clare Hollingworth of the Kemsley newspapers, the veteran of Poland and Romania, was in Cairo and American officers attached to the Eighth Army finagled to bring her into Tripoli. Montgomery was furious. "I'll have no women correspondents with my army," he told his aides. "Don't let her into Tripoli. Get rid of her. I don't care if the Americans did bring her up, she can't stay." She was flown back to Cairo, then left to join U.S. forces in Algeria. Boasting of her ability to put up with desert conditions, she wrote: "It was essential to be able to go without washing, sleep in the open desert and live on bully beef and biscuits for days on end. Many male correspondents got themselves sent back to Cairo because they could not take it."[45]

Alexander Clifford, who had left Egypt in July, found he had not washed the desert out of his system. "I realized with astonishment how much I knew about it, and how interested I was in it." Certain that a British offensive would soon begin, he rushed back—arriving just after the offensive started. One afternoon he took a break to strip off and wash with water from a military truck. Still naked, he sat down to write an article just as a Messerschmitt flew over very low. As more German fighters appeared, he started running. "One fighter swung round after me. I saw the earth was being ripped into sudden ruts ahead of me and I knew I was coming into another plane's field of fire." He fell among prickly thorn while Bill Munday of Sydney's *Morning Herald*, equally naked, "was still galloping about." The planes went on their way and Clifford drew another mugful of water to wash himself again. "That was a fairly representative desert afternoon," he wrote.

He was present at the fall of Misurata, east of Tripoli. With no means to get his story out, Clifford had to go back 150 miles and hand his dispatch to the crew of a plane heading for Cairo.[46]

* * *

American, British and Canadian correspondents were sent from England to cover landings in Algeria and Morocco. During the voyage, Leo Disher of UP fell and broke his ankle. Officers wanted to put him ashore at Gibraltar, but he found crutches and refused to disembark. As his ship approached the Algerian port of Oran on the night of November 7, correspondents were transferred to the U.S. Coast Guard cutter *Walney*. Disher put a life preserver around his injured leg and strapped another to his chest. The *Walney* came under fire, took two direct hits and began drifting without power. An American officer appealed to the French over a loudspeaker: "Cease firing. We are your friends. We are Americans."

But the French navy sought to repel the landing. A destroyer and cruiser raked the *Walney* with fire. Dead and wounded littered the decks. Disher fell, wounded in both legs, his crutches slipping away. The men were ordered to abandon ship. Disher jumped and the life preserver around his leg inflated automatically, but the one around his chest had been punctured by shell fragments. His head was under water, his injured leg sticking out. Pulling off the preserver, he started swimming to the pier. A man with just one hand—the other had been shot off—reached down and pulled him to shore. But the French were still firing and a bullet hit his broken ankle while another ricocheted from a wall across his temple. Another bullet struck him in the backside. Later a French patrol found him, and a doctor who treated him counted twenty-six wounds.[47]

U.S. General Mark Clark held a news conference to announce the Allies had chosen Adm. François Darlan to head a French administration in North Africa. Darlan, who had come to Algiers days earlier to visit a son stricken with polio, was Admiral of the Fleet for the Vichy regime and had served as its deputy leader.

"The story was something out of Alice in Wonderland being told, not by a Mad Hatter, but by an apparently sane and collected American general," John MacVane of NBC wrote. Censors suddenly received orders to censor all political stories, clearly intended to avoid criticism of the appointment. "Both correspondents and censors disagreed with the decision to bolster a Fascist regime by stifling the truth," MacVane wrote. Eventually he got past censors a broadcast that gave some indication of the true situation. Allied headquarters received angry cables from Washington asking how the broadcast was allowed to go through.[48]

Charles Collingwood of CBS also criticized the appointment, and one Eisenhower aide tried in vain to persuade CBS to transfer him to another front. Philip Jordan of the *News Chronicle*, who after the war would become press spokesman for Prime Minister Clement Attlee, wrote a long "open letter" to Eisenhower, complaining that Allied conduct in working with a Vichy regime was "jeopardizing our victory in peace[time]."[49]

Eisenhower had told correspondents that he regarded them as quasi staff officers, so protests offended his sense of military discipline. "As staff officers your first duty is a military duty, and the one fact which you must always bear in mind is to disclose nothing which would help the enemy," he said.[50]

Another correspondent who made clear how he felt about the subject was a Scripps-Howard columnist, Ernie Pyle. "We have left in office most of the small-fry officials put there by the Germans before we came," he wrote. "We are permitting Fascist societies to continue to exist . . . The loyal French see this and wonder what manner of people we are . . . Our fundamental policy still is one of soft-gloving snakes in our midst." It was never discovered how Pyle got this past censors.

He wrote that Allied communiqués were giving the false impression that the campaign was a walkover, U.S. losses were few and "the French here love us to death." In fact, he noted, the American army was stalemated and would take months of fighting to gain the experience the enemy enjoyed.

Born in Dana, Indiana, in 1900, Pyle worked on newspapers in Indiana, Washington and New York before setting out in 1935 as a wandering columnist, traveling around America with his mentally unstable wife Jerry. Relatively few newspapers carried his syndicated column but he acquired a devoted following. After briefly covering the Blitz in London, he returned home because of personal troubles and his wife's mental state. He divorced her in 1942 and returned to the war, landing in Algeria with "one of the Ten Best Colds of 1942." Hal Boyle encountered him in a drafty Oran hotel, sprawled on a bed, "mopping his nose and gently cursing the people who had reported that Africa was a warm country [sic]."

A writer who soon gained a following of millions of readers, Pyle found his metier in writing about GIs slogging it out on the battlefield. The infantry would remain the prime focus of his dispatches. In one column that would become famous, he wrote:

Now to the infantry, the God-damned infantry as they like to call themselves. I love the infantry because they are the underdogs. They are the mud-rain-frost-and-wind boys. They have no comforts, and they even learn to live without the necessities. And in the end they are the guys that wars can't be won without.

After one battle he wrote of "an ineradicable picture" in his mind of a line of men on a narrow path like a ribbon over a hill:

For four days and nights they have fought hard, eaten little, washed none and slept hardly at all. Their nights have been violent with attack, fright, butchery and their days sleepless and miserable with the crash of artillery . . . Their walk is slow, for they are dead weary . . . Every line and sag of their bodies speaks their inhuman exhaustion . . . There is agony in your heart and you almost feel ashamed to look at them . . . No matter how hard people work back home they are not keeping pace with these infantrymen in Tunisia.

Once in Tunisia, sitting under a tree, he wrote his column with a pencil while under fire from a German sniper. "Four times in one day that fellow chased me out of my shady place," Pyle wrote. "The fourth time three bullets went past so close they had fuzz on them." He abandoned his shady spot and took refuge in a foxhole, with GIs reading over his shoulder as he wrote.

Across America, newspapers began running his column. The *New York World-Telegram* carried it daily on page one in large type, and other papers sometimes also put it out front. Soon he had millions of followers. He remarried Jerry by proxy in a cable ceremony. The singer Al Jolson, in North Africa to entertain troops, said: "Everywhere I went the soldiers told me how wonderful Ernie Pyle was. Heck, he doesn't sing or dance and I couldn't figure out what he did to entertain them, but they acted like he was Mr. God." A. J. Liebling of the *New Yorker* wrote in an article for *Esquire*: "War for him meant not adventure . . . a crusade . . . an enthrallment . . . or a chance to be a prima donna . . . He treated it as an unalleviated misfortune."[51]

MacVane was asked on short notice to compile an hour-long program that would include interviews with troops. Before he went on air, NBC had changed its mind and wanted only a five-minute broadcast, but he never got the message. A Signal Corps officer congratulated him afterward, saying it was the "best broadcast I ever helped put on the air." But it was never received in New York; the Algiers engineers switched frequencies to fool the Germans, and fooled engineers in London and New York as well. A British Spitfire pilot heard it while in the air and said "it was a grand show." A local French-language newspaper carried a description of the program "broadcast from Algiers and heard by millions of Americans yesterday."

But one MacVane broadcast that did go out included interviews with American pilots back from bombing raids and soldiers who had been wounded. He commented:

> Most of them never knew what war was all about until they hit Africa. But they know now—what nobody *ever* knows until that bomb or that shell starts coming at you, and you suddenly realize that someone is really trying to kill you—that war isn't something in a book or a picture, but friends of yours getting battered to pieces a few yards from you. War is kids writing home to Manchester or Philadelphia, writing: "Dear Mom, I am feeling fine," after they have been pounded by shells or dive bombers for hours. War is a bunch of American boys behind a big gun whanging away at German tanks like you whang at the ducks in a shooting gallery. And war is the two young British navy sub-lieutenants I saw the other day buying a whole armful of carnations from an Arab flower-seller and cramming them into the arms of a French girl who smiled at them.

Anyway, that is war in North Africa tonight, and I thought you might like to hear about it. The thing that strikes an observer who has knocked around Europe for a few years, right in the eye, is that these American boys who have gone out to Tunisia to fight are the same ordinary boys you used to see on Congress Street or Main Street, fellows who are still interested in Superman and Lana Turner and who'll win the Rose Bowl game—if they are still playing the Rose Bowl game.[52]

On December 24, 1942, Darlan was assassinated by a young Frenchman, who was quickly tried and executed. MacVane got on the air first with the news, but NBC received only a portion of his broadcast. Collingwood, 25, a Kansan and former UP man, was content to let MacVane and another competitor broadcast first; he figured the later the broadcast, the better the chance that ham radio operators would pick it up and alert CBS. Thus he got the first full report on the air, and it was published on the front page of the *New York Times*.[53]

Wes Gallagher, heading the AP bureau in Algiers, made no attempt to hide his dismay when Ruth B. Cowan showed up. A woman! In a battle zone! He gave her the cold shoulder and Cowan threatened to write to Eleanor Roosevelt about discrimination against women correspondents. "He didn't want any women on his staff," Cowan wrote. "I heard him say, 'Put them on the boat and send them back.' It upset me very much."

Cowan had covered the Texas legislature for UP in 1929 until a visiting executive discovered that the byline R. Baldwin Cowan belonged to a woman. He fired her and she joined the AP. Later, in Sicily, General Patton asked her: "What is the first law of war?" She replied: "You kill him before he kills you." Patton said: "She stays."[54]

Three AP correspondents in Algiers won Pulitzer Prizes during the war— Larry Allen, De Luce and Hal Boyle. Two others, Relman "Pat" Morin and Whitehead, won two Pulitzers each after the war. "I believe this staff was the best group of reporters ever assembled," Ed Kennedy wrote.

Boyle, like Pyle, mostly wrote personal stories about GIs and referred to himself as the poor man's Ernie Pyle. "I regarded Boyle's writing as superior to Pyle's and his observations more penetrating," Kennedy wrote. "Ernie, however, had a popular appeal that no other correspondent achieved." Boyle himself described Pyle as "my war comrade and mentor" and wrote that he "was one of the most beautiful friends any man is lucky to have in a lifetime. I thought he had the most sensitive understanding of people of any man I ever met." During the Tunisia campaign Boyle delivered a speech to Arabs in a village and ended with "Vote for Boyle, the son of toil. Honest Hal, the Arab's pal." When Allied troops arrived, they were astonished to hear the Arabs repeating these words.[55]

In January 1943, military authorities invited correspondents to go to Casablanca for a story whose nature they could not divulge. William Stoneman of the *Chicago Daily News* declined, saying he had a war to cover. Thus he missed the January 14–24 Casablanca conference between Roosevelt, Churchill and Stalin. Correspondents flying to the conference were surprised when their plane began to descend at the Spanish port of Larache. They assumed the plane had developed engine trouble. The Spanish opened fire. Edward Baudry of the Canadian Broadcasting Corporation was lying on parachutes and a bullet struck him in the head. "With a slight sigh, he leaned slowly over backward—and his left temple had been blown away," Alan Moorehead wrote. "Blood and gray brains were pumping out of the wound and spilling down his cheeks." The plane turned away, the Spanish still firing at it, and went on to its correct destination, the French Moroccan port of Lyautey. Baudrey died that afternoon.[56]

* * *

In March 1943, Whitehead was in Medenine, Tunisia. A British Captain Forwood, former equerry to the Duke of Windsor, appeared, hunting for correspondents he was shepherding. One was a Russian named Solodovnik, working for the TASS news agency. "My little chickabiddy!" Forwood exclaimed when he found him. "Where have you been? Have you been a naughty boy? I was afraid something had happened to you. Are all my chicks safe?"

Solodovnik was baffled and asked Whitehead: "What does he mean by 'chickabiddy'? I look in dictionary. I no find any chickabiddy. No one can tell me what it mean. He ask if I'm naughty. I look up word naughty. It mean 'bad.' Why do he think I been bad?" Whitehead said Solodovnik told him he had been a lieutenant colonel in the Red Army. He had a row with a censor, who told him: "You simply cannot say that General Eisenhower should be removed!" Almost a year later, Whitehead encountered him in the Naples airport. Then a member of the Russian mission to the Italian front, he wore the insignia of a major general. Solodovnik had learned of an Allied failure to bring guns to the front over muddy roads and said: "You have shot the brigadier, of course?"[57]

Pyle, who became one of Whitehead's close friends and admirers, quoted him in a column that was reprinted in Whitehead's hometown newspaper in

Harlan, Kentucky. The two men "got the giggles like children," Pyle wrote, when they saw the headline: Harlan Man Talks in Foxhole.[58]

* * *

Hal Boyle came under fire in Tunisia in January 1943. "What the hell business have I got lying flat on my face with my nose two inches from an African snail and Germans pinging at me?" he wrote. He described American 105mm shells being fired at the Germans as having "a murmurous sound like a line from Keats or Tennyson."[59]

In February 1943 Moorehead and three other correspondents got wind of the fact that two advance patrols of the British First Army coming from the west and the Eighth Army coming from the east had met in the Mareth Oasis in southern Tunisia. The correspondents raced forward, stampeding a herd of camels, and in a hotel they encountered a French parachutist fighting with the British. He led them to mud huts where they found four Allied soldiers, all in tattered clothing and living on one tin of sardines per man per day. Two New Zealanders among them had been slightly wounded and they had walked for five days before reaching the village. The Germans had moved out after committing what Moorehead called "fantastic atrocities." The 13-year-old son of the hotel owner had been taken to Germany as a hostage, and people who hid goods from the Germans were shot out of hand. "All areas through which I have passed have been denuded of cattle, and even seed for potatoes and wheat crops has been taken away," Moorehead wrote.[60]

Jack Belden and three other correspondents witnessed the first meeting of British Eighth Army and American troops in Tunisia. Hundreds of men on a ridge walked up a road toward them, rifles held menacingly, and one of them said: "Good morning. I expect you're the English army."

"That's how the Americans on the Maknassy Road made their junction with the Eighth Army," Belden wrote. "That and nothing more." He noted that a formal junction was expected in a few days, adding: "I get more of a kick out of shaking hands with a bum from Manhattan out here in the desert than I will in shaking hands with generals in their headquarters."[61]

John D'Arcy Dawson of the Kemsley Newspapers, a soldier in World War I and afterward briefly a member of the RAF, complained frequently about the failure of the Allied Command to facilitate filing of news dispatches. Correspondents sometimes had to drive up to 200 miles to put copy on a plane for Algiers, and many reports were lost in transit.

He entered Kairouan and was mobbed by cheering Jews tearing off their yellow Stars of David. Many had been forced to work on roads for twelve hours a day without pay, and had been required to repair blown-up roads under shellfire.

William Stoneman set out to visit American troops and packed five bottles of whisky to share with them. En route, he came under machine-gun fire and, after he had jumped out and been shot in the buttocks, his car burst into flames. The whisky went up in the bonfire, but Stoneman crawled back to British lines.[62]

Drew Middleton, who had left the AP for the *New York Times*, was with correspondents who came under fire when Allied troops advanced into Tunisia. An American sergeant drove up and said: "Drag ass out of here. There's 30 German tanks comin' this way." The correspondents came under fire repeatedly that day and were accidentally shelled by British tanks. The next day Middleton got a lift from Darryl Zanuck, then a colonel in the Signal Corps who was making a movie about the campaign. As the Allies advanced, Middleton wrote, "I seldom felt exultation in the war. Fear, often; acute physical discomfort, yes. Exultation came sparingly and fleetingly. This was one of the times . . . I felt at last the taste of victory."[63]

By now Pyle could barely look at dead bodies without flinching. "At least the enormity of all these newly dead strikes me like a living nightmare. And there are times when I feel that I can't stand it all and will have to leave."[64]

* * *

The full meeting of British and American armies took place on April 7 in Tunisia and they received a rapturous welcome in Sfax. "The entire center of town was smashed to bits by Allied bombing, but people said nothing of this," Russell Hill reported. "What they complained of was the way the town had been ravaged by the Nazis." Hill "suddenly felt terribly sick of the war and of seeing battles . . . In order to keep one's sanity, one had to convince oneself that war was exciting, interesting, that it had a point. Nevertheless, it was hard to forget sometimes that the war was in fact dirty, bloody, pointless and usually boring." He thought he could escape his depression only by a change of scene; he left the Eighth Army and joined the Americans.

Arriving at a Bizerte devoid of its civilian population, he and American troops came under fire, with shells and bullets "ripping over our heads and burying themselves in the houses across the street." He was the first correspondent into Bizerte. An American sergeant told Hill he had spent three days on an Axis prison ship that survived twenty-three attacks by Allied planes. The Italian captain beached the ship, and Germans and Italians scrambled ashore, then started shooting at prisoners from the shore.[65]

When Gallagher and other correspondents drove out of Bizerte to reach a filing point, a French Marine riding a bicycle suddenly appeared in the middle of the road. To avoid hitting him, the driver crashed into rocks, the car turned over and Gallagher was pinned beneath it with a fractured spine. Months of recovery lay ahead.[66]

MacVane, Will Lang of *Time* and Robert Raymond of the *Echo of Algiers* were in Tunis when it fell on May 7. "No other correspondents had been within a mile of the Tunis gates," MacVane wrote. "The next day we heard other correspondents had sent Tunis-datelined stories." They entered the Casbah, then the city proper. "Arabs sullenly stared at us as we went through their narrow streets," Lang wrote. "But on reaching the Jewish section our car was greeted by storms of hand-clapping. Civilians poured out into the streets . . . One old man unrolled a large photograph of Roosevelt . . . Each intersection flushed new throngs of happy, hysterical Frenchmen." One young man ran alongside the correspondents' car exclaiming: "Now we can again see American films, Robert Taylor and Greta Garbo."

Philip Jordan talked to one prisoner. "That's my Führer," the German said, taking a photo from his pocket. Then, giving vent to a torrent of obscenities, he tore the photo into shreds. "Fuck my Führer."[67]

After the liberation of Tunis, Moorehead and Clifford drove to a nearby town to write their dispatches. "When a Spitfire belly-landed beside us on the way and burst into flames," Clifford wrote, "we scarcely turned to watch. We were still utterly absorbed with the greatness of this day."[68]

The campaign over, Collingwood was soon shipped back to London with gonorrhea. The two authors of a book entitled *Murrow's Boys* wrote: "His art collecting, foppishness, compulsive gambling and partying led some to consider him a dilettante." He went on to a distinguished postwar career with CBS.[69]

CHAPTER 11

STALINGRAD AND LENINGRAD

The Russian victory at Stalingrad in February 1943 was a major turning point of the war. It set the stage for a series of Russian offensives that would result in the final defeat of Hitler. In the summer of 1942, Hitler ordered Gen. Friedrich von Paulus to begin a drive toward Stalingrad, a move opposed by most German generals because it diverted troops from securing Caucasus oilfields. On August 21, Paulus reached the Volga River just north of Stalingrad and German troops entered the city on September 12. Stalin sent Marshal Gheorghi Zhukov to oversee Stalingrad's defense. Soviet tanks carried out an envelopment behind the Sixth Army and Paulus wanted to withdraw but Hitler refused to allow it. In the winter fighting of 1942–3, Germany lost a million dead. Paulus surrendered on February 2 and 250,000 Axis troops became prisoners.

Vasily Grossman left Moscow on August 23 to cover the battle. "Stalingrad is burned down," he wrote. "It is dead. People are in basements. Everything is burned out. The hot walls of the buildings are like the bodies of people who have died in the terrible heat and haven't gone cold yet." A sniper, Anatoly Chekhov, who worked from a building facing a house occupied by Germans, told Grossman: "I knocked down nine on the first day. I knocked down 17 in two days. They sent women, and I killed two out of five. On the third day I saw . . . a sniper. I waited and fired. He fell down and cried out in German. They stopped carrying mines and getting water. I killed 40 Fritzes in eight days."

Grossman's editor in Moscow, Gen. David Ortenberg, marveled at his reportorial skill. "All the correspondents attached to the Stalingrad Front were amazed how Grossman had made the divisional commander, General Gurtiev, a silent and reserved Siberian, talk to him for six hours without a break, telling him all that he wanted to know, at one of the hardest moments."[1]

In October Grossman gave this graphic account of the Russian experience under relentless bombing:

> For eight hours on end Junkers 87s dived and swooped over the [Siberian] Division's defenses . . . sirens howled, bombs shrieked, the earth quaked and the remains of brick buildings crashed . . . the air was filled with clouds of smoke and dust, and shells and bombs whined their death song. Anyone who has . . . lived through a harrowing ten minutes' raid of German aircraft will have some idea of what eight hours of intense bombing by dive bombers means.

The Russians went on the offensive, advanced 1 km and dug in. The battle raged for several days, then German pressure began to subside. "The Siberians had successfully stood this superhuman strain."[2] Pyotr Lidov of *Pravda* wrote: "There is smoke over the city. From a distance it looks as if the city were alive, as if the great factories were breathing. But it is not the breath of life, but the breath of death . . . And now, at nightfall, you . . . only see flames. In many places Stalingrad is still burning. Let it burn! We shall hold it, and make it rise from its ashes!"[3]

In a letter to his father on November 13, Grossman wrote: "I work a lot, the work is stressful and I am pretty tired. I have never been to such a hot spot as this one."

Six days later, the Soviets launched their offensive. Grossman wrote: "Troops are marching. Their spirits are higher now . . . Our soldiers are sitting among the corpses, cooking in a cauldron slices cut from a dead horse, and stretching their frozen hands toward the fire." By November 26, Paulus's Sixth Army was surrounded. Grossman wrote:

> The Germans have crawled into deep holes and stone cellars; they have crawled into concrete water tanks, into wells and sewage pipes, into underground tunnels . . . The sun . . . shines . . . on the twisted metal girders of the factories, red and rust, and on the common graves of our soldiers . . . This is holy soil . . . There is no sun for [the Germans] . . . Here, among the dark, cold ruins, with no water and only scraps of horseflesh to eat, they will meet with vengeance; they will meet with it under the cruel stars of the Russian winter night.

In December he wrote to his wife that he was upset at cuts and distortions that editors had made to his dispatches. Writing to his father that same month: "My nerves have suffered a lot. I've become angry and irritable. I keep attacking my colleagues. They are frightened of me now."

Having covered some of the most grueling weeks of the battle, Grossman would be denied the glory of reporting the final victory. His editor ordered him to the south and assigned Konstantin Simonov, a decision that Ilya Ehrenberg of *Pravda* found unjust and illogical. Another humiliation occurred when the commission that chose the winner of the 1942 Stalin Prize voted unanimously for Grossman's novel *The People Immortal*; Stalin ignored the choice and gave the prize to Ehrenburg's novel *The Fall of Paris.*[4]

In one report, Simonov wrote:

Stalingrad is now a gray, smoking city above which fire dances day and night and ashes float in the air . . . The wounded go to hospitals but the dead are laid out for burial on the shore. Already many streets of the city no longer exist. Others are pitted with craters or are full of crashed bombers. Women and children, still left in the city, are living in cellars or digging caves in the river bank . . .

He quoted a Ukrainian woman, a doctor's assistant, who said she had been wounded twice. "But I don't believe I'll die yet because I haven't begun to live."[5]

* * *

Henry Shapiro, the UP bureau chief in Moscow, grumbled to Ehrenburg about not being able to go to the front, and was particularly upset when Stalin gave two scoops to his AP rival, Henry Cassidy. "Shapiro came to me in a great state: 'I sent a questionnaire too. Associated Press is far more right-wing than UP. Does Stalin want to ruin me?' " Ehrenburg recounted. "It was impossible to calm him down." Ehrenburg, himself a Jew but a Communist, told him his Jewish name would never endear him to Stalin. As a "consolation prize," Shapiro was allowed to visit the Stalingrad front in November.

During the four days he was in the city itself, he found among officers and soldiers "an air of confidence the like of which I had never seen in the Red Army before. In the battle of Moscow there was nothing like it." Born in Romania, he talked to hundreds of Romanian prisoners and all told him it was not their war but they had been forced into it. Many were begging to be taken prisoner.

On the approaches to Stalingrad, he later told fellow correspondent Alexander Werth: "The whole goddamn steppe was full of dead horses . . . Ten thousand horses had been killed by the Russians in the breakthrough." German prisoners were nearly all 19 or 20 years old and "very miserable," with hardly any winter clothing. "Morally, the Germans were completely stunned, in addition to being starved and frozen. They did not seem to understand what the devil had happened."

Shapiro wrote eight articles, commenting in one that "the Germans are doomed." Nikolai Palgunov, head of the press department, refused to pass them because they were "too optimistic." Shapiro sent copies to Stalin and soon afterward Palgunov told him he would let the articles go out. But he required Shapiro to make a few cosmetic changes. Palgunov balked, however, at allowing him to name the commanding general at Stalingrad. Shapiro pointed out that thousands of leaflets had been dropped over German lines, signed by Gen. Konstantin K. Rokossovsky. Palgunov said this had not been officially confirmed, so Rokossovky could not be named.[6]

About a dozen foreign correspondents were finally allowed to visit the Stalingrad area on January 7. Eddy Gilmore of the AP saw something that "shocked me as much as anything during the war." A Soviet soldier held a rope attached to the neck of a wild-eyed Romanian private. "As he reached me, the Russian soldier saluted, said something to the man he was leading like a dog. The prisoner dropped to all fours and loped along behind his captor, looking at me and smiling, an expression of horrible and pathetic embarrassment on his face." The soldier called out another order, the prisoner got to his feet and brushed off the snow, and they shuffled on down the street. "Nothing affected me as much as that Romanian being led down the street by his neck."[7]

Foreign correspondents were back in Stalingrad on February 4, two days after the German surrender. Bill Downs of CBS said in a broadcast: "There are sights and smells and sounds in and around Stalingrad that make you want to weep and make you want to shout and make you just plain sick at your stomach." He later went on a lecture tour in the U.S. and expressed sympathy for the Russian people. Some listeners branded him a liar or a Russian agent.[8]

A captain told of finding an open-air concentration camp for Russian prisoners. "It was dreadful," Alexander Werth wrote. Of 1,400 men there, only 102 survived. The Germans themselves had nothing to eat, but they began starving prisoners even before they were encircled. After liberation, Russian soldiers gave bread and sausage to survivors, and many died because they could no longer absorb such a rich diet. Werth visited a basement in which 200 Germans were dying of hunger and frostbite. "We haven't had time to deal with them yet," a Russian told him. "They'll be taken away tomorrow, I suppose."

The correspondents were taken to see captured generals, held in cottages outside Stalingrad. "We were not allowed to enter the room, and had to inspect them from the passage through the door," Werth recounted.

> We could speak only to those who were near the door and were willing to talk . . . It was rather like being at the zoo, where some animals showed interest in the public and the others sulked. Some of those in the background looked slovenly and unshaved . . . The first thing that hit you in the eye was their crosses, orders, medals and whole mantelpiece ornaments pinned to their uniforms. Many were wearing monocles. They were almost too good to be true. Erich von Stroheim was mild in comparison.

Werth was struck by the fact the generals looked healthy, suggesting they had regular meals while their soldiers starved.

> The only man who looked in poor shape was Paulus himself. We weren't allowed to speak to him; he was only shown to us . . . Paulus looked pale and sick, and had a nervous twitch in his left cheek. He had more natural dignity than any of the others, and wore only one or two decorations.

Paulus had been promoted to field marshal by Hitler a few days before his surrender.

The most unforgettable German, Werth wrote, was Lt. Gen. Sixt von Arnim, "enormously tall, with a long, twisted nose and a look of fury in his long horse-like face with its popping eyes . . . One felt that here was a maniac capable of anything." Von Arnim said he had been treated correctly by Russian officers, but not their men. "They stole all my things. Eine Schweinerei! . . . Four whole suitcases, and they stole them all." Werth commented: "They had looted the whole of Europe, these people; but what was that compared with his four suitcases!"

A Russian soldier said a Red Army woman barber shaved the generals every morning. One got fresh with her and pinched her bottom. She slapped his face. "He got so scared of having his throat cut, he won't shave any more and is now growing a beard," Werth wrote.

Lt. Fyodor Mikhailovich Elchenko told of his capture of Paulus inside the Univermag department store. A German general summoned him and said, "Our chief wants to talk to your chief." Elchenko told him the Russian chief was busy and the German would have to talk to him. He was shown inside. "It was packed with soldiers—hundreds of them," he said. "They were dirty and hungry and stank. And did they look scared!"

Paulus was lying on a bed, wearing his uniform. "He looked unshaven and you wouldn't say he felt jolly," Elchenko remarked. He commented to Paulus, "Well, that finishes it," and the field marshal gave him a miserable look and nodded. A German general said to Elchenko: "You must have him taken away in a decent car, under proper guard, so the Red Army soldiers don't kill him, as though he were some vagabond."

One Russian soldier commented about the Germans: "Funny blokes, really. Coming to conquer Stalingrad, wearing patent-leather shoes. Suppose they thought it would be a joy ride!"[9]

Richard Lauterbach of *Time-Life* visited weeks after the German surrender and found people still living in underground shelters, crude caves and huts. Factories were operating again, without roofs and windows. As he left by train, he passed the village of Koorman and "probably the greatest junk heap in the world . . . As far as the eye could see were captured Nazi cannons, light and heavy tanks, anti-tank guns, mortars, carriers, machine guns, assorted vehicles of all sizes." Along the tracks were dozens of dismantled German locomotives, many overturned, and hundreds of railway cars.[10]

* * *

Werth went to Kharkov in February 1943. A boy told him how the Germans took 16,000 Jews to a brick works and killed them. He said they also sent thousands of people to Germany for slave labor, and had taken some sailors to a river and drowned them. Other people had been hanged at Gestapo headquarters.

Werth wrote that many professors at Kharkov University and other colleges had been shot. Some professors had committed suicide or died from starvation, and several university buildings had been destroyed. Werth visited three towns in the area and wrote that most houses, other buildings and churches had been destroyed, the populations starved and 15,000 people deported to Germany.[11]

In the spring of 1943 Ehrenburg reported on atrocities in Shchigry, north of Kharkov. After partisans blew up a bridge to cut off escape, the Germans shot fifty hostages, hanged six women and destroyed much of the village. One woman caught sight of a girl with rouged cheeks and shouted: "Shame on you, you German mattress."

In Piryatin, a man told Ehrenburg he had been forced to dig a pit into which the Germans dumped the bodies of 600 Jews. One friend, his face covered with blood and an eye gouged out, pleaded with him: "Finish me off." A woman resident said: "They buried them alive, the earth heaved." At Koryuchkovo the priest went out carrying a cross, begging the Germans to spare his village. They shot him and his wife.[12]

* * *

Edmund Stevens covered war crimes trials in Kharkov before a military tribunal. The defendants, he reported, "almost seemed to revel in their wickedness," eagerly confessing how they had ordered Russian prisoners beaten and shot. By their own testimony they slaughtered 30,000 people. In a December 20 dispatch, Stevens told of the execution of three Germans and a Russian traitor, Mikhail Bulanov. Bulanov fainted, two of the Germans turned white and "drooled at the mouth," while only one man "remained stiff as a ramrod throughout, never once flinching."

There was no emotion in the watching crowd. "Then I realized," Stevens wrote, "that in the past two years these people had lived in such constant daily contact with this kind of thing that they had become hardened and used to it. It was as though their cup of feeling and emotion had evaporated. From now on nothing could phase [sic] them."[13]

* * *

After Stalingrad, Moscow-based correspondents went to a Foreign Ministry news conference. The strains among them were intense. Harold King of Reuters was enraged by the presence of Ralph Parker of the Communist *Daily Worker*. King denounced Parker and implied his secretary was a police informer. Parker punched King on the nose. Eddy Gilmore grabbed Parker by the arm to break up the fight, but Ronald Matthews of the *Daily Herald* reached over his shoulder and slugged Parker "a beautiful full clout on the nose." Parker's secretary jumped on Gilmore's back, cursing and clawing. He shook her off and she flew across the room, shattering a glass door panel. At the far end of the room, an official emerged to say the foreign minister was ready to see the press. Battered and bleeding and without his glasses, Parker was unable to attend. The Foreign Ministry press department ignored the entire matter.

Parker, who was English, had come to Moscow for *The Times* of London, having previously covered Eastern Europe. He became a Soviet sympathizer and was fired as a stringer for the *New York Times* by William Lawrence, the bureau chief, so he switched to the *Daily Worker* and remained in Moscow for the rest of his life.

Ilya Ehrenburg reported that correspondents sometimes came to blows, and claimed one American punctured the tires of a rival's car. "There were also some unpleasant types," he wrote. One "breezy fellow" arrived at his apartment and put a pound of sugar on the table. Ehrenburg's wife Lyuba came in and, not knowing who the guest was, asked: "Are you selling sugar?" Ehrenburg insisted on the American taking back his sugar. Later he told this story to novelist Alexei Tolstoy, who said the correspondent also had brought him sugar. Tolstoy felt he had to give something in return but had nothing handy so offered him a Waterman fountain pen. "And he took it, the bastard."

On another occasion Mike Handler of UP knocked down Shapiro and threatened to choke him to death because he was convinced Shapiro had given authorities the name of a Russian girl with whom he was having an affair. Harold King got into a brawl with Shapiro, and they stopped speaking until a colleague persuaded them at least to acknowledge each other's presence when they met. One day King phoned Shapiro and said that, having realized they were now back on speaking terms, he wanted him to know he still thought he was a son of a bitch.

Born in Romania in 1907, Shapiro emigrated to the U.S. in his youth, earned a law degree from Harvard and, on the advice of a professor, went to Moscow in 1933 to study Soviet law. He soon began working part time as a translator for American and British correspondents, then joined UP in 1936. A year earlier he had married Ludmilla Nikitina, the daughter of a University of Moscow professor, and remained in the Soviet Union for thirty-nine years—the longest continuous stretch of any correspondent. He retired in 1972 and from 1973 to 1979 he was a professor at the University of Wisconsin School of Journalism. He died of a stroke in 1991 at age 84. A personal note: I succeeded Shapiro as UPI's (United Press International) Moscow bureau chief in 1972.[14]

Harold King had been a part-time Reuters correspondent in Paris before the fall of France, then had been sent to Moscow, where he taught himself Russian. In May 1943 he scored a major beat when he obtained from Stalin a statement announcing dissolution of the Comintern. King served as Paris bureau chief of Reuters for twenty-three years after the war, and died in Paris in 1990, aged 91. He was born Harold Koenig in Berlin but the family moved to London and his father changed the family name with the outbreak of World War I.[15]

Edmund Stevens returned to Moscow in 1946, worked there three more years, then served as the *Christian Science Monitor*'s chief Mediterranean correspondent for six years. Returning to the Soviet Union in 1956, he remained there until his death in May 1992 at age 81. He and his Russian wife, Nina Bondarenko, became well-known collectors of Russian art and icons. In 1950 he won the Pulitzer Prize for a series of articles on life under the Stalin dictatorship.[16]

Alexander Werth returned to Moscow after the war for the *Manchester Guardian*, serving from 1946 to 1949. The author of eighteen books, most dealing with the Soviet Union and France, he later moved to Paris, where he died in March 1969, aged 68.[17]

* * *

The siege of Leningrad by Germans to the south and Finnish troops to the north and east lasted for 872 days from September 8, 1941, to January 27, 1944. An estimated 1.5 million Russians died and 1.4 million, mostly women and children, were evacuated. The Russians opened a corridor via Lake Ladoga in 1943, and a million people took part in building fortifications that helped save the city. It was not until January 1944 that the Red Army was able to push the Germans back beyond artillery range of the city. Stalin declared it liberated on January 27.

Leningrad was potentially one of the great news stories of the war, but relatively little of its agony was known to the outside world. The city was off limits to foreign correspondents until virtually the end of the siege, and even then few were allowed to travel there. But one spent several months with the besiegers. Curzio Malaparte was back in Russia in September 1941, this time with Finnish troops on the eastern flanks of Leningrad.

"The countryside is a nursery of mines," he wrote. "Mines are placed everywhere—in isolated houses, public buildings and private dwellings. They are in sofas, telephones, drawers, under carpets. They explode when the light is switched on." By the following April, when Leningraders had started dying by the thousands, his sympathy was evident. "The informers, the prisoners, the deserters are agreed in describing the siege of Leningrad as a taciturn, obstinate agony. A slow death, a gray death . . . The secret of the resistance of this immense city, more than in arms, more than in the courage of its soldiers, consists in its incredible capacity to suffer."

The trench warfare on the outskirts reminded him of World War I, when he was a soldier in the Italian Army:

Those dead lying among the barbed wire, those frozen cadavers, fixed forever in the final gesture and that Soviet soldier down there, on his knees among the barbed wire, with his face turned toward us, the dark forehead in the shadow of the sheepskin hat covered by a layer of snow, how many times have I seen them, for how many years have I known them? Nothing has changed in these 25 years . . .

For those not caught up in "the immense cage of the siege," he wrote:

the agony of Leningrad cannot be anything else, by now, than a terrible performance . . . There is no Christian sentiment, nor piety, nor compassion, that is so great, so profound, as to be able to embrace and sympathize with a similar tragedy. It is like certain scenes of Aeschylus or Shakespeare: the mind of the spectator is overcome by such horrible force . . . outside the history of human events.

He came upon the remains of two Soviet parachutists in a forest. Finnish soldiers had arrived with ladders to take down the bodies and bury them. The Finns had shot them as they were falling from the sky. "I believe William Blake in his visions of hell never saw anything of such terrible grandiosity. One of the 'fallen angels' held in his fist something shining. It was a large pistol. Around the tree, on the snow, were some spent shells. He came down from the sky shooting."

Leaving in November 1942, Malaparte wrote of "an infinite sadness" at going away. In February, many had predicted the imminent surrender of the city but he had not shared that view. The city's current condition, he wrote, was much better than the previous winter and a great part of the population had escaped via the Lake Ladoga lifeline. Fresh troops also had moved in to replace those worn down during the terrible winter months.

There is no longer the hard war of siege of the last months, that continuous hammering of heavy artillery on the industrial suburbs of the southwest, that ferocious rhythm of attacks and counterattacks. Something mature, and tired, is in this air suspended on the roofs of Leningrad. The air of an imminent threat, and at the same time of an unconscious rest.

After the overthrow of Mussolini, Malaparte served the American High Command in Italy from 1943 to 1946. Then this one-time Fascist became a member of the Communist Party. In 1947 he settled in Paris and embarked on a career as a moderately successful playwright and film director. He died in Rome of lung cancer in July 1957, aged 59.[18]

* * *

Pravda correspondent Lazar Brontman reported that Leningrad people used grass to make soup and bread. "Grass cakes found their own price in the market." He also wrote that many people ignited kindling with magnifying glasses, when there was sun, because matches were so scarce. While most residents resorted to killing and eating their pets, one of his friends clung to his, "probably the only surviving dog in Leningrad."[19]

Werth, born in the city in 1901 when it was still called St. Petersburg, became the first foreign correspondent to witness Leningrad's suffering when he was flown there on September 23, 1943. He found vegetables growing on lawns of the Senate Square, cabbages in the Champ de Mars parade ground.[20] Anna Andeievna, an attendant in his hotel, told him of the worst years of famine: "You just stepped over corpses on the street and on the stairs. You simply stopped taking any notice ... Some people went quite insane with hunger. And the practice of hiding the dead somewhere in the house and using their ration cards was very common indeed."[21]

Werth found the bombed area around his former home shabby and deserted. The doors to his old apartment were locked and "there was a smell of death about the house." A city architect told him 8 per cent of Leningrad housing had been destroyed—much less than in some other Russian cities. Werth visited a school where none of the pupils had died from hunger, but several teachers had. Shown essays that the children had written, he commented: "Curious that in all these ultra-patriotic essays there was not a single mention of Stalin."

A Russian officer said the Germans used to run around openly, gathering in hay, in the city's outskirts, but now "stay in their rat holes" because of snipers. "We bomb them every day ... and when we answer their shelling, they soon shut up," he told Werth. A colonel said Germans were prone to run away from a fight unless they had a big advantage. "They've lost all their best men, and we've lost most of ours."

A factory manager told Werth that, during the worst period of the siege, people ate carpenter's glue and tried to stay alive on hot water and yeast. Of 5,000 working at the factory, several hundred had died of starvation. Members of the Writers Union revealed that, during the siege, divers went down in the icy waters of the port and retrieved more than 4,000 tons of coal that had fallen in over the years during unloading from ships.

Werth returned in February 1944 after the siege had been broken. "The city now stands in the middle of a desert. There is nothing left of thousands of country houses around Leningrad. Peterhof is wiped out and little more than a heap of ruins is left of Tsarskoye Selo, Pavlovsk and Gatchina . . . The famous Imperial Palaces and their beautiful parks . . . have practically disappeared . . . The destruction of these palaces and parks has aroused among the Russians as great a fury as the worst German atrocities against human beings."[22]

* * *

The German war against the Soviet Union brought about a gradual shift of opinion within the Reich, as recorded by one of the few credible correspondents remaining there. Arvid Fredborg of Stockholm's *Svenska Dagbladet* detected growing unrest in Berlin as the winter of 1941–2 approached. "Hitler was still sacrosanct. But the Party was criticized more and more." The regime began to step up anti-American propaganda and Fredborg commented: "Even the most devoted Nazis did not want a war with America. All Germans had a high respect for her strength." The German people received news of Hitler's declaration of war on the United States "without the slightest sign of enthusiasm."

More stringent press restrictions had been imposed and new campaigns initiated against listening to foreign broadcasts. The wearing of the Star of David was imposed for Jews in September 1941. "Now and again there were small demonstrations *in favor*" of the Jews, Fredborg wrote in a book published after he left Berlin.

As fighting in Russia continued, he saw signs of growing war weariness. Black marketeering had assumed enormous proportions. The death penalty was imposed for traffickers and those who tried to print their own ration cards. From the beginning of 1943, he wrote, fear of the consequences of a German defeat had become the dominant emotion, and surveillance was tightened. "People were simply worn out," partly as a result of a cut in food rations. There were now daily instances of workers collapsing at their machines.

Fredborg went to Vienna and found Austrians taking out their war weariness by treating Germans with contempt. Waiters were rude until he revealed he was Swedish.

During the first half of 1943 moral disintegration reached such a point that hardly a single German remained quite loyal. Everyone was involved in some little "black" business. An increase in working hours—10 hours was practically the minimum, 11 or 12 being the average—contributed to the exhaustion of the people. Housing facilities also were reduced by Allied air attacks, and any family with more than one room per person was required to take a lodger.

A new wave of deportation of Jews swept Berlin in spring 1943. "The Jews were collected under incredibly brutal circumstances . . . The last Jews were evacuated from my district in early May . . . There were many signs of increasing popular disapproval of the brutal treatment of the Jews."

He did not escape suspicion and felt that, by the end of spring 1943, his position had become untenable. "I noticed I was being watched, and the phone became more and more troublesome. Friends gave me quiet warnings." He left for Sweden on May 31.[23]

CHAPTER 12

THE BATTLE FOR ITALY

Allied forces carried the war to Sicily on July 10, 1943, disembarking 180,000 troops by sea and air on the south coast. The four Italian divisions on the island offered little resistance and Axis counterattacks were repulsed. On July 25, King Victor Emanuel III and Marshal Pietro Badoglio had Mussolini arrested, preparing the way for surrender. In Sicily, the Allies failed to cut off a German escape across the Straits of Messina to the Italian mainland. Harder fighting lay ahead there.

Hours before going ashore in Sicily, Allied troops and correspondents alike rode out a storm, their 2,000 ships buffeted by mountainous waves and winds of 40 miles an hour that delayed landings until the winds dropped and the sea was calmer.

Ross Munro of the Canadian Press news agency went ashore under machine-gun fire but enemy guns soon went silent and prisoners started coming in. He sat down on the beach to write his dispatch, then sent it to the headquarters ship where it was relayed to London. "It was a world beat by seven and a half hours," he wrote. "Coming as we did directly from England, we had not yet become bound by official red tape on communications and censorship." Allied headquarters in Algiers was furious. Unknown to Munro, officers threatened to arrest him and expel him for not going through censorship. But a Canadian public relations officer managed somehow to placate them.[1]

Mark Watson, 55, of the *Baltimore Sun* wrote: "We have seen Allied warships steam up against Italy's shores without shaming so much as a single Italian motorboat into a single desperate effort to launch one torpedo for defense of the land. The Italian army . . . has made only a feeble defense of Sicily."[2]

Don Whitehead went ashore at Gela with the U.S. First Division. "I tried to appear calm and indifferent to the sounds of battle before these veterans of Tunisia, but my heart was pounding with excitement." Civilians swarmed out of hiding places, cheering and weeping. "The American boys were bewildered . . . They did not know how to cope with the laughter and happiness of an enemy." An old crone mouthed curses, but the crowd booed her and shouted, "Viva America!"

During the night American paratroopers came over. Then Allied naval guns fired on the planes carrying them. Jack Belden of *Time* began shouting, "Oh God, No! No! Stop, you bastards, stop! Stop shooting!" More than twenty-five planes were shot down. Additionally, some paratroopers who jumped were blown out to sea and drowned, and several gliders caught in high winds crashed. Censors banned reporting of these incidents, and of a munitions ship that blew up in Algiers harbor, killing a thousand men.

Byron Price, a U.S. censor, thought "newspapers . . . and broadcasting stations must be as actively behind the war effort as merchants or manufacturers." John Steinbeck later wrote: "Facts available in any library in the world came to be carefully guarded secrets, and the most carefully guarded secrets were known by everyone."[3]

John Thompson of the *Chicago Tribune* parachuted with the troops. He cracked a rib and wrenched a knee on landing, then received a cable from Chicago: JUMP NO MORE MCCORMICK. The cable was from editor Robert R. McCormick. Thompson had undergone paratroop training and previously jumped with troops in Algeria.[4]

As U.S. Rangers moved inland to Butera, Capt. Charles Shunstrum shoved .45 pistols into the hands of Whitehead and Belden. "We're not supposed to go armed," Whitehead told him. "To hell with that," Shunstrum replied. "If there is any shooting I want everybody with me to shoot back." Whitehead felt like a kid in a game of cops and robbers. "I looked around and Belden grinned at me sheepishly. We were a couple of Boy Scouts playing at war in the moonlight." After the war Shunstrum became unhinged and was charged with armed robbery in Los Angeles. He pleaded guilty by reason of insanity before a sympathetic judge who said he had changed from "a daring, reckless young officer to a man . . . filled with hatred for people he thought would not allow him to earn a livelihood." He freed Shunstrum "to begin life anew."

Once the Americans were well established, General Patton, commander of the Seventh Army, raced north to Palermo, the capital, instead of east to cut off the German retreat. Palermo surrendered without a battle. "One of the incongruous sights was to see Italian soldiers still in uniform standing on the curb and cheering the Yanks as wildly as the civilians," Whitehead wrote.[5]

Pyle went ashore near Licata, west of Gela. In a letter to his wife, he wrote: "I'm getting awfully tired of war and writing about it. It seems like I can't think of anything new to say—each time it's like going to the same movie again."

He ran into comedian Bob Hope. "He had the right touch with soldiers. He could handle himself as well in a hospital full of suffering men as before a rough audience of 10,000 war-coarsened ones." Hope played closer to the front line than any other entertainer. "No matter what narrow-escape story Bob tells about Sicily, it's true."

From July 31 to August 6, Americans fought a hard battle with German and Italian troops dug in around Troina in central Sicily, and Pyle wrote of the disorientation that can come over weary soldiers in such conditions. A company runner arrived and said excitedly, "I've got to find Captain Blank right away. Important message." The captain said, "But I am Captain Blank. Don't you recognize me?" The runner turned away, saying: "I've got to find Captain Blank right away." He dashed off and other troops had to run to catch him. This same sort of mind-numbing weariness also overcame correspondents at times, Pyle recounted in a dispatch:

> We were usually under fire only briefly and . . . we lived better than the average soldier. Yet our lives were strangely consuming in that we did live primitively and at the same time had to delve into ourselves and do creative writing . . . Most of the correspondents actually worked like slaves . . . We traveled continuously, moved camp every few days, ate out, slept out, wrote wherever we could and just never caught up on sleep, rest, cleanliness or anything else normal . . . We'd drained our emotions until they cringed from being called out from hiding. I am not writing this to make heroes of the correspondents, because only a few look upon themselves in any dramatic light whatever. I am writing it merely to let you know that correspondents, too, can get sick of war—and deadly tired.

He told Whitehead: "I know the longer we stay with this, the smaller our chances are of getting out. It's the inevitability of death in war that finally gets you down." When the Sicilian campaign ended, he returned to the U.S. on leave. "I had come to despise and be revolted by war clear out of any logical proportion. Through repetition, I had worn down to the nub my ability to weigh and describe."[6]

Noel Monks of London's *Daily Mail* had long talks with Pyle "and he convinced me, as he did himself, that he would not survive the war. He made no bones about being scared stiff every time he visited the front." But Pyle was so cherished by the troops, he added, that "for morale purposes, he was worth an armored division to the Yanks."[7]

Herbert Matthews covered the German surrender at Troina on August 6. He confessed that he did "a pretty poor job of coverage for the *New York Times*" because of boredom. In Troina he found "a town of horror, alive with weeping, hysterical men, women and children who had stayed there through two terrible days of bombing and shelling, seeing their loved ones killed or wounded, their houses destroyed and whatever was left pillaged ruthlessly by departing Nazis." Later he witnessed the capture of Messina, but his dispatch arrived in New York a day late. "I returned to Algiers bored and disgusted."[8]

South of Troina, American planes mistakenly bombed U.S. and Canadian troops, but censors refused to allow correspondents to report this.[9]

Whitehead described a scene where General Patton and Sen. Henry Cabot Lodge met troops and Lodge made a speech. "All at once the whole little tableau sickened me. I wanted to get away from the voices of the general and the senator. The dead scattered on the hillside and in the lemon grove spoke eloquently enough."[10]

* * *

On August 3, Patton visited wounded soldiers at a field hospital where Pvt. Charles H. Kuhl, 18, was bedridden with post-traumatic stress syndrome, then known as shell shock. When Patton asked what was the matter with him, Kuhl replied, "I guess I can't take it." Enraged, Patton slapped him, put his hands on his pistols and shouted: "Get up, you swine! You should be shot!" Turning to a doctor, he said: "Get this man on his feet and send him back to his unit." Monks and H. R. Knickerbocker of the *Chicago Sun* arrived as Patton emerged from the hospital tent. "There's no such thing as shell shock," he declared. "It's an invention of the Jews."

About twenty American correspondents assembled to discuss the incident. They decided no one would send the story. Patton was acknowledged as a resourceful general and correspondents feared the war effort might be damaged if they wrote a story that resulted in his removal. They decided to send Demaree Bess of the *Saturday Evening Post* to Algiers with a letter to

Eisenhower, asking that Patton be made to apologize to the soldier he struck. While Pyle agreed not to write the story, he "hated Patton's guts," according to Whitehead. "Patton's bluster, show and complete disregard for the dignity of the individual was the direct antithesis of Ernie's gentle character."

On August 10, Patton visited another hospital and erupted again at a traumatized soldier, Pvt. Paul G. Bennett. Calling him "a goddamned coward" and a "yellow son of a bitch," Patton shouted: "I won't have these brave men here who have been shot seeing a yellow bastard sitting here crying." He pulled his pistol, shoved it in Bennett's face and slapped him, then ordered the hospital commander to "get this man out of here right away. I won't have these boys seeing such a bastard babied." This incident did not receive the attention of the earlier one.[11]

Ed Kennedy, the AP manager in Algiers, learned of the incidents. He urged Eisenhower to release the story and cautioned that if it broke in an irregular manner the emphasis would be on the fact it had been suppressed. Eisenhower agreed in principle but couldn't bring himself to approve publication. He had not prohibited correspondents from sending the story but said any attempt to do so would be an embarrassment to Patton, himself and the war effort.[12]

Demaree Bess and Merrill Mueller of NBC went to Algiers, carrying signed statements from doctors and patients who witnessed the first incident. They were told Eisenhower had not slept for two nights, worrying about how to handle it. The general listened to them, smiled and said: "You men have got yourselves good stories and, as you know, there's no question of censorship involved." Bess told him the correspondents had concluded they would not file because "we're Americans first and correspondents second. Every mother would figure her son is next." Eisenhower revealed that Patton already had apologized to the soldiers and their officers, on his orders.[13]

The columnist Drew Pearson broke the story in a radio broadcast in Washington on November 21, after hospital staff and soldiers wrote home about it. There was an uproar in Congress and the press, but already Patton had been stripped of his command and left in Palermo. Eisenhower's office denied he had been removed from command or reprimanded. "It would be difficult to imagine a more dishonest statement," Ed Kennedy wrote. "Its whole intent was to deny the Pearson report by deceit." Patton had been tipped to command U.S. forces for the invasion of Normandy, but that role went to Gen. Omar Bradley. Not until January 1944 did Eisenhower summon Patton to England to command the Third Army.[14]

Leonard Shapiro of the *Montreal Gazette* landed with troops south of Syracuse. "I walked ashore like a summer tourist. Two Italian prisoners rushed forward to carry my baggage." Hundreds more Italian troops hastened to the beaches to surrender and were put to work unloading ships. When the troops landed, Shapiro wrote, one Italian grabbed an army chaplain and locked him in a small hut. As troops moved toward the hut, the Italian opened the door and threw in a live grenade. The troops shot him.

Later Shapiro covered a battle on the Catania plain, below Mt. Etna. German dead were scattered in a shallow trench. "The heat was intense and the smell overpowering. When I met the first sizable batch of prisoners being escorted back of the lines, Hitler's warriors were green with vomit and jittery as a Bowery bum after a banquet of nickel whiskey."

Italians had fought well in the final stages of the Tunisia campaign, he noted, but many in Sicily "streamed into our lines, grinning like Oriental beggars . . . What was there to defend? Poverty? Illiteracy? Filth? Exploitation? Of course they let us in!"

When Canadian troops entered Valguernera, the local leader told their commander he had arranged for thirty women to be made available for the pleasure of his troops. "The Fascist seemed genuinely upset when the women were returned to their homes, and he was appalled when the commander promptly threw him in jail," Shapiro wrote.[15]

Belden and Whitehead went ashore again with American troops at Brolo, on the north coast, 35 miles west of Messina. They climbed a hill and stepped into a ditch where eight German soldiers slept under one blanket. The Germans staggered to their feet with hands up. Then both the Americans and Germans came under heavy machine-gun fire, and Belden found himself crouching in a foxhole with two German prisoners.

German tanks moved up, followed by artillery and ammunition. "We were cut off and trapped on the hill," Belden wrote. "We were without food and almost out of ammunition." Then Allied planes came over and bombed German positions and the Germans disappeared. A week later, Messina fell to the Allies.[16]

* * *

Christopher Buckley of London's *Daily Telegraph* accompanied British troops on an unopposed landing on the east coast. They met 200 Italian soldiers, marching in to surrender with their hands up, some laughing and joking. Noto fell without a fight. The mayor invited Buckley and a British major to join him for a glass a wine. "We filled our glasses; we raised them; there was a moment of embarrassment as we wondered what was the appropriate toast under the circumstances. The mayor solved the problem for us. 'To Winston Churchill!' he said gravely."

A veteran of North Africa coverage, Buckley, 38, had studied military history at Cambridge and, anticipating the war, had traveled widely to familiarize himself with prospective battlefronts. In Cairo he had a brief romance with Clare Hollingworth, who described him as slim, tall and with a slight stoop. "He wore thick glasses and, although he was basically good looking, few women noticed him," she wrote. "He knew North Africa better than any other Allied war correspondent." The philosophical Buckley wrote:

> To accompany the soldier in the field is also to experience the genuine Aristotelian catharsis, to purge one's soul with pity and terror. It is not an ignoble experience to meet men who have just come from the Shadow of Death. You may even, for five fleeting minutes, be privileged to share their own routine battle experience, and it is worthwhile, for you will write all the better for it. Besides, you will have the pleasure of going back and telling your friends (who were not there) how brave you have been.

Buckley was in Giardini with Moorehead and Clifford when a group of Italian soldiers ran forward calling, "We surrender." "There was something essentially childish in their dark and troubled faces," Buckley wrote. "They were tired and hurt and frightened, and it was embarrassing to feel their deflation." The correspondents climbed a goat track to Taormina and were met by an enthusiastic crowd. An Italian officer addressed them: "My lords, we have waited too long for you!" He said the last Germans had left Taormina after a street battle in which they had been routed by Italian troops. "We politely pretended to believe him," Buckley wrote.[17]

* * *

Italy surrendered on September 8, 1943, and Allied troops landed at Salerno the next day against bitter German resistance. Mussolini was freed from imprisonment on September 12 by the Germans and installed as head of a puppet government in northern Italy. The so-called "soft underbelly" of the Axis empire proved anything but soft in Italy's mountainous terrain. The Germans did not surrender until May 2, 1945, six days before the end of the war in Europe.

Before the Italian surrender, correspondents heard reports it was near. "I expected that," Reynolds Packard told Quentin Reynolds. "I have complete faith in the Italians. They've double-crossed every ally they ever had. Now it's Hitler's turn."[18]

Packard, Reynolds and Leonard Shapiro were aboard the ship carrying Gen. Mark Clark, commander of the U.S. Fifth Army, for the landing at Salerno. Forty German bombers appeared and their bombs narrowly missed the ship. The correspondents made it safely ashore. Three days later, the Germans began a counterattack and broke through to within 2,500 yards of the headquarters camp. "Instinct kept pounding words of panic into my mind," Shapiro wrote. "Why not run? Anywhere. Just run." Then he decided panic would be disastrous. He, Packard and Herbert Matthews sat down on a log. Capt. John Boettiger, son-in-law of President Roosevelt, strolled over and said he had an extra revolver. "One of our group took it," Shapiro wrote. The German attack was repulsed and on September 14 a huge air and naval bombardment "tore German forces from their moorings."[19]

"Normandy was a picnic compared with Salerno," wrote Monks. He denounced the "crass stupidity" of announcing Italy's surrender before the men hit the beaches and called it "the greatest psychological blunder of the war." The Germans had 300,000 men on Italian soil when the "shoestring" U.S. Fifth Army of 75,000 landed. The Germans let the first wave of troops ashore, "then opened up with everything they had . . . The sea was a cauldron of bursting shells and exploding bombs."

As German planes appeared, a young soldier ran past Monks, shouting, "Nazi plane . . . strafing." Monks shouted to him to get down but he kept running until he was struck by machine-gun fire from a Messerschmitt 109. A tank appeared in front of Monks and he thought: "I'll be joining this poor chap any second now."

"I found myself wishing I had a gun, a revolver, anything legal . . . to defend myself with." He fell into a hole where two dead GIs lay. The German tank passed by two yards away. Someone fired an anti-tank gun and it blew up.

A landing craft was returning to Monks's ship and he got aboard, hoping to file from there, but was refused permission. The ship was leaving for Oran, Algeria, and there was no way he could return to the beach. He went to Cairo, just in time for a secret conference of Churchill, Roosevelt and Chiang Kai-shek, held November 22–6, 1943. None of the nearly one hundred correspondents on hand even glimpsed the three leaders and dispatches were held up for ten days as the leaders went on to Tehran to meet with Stalin. On return to Cairo, Churchill gave correspondents a half-hour meeting but no questions were allowed.[20]

Whitehead would have had one of the great scoops of the war at Salerno had it not been for Navy censors. An Italian officer coming from Rome told him Mussolini had been arrested and imprisoned but escaped with German help. Whitehead filed a dispatch but censors held it for a week. By then official sources in Rome had released the news.[21]

Belden was with troops who made their way through barbed-wire barriers and emerged onto a highway. A German truck approached, the Americans opened fire and the truck stopped. Belden began climbing onto a wall as a German opened fire. "Something like a baseball bat hammered into my leg. I flew off the wall. A loud, involuntary howl of anguish escaped my lips." He tried to get up and fell back. Four medics arrived and gave him morphine. Belden asked them to take him to the beach but they put a splint on his leg and went away. He eventually was carried to the beach and transferred to a ship, where a doctor told him the splint probably saved his leg. Afterward he always walked with a limp.[22]

Matthews went ashore suffering from dysentery and running a high fever. "It was hard enough for 10 days or more to turn out, each day, one to four stories of a mediocre nature for my newspaper." Later, when troops were pushing toward Naples, he was among correspondents caught up in a tank battle at Scafati. A German shell struck the corner of an alley, killing Stewart Sale of the *Daily Herald*, A. B. Austin of Reuters, William Munday of the *Sydney Morning Herald*, a British soldier and two Italian civilians. B. H. T. Gingell of the British Exchange Telegraph was slightly wounded.[23]

Monks and Packard drove into Naples on October 1, 1943, as Germans began evacuating the city. Germans were sniping from rooftops, while German engineers laid booby traps in public buildings. Packard reported no bodies had been buried in Naples for two weeks and "the smell of death was everywhere . . . Hospitals were piled with decomposing bodies. Private houses also contained corpses." He and Monks were blown out of their Jeep and knocked unconscious by an explosion in the central post office. The Germans had been gone nearly two weeks by then but had left time bombs behind.

Monks and Packard doubled back to Sorrento, where well-dressed Italians were preparing to dine at the Grand Hotel. "Against the background of the filth and destruction and hunger of Naples, just across the shimmering bay, it was a fantastic scene," Monks wrote. Packard demanded they be given rooms and lunch and the haughty manager refused. Several days later, they told General Clark of the incident and he requisitioned the hotel as a convalescent hostel for sick and wounded soldiers.[24]

Mark Watson entered Naples in October. "The highway was lined with exuberant people. Some of the prettiest girls I ever expect to see came running with flowers and bouquets." But he reached a waterfront devoid of people, all of its piers and warehouses destroyed or damaged, its ships sunk or capsized. "This might have been as completely a dead city as Pompeii itself."[25]

In November 1943 Pyle ended a two-month leave at home and left for Italy. "I hate to go back to the front. I dread it and I am afraid of it. But what can a guy do?" He had been in Naples less than two hours before he felt he couldn't stand it. So it was off to the battlefront, "up in the mud again, sleeping on straw and awakening throughout the night with the old familiar crash and thunder of the big guns in my reluctant ears." He was drinking heavily by then. Towns northward from Salerno had been reduced to rubble. "Most inhabitants took to the hills," Pyle wrote. "Some to live in caves, some to relatives in the country. In every town there were people who refused to leave no matter what happened, and many were killed . . ."[26]

Sgt. Jack Foisie of *Stars and Stripes* referred in a dispatch to German destruction of Naples's water, sanitation, electric power and heating. He termed it a city of 700,000 candles—one for each inhabitant:

A city of empty, looted buildings, apartment houses and hotels. The windows were knocked out because of the bomb blasts, but the looting was done by the Germans or by incited Italians under the watchful eye of German propaganda cameras . . . Garbage is dumped in the nearest vacant lot . . . Flies are the thickest I've ever seen . . . I can see a mob milling at one of the few civilian water points in the city; they are like thirsty cattle at a waterhole.

Pyle wrote an affectionate portrayal of the 24-year-old Foisie, who became a correspondent of the *Los Angeles Times* after the war. According to Pyle, Foisie had an "ephemeral and intuitive ability to express the soldiers' viewpoint . . . Among correspondents he had the reputation of always being willing to go anywhere and do anything. But he was shy, and for the most part he kept in the background." When Pyle first met him in Sicily, he had a hesitation in speech but when they met again on the mainland that was gone. "I spoke to him about it and he said he thought it was because he had gained more confidence in himself," Pyle wrote.[27]

Moorehead came into Naples and was appalled by rampant corruption and degeneracy. Children of 10 and 12 were being offered in brothels, and raw alcohol mixed with flavoring was being sold with fake labels. Fake jewelry was on sale and 6-year-old boys were selling obscene postcards, "selling their sisters, themselves, anything." Sixty or seventy vehicles were stolen every night, not always by Italians.

Moorehead wrote that typhus broke out and began to develop into an epidemic. "The unwashed, cold and hungry people died very quickly. The cars came round at night and took the bodies away." Not until January was the epidemic brought under control. Then the American Army was confronted by widespread gonorrhea. "Before Christmas we were taking more casualties in Naples through gonorrhea than we were through enemy action on the whole of the front line." Eventually that, too, was brought under control.[28]

Packard wrote that desertions among U.S. troops became wholesale in Naples. GIs would "shack up with Italian girls and not bother to return to their regiments." Later, deserters teamed up and became heavily involved in black market operations. Censors blocked Packard's attempt to report this.[29]

In mountains east of Naples, Richard Tregaskis had a narrow escape when German artillery opened up outside Altavilla and shrapnel dented his helmet. Tregaskis was diabetic; it might have kept him from military service but not from frontline journalism. "The lure of the front is like an opiate," he wrote. "After the abstinence and the tedium of workaday life, its attraction becomes more and more insistent."

An officer told him that troops on nearby Mount Corno were having a "pretty hot" time with Germans sheltering in caves. Tregaskis started up the mountain with two officers. Just below the 1,054-meter crest, troops were dropping mortars on German positions. The two officers soon headed back down the mountain, but Tregaskis stopped to talk to Rangers. "For the first time in several weeks, I had a bang-up eyewitness story of an action at a crucial sector of the front," he wrote. Afterward he hurried to catch up with the officers, then heard the scream of an incoming mortar—and felt an explosion. He was unconscious for a moment, then woke and knew he was badly wounded.

His helmet lay a few feet away, gashed in at least two places. Men were running past and he tried to shout, "but only incoherent sounds tumbled from my mouth." He tried to tell a soldier he needed help. The soldier replied: "I can't help you, I'm too scared." He ran off. A medic dropped beside Tregaskis, bandaged his head, gave him a shot of morphine, then disappeared. "I knew if I wanted to get back to a field dressing station, I would have to go under my own power." He tried to pick up his glasses with his right hand but that arm was useless. Grabbing the glasses with his left hand and picking up the helmet, which he thought would be a fine souvenir, he started downhill. There was another explosion. "I saw tall spouts of smoke and high explosive jumping up all around me. A red drapery of blood ran down over my glasses and blurred my vision." He took refuge in a cave, then staggered out and saw Col. Bill Yarborough and Capt. Edmund Tomasik, with whom he had gone up the mountain, bending over a wounded man. Yarborough helped Tregaskis down the trail to a command post. Army surgeons operated on him for four hours.

For several days, he vomited every time he woke up. His voice was even less coherent than before and the right side of his body was numb. His right eye wouldn't focus. A doctor told him he had been hit in the left side of the brain, the region that controlled speech in a right-handed person. The doctor said he would need at least six months to recover and surgeons would have to patch his skull with a metal plate. Bone fragments had been driven into his brain but these had been removed.

"One afternoon I felt an electric sensation in my arm, then my shoulder and neck. My whole field of vision snapped out of joint." His speech thickened, but later he had more feeling in his arm and could see better. On December 10, he was moved to a hospital north of Naples and soon could walk downstairs. On December 26, he and sixteen other wounded men were put aboard a DC-3 and flown to North Africa. Then on January 14, 1944, he boarded another plane for home. While he was still in hospital in Italy, Pyle visited him and wrote that it was a miracle he was alive. "If I'd had his wound, I would have gone home and rested on my laurels forever," Pyle wrote. "But he was back in action in France in 1944."[30]

Pyle left Naples to cover fighting in the mountains, following a mule-pack outfit that served an infantry battalion. The men there fought ten days and nights, and when they came off the mountain fewer than one-third were still alive. On this occasion, Pyle produced a dispatch that remains the best known of his career. He wrote:

> In this war I have known a lot of officers who were loved and respected by the soldiers under them. But never have I crossed the trail of any man as beloved as Capt. Henry T. Waskow, of Belton, Texas.
>
> Captain Waskow was a company commander in the 36th Division . . . He was very young, only in his middle twenties, but he carried in him a sincerity and a gentleness that made people want to be guided by him.
>
> "After my father, he came next," a sergeant told me.
>
> "He always looked after us," a soldier said. "He'd go to bat for us every time."
>
> "I've never knowed him to do anything unfair," another said . . .

I was at the foot of the mule trail the night they brought Captain Waskow down. The moon was nearly full, and you could see far up the trail, and even part way across the valley below . . .

Then a soldier came into the cowshed and said there were some more bodies outside. We went out into the road. Four mules stood there in the moonlight . . . The soldiers who led them stood there waiting.

"This one is Captain Waskow," one of them said quietly . . .

The men in the road . . . stood around, and gradually I could sense them moving, one by one, close to Captain Waskow's body . . . One soldier came and looked down, and he said out loud, "God damn it!"

That's all he said, and then he walked away.

Another one came, and he said, "God damn it to hell anyway!" . . .

Another man came. I think he was an officer . . . The man looked down into the dead captain's face and then spoke directly to him, as though he were alive, "I'm sorry, old man . . ."

Then the first man squatted down, and he reached down and took the captain's hand, and he sat there for a full five minutes holding the dead hand in his own and looking intently into the dead face. And he never uttered a sound all the time he sat there.

Finally he put the hand down. He reached over and gently straightened the points of the captain's shirt collar, and then he sort of rearranged the tattered edges of the uniform around the wound, and then he got up and walked away down the road in the moonlight, all alone.

The rest of us went back into the cowshed, leaving the five dead men lying in a line, end to end, in the shadow of the low stone wall. We lay down on the straw in the cowshed, and pretty soon we were all asleep.

The article, played on front pages across America, caught the public imagination and the death of Captain Waskow was retold in the Hollywood movie, *The Story of GI Joe*, and in the John Huston film, *The Battle of San Pietro*. On the night he wrote the piece, Pyle told his colleagues: "I've lost the touch. This stuff stinks. I just can't seem to get going again." He tossed the column to Whitehead. "The simplicity and beauty of that description brought tears to my eyes," Whitehead wrote. "This was the kind of writing all of us were striving for . . . 'If this is a sample from a guy who has lost his touch,' I said, 'then the rest of us had better go home.'" He told Pyle, "My God, Ernie, if you've lost your touch writing that story, I hope I can lose mine!"[31]

Pyle also spent time with American pilots. "I never heard an American pilot make a disparaging remark about a British flier," he wrote. "Our pilots said the Brits were cooler under fire than we were." He listened to RAF pilots talking to each other by radio and heard one call out: "I say, old chap, there is a Jerry on your tail." The imperiled pilot replied: "Quite so, quite so, thanks very much, old man." One American piloting a damaged dive bomber was "easy meat" for any German fighter as he headed for his base. Then he heard over his earphones a distinctly British voice saying, "Cheer up, chicken, we have you." Two Spitfires, one on either side, mothered him back to his home field.

In February 1944 Pyle learned that Raymond Clapper, his Scripps-Howard syndicate colleague and a distinguished Washington columnist and broad-caster, had been killed. Clapper, 52, was aboard a navy bomber in the Marshall Islands. The squadron commander, to give him a better view of an operation, flew in close and out of formation, colliding with another plane. Pyle paid tribute to his old friend in his column:

> Ray Clapper's passing hit us hard. He had many friends in the war theater ... We had known each other for 20 years. He was always generous and thoughtful of me. Time and again he went out of his way to do little things that would help me, and to say nice things about me in his column, and I cannot remember that I ever did one thing for him ... It made us wonder who would be next.[32]

* * *

Frank Gervasi of *Collier's* entered a cave in the Rapido River valley and saw:

> the most gruesome sight I had ever beheld. Under a crudely lettered sign that read PIECES lay several burlap bags containing the unidentified— and probably unidentifiable—arms, legs, hands and feet of Texans dismembered ... by enemy mines, shells and rockets. I had seen many wounded, but never before gunny sacks lumpy with the bloody *remains* of men ... The horror of the scene in that damp, murky, malodorous cave recurred in the nightmares that troubled me for several years after the war.

He eventually had to seek psychiatric help.

Censors suppressed his description of the scene and his comments on mismanagement of battle by Fifth Army command. Also, he was not allowed to say that some boats intended for use in crossing the river had no paddles, and not permitted "to describe the utter futility of the battle itself." During one battle, he and Hal Boyle came under machine-gun fire and Boyle was shaking as though he had been hit. "I snaked up to him as fast as I could, but he wasn't hurt; he was laughing. Before I could cuss him out for scaring me out of my wits, he chortled, 'It just occurred to me, Frank, that you and I are a bit too old for this sort of thing . . .'" Gervasi was four days short of his 36th birthday, Boyle 32.[33]

Tom Treanor was with the 34th Division when it began an attack across the Rapido. Afterward, he reflected on the nature of war reporting:

> The principal trouble with newspaper war stories is that they are true and still give a false impression of battle. Probably the hero story, more than any other, is responsible for this falsification through truth. Hero stories are insidious because they are true . . . But . . . a battle doesn't have the adventurous-hero feeling. It's too exhausting. There's no dash and devil-may-care feeling left in a man after he's been sleeping on the ground for weeks, soaked and frozen . . . He just isn't in a hero mood . . . So in a sense I always felt a little reluctant to write a hero story.

Treanor wrote that troops in the Rapido attack were caught in minefields and "crucified by mortar and machine-gun fire." But he suggested there may have been an excess of caution among the Americans. "There is still an inclination, even in the Army, to think of our soldiers not as soldiers but as American boys whose lives must be cherished. We become too cautious and in the end defeat our own purpose of saving those lives. Our actions, as Shakespeare put it, are sometimes 'sicklied o'er with the pale cast of thought.'"

Every few days Treanor had to break away from coverage and thumb a ride to press headquarters to file his stories. On one such trip, he expected to find a congratulatory cable from his newspaper on his exclusive coverage. There was none, so he sent a gentle reminder. "Their answer was to the effect, 'Didn't you know that two weeks ago we discontinued your column until you got to England?' "

"I didn't have the face to go back to the 34th Division and explain to the boys that, after all, I hadn't made them famous in every hamlet, village, town and city. I wired the [*Los Angeles*] *Times* for permission to come home and meanwhile went up to visit the beachhead, which seemed to be on the verge of falling apart." He referred to the beachhead at Anzio.[34]

On January 22, 1944, the Allies had attempted to leapfrog ahead of the Germans and begin a drive toward Rome by landing at Anzio, 33 miles away. It was a disaster, owing mainly to the fact that American Major General John

R. Lucas kept troops on the beaches until Germans arrived in force and pinned them down. The battle went on until June 5.

Whitehead was one of the first correspondents ashore, and he raced to a truck containing a radio for transmission of news copy. His arch rival, Packard, arrived at the same moment and they argued as to which would file first. Packard finally conceded and, after Whitehead's dispatch was sent, the radio broke down. So for 24 hours his was the only story from the beach.[35]

Gervasi headed for Anzio with General Clark aboard a PT boat, but a U.S. minesweeper misread the boat's signals and opened fire. "I was stupefied with fear; I could feel my hair thrusting upward under my helmet, and my voice stuck in my throat as I tried to cry out," Gervasi wrote. Five men were wounded and Gervasi was hit by shrapnel that failed to penetrate his thick clothing.[36]

British General Sir Harold Alexander, supreme Allied commander for the Mediterranean, was incensed by negative coverage of Anzio. On February 14, he met with correspondents and accused them of "blowing hot and cold" in their dispatches, thereby damaging morale at home and comforting the enemy. He referred to "pessimistic rubbish" in their reports and refused to continue allowing them use of military radio facilities for filing. A British correspondent responded indignantly, asking Alexander to give specific examples of "rubbish" reporting. He couldn't. But a brigadier general told the correspondents: "You don't get the radio back until you follow the line."

Homer Bigart took issue with Alexander in no uncertain terms. "If the stories blew hot and cold," he wrote, "that is exactly the way the battle ran . . . Basically the issue is this—shall the public receive accurate day-by-day reports of the changing fortunes of battle or shall we maintain an 'even tone,' speaking only vaguely of reverses." In a dispatch published March 26, he wrote that the invasion force was too small and the beachhead thinly defended. "To this observer it seems awfully late in the war to attempt so dangerous an operation without first securing such preponderance of strength that the outcome is never in doubt once the landings have been secured." A general in charge of beachhead operations told correspondents Alexander had never consulted him before giving vent to his anger. "I have since told him that I am certain no such stories came from the beachhead." Two days later the radio was restored.[37]

Pyle was among a dozen correspondents sharing a waterfront house with five officers and twelve enlisted men. One morning, American anti-aircraft guns started firing and a bomb blast threw Pyle into the middle of the room. Half of the window flew past. One huge explosion after another followed, and a wall blew in, burying Pyle's bed. Doors were ripped from hinges. On the floor below, the ceiling came down on sleeping men, but no one was killed and Pyle emerged with only a tiny cut on his right cheek. The Germans had dropped a stick of 500-pound bombs and some had hit within 30 feet of the house. Days later Pyle wanted to take his comb out of his shirt pocket; instead, he withdrew his handkerchief and starting combing his hair with it. "Me nervous?" he wrote. "I should say not."[38]

Lee McCardell of the *Baltimore Sun* wrote of the shelling at Anzio and told readers: "Don't get the idea we're brave. We're not. We're badly frightened and close to panic when a close barrage blows open latched shutters and jars. Creeping out [of cellars] by morning light, we thank God for having seen us through another night."[39]

Bigart had a close call when he took a day off. He went out in a rubber boat and a German plane appeared and began firing at him. Bullets hit the water all around but missed the frantically rowing Bigart.[40]

In May 1944, at Pyle's repeated urging, Congress passed a bill granting all U.S. soldiers 50 per cent extra pay for combat duty. It would always be known as "the Ernie Pyle bill."[41]

* * *

Christopher Buckley followed Canadian troops into Ortona on the Adriatic coast. In a cottage he found an old woman moaning and keening while the corpses of four children lay on the floor. Buckley soon found an ambulance to take care of her. In one house he found a handful of soldiers, old women and children around an old man who was dying. One woman produced a jeroboam of Marsala wine and filled soldiers' glasses. "The children clambered around the Canadian soldiers and clutched at them convulsively every time one of our antitank guns fired down the street," Buckley wrote. "Soon each one of us had a squirming, terrified child in his arms. And the old lady went on distributing Marsala."

From Ortona, he went across Italy to cover the battle for Cassino:

I used to drive up to an observation post on the road near Cervaro and gaze across the open meadows toward Cassino, remembering how Hannibal must have stood and pondered perhaps on this precise spot when Fabius had bottled up his troops in the valley below . . . I saw the defensive potentialities of the place, and I knew that it was going to provide us with the toughest obstacle we had yet encountered.

The Allied Command was convinced the Germans, despite assurances to the contrary, had occupied the Benedictine abbey on Monte Cassino, giving them a magnificent observation post. Thus in February the decision was made to bomb the abbey—a major mistake. The ruins provided the Germans an excellent defensive position for fending off attempts to capture the stronghold. Nearly 300 planes took part in the initial raid. "It was as though some vast malevolent giant had poured a sackful of rocks upon it, but essentially the building was still standing after four hours of pounding from the air," Buckley wrote. Then a formation of Mitchell bombers passed over, and flame and smoke obscured the abbey. When it became visible again, "its whole outline had changed. The west wall had totally collapsed, and the whole side of the building along a length of about a hundred yards had simply caved in."

Allied infantry attacked and was beaten back with heavy losses. To Buckley, the artillery bombardment preceding the infantry attack was "about as militarily significant as a display of fireworks." Alexander broke off the attack but on March 15 more than 500 planes took part in a raid to flatten the town of Cassino. Buckley wrote: "I remember no spectacle in war so gigantically one-sided. Above, the beautiful, arrogant, silver-gray monsters performing their mission with what looked from below like a spirit of utter detachment; below, the silent town, suffering all this in complete passivity . . . The men within the town must be very brave indeed."

Buckley expressed a reluctant admiration of the German First Parachute Division. "For sheer dogged fanaticism I know of no finer Division in the world. I wish it were not necessary for me to say that. I loathe their doctrines and the evil god which they serve, but their resolute courage in defense of that Golgotha leaves one reluctantly spellbound." He watched Allied tanks going in and wrote: "Almost none of our tank men came alive out of Cassino that week." He judged that the attack failed because the Allies committed fewer troops than were needed.

"A wave of total and overwhelming despair swept over me. One had to steel oneself to recall the shrill hysterical screeching of Hitler, Göring's brutally triumphant smile at Munich and all the obscene bestialities done in secret in the black night of a concentration camp. That was why they were dying in Cassino now." By the night of May 16, Germans began withdrawing. Buckley had left for England by then; he would be killed several years later while covering the Korean war when his Jeep hit a mine.[42]

Roderick Macdonald of the *Sydney Morning Herald* and Cyril Bewley, 39, of Britain's Allied Newspapers were killed when they went into a field and stepped on a mine. Pyle wrote of the Scots-born Macdonald, who died two days short of his 32nd birthday: "Among Americans he was the best-liked British correspondent I have ever known."[43]

Bigart and Kenneth Dixon of the AP were the first correspondents to enter the town on May 19. "Cassino is a bleak, gray, smoking ruin which, with a little sulphur added, would be more grim than a Calvinist conception of hell," Bigart wrote.[44] Price Day of the *Baltimore Sun* encountered an Italian boy selling kumquats, and farmers were in their fields again. "They stopped only when the armies fought through as other farmers stopped in the third century B.C. when Hannibal's polyglot army of Spaniards, Libyans, Carthaginians and Senegalese passed through here in his vain attempt to reach Rome from the south after his victory at Cannae," Day wrote.[45]

Peter Stursberg of the Canadian Broadcasting Corporation wrote of Monte Cassino:

> I have never seen such a grisly sight . . . There were the dead that had stormed and taken this fortress only yesterday. And there were the dead that had tried to take it months ago. I almost stumbled over a head that had almost mummified. It was not the sight of the dead . . . that turned our stomachs but the stench, a horror that I did not mention in my broadcast.[46]

Graham Hovey of INS wrote on February 15, 1944: "I wondered . . . if it was necessary to do this job. Then I . . . saw two giant red crosses on the ground marking army hospitals where broken soldiers were fighting for life after suffering at enemy hands in the fight for Cassino. Yes, I'm sure it was necessary to bomb the abbey."[47]

Near Valmontone, southeast of Rome, Eric Sevareid "walked into a veritable lake of stench":

> The bodies must have been dragged into the brush just off the road, but the hot sun was directly on them . . . I began to choke, and water streamed from my eyes . . . All my insides were convulsed, and I felt vomit in my throat. I was almost in a fainting condition . . . and I stayed sick for hours afterwards. The sight of death is nothing like its smell.[48]

* * *

The Germans decided not to fight for Rome, moving out to a defensive line further north. Daniel De Luce and Packard raced ahead of troops to try to get to Rome first, followed by the BBC's Denis Johnston, but they ran into a

German armored car. Beating a quick retreat, they berated an American general because his brigade was slow in moving up. The general sent some tanks forward and correspondents followed. But the first two tanks were knocked out by German artillery and the correspondents retreated.[49]

"There are many snipers," Price Day reported from the outskirts of Rome on June 4. "The crack of rifles and the squirt of German machine pistols sound every few minutes . . . We did not choose to be here. It was the roses that fooled us. As we came up the road in the dewy dawn, Italians lined along the road with great masses of rambler roses. From the cheers of the Italians we felt certain everything in front was clear."[50]

The Allies entered Rome on June 5. Along a main artery "jubilation gave way to frozen panic and sudden death," Bigart wrote. The Germans had sent a flak wagon—heavy anti-aircraft guns mounted on a half-track—into a column of American troops near the Bank of Italy. "We were within a few hundred yards of the Forum of Trajan at the end of the Via Nazionale when the flak wagon careened around a bend, its guns streaming red tracers into the throngs outside the Bank of Italy. I shall never forget that dreadful moment of panic." Correspondents leaped over an iron guard rail and ran into a department store. A Sherman tank disabled the flak wagon, leaving two Germans killed outright, a third dying and three taken prisoner.[51]

Denis Johnston, sitting beside the Colosseum after letting two colleagues enter Rome ahead of him, felt not the elation of victory but "melancholy, and a deep lassitude. I was sorry for my missed opportunities . . . and above all for not caring more than I did."

A day later, the Allies invaded Normandy and correspondents in Rome realized public interest in their dispatches would now be minimal. "All of a sudden, as good as unemployed, we went to the bar and had a vermouth," wrote Price Day. The BBC's Godfrey Talbot told colleagues: "Boys, we're on the back page now. They've landed in Normandy." Johnston was not dismayed. "Well, thank God for that!" he wrote. "Now we could take a few deep breaths and relax . . . Normandy was welcome to all the headlines."[52]

Winston Burdett got into Rome the night before liberation and drove around almost alone as sniper shots rang out. "He wrote one of the most dramatic and beautiful broadcasts I have ever read," wrote Sevareid. "It would have been one of the memorable essays of the war; but the operators at the Naples relay station, doubtless exhausted themselves, had not been monitoring us, so his words were lost."[53]

Herbert Matthews witnessed the lynching of Donato Carretta, deputy director of Rome's Regina Coeli prison, on September 18. A mob set out to lynch Pietro Caruso, the Rome police chief, who was to have been brought to trial that morning, but fell upon Carretta en route. Matthews commented that the mob "lynched an innocent man under conditions of the most sickening cowardice and atrocity. I was shocked and infuriated." His dispatch to the *New York Times* brought down upon him the wrath of many Italians, who thought Carretta deserved to die.[54]

Herbert Mitgang of *Stars and Stripes* was in Florence on August 31 and witnessed an exchange between an elderly British woman and a British captain. "I am a British subject," she told him. "The Germans have moved into my home in Fiesole and I'm afraid that they are going to steal my dishes and silverware. Would you please send a detachment of your men to safeguard my possessions?"

"Madam, I too am a British subject," he replied, "but I did not join his majesty's army in order to save your crockery. Good day."[55]

If that reads like a scene from the film *Tea with Mussolini*, consider this: the Marchesa Torigiani, formerly Lucy Davis of Worcester, Boston and Philadelphia, complained to Burdett of hardships she had to endure, with butter and coffee so expensive and as many as nine German officers in her salon at one time. The greatest outrage she suffered occurred when her chauffeur deserted to become a partisan leader. However, she assured Burdett that a British officer had given the man a good talking-to when she complained about him. "I'm taking him back on probation only," she said.[56]

Mitgang, who joined the *New York Times* after the war and founded its op-ed page, covered the all-black 92nd Infantry Division and asked a white captain about his men. "They're good at drilling because they've got natural-born rhythm, but I'm afraid they won't stand up in combat," he replied. Mitgang declined to use the comment.[57]

* * *

Like other women correspondents, Martha Gellhorn was barred by the Allied Command from covering fighting in Normandy, so she left England in July 1944 to report from Italy. She attached herself to the Carpathian Lancers, a Polish unit. They told her they did not believe Russia would relinquish their country after the war. "We talked of Russia and I tried to tell them that their fears must be wrong or there would be no peace in the world. But I am not a Pole; I belong to a large free country and I speak with the optimism of those who are forever safe." *Collier's* never published her piece, possibly because of the Poles' critical comments about Russia.[58]

On August 4 she was in Rome and, in a letter to a friend, described the uncovering of the graves of 335 hostages who had been murdered by Germans a year earlier in retaliation for a partisan attack that killed 32 men. The bodies had been buried in the Ardeatine caves south of Rome. "Yesterday I saw the worst thing I have ever seen in my life," she wrote:

> The smell was something utterly unimaginable and that garbage of human bodies, with nothing of human dignity left, was the most ghastly sight I have ever seen. A great pit full of decomposing bodies which had melted into each other, and shrunken. What a race are these Germans: considering that we have tried to exterminate the anopheles mosquito, I think we could most easily devote time to exterminating the German who brings surer and nastier death.

She was soon back in France.[59]

CHAPTER 13

D-DAY LANDINGS IN NORMANDY

The Allied invasion of France began on June 6, 1944, postponed by a day because of rough weather. Paratroopers dropped into Normandy in the early hours, followed by troops in gliders, then landings on the coast. The British and Canadians went ashore at beaches code-named Sword, Juno and Gold, while the Americans landed farther west at Omaha and Utah. By far the stiffest resistance occurred at Omaha, where Germans firing down from pillboxes killed more than 800 Americans. But by nightfall the beaches had been secured. At the end of the second day, 450,000 men had been deployed in the greatest invasion in history.

In the months leading up to D-Day, England was invaded—by a small army of correspondents eager to be on hand for this historic news story. "If the Army failed to get ashore on D-Day," Ernie Pyle wrote, "there would be enough American correspondents to force through a beachhead on their own." He estimated their number at 450. Wes Gallagher was among London-based correspondents asked by Army public relations to choose a relative handful to go ashore with the first invasion force. A. J. Liebling of the *New Yorker* never forgave him for omitting him from the list.[1]

In what could have proved a disastrous security breach, the AP mistakenly sent this flash on June 4: EISENHOWER HQ ANNOUNCES ALLIED LANDINGS IN FRANCE. The flash had been prepared in advance so the AP could try to be first with the news, and teletype operator Joan Ellis sent it in error. The AP quickly killed the report, but not before it had been broadcast in the U.S. At a New York Giants–Pittsburgh Pirates baseball game, play was halted for one minute so the crowd could pray for the success of the Allies. In

London, Joan Ellis collapsed. A colleague gave her a sedative and sent her home. Fortunately, the Germans did not take the report seriously.[2]

Danger aside, D-Day was fraught with frustration for correspondents. Because of delays in setting up communication facilities, few dispatches made it back to England on the day, and some simply disappeared. Gen. Omar Bradley, commander of Allied ground forces, further tightened censorship by decreeing that all quotes of general officers in 12th Army Group would have to be approved by him personally. As Col. Barney Oldfield, the chief public relations officer, noted, this made him the highest-ranking military censor of all time. Oldfield wrote that Bradley had an aversion to "talking generals," and an unsigned memo stated that Patton should never be quoted.[3]

Pyle wrote of the mood among correspondents who already had seen too much combat:

> In more pensive moments we conjectured on our chances of coming through alive. We felt our chances were not very good. Men like Don Whitehead and Clark Lee . . . began to get nerves. Frankly, I was the worst of the lot, and continued to be. I began having terrible periods of depression and often wild dreams, hideous dreams. All the time fear lay blackly deep upon our consciousness. It bore down on our hearts like an all-consuming weight.

But later he wrote, "My devastating sense of fear and depression disappeared when we approached the beachhead . . . The war was prosaic to me again." Onshore, he caught up with Whitehead and Jack Thompson, who had gone in on D-Day. Thompson told him: "You've never seen a beach like this before. Dead and wounded men were lying so thick you could hardly take a step. One officer was killed only two feet away from me." Whitehead remarked: "I don't know why I'm alive at all. It was really awful . . . After a while you didn't care whether you got hit or not." When the smoke and fire cleared, he helped bury German dead.[4]

Fifty years later, Thompson revisited the beach and recalled: "As we neared shore, German artillery bracketed our fragile steel box while machine-gun bullets ripped against our landing ramp and sides. This was enough for our coxswain . . . He shoved the motor into reverse and backed off." Col. George C. Taylor, commander of the 16th Infantry Regiment of the First Division, screamed: "Coxswain! Take us in! Regardless! My men are in there! Take us in!" The men came ashore with "gallons of blood drenching the cold sands beyond the sloping shingle ridge of pebbles against which massed soldiers huddled, in life and in death."[5]

Ten days after going ashore, Pyle wrote to a friend: "I haven't had too bad a time, and yet the thing is about to get me down . . . I'm so sick of living in misery and fright."[6]

As John MacVane's landing craft approached shore, buffeted by heavy waves and a cold wind, a young soldier next to him vomited. The wind whipped it across MacVane's face and he threw up. "I continued to be wet and sick and cold for most of the next four hours. The whole scene . . . could have been a study in gray by El Greco, weird streaks of black and gray, gray seas with frothing peaks." MacVane thought of Shakespeare:

> *Gentlemen in England, now abed*
> *Shall think themselves accursed they were not here . . .*

Feeling numb and tired, MacVane "wanted to trot across the sand and stones toward the bluff ahead of me, but I could hardly walk. The dead lay rolling in the incoming tide at the water's edge, and some still floated on the sea . . . I began digging a foxhole in the sandy bank . . . I had only one thought, to get as deep into the ground as I could."

He wrote several short dispatches and gave them to an Army public relations officer, who promised to make sure the Navy took them to England. None ever reached London. MacVane was unable to broadcast because all four military radios expected in his area had been sunk. The next night, he found a radio, but Army Signal Corps bureaucrats in London had been told to expect no broadcasts for three weeks, so they decided MacVane's was unauthorized and refused to transmit it to New York. Ashore only a few days, he broke an ankle jumping across a ditch and was sent back to London. Before going into hospital, he broadcast a 15-minute account of the invasion.[7]

The BBC's Robin Duff headed to Omaha Beach after it had been pounded by planes and naval guns. An American commander assured him: "Not even a rabbit could be left alive on those beaches."[8]

Vincent L. "Roi" Ottley, an African-American correspondent for the New York newspaper *PM* and *Liberty* magazine, arrived off the beachhead and, every once in a while, a leg, arm or torso would float past. He also witnessed German dive bombers coming down "with a roar sufficient to drive a man crazy" and strafing landing craft. "I make no bones about it—I was scared as hell." He interviewed German prisoners and reported they seemed "definitely without prejudice for Negroes, but this may have been a pose."[9]

Tommy Grandin of the Blue Network (later ABC) and his army press escort ran to the foot of the cliff overlooking Omaha Beach. German artillery opened up and they fell face down—into an open latrine. They had to remain there for a half hour. Then they hopped onto a boatload of wounded men as it shoved off for England.[10]

Holbrook Bradley, 28, of the *Baltimore Sun* went ashore the morning after D-Day. A Yale graduate, he had married Sarah Bergen, daughter of the newspaper's managing editor, but they separated in the spring of 1943 as he prepared to go to England. On the beach, he picked up a Walther .38 revolver from a dead German, carrying it until he left Europe in 1945.[11]

One of the first broadcasts to reach America came from a recording made by Charles Collingwood, his report enlivened by the sound of gunfire and exploding shells:

> We're standing here. It's an absolutely incredible and fantastic sight. I don't know whether it's possible to describe it to you or not. It is late in the afternoon, the sun is going down. The sea is choppy and the beach is lined with men and materials and, uh, guns, trucks, vehicles of all kinds. On either side of us there are pillars of smoke perhaps a mile, two miles away, which are rising from enemy shelling, and further back we can see the smoke and results of our own shelling . . . This place even smells like an invasion. It has a curious odor, which we always associate with modern war, it's a smell of oil, and high explosives and burning things.

The report was played over and over on CBS.[12]

A more dramatic report, hailed by the *New York World-Telegram* as "the greatest recording yet to come out of the war," was a pool broadcast that evening by George Hicks of the Blue Network. Standing on the deck of U.S.S. *Ancon* 8 miles off the coast, he began calmly: "You see the ships lying in all directions, just like black shadows on the gray sky . . . Now planes are going overhead . . . Heavy fire now just behind us . . . bombs bursting on the shore and along in the convoys." As darkness fell, German planes began attacking and Hicks maintained an even tone while the sound of planes, ships' air-raid sirens, exploding bombs and machine-gun fire brought the war vividly into living rooms across America. At times Hicks's voice became excited: "Here we go again as planes come over . . . Give it to 'em, boys! . . . Something is falling down through the sky. It may be a hit plane . . . Here they go . . . They got one! They got one!" Behind him, sailors could be heard cheering. Then, after a quiet recap, reporting no ships had been hit, Hicks signed off at 12:10 a.m., June 7.[13]

On the evening of D-Day, Richard Dimbleby was aboard a bomber flying over France and later described "long stretches of empty roads, shining with rain, deserted, dripping woods and damp fields—static, quiet—perhaps uncannily quiet, and possibly not to remain quiet." Three German soldiers ran across a road while a solitary French farmer was harrowing his field, "up and down behind the horses, looking nowhere but before him and at the soil."[14] George Blake, writing in the Glasgow *Evening Citizen*, said Dimbleby "brought back a picture of Normandy that I, for one, shall always count as one of the best bits of descriptive reporting in this war."[15]

Several days after the invasion, Andy Rooney arrived on Utah beach. "I waited to be raked with machine-gun fire but there were no German soldiers within two miles of where I was. My output as a reporter was small and the stories I wrote for the paper were petty. I was not experienced enough to understand that everything I saw was a story."[16]

* * *

The UP bureau in London had decided Walter Cronkite would remain in London and help write the lead story on the invasion. But at midnight June 5–6, a U.S. Air Force major arrived at his apartment. "Cronkite, you've drawn the straw to represent the Allied press on a very important mission," he said. "It will be dangerous. No guarantee you'll get back. But if you do, you'll have a great story." The major told him he could not inform his office of the mission. Cronkite accepted. He flew with a squadron of heavy bombers ordered to attack German artillery emplacements at a low level. But, as they approached, cloud cover forced them to fly back to England with bombs still armed.

The Germans soon unleashed V-1 rockets on London from bases in the Pas-de-Calais region. Cronkite saw one land in Bloomsbury and later read a communiqué that ascribed the explosion to a gas leak. Another V-1 bomb hit the Guards Chapel near Buckingham Palace, close to his apartment. He had just rung George, the building's ancient servant, for breakfast. Hall doors blew off, the plumbing broke and there was blinding dust. Then a knock on the door. George, holding a towel over a bleeding eye, said: "Did you ring, sir?"[17]

Richard L. Tobin of the *New York Herald-Tribune* was blown out of bed in London by a V-1 bomb that struck a hospital 350 yards away on June 16. It was his baptism of fire, and he was terrified. "I shall never forget its detonation . . . My heart was pounding, pounding . . . I had been frightened before, but not so frightened that my heart felt as though it would break through my breast. But it pounded that way tonight."

He was so shaken he had trouble putting on his clothes. Going out to investigate, he found half a dozen children in hospital maternity wards had been killed and a score of others lay in the rubble. Some nurses also were killed. One woman had been undergoing an appendectomy, but surgeons carried on working and, after completing the operation, moved her to another hospital. Later Tobin came even closer to a V-1 explosion as he waited in a car near an air base for a lift back to London. When the bomb engine cut out, he ran but was knocked off his feet and slammed against the side of a building when the bomb smashed into it.[18]

* * *

On the British and Canadian flank, Ross Munro of the Canadian Press news agency watched initial fighting from the deck of a ship. With information from shore flooding in over a wireless radio, Munro batted out his first dispatch, well ahead of those from correspondents who had gone ashore, and a destroyer returning to England carried it back, giving him a notable news beat. When shelling stopped, he walked into Bernières. "A girl handed me a crimson rose and there were tears of despair and joy in her eyes as she said: 'There is my home, over there. It is gone. It is ruined by the bombardment, but the Allies are here! The Canadians are in our village now, and the Boche has gone.'"

Munro was told German parachute landings could be expected that night:

> It was the jumpiest night I can remember and I lay in my slit trench . . . miserable with the cold and wondering why I was in this hole in Normandy waiting for some German to come out of the air and land in our orchard . . . Wild, unsettling thoughts raced through my mind and then I tried to be rational about it and put it down to inevitable D-Day nerves.

The paratroops did not come, but German bombers did. "I never got used to it and never would."

Munro tried to send dispatches back by landing craft or carrier pigeon, "but these perverse birds all seemed to fly toward the German lines. We had brought about 20 with us but I never heard of one getting back to its English loft." Soon he had a small wireless set and could send brief dispatches.[19] Reuters and INS also used carrier pigeons. Charles Lynch, a Canadian correspondent for Reuters, was dismayed as they flew toward German lines. "Traitors! Damned traitors!" he shouted after them. Other Reuters pigeons made it to a police station on the Isle of Wight fifty-six hours after D-Day. But Joseph Willicombe of INS was luckier: his pigeons arrived at the Ministry of Information in London within hours.[20]

John D'Arcy Dawson, shuttling between British and American battle-fronts, noted that the Americans had high-speed transmitters capable of sending 500 words a minute, while the British had more rudimentary sets that could send fewer than 70. British sets also broke down frequently. Some copy reached London by plane but sometimes was held up at Allied headquarters for six hours before reaching newspapers.

"It was heartbreaking to get good action stories and then have them delayed so long that when they arrived they were of little use." But he was more scathing about "a horde of untrained young American censors. For the greatest invasion in history the Press of the world was placed at the mercy of youngsters who did not even know the rudiments of their job . . . Heads were buried so deeply in the sand that even an ostrich would be suffocated . . . We flounder along in a morass of ignorance and inefficiency."[21]

Doon Campbell, 24, of Reuters, ineligible for military service because he was born without a left forearm and wore an artificial limb, landed on Sword with British Marine commandos. "It is a miracle that I'm alive to write this dispatch—that I've survived 24 hours on this beachhead bag of tricks," he wrote. "Much of my 24 hours have been spent flat on my face burrowing into sand or earth . . . The front is fluid, so fluid that I crouched for two hours in a ditch before realizing I was a good 100 yards ahead of the forward troops."[22]

Noel Monks stepped into water up to his chin, holding his typewriter above his head. Once ashore, he half crawled and half ran through shell fire to a house where twenty French people sheltered in the cellar. A wounded Army Film Unit man handed him film to go back to London, and Monks put it in a bag with his dispatches. The film was shown in London newsreel theaters two days later but his dispatches were lost.[23]

Moorehead went into Bayeux and a crowd of French people appeared, driving an old man in front of them. His shirt was torn off, there was blood running down his face and his eyes were wide with fright. The crowd beat and scratched him viciously, shouting "*Collaborateur.*" Then more victims were beaten in the square in front of the hotel.[24]

Robert Casey of the *Chicago Daily News* approached Ver-sur-Mer aboard a British ship. "We were in the middle of a congestion like Main Street in Christmas week and guns were popping off on all sides of us. We rode literally through masses of flame."

Casey was back in London when Hitler unleashed V-2 rocket attacks and he heard a motor cut out. "I could have sworn that it was squarely above me, though it was probably two or three blocks to the north. A few seconds later, fire squirted upward through the near distance . . . and the sky glowed red.

The pavement trembled underfoot, a sudden concussion pressed against my stomach and a snarling roar came back to us."

Bombs wrecked three buildings while Larry Rue of the *Chicago Tribune* was in them. Casey himself was blown out of five different hotels in a week. The casualty list from V-2 raids eventually reached more than 8,000 and several people Casey knew were killed.[25]

Phil Bucknell of *Stars and Stripes* became the first correspondent casualty of the invasion on June 6 when he parachuted with troops near St. Mère Église, landed hard and broke a leg. A paratrooper propped him against a tree and Bucknell pleaded not to be left behind. The paratrooper was adamant: "If I were you, I'd just stay here real quiet-like. If you make any noise, you may attract someone you won't want to see." Then he took off. Bucknell was later rescued by medics.

Bill Walton of *Time* parachuted onto a pear tree, "a rather good shock absorber." His 'chute harness slipped up around his neck and was about to strangle him when a sergeant cut the cords. "I fell like an overripe pear." Walton accompanied paratroops through a swamp, carrying his typewriter above his head. Most of the men crossed safely but some drowned.[26]

After Robert E. Reuben of Reuters landed with paratroops, he made his way to the beach, went aboard Maj. Gen. J. Lawton Collins's command ship and dictated to Collins's stenographer a report on the 101st Airborne Division's drop into France. His dispatch, sent by carrier pigeon, arrived at Dover. Collins asked Reuben if he had had any sleep and he shook his head. "Give him a batch of ham and eggs and let him have my bunk," the general instructed an assistant.[27]

Col. Barney Oldfield, a former newsman who directed press operations for the Allied Command, wrote that three women correspondents volunteered to make drops with the paratroops but few male reporters were interested. All who did agree to do so had to undergo paratroop training before D-Day. Larry LeSueur was one of them, but Oldfield wrote that LeSueur bowed out before training started, saying he had badly sprained his ankle when he fell off a curb. "Bob Landrey of *Life* used the same excuse," Oldfield wrote. None of the women were taken with the paratroops. LeSueur covered landings at Utah beach but none of his dispatches, which were to be sent back by ship, ever showed up. More than a week passed before he could begin broadcasting.[28]

Peter Paris, a soldier correspondent with the army's *Yank* magazine, went ashore with the infantry and was killed, becoming the first beach fatality among journalists. Ian Fyfe of the *Daily Mirror* was also killed when he went in aboard a glider.[29]

David Woodward of the *Manchester Guardian* flew into Normandy and was lightly wounded. He returned to England for treatment and wrote a graphic account of the operation, describing how on the evening of June 5, the troops, their faces blackened, headed off to an airfield "singing, incredible as it seems, the notes of the Horst Wessel song at the tops of their voices." The words were not the original German. In French villages, people gathered at windows and street corners to watch the paratroops landing. "They were a little shy and a little reserved for the most part." Woodward thought that was because they remembered a statement by Churchill that feint landings would take place, and if this was a feint they did not want to bring down German wrath upon them. "These considerations did not affect some of them, however. One elderly Frenchman walked into a cemetery where British wounded were being collected among grotesque examples of French funerary art and laid upon the stretcher of one of the most seriously wounded men a huge bunch of red roses."

The next morning, Woodward went to the beachhead. "The countryside looked empty, but it still looked like posters advertising summer holidays in Normandy." At a dressing station where wounded British and Germans were being treated, a German NCO was showing three British soldiers picture postcards of Paris he had brought from a recent visit. When Woodward returned to England with some of the glider pilots, they landed at a port that had received men evacuated from Dunkirk in 1940. One pilot remarked: "The people cheered us then, and now they just watch us go by. Do you suppose the English ever cheer their victories?"[30]

In London, Ed Murrow noted a similarly subdued atmosphere. "People go about their business calmly. There was no excitement. Walking along the streets of London, you almost wanted to shout at them and say, 'Don't you know that history is being made this day?' They realized it all right, but their emotions were under complete control."[31]

Molly Panter-Downes wrote along similar lines for the *New Yorker*: "The principal impression one got on the streets was that nobody was smiling . . . Everybody seemed to be existing wholly in a preoccupied silence of his own, a silence which had something almost frantic about it . . ." At a rail crossing, she observed trainloads of wounded passing by, while "waiting women, shopping baskets on their arms, don't know whether to wave or cheer or cry. Sometimes they do all three."[32]

Marshall Yarrow, a Canadian correspondent for Reuters, gave BBC listeners on June 11 an account of landing by glider on D-Day: "Great balls of fire started to stream through our glider as we circled to land . . . I was thrown to the floor as our glider smashed and jarred on the earth, slid across the field and crashed into a ditch. For a moment I lay half stunned, but the red-hot zip of machine-gun bullets an inch or two above my head revived me in a hurry."

He jumped into a ditch filled with smelly water. "I was—and I admit it—in a panic. My one desire was to get back home . . . I clung to the mud and prayed." Later in the day the paratroopers reached a little town that had been captured by Americans. "Those khaki uniforms were the loveliest sight I had ever seen. An old French woman came out with a bottle of cognac which I gulped for medicinal purposes only."[33]

* * *

Martha Gellhorn had entreated her husband, Ernest Hemingway, to leave their home in Cuba and join her on the war front, but he had resisted until D-Day approached. Then he showed up in England. As *Collier's* could have only one correspondent with the invasion force, his editors selected him. Several days before D-Day, he was in a car driven by a drunk that smashed into a water tank in London. His head struck the windshield and, for months afterward, he was tortured by headaches. Gellhorn arrived in England and burst out laughing when she saw him. He felt deeply hurt.[34]

Before she arrived, Hemingway had met Mary Welsh of *Time*, then married to Noel Monks, who was in Cairo at the time. Welsh heard that Monks was "squiring a pretty girl" there: "I decided not to worry about it." She was lunching with the budding novelist Irwin Shaw at a restaurant when she met Hemingway. After a relatively short time, he told her he wanted to marry her.[35]

On D-Day, Hemingway watched as the battleship *Texas* fired over troops at a tank barrier. "Those of our troops who were not wax-gray with seasickness were watching the *Texas* with looks of surprise and happiness. Under the steel helmets they looked like pikemen of the Middle Ages to whose aid in battle had suddenly come some strange and unbelievable monster." The big guns of the *Texas* "sounded as though they were throwing whole railway trains across the sky."

Hemingway could see infantry working their way up the bluff behind Omaha Beach, "moving slowly . . . like a tired pack train at the end of the day." Destroyers moved in almost to the beach to blast pillboxes and Hemingway saw "a piece of German about three feet long with an arm on it sail high up into the air . . . It reminded me of a scene in *Petroushka*."[36]

Gellhorn, like other women correspondents, continued to be denied the privilege of covering combat troops. She denounced the "doctrinaire bunch" of Army public relations officers who took this decision. "My job . . . was not to report the rear areas or the women's angle."

On D-Day Plus 1, she witnessed the arrival at a British port of a ship loaded with German prisoners and was surprised by the sight of "such unhealthy, undersized men," concluding that they must be from a labor battalion. "There was no sense in imagining the entire Wehrmacht would turn out to be five feet four and hangdog." One German asked her how much 100 francs was worth in English money. She found it difficult to reply because "it would mean explaining to the German that you can't get away with everything forever, and you can't expect to trade false inflation money, imposed on a defeated nation, for good money that free men have earned." She told him his money was worthless in Britain and he "seemed to feel cheated."

Days later she stowed away on a hospital ship so she could get a glimpse of Normandy. Just four doctors, six nurses and fourteen orderlies tended 400 wounded men, and they worked twenty-nine hours without a break until the ship reached England. "Only one soldier died on that ship and he had come aboard as a hopeless case."

When the ship reached Normandy, a water ambulance could not go inshore so Gellhorn and the medical personnel waded in to assemble the wounded in a landing craft until the ambulance could return. Everyone aboard the beached craft was German. A stretcher-bearer told her: "If anything hits this ship, dammit, they deserve it." Through the night the stretcher-bearer joked and toward morning, Gellhorn wrote, the two of them really began to enjoy themselves. "There is a point where you feel yourself so small and helpless in such an enormous, insane nightmare of a world, that you cease to give a hoot about anything and you renounce care and start laughing."

Two German planes were shot down and fell onto the beach to the right and left of them. Then the water ambulance returned and took the wounded to the ship. Most had not eaten for two days and were "a magnificent enduring bunch of men. Men smiled who were in such pain that all they really can have wanted to do was turn their heads away and cry, and men made jokes when they needed their strength just to survive." A badly wounded lieutenant realized that a German, also seriously wounded, lay in the bunk behind him. "I'd kill him if I could move," he told Gellhorn. When the ship reached England, Gellhorn was arrested by military police and sent to a nurses training camp. She wrote a memorable and moving article for *Collier's* about the ship experience.

On June 24, she sent a letter to a colonel in Allied public relations, complaining of the army's refusal to let women cover the war. She pointed out that nineteen women correspondents were accredited to Allied forces, six had

had war reporting experience and two—including herself—had been covering wars for seven years. "This curious condescending treatment is as ridiculous as it is undignified," she wrote. "Since I am helpless to fulfill my obligations here I wish to return to Italy where I always found the greatest cooperation for the Press." Soon after, she was in Italy.[37]

* * *

Lee Miller, a 37-year-old writer and photographer, was permitted to visit the 44th Evacuation Hospital in Normandy and filed a dispatch that *Vogue* published on August 2. She resented her heart softening involuntarily toward German wounded. "A group of Krauts we interviewed were astonished that we lived and worked in buzz-bombed London, and that the secret weapon was not ending the war for them." Born in Poughkeepsie, New York, Miller was "discovered" by Condé Nast in 1927, when she was 20 years old, as a prime beauty of her generation. She became a fashion model, protégée and lover of the artist Man Ray. When war broke out, she was living in Britain with Roland Penrose, an artist, historian, poet and the official biographer of Pablo Picasso.[38]

* * *

After the invasion, Ruth Cowan of the AP and Rita Bellingham of Reuters were assigned to the ship carrying General Patton, but he declared: "These women can't come aboard here." The Navy insisted on its right to decide who could come aboard its ships and the two women sailed to Normandy.

Before the war, Iris Carpenter, a slender, blue-eyed blonde, had been a film critic for the *Daily Express*, then switched to the *Daily Herald* to cover the Blitz. Denied permission to cover fighting in Europe, she went to work for the *Boston Globe*. At the time of D-Day, she was reporting for both newspapers, but her problems still had not ended. The British War Office said flatly of women war correspondents: "We will not tolerate them." But the Americans admitted that "certain phases of the war should be covered by women."

Carpenter, 38, a mother of two, had to settle for flying on D-Plus-Four to a new landing strip in France, where she saw African-American troops putting bodies in shrouds and carrying them to a cemetery. Later she followed troops into Cherbourg. Under the city's arsenal, the Germans had built a fortress city. Underground rooms were centrally heated, had hot and cold running water and electric light and were furnished with silk tapestries, fine rugs and expensive furniture. Carpenter wrote that the fortress contained enough food to keep the garrison for a year. Wardrobes were full of women's clothes, as officers and men were allowed to keep mistresses with them.

Before the German surrender, the commander gave a party, and Allied troops arrived to find tables littered with bottles of cognac, champagne and wines of priceless vintage. "There was a flagellation whip and bloodstains among the wine and food spatters on the tablecloth," Carpenter wrote. Across the road, the Pasteur Hospital contained 300 wounded German soldiers lying "in misery and filth beyond description. Every bed was soiled, every latrine choked." Behind the hospital were stacks of amputated limbs and mangled bodies. Allied nurses, doctors and orderlies hauled in water, cleaned the Germans and dressed their wounds. "When they had finished, the stench of death still hung so heavily you could almost reach a hand out and touch it."

When Carpenter returned to London, she faced what she termed a court martial. Military authorities complained she had violated orders not to leave the beachhead and had gone to Cherbourg without authorization. They threatened to take away her accreditation. She challenged their definition of beachhead, and how far inland it extended. Unable to give a specific answer, they backed down, and soon she was in Normandy again.[39]

* * *

On June 14, General de Gaulle arrived in France and proceeded to Bayeux, which he proclaimed the capital of Free France. Monks reported: "He walked through Bayeux like the Pied Piper . . . He strode along the cobbled roadway until hysterical French men and women halted him by throwing themselves at his feet. Others fought to kiss his hands, or just to touch him . . . Tears were streaming down his face. I saw them, and wept with him and the crowd."[40]

John D'Arcy Dawson was present when de Gaulle visited Isigny, a small town that had been reduced to rubble by Allied bombing. De Gaulle wept when he saw "the proud, unbroken spirit" of its people. NBC's W. W. Chaplin was present when de Gaulle made a speech in a liberated village. A mother in the crowd stood before a wheelbarrow containing the body of her child, killed in an Allied bombardment. A censor deleted this detail from Chaplin's report.[41]

* * *

Moorehead and Clifford witnessed the destruction of Villers-Bocage, southwest of Caen. After British tanks moved in, they were standing in the central square when Germans opened fire. They beat a retreat out of town. Moorehead reported that German snipers were deadly, "something new in our experience." The British called up bombers, which pasted the little town of 1,000 people, but the Germans had withdrawn, escaping serious losses. Bulldozers arrived and "it was like an archeological excavation into a lost world . . . The bombing accomplished nothing. One after another Normandy villages were obliterated like this."

Moorehead and Clifford saw Cherbourg burning. "Army horses were roaming about or lying dead among the dead cattle and the dead men," Moorehead wrote. "We must have seen a thousand dead cows in Normandy, perhaps two thousand, and one could never get used to that appalling sweet, sickly stench. There was only one thing worse, the sweet smell of dead men."

A Frenchman invited them into his café and opened champagne, Calvados and cognac while women were making omelettes. An American soldier appeared and said: "Get out of here quick. There's a German with a machine gun coming through the garden." The Frenchman ignored this warning and invited the soldier to come inside and take a glass. One of the women said to the correspondents: "You must have a little more omelette." And the man cried: "Vive la liberation!" The soldier banged at the door again. "He's getting over the garden wall. You better get out of here."

"Away, away!" roared the patron. "You are spoiling the lunch. These gentlemen are my guests." Moorehead wrote that he didn't remember the upshot of this incident, but after some confusion in the garden the meal went on peacefully.[42]

In the last stages of the battle for Cherbourg, an American tank was blown up and the crew emerging from it ran toward a street corner where Pyle had taken shelter. "Some of those fellows . . . knew me from my picture so I had to stop and talk," he explained.[43]

Richard McMillan of UP was in a field outside Cherbourg when a shell landed 30 yards away:

In a flash I knew I had been hit. I knew, too, the man on my left was dead. The young captain to my right came towards me on his hands and knees . . . He had a wound in his back the size of a pudding basin and I could see his spine. As he crawled towards me with appeal in his eyes, he mewed— yes, he mewed like a wounded cat.

McMillan found he could stand. A piece of shrapnel had entered his back, struck a bone and traveled alongside his spine to lodge in a muscle. A dog he had picked up and named Tilly was wounded, too, on her forehead. Later, in the battle for Caen, Tilly was killed when a tank ran over her.[44]

Dawson went into Cherbourg the day after its capture on June 26 and found it "a sad city of deserted streets, ankle-deep in broken glass." The Germans' last redoubt was the seaside Fort de Roule, and when American troops approached they shouted to the men inside to surrender. A white flag was pushed through an embrasure, followed by shots, screams and howls of anger. German officers had shot men who wished to surrender. The Americans blew open the doors with bazookas and most men surrendered. But some fought on for two days.[45]

After Cherbourg's capture, Lee McCardell of the *Baltimore Sun* was caustic about visiting celebrities at the front:

> Sightseers and visiting firemen and one-day journalistic wonders pour into the ice-cream front, usually arriving by upholstered plane. They wear neckties and sleep in pajamas and complain about the shortage of clean towels . . . They bring back German helmets as souvenirs and tell hair-raising tales about the shells they heard explode in the distance.[46]

On the seventh day of the invasion, Clark Lee rushed back to the beachhead from fighting around the Cotentin peninsula and was told Hank Gorrell of UP already had filed an exhaustive piece on it. Lee, who had left the AP for a higher salary at INS, looked at the clean-shaven and unfatigued Gorrell and expressed doubt he had even been in Cotentin. Gorrell explained that he got his story by interviewing wounded soldiers as they were evacuated. Lee, still angry, doubled up his fists but was dissuaded from attacking his competitor. Two photographers christened Gorrell "X-ray Eyes" because they said he had a habit of writing stories with datelines of towns the Allies had not yet quite reached.[47]

BBC correspondent Kent Stevenson was killed on June 22 when the Lancaster bomber on which he was flying over northwest Germany was shot down. He had joined the BBC three years earlier.[48]

* * *

When he entered Cherbourg, Roi Ottley reported that the American Red Cross was preparing to open a club for white soldiers only. Red Cross officials told him the army command had forced them to do so. The army, he reported, also allowed brothels to operate, and African-American soldiers "were assigned their *own*. Imagine!"

Ottley wrote of a black Frenchman, Antoine Montbrun from Martinique, who had been in a German prison camp but had been released after he pretended to be insane. On a Cherbourg street, as he was talking to three French girls, American soldiers knocked him down, kicked him and dragged the girls off. "The conduct of the American soldiers is disorderly, crude and domineering," Ottley commented.

Earlier, while he was in England awaiting the invasion, Ottley wrote: "The Negro troops are full of injustices done them by various army officers, even of threatened lynching by officers when they meet in pubs. Americans deeply resent what little freedom Negroes enjoy here." He also reported that at least 600 babies in Manchester had been born to British women with black soldiers as the fathers, and most of the babies had been abandoned on doorsteps of Red Cross clubs. Many of the women, he wrote, were married and their husbands were away on military duty. Africans resident in Manchester were raising money to build a home for the foundlings.

Ottley went on to report from Paris after its liberation. After the war he became a foreign correspondent for the *Pittsburgh Courier*, a black newspaper, covering Europe and the Middle East. Then he returned to the U.S. as a columnist for the *Chicago Defender*, another black newspaper, and the *Chicago Tribune*. He died of a heart attack in 1960, aged 54.[49]

CHAPTER 14

THE BATTLE FOR FRANCE

As the Allies pushed inland, major battles were fought at Caen, St. Lo and the Falaise pocket. All were reduced to rubble before the Germans were driven out. On August 15, American and Free French troops landed in southern France against relatively light opposition. Hitler ordered a strategic withdrawal from Normandy that day. The Germans suffered 240,000 casualties in Normandy, but a large part of their forces escaped entrapment at Falaise and retreated across the Seine. The way was now open to Paris.

Caen, 10 miles south of the Normandy coast, dates from the time of William the Conqueror, who is buried there. The Allies had expected to capture it on D-Day but the Germans held out until July 7. Bill Downs of CBS, one of the first correspondents into the city, wrote to his parents: "I get shelled or mortared frequently and have become adept at hitting the ground faster than it takes to blink an eye."[1]

Moorehead wrote:

We . . . came at once upon such a desolation that one could think only of the surface of the moon. Where three- and four-storey houses had been, there were now merely hollows in the ground . . . There were no longer streets or footpaths or any decided evidence that human beings had once been here and lived . . . This was the end of the world, the end of the war, the final expression of man's desire to destroy.[2]

Mark Watson of the *Baltimore Sun* mourned the loss of historic churches and the university. "The dreadful destruction to buildings of the most profound interest to architects, artists and antiquarians cannot be readily wiped from memory. Time will, perhaps, determine whether so much destruction was necessary."[3]

John D'Arcy Dawson wrote: "When I saw what we had done to a friendly people, I expected to be greeted with anger. Yet they scrambled from the ruins and greeted us with the Marsellaise." He thought the indiscriminate bombing of French cities was "wrong militarily and morally." Alan Wood, an Australian-born correspondent of the *Daily Express*, wrote: "You might think you were touring the ruins of ancient Rome, not of a city which was living two months ago." Lee McCardell of the *Baltimore Sun* was equally saddened by the destruction of a nearby village. "It must have been a pretty village . . . among its rolling hills and orchards. But now it makes you sick at heart to see it."[4]

Richard McMillan met a woman café-owner. When Caen was about to fall, she told him, SS troops went berserk, pillaging, shooting, robbing and raping. They came to her café and smashed it up. When her husband tried to stop them, one youth threw him to the floor and shot him in the thigh. He was taken to hospital but the SS dragged him from an operating table, put him against a wall outside and shot him repeatedly. After the liberation of Brussels, McMillan made a speech to townspeople in which he described this atrocity.

In a village near Caen, he saw three women hustled across a square by a young Frenchman threatening them with a revolver. They were a grandmother, daughter and granddaughter. The man took them to a barber shop and began to shave the granddaughter's hair, threatening to brand her with a swastika. He claimed all three had slept with German officers. McMillan urged him to hand the women over to proper authorities. A crowd gathered and agreed with him and the women were allowed to return home. "It made me sick to think that French people could be guilty of such brutality towards their own folk, their own womenfolk, without any real proof of guilt."[5]

In Courville, Dawson witnessed a similar incident. "The scene was revolting. Several of the women wept bitterly . . . Others took it with a defiant courage which compelled admiration . . . Women and men . . . roared with laughter at any signs of distress." He thought some girls whose heads were shaved were innocent and had been denounced by jealous neighbors. Iris Carpenter described another such scene in yet another village. After several girls' heads were shaved, they were driven around in a cart while one pleaded: "No more. It is enough. Please, oh, *please*, let it be enough." A teenage boy hurled manure at them.

Carpenter was also dismayed by the Allied Command's continued discrimination against women correspondents. Men had access to Jeeps and drivers,
and teletype and radio transmission of copy. Censors traveled with them
so they knew what was cut from their stories before they were filed. They were
briefed twice a day. None of that was available to women, mostly confined to
coverage of field hospitals. These were often nearer enemy lines than press
camps for men, and several women ventured through enemy lines without
realizing it. Carpenter came under strafing while heading toward a village
that, unknown to her, was still in German hands. "Why none of us ever got
killed, hurt or taken prisoner, no one will ever know." Articles written by
women were put in a press bag, flown to England and taken to the Ministry of
Information to be censored, then transmitted. Newspapers often got them four
days to a week after they were written. If flying weather was bad, it could be
longer.[6]

* * *

While the British and Canadians fought to dislodge Germans around Caen,
the Americans were trying to capture St. Lo, just below the Cotentin peninsula. Some American bombers were hit by anti-aircraft fire, and Ernie Pyle
saw one airman bail out, only to have his parachute caught on the tail of his
plane. "Men with binoculars could see him fighting to get loose until flames
swept over him, and then a tiny black dot fell through space, all alone."

A smoke line on the ground, intended to pinpoint targets, began drifting
back and the planes bombed their own troops. Pyle took cover in a wagon
shed. "Our ears drummed and rang. We could feel quick little waves of
concussion on the chest and in the eyes . . . Men went to pieces and had to be
sent back. And yet the company attacked on time." Within an hour troops
had advanced 800 yards. "The American soldier can be majestic when he
needs to be," Pyle wrote. A German shell struck 20 feet behind him, and he
was deaf in his right ear until the next day. He left a command post in a farmhouse just 10 minutes before it was hit by an armor-piercing shell. A man he
knew had a leg blown off.

Two soldiers spotted a wrecked British plane, upside down, and the pilot
lay on his back in the cockpit. The soldiers gave him a cigarette and Pyle
helped free him. He had lost track of time but knew the date he flew—eight
days earlier. His left leg was broken and punctured by an anti-aircraft burst,
and his back was terribly burned by gasoline. "In his correct Oxford accent he
even apologized for taking up our time to get him out."

After his experience at St. Lo, Pyle told a fellow correspondent: "I damn near had a war neurosis. About two weeks more and I'd have been in a hospital. I'd become so revolted, so nauseated by the sight of swell kids having their heads blown off, I'd lost track of the whole point of the war. I'd reached a point where I felt that no ideal was worth the death of one more man."[7]

Roi Ottley was in a foxhole nearby when Lt. Gen. Lesley J. McNair was killed by the American bombs. Curiously enough, he did not report it. "You don't write that sort of thing because people get the impression that you are laying it on thick." Presumably he referred to his own near escape from death.[8]

AP photographer George Bede Irvin, 33, was also killed by an American bomb during the St. Lo battle.[9]

Ross Munro reported that American planes dropped bombs on Canadian lines at Vaucelles, near Bayeux, and several nearby towns. "Bombs hurtled into our gun lines, into ammunition dumps and near troop concentrations. It filled me with terror to see this havoc even from a mile away."[10]

Carpenter and Ruth Cowan of the AP, while trying to thumb a ride to a hospital near Cherbourg, came under bombardment at St. Lo and had to take cover beside the wall of a jail. Under it lay the bodies of at least fifty French political prisoners. The Germans had chained them there to be killed by Allied bombing. Carpenter suffered a shattered eardrum and later had to be treated in a Paris hospital.[11]

Ira Wolfert of the North American Newspaper Alliance was inside an American farmhouse headquarters outside St. Lo when a German tank shell struck. "Dust flew up my nose with the force of gravel. The dust flew way high up into my head." In the next room, a captain was looking dazedly at the stump of a leg blown off. "The shock of the amputation had been so sudden that it had not yet reached his mind."[12]

Holbrook Bradley of the *Baltimore Sun*, covering the 29th Infantry Division, encountered a lieutenant who told him he was short of men. He asked if Bradley would like to fill in. "It might be interesting," the reporter replied. He wrote in his memoir that the idea intrigued him, as he had "never really tested myself in battle." By his own account, Bradley tested himself a number of times subsequently and must rank as one of the most egregious violators of the Geneva conventions forbidding correspondents from carrying weapons or engaging in battle.

The lieutenant gave him two grenades. Bradley and a group of soldiers went out through German lines to try to locate a headquarters suspected of resupplying Germans in St. Lo after dark. Crawling forward, he lost the grenades. Shortly afterward, the lieutenant in charge decided it was time to head back.

Returning to the battlefield at Vire, 25 miles south of St. Lo, Bradley again went armed. He claimed he had never come across a correspondent in a combat zone who didn't at least carry a pistol for self-defense. This must be weighed against other memoirs in which correspondents wrote of their unwillingness to carry arms, though some admitted having done so. Bradley took shelter in a wrecked house with American officers while artillery exchanges went on outside. He decided to join soldiers along a nearby hedgerow and was halfway across when he heard the sound of a mortar being dropped into a tube. It went off over his head and he felt as though someone had hit him with a baseball bat in the left thigh. His military escort examined his wound, swore and raced back to the farmhouse. A Jeep soon pulled up and drove Bradley to an aid station. He was transferred to England and spent two weeks in hospital before returning to the fighting.[13]

At St. Lo, Germans holding out in a chateau called for a truce and asked permission to send out all of the French still sheltering in the town. Lee Miller wrote: "A long stream of people came out into view . . . the injured and ill first, then old women with bundles and dazed eyes . . . couples with babies . . . boys, men shambling from shock—prim, snotty women, nuns in immaculate white and whores." The Germans had said they were sending out 600 people but twice that number appeared. "There were two collapsed girls who had been given morphine for hysteria, a woman with four babies . . . a tottering old couple with no shoes, an indignant dame in black taffeta who froze us with her ingratitude."

Afterward a German colonel holding out in a fort called Cité d'Aleth announced he would resist to the last man. Allied planes bombed the fort and Miller, 700 yards away, wrote: "Our house shuddered and stuff flew in the window—more bombs crashing, thundering, flashing—like Vesuvius—the smoke rolling away in a sloping trail." She took shelter in a German dugout and her heel ground into a detached hand. "I cursed the Germans for the sordid ugly destruction they had conjured up in this once beautiful town . . . I picked up the hand and hurled it across the street and ran back the way I'd come . . . Christ, it was awful."[14]

William Casey of the *Chicago Daily News* came into St. Lo after its capture. "Now it is flat, a pile of powder that could be shaken out of a sugar sifter, and of importance only as a classic example of destruction. I never felt any consciousness that people had lived there once, that these broken, windowless houses had ever been populated by anything but corpses."[15]

Hemingway appeared on August 3 just outside Villedieu-les-Poeles, southwest of St. Lo, and was told the infantry had bypassed a cellar full of SS men.

He armed himself and his driver, Pvt. Archie Pelkey, with grenades and went to the house, yelling down the cellar in French and German, demanding the men come out with their hands up. There was no reply, so they tossed down three grenades. Although it was unclear if Germans actually were in the cellar, Hemingway boasted later he had killed "plenty" of them.[16]

* * *

Back on the Caen front, the British and Canadians were engaged in a difficult battle as waist-high crops, hedgerows and orchard walls gave an advantage to the defenders. Alan Wood of the *Daily Express* wrote:

> In my experience, I know of nothing in this war which exceeds the bitterness and strain of the battle the British and Canadians are fighting here now, except the battles the Australians fought in New Guinea. The Germans are fighting with almost the same fanaticism as the Japanese, and they are digging in in the same way . . . There is the same feeling of fighting blind against an enemy you cannot see but who can see you.

The plight of Allied troops grew worse when British Lancaster bombers mistakenly targeted them on August 14. Wood, driving toward Falaise, wrote afterward: "It was one of the occasions where you either drive like hell out of it or stop and jump into a hole. We drove like hell out of it, and our luck held." When the bombing was over, the casualty count was not as high as many feared but tanks and transport were "badly smashed about."

With Allied troops in sight of Falaise, thousands of Germans began coming up the road to surrender. "In the woods you come across rabbits with their ears dropping down," Wood wrote. "I suppose it is some odd effect of bomb blast or bomb daze. And in one spot some horses, numbed and deaf to any human voice, wander vaguely round and round in circles." Falaise fell on August 17.[17]

Afterward Ross Munro looked out upon a road that was a long open grave of men, horses, vehicles, guns and equipment:

> The fetid stench of this mass of death filled the air and shocked the senses. I saw the remains of the massacre of an army, a sickening, terrible, inhuman gross spectacle . . . There were the men of the Reich who had stormed through Europe and had pillaged and looted and forced endless disorder and grief on the world . . . I hate the sight of death, but this afternoon I

liked it. I got an insensate pleasure out of this disaster to the men of the German Army . . . Misguided fools, dead in the mud, slime and blood of the ditches.

Munro went on to St. Lambert-sur-Dives. "The carnage eclipsed anything I had ever seen. Hundreds and hundreds of Germans had been cut down like wheat by a reaper . . . Bodies had to be cleared from the road to permit our transport to pass through."[18]

Dawson wrote:

The stench of battle lay over Normandy, where thousands of men, cattle and horses rotted under the sun. A journey through the battlefield was a nightmare of dead, tortured shapes; of cattle grossly swollen, of men lying blackly in ditches . . . fleshy gargoyles putrefying amidst the scene of wild flowers. No sonorous organ in a dim cathedral pealed out the grand chords of a requiem for them; only the softly waving grass and the menacing buzz of millions of lovely green-bronzed flies, feeding on this wreckage of humanity, sounded their passing . . . The smell of human corruption mingled with the scene of the wildflowers combined in a macabre perfume which blew softly and horribly against our bodies."[19]

After the battle, Moorehead informed *Daily Express* readers: "If I were to be allowed just one more dispatch from this front this would be it; not because the dispatch itself is important, but because we have begun to see the end of Germany here in this village of St. Lambert today." In one of his most descriptive war pieces, he told of the wholesale destruction of von Kluge's army:

This is the most awful sight that has come my way since the war began. It begins in the back streets of St. Lambert, where the German columns first came in range of the British fire. The horses stampeded. Not half a dozen, but perhaps 300 or more. They lashed down the fences and the hedges with their hooves, and dragged their carriages through the farmyards. Many galloped for the banks of the river Dives, and plunged headlong with all their trappings down the 12-foot banks into the stream below, which at once turned red with blood. Those animals that did not drown . . . or die in falling, kept plunging about among the broken gun-carriages, and trampled to death the Germans hiding under the bank. The drivers of the lorries panicked in the same way. As more and more shells kept ripping through the apple trees, they collided their vehicles one against the other, and with such force that some of the lighter cars were telescoped with their occupants inside.

At some places for stretches of 50 yards, vehicles, horses and men became jammed together in one struggling, shrieking mass. Engines and broken petrol tanks took fire, and the wounded pinned in the wreckage were suffocated, burned and lost. Those who were lucky enough to get out of the first collisions scrambled up the ditches and ran for cover across the open fields. They were picked off as they ran. One belt of shellfire fell on the Dives river bridge at the moment when two closely packed columns were converging upon it. Those vehicles and beasts and men on the center of the bridge were all pitchforked into space at once. But so many fell that soon the wreckage piled up level with the bridge itself and made a dam across the river.

At the far entrance to the bridge . . . a blockage was caused and took fire. Those in front apparently tried to struggle back. Those behind, being utterly bewildered, tried to push on. And so the whole column was wedged immovably until it was reduced to flames . . . The beaten Wehrmacht is a pitiable thing.[20]

Near Chartres on August 15, two German armored cars emerged from a side road and fired on a Jeep. Paul Holt of the *Daily Express* escaped, but William Makin of the *Daily Sketch* and the Kemsley Newspapers was shot in the stomach four times. Alexander Gault MacGowan, a Scottish-born correspondent of the *New York Sun*, was taken prisoner. They were driven 50 miles to Chalons-sur-Marne, where a German doctor removed two of the bullets in Makin's stomach. But when the Germans evacuated, he was left behind with nuns lacking medicines to care for him. Holt found him and moved him to a hospital where he died.[21]

On September 14, as MacGowan was being taken by train to Germany, he escaped. His guards were changing shifts at 2 a.m. and he took advantage of the blackout to jump out. The new guard shouted, the train halted and a fusillade of bullets "hit everything but me." After hiding in farm outhouses, he came upon a group of Maquis who returned him to American lines.[22]

On August 17, Bill Stringer, 27, an American correspondent for Reuters, and Acme News photographer Andy Lopez were in a Jeep driven by Pvt. Lawrence Sabin near Dreux, 60 miles west of Paris, when Germans fired an anti-aircraft gun. The shell hit Stringer over the heart and passed through his body. He died immediately. Lopez and Sabin, slightly wounded by shrapnel, jumped into a ditch and crawled for a half mile under shelling. After hiding in woods for thirty-six hours, they ran toward Allied lines and were stopped by the Maquis. One Frenchman, for no apparent reason, shot and killed Sabin.

Stringer and his wife Ann, University of Texas sweethearts who had married in their senior year, had both been UP correspondents but Stringer chafed at UP's reluctance to make him a war correspondent. So he joined Reuters and was sent to Europe in time for D-Day. Ann left UP for Reuters for the same reason and was waiting to sail to England when she got word of his death. She canceled her departure plans, and UP President Hugh Baillie persuaded her to return to UP with the promise of a war assignment. In November 1944, she sailed for England and would become one of UP's star correspondents.[23]

On August 22, Tom Treanor was killed at age 35 when his Jeep was crushed by an American tank northwest of Paris. Treanor was conscious when he was taken to a hospital but failed to realize the gravity of his injuries. "Hurry up and get this job over so I can file my story," he told the surgeons. Just six days earlier, Treanor had prepared a broadcast for NBC, telling with his usual whimsy that he had a dream of walking down the middle of the Champs Élysées in Paris, flowers under his feet and a thousand hands holding out glasses of champagne. He died three days before that dream could have become reality.[24]

* * *

Allied troops landed in southern France on August 15 and met relatively light opposition. Frank Gervasi of *Collier's* reported: "The French welcome was warm and dignified, utterly lacking in the wild acclamations we had known in Italy."

On a rainy day in Grenoble the reporters witnessed the public execution of six young men, ranging in age from 17 to 26, who had served in the pro-German Milice (militia). Carl Mydans wrote that the prisoners were "surrounded by an ocean of tossing faces all contorted with hatred and filling the air with screams and hoots of derision." The young men did not deny their guilt but said they had been misled by Vichy propaganda. They were tied to iron posts. "The boys' eyes darted and their bodies tensed," Mydans wrote. "They looked confused, and pitifully frightened . . ." He took a photograph of each one, and "a look of courage came into their faces." A firing squad cut them down and they slid to their knees. Small boys spat on the bodies.[25]

"As the last shot was fired, the terrible, savage cry arose again from the crowd," Eric Sevareid noted. "The scene was barbarous." Gervasi wrote:

Two or three of my colleagues were outraged by what they had witnessed and loudly denounced the executions as Maquis "drumhead justice." I found myself in total disagreement. The animalistic reaction of the mob had been as distasteful to me as it was to them, but . . . the men who died had actually fought fellow Frenchmen on behalf of the Nazis. Traitors had met the end traitors deserve.

On September 1 Sevareid invited three colleagues to join him in a search for Gertrude Stein, then 70. She and her companion Alice B. Toklas had left Paris after the French collapse and were known to be living north of Grenoble. En route, the correspondents met Col. William Perry of the 45th Infantry and Sevareid told him they were on their way to "liberate" Stein. "Forget it," he said. "Gertrude Stein's already been liberated—by damn near the whole United States Army. We spent the night in her home—in beds the Germans had slept in only a few nights ago." He said the two women lived in Culoz.

When they arrived, the correspondents apologized for having come dirty and unshaven. Stein replied: "Can you get it through your thick heads how wonderful it is to see American children?" She threw her arms around them. Sevareid, who had known her in Paris, wrote: "The iron-gray hair was still closely cropped, and the small eyes were as direct and searching as before, but she was just a trifle more bent, a trifle heavier in her walk."[26]

Price Day of the *Baltimore Sun* commented: "By staying she got one of the great stories of the war, for it was in the region of cloud-filled valleys and rugged peaks that the Maquis arose in their fullest strength." He reported that she kept a manuscript in illegible shorthand so it could not be deciphered if it fell into German hands.[27] On four occasions German officers had occupied part of her house but, according to Sevareid, they were "too stupid to realize they were dwelling with the enemy, and that the lady of the house was not only a Jewess but a famous writer whose works were on Goebbels's blacklist." She told him the Germans were "just unpleasant at times but never really bad while they were here . . ."

When the Germans began rounding up enemy aliens, the mayor conveniently forgot to tell them about Stein. He told her: "You are obviously too old for life in a concentration camp. You would not survive it, so why should I tell them?"

Stein ran low on money until a friend from Paris bought Cézanne's portrait of his mother from her. "With all the difficulties, the isolation from lifelong friends, these had been the happiest years of her life, she said, and one could only believe her," Sevareid wrote. She explained she had learned more about the French in her village than she had in thirty years of living in Paris.[28]

Gervasi reported she was full of questions about Hemingway, whom she obviously disliked, and Thornton Wilder and Carl Van Vechten, whom she equally adored. She asked him to get her manuscript to Bennet Cerf, the Random House publisher. Then she gave him a ballad she had written commemorating the correspondents' visit. On his return to New York, Gervasi offered the manuscript to *Collier's* but its editors were not interested. Cerf published it as *Wars I Have Seen*, to excellent reviews.[29]

When the correspondents left, their Army driver asked: "Who'n hell is that old battle ax?" They told him Gertrude Stein. The name meant nothing to him. Sevareid later drove Stein 40 miles to Voiron where he could get a broadcast connection to New York and let her speak to CBS listeners.[30] He also broadcast a thoughtful commentary about the nature of war and its effect on the men who fight it, and about the role of correspondents:

> Only the soldier really lives the war; the journalist does not. He may share the soldier's outward life and dangers, but he cannot share his inner life because the same moral compulsion does not bear on him . . . Their worlds are very far apart, for one is free—the other, a slave . . . We can tell you only of events, of what men do. We cannot really tell you how, or why, they do it. We can see, and tell you, that this war is brutalizing some among your sons, and yet ennobling others. We can tell you very little more. War happens inside a man. It happens to one man alone. It can never be communicated. That is the tragedy—and, perhaps, the blessing. A thousand ghastly wounds are really only one. A million martyred lives leave an empty place at only one family table. That is why, at bottom, people can let wars happen, and that is why nations survive them and carry on. And, I am sorry to say, that is also why, in a certain sense, you and your sons from the war will be forever strangers.[31]

Ed Kennedy of the AP went to Oradour-sur-Glane, where SS troops carried out one of their worst atrocities on June 10, 1944. Told that the Maquis had captured a German officer in Oradour-sur Vayres, 15 miles away, the SS mistakenly descended on Oradour-sur-Glane. Women and children were locked in a church and the men marched to barns and cut down by machine-gun fire, with the barns then set on fire. The Germans moved a chest of explosives into the church, set fuses and went out. Those not killed in the explosion were shot. Altogether, 642 people died. The corpses were burned.

"Although the ashes had been removed and the church cleaned," Kennedy wrote, "we found bits of flesh, bone and gristle, locks of children's hair, pieces of the toys they had held in their hands and little metal pieces from baby carriages."[32]

* * *

In northern France, Hemingway met two truckloads of Maquis troops on the road to Paris and they told him the German infantry had abandoned Rambouillet, west of the city, that morning. But they had felled trees to create a roadblock and planted forty mines among the tree trunks. In Rambouillet, Hemingway acquired arms from the Second Infantry and set up a command post at the Hotel du Grand Veneur with a group of ten French boys he had recruited. He later boasted to Mary Welsh that the First Division commander counted on him to carry out reconnaissance missions in forward areas and supplied him with arms and ammunition. When other correspondents arrived, he told them he and his French boys had defended Rambouillet against the Germans.[33]

"As there was no reason for any Germans to try to take Rambouillet, this sort of talk made something less than a sensation," commented John MacVane. He wrote that Hemingway would yell at one of his boys to "go out and check the Germans" on such and such a road. The boy would bow or salute, "Oui, mon colonel," and leap onto a bicycle.

MacVane wrote that Hemingway was draped in pistols and seemed like a small boy playing soldiers, "swaggering about and taking himself as seriously as though he were commanding the legions of Rome." He kept in his room an arsenal of grenades, mines, tommy guns and pistols.[34]

Bruce Grant of the *Chicago Times* confronted him. "Look, Hemingway, why don't you stop trying to be a chickenshit general with your chickenshit little army?" Grant said. "You're just making a chickenshit spectacle of yourself. Come on down to earth and act normal."

Hemingway grew red in the face and clenched his fist. MacVane and another reporter stepped between them, with Hemingway shouting: "I'll beat the bastard's brains in. He can't say that to me. I'll kill the bastard." Grant, 15 years older and 100 pounds lighter, sat down in the hotel garden, sipping cognac, and said: "Horseshit, Hemingway. Go play with your little soldier boys." Hemingway allowed himself to be led away.

His biographer, Carlos Baker, wrote that none of his dispatches from Normandy was completely accurate and some of it was factional, containing invented dialogue. Hemingway wrote a piece called "The General" and showed it to Charles Collingwood of CBS. "I told him it read to me like somebody's parody of Ernest Hemingway," Collingwood wrote. "I don't think he spoke to me again until we got to Paris."[35]

Hemingway's blatant violations of Geneva conventions led other correspondents to lodge a complaint with the American military, but that didn't end his use of firearms. The complaint prompted a formal investigation that will be discussed in Chapter 16.

CHAPTER 15

THE LIBERATION OF PARIS

*As the Germans withdrew from Paris, Eisenhower decreed that the Free French
Second Armored Division under Gen. Jacques Philippe Leclerc should have the
honor of being first into the city. They were followed by other Allied forces.
French citizens lined the streets to cheer and greet them even as a German
rearguard and collaborationists continued to wage losing street battles.*

In the journalistic race to be first into Paris, Don Whitehead headed the pack.
He and several other correspondents joined a military column at Longjumeau,
6 miles south of the capital, at 7 a.m. on August 25, 1944. One mile short of
their destination, a French captain insisted no one could enter Paris without a
written permit, warning three British reporters they would be shot if they
tried. An American colonel said the captain was acting without authority. "I
drove to the blockade and suddenly my Jeep lurched forward into the column
of troops," Whitehead wrote. "It was too late to turn back, so I kept going . . ."[1]

Andy Rooney of *Stars and Stripes* was halted along with Whitehead and
other correspondents by German tanks in the suburb of St. Cloud:

> The only smart reporter . . . was Whitehead, who asked a resident if he
> could use their phone. He called the U.S. Embassy in Paris and got from
> the caretaker a first-hand report on the situation . . . It never occurred to
> any of the rest of us that anything so normal as telephone service was avail-
> able and we wouldn't have thought to call the Embassy if we had.

The embassy had been closed since Germany declared war on the U.S., but a
French caretaker staff remained.[2]

The French column approached the Luxembourg Gardens and came under machine-gun fire from housetops and windows. French tanks fired back. Whitehead and his driver took cover behind a tank, bullets glancing off the pavement around them. "The crowds, which a few minutes before lined the streets, melted as if a blast from a furnace had hit a snowbank. Then the streets were terribly lonely and barren except for armor with guns clattering . . ."

Later Whitehead saw four women whose heads had been shaved, surrounded by jeering people who accused them of having "kept company" with Germans. A woman pointed to one bald woman and told Whitehead: "That woman had a husband in Germany as a prisoner. He escaped and returned to her, but she betrayed him to the Germans and he was shot."

Returning to Rambouillet, Whitehead encountered correspondents still waiting for word as to when they could move into Paris. "Where have you been, Don?" one asked. "Paris," he replied. He wrote a 1,600-word account of the capture of Paris, his biggest scoop of the war.[3]

Quentin Reynolds told of a gathering of correspondents at the Hotel Scribe in Paris toward the end of the war. They began discussing which correspondent had done the best job of reporting, then took a vote. Among the 23 present, 21 votes went to Whitehead.[4]

In another part of Paris on August 25, Rooney saw a crowd shave the heads of three women. "It was a form of lynching." Near the Arc de Triomphe, troops captured several German soldiers and one burly Frenchman swung a wine bottle over his head and brought it down with full force on the skull of a German. "There was a sickening thud. Blood spurted from the German's head and face as he sank to the ground. I'd never seen hatred so deep."

To his deep dismay, his story on the liberation of Paris never reached his newspaper. He gave a copy to a Piper Club pilot who was flying to Rennes, where *Stars and Stripes* was then being printed, but the pilot was forced down with engine trouble shortly after takeoff. "It was the single most disappointing event in my three years as a war correspondent. I hadn't paid off on the biggest story of my life."[5]

The night before the entry into Paris, Charles Collingwood wrote a detailed account of the liberation and filed it to London, with a hold-for-release warning at the top of his copy. Somehow CBS managed to overlook that and Richard Hottelet read Collingwood's dispatch on the air more than twelve hours before the Allies entered Paris. King George VI heard the report and went on the BBC to make a formal announcement. Ed Murrow defended Collingwood, saying the copy was clearly marked "hold for release" but that had been overlooked.[6]

En route to Paris, Richard McMillan passed a field filled with Allied spotter planes. One pilot, a lanky young Texan, exclaimed: "Just seen Paris! What's that oil derrick in the middle?" McMillan told him it was the Eiffel Tower. "So that's it!" the pilot replied. "I thought I was back in Texas!"[7]

Henry Wales of the *Chicago Tribune* drove toward Paris with Ann Stringer, one of the most beautiful of the women correspondents, and along the road GIs started waving and wolf-whistling. "You'd think these guys had never seen a Jeep before," Wales remarked.[8]

Ernie Pyle rode in with Hank Gorrell. "We all got kissed until we were literally red in the face, and I must say we enjoyed it," he wrote. "The fact that I hadn't shaved for days and was gray-bearded as well as bald-headed made no difference." Clark Lee of INS was on a hotel balcony with him, watching the celebrations, and quoted him as saying: "Anybody who doesn't sleep with a woman tonight is just an exhibitionist." But Pyle couldn't find the words to write of liberation. "I felt totally incapable of reporting it. It was so big I felt inadequate to touch it. I didn't know where to start or what to say. The words you put down about it sounded feeble to the point of asininity." He wrote to a soldier friend later: "When I was there I felt as though I were living in a whorehouse—not physically but spiritually." Within two days, he was preparing to return to the U.S. "I have had all I can take for a while," he told his readers. "All of a sudden it seemed to me that if I heard one more shot or saw one more dead man, I would go off my nut . . ." Later he wrote: "You begin to feel that you can't go on forever without being hit. I feel that I've used up all my chances. And I hate it . . . I don't want to be killed."

He finished his book, *Brave Men*, in a French orchard. "For me war has become a flat, black depression without highlights, a revulsion of the mind and an exhaustion of the spirit . . . The Pacific war may yet be long and bloody . . . It would be disastrous to approach it with easy hopes." Pyle returned home in September after his good friend, Gen. Omar Bradley, advised him: "Go home and stay home." At the time Hollywood was making a film based on his dispatches from Italy, with Burgess Meredith playing him in *The Story of GI Joe*.[9]

When Noel Monks entered Paris, he lost face with two less emotional colleagues "by blubbing like a child." At the Place de l'Opéra, German soldiers were frogmarched past his car. "Women were kicking them and clouting them over the head. Men were hitting them with their fists . . . I was sickened at this barbarous display."[10]

Moorehead was not among those caught up in the rapture of liberation:

I found it impossible to feel any of the expected things, either the sense of accomplishment or triumph, of release or joy, of reverence or excitement; not even any deep feeling of delight . . . One had been prepared and braced to plunge down to God-knows-what excesses of emotion and hysteria. But here was nothing, absolutely nothing. An utter ordinariness, an acceptance.

He came across military men who had hid out in Paris and had now taken a number of prisoners, mostly French snipers. A Dutchman told him they had court-martialed a dentist who used to give his patients away to the Gestapo. "We took evidence on his behalf before we shot him," the Dutchman said.[11]

Bill Walton of *Time* drove into Montmartre, where a girl climbed onto the hood of his Jeep and did the can-can, revealing that she wore no panties.[12]

William J. Casey saw smoke rising from the Hotel Crillon and the Ministry of Marine in the Place de la Concorde. Partisans were crouched behind every statue, pillar and wall and a large crowd watched as the French exchanged fire with Germans in the two buildings. One German officer "who looked like a general" lay dead in a gutter and other bodies were scattered in the street. The battle stopped suddenly and surviving officers came out of the hotel with hands clasped at the back of their necks. "Pompous, immaculate, and properly dressed for the occasion," Casey wrote. "They were stiff and erect as if they'd been cast for their parts by a Hollywood director." Mark Watson wrote: "It was the end of the Master Race in the City of Light and it did not look at all like the visions Hitler had painted."[13]

Casey, who had been in Paris when France surrendered in 1940, had been given a ticket for parking with lights on during a blackout on the night before he left. Now, in a light-hearted mood, he went to a police station to turn himself in. A lieutenant looked at the date on the ticket and declared that Casey would have to go before a judge and explain why he flouted the law. Casey began to wonder why he had thought there would be humor in the situation. Then he read a summons the lieutenant had written. The date for his appearance was fixed for August 28, 1999. "I can hardly wait," he wrote.[14]

John MacVane made it into Paris with Wright Bryan, managing editor of the *Atlanta Journal*. As they drove in, a civilian in a black homburg jumped onto their Jeep. MacVane ordered him off. The man grinned and said he was an American agent of the Office of Strategic Services and had been in Paris for three months preparing for the Allied entry. Eventually he jumped off with thanks.

MacVane parked near Notre Dame and shooting broke out. When it was over, he and Bryan were approached by two men wearing the uniforms of

Paris firemen. They were American fliers who had been shot down and had been hiding for a month with the Fire Department. MacVane went on to the Paris Préfecture and was offered the use of a radio to broadcast to America, but he declined with thanks. He had signed an agreement that all broadcasts would be passed through censorship.

After clearing a script with censors, he went to a clandestine radio station to broadcast, and was stunned to find studios crowded with British and American broadcasters. An American told him he had broadcast an hour earlier, and so had several others. The correspondents who had evaded censorship were given a sixty-day suspension of filing privileges, later reduced to thirty. They included Larry LeSueur, Jim McGlincy of UP and three British correspondents.[15]

Alan Wood, the *Daily Express* man, observed that the Parisian rich "have been having a fine time" during the occupation.

> There was plenty of food for those who could buy at black market prices, plenty to drink . . . Walk through the streets, the windows of all the shops still displaying every kind of luxury and finery, the girls as smart and colorfully dressed as ever, the strings of gay flags on every building, everything a contrast to drab, dirty, war-battered London, and you might think you were visiting Paris on some gala day of peace.[16]

* * *

At the Gare Montparnasse, Gen. Dietrich von Choltitz surrendered to General Leclerc and the only correspondent present was Harold Denny of the *New York Times*. Denny, who had returned to reporting after his capture in North Africa and internment in Germany, gave his story to a military public relations officer who took it back to the Hotel Scribe press center, where it was lost. Denny died less than a year later at age 56 and A. J. Liebling of the *New Yorker* speculated: "I've sometimes wondered how much the lost scoop had to do with it."

Alan Moorehead checked in at the Ritz, thinking for a moment he might liberate it. "It was a little galling to find Ernest Hemingway sitting in the dining room over a bottle of Heidsieck."[17] The next day Helen Kirkpatrick left a lunch with Hemingway, over his protests, to cover a victory parade and happened upon one of the great news stories of the liberation. She followed General de Gaulle down the Champs Élysées, then into Notre Dame Cathedral for a service of thanksgiving:

The general's car arrived on the dot of 4:15. As they stepped from the car, we stood at salute and at that very moment a revolver shot rang out. It seemed to come from behind one of Notre Dame's gargoyles. Within a split second a machine gun opened up from behind the Hotel de Ville. It sprayed the pavement at my feet.

De Gaulle and his entourage proceeded as though nothing had happened. Kirkpatrick went down the main aisle, a few feet behind the generals:

People were cowering behind pillars. Someone tried to pull me down . . . Suddenly an automatic opened up from behind us . . . Other shots rang out and I saw a man ducking behind a pillar above. Beside me FFI men [resistance fighters] and the police were shooting . . . Spontaneously, a crowd of widows and bereaved burst forth into the Te Deum as the generals stood bareheaded before the altar. For one flashing instant it seemed that a great massacre was bound to take place . . . I could only stand amazed at the coolness, imperturbability and apparent unconcern of French generals and civilians alike, who walked as though nothing had happened. General [Marie-Pierre] Koenig, smiling, leaned across and shook my hand . . .[18]

Koenig was the newly appointed military governor of Paris. Robert Reid of the BBC reported:

Well, that was one of the most dramatic scenes I've ever seen . . . General de Gaulle was trying to control the crowds rushing into the cathedral. He walked straight ahead in what appeared to me to be a hail of fire . . . But he went straight ahead without hesitation, his shoulders flung back, and walked right down the central aisle even while the bullets were pouring around him. It was the most extraordinary example of courage that I've ever seen.[19]

Moorehead watched a crowd hitting the ground outside the nearby Hôtel de Ville and wrote: "It was like a field of wheat suddenly struck by a strong gust of wind. Everyone with a gun began firing at housetops." The shooting stopped in the cathedral but outside it went on. "It was a last defiant gesture against society, the instinct of the gangster at bay."[20]

* * *

John D'Arcy Dawson arrived with a determination to track down British author P. G. Wodehouse, who had disgraced himself in England by making five broadcasts from Berlin after he was caught in the 1940 fall of Paris. He learned that Wodehouse was staying at the Bristol Hotel, but he was worried that his potential scoop might not see print; in his few days in Paris he had written more than ten stories but few reached London, either because of communications problems or censorship. Dawson decided to share his story with Ed Beattie of UP because Beattie was well plugged in with the U.S. Air Force. Beattie was working with another American correspondent, Ned Russell, and Dawson agreed to share with him also, provided he retained British rights to the story for 48 hours.

Wodehouse was not enthusiastic about talking to them until Dawson pointed out he was "rather in a jam" and the sooner he gave his side of the story, the better for him. Wodehouse asked what the British people thought of him. Dawson shocked him by replying that they regarded him as a traitor who should be tried and, if found guilty, hanged. Wodehouse explained that he was put in a concentration camp and certainly had made a great mistake in agreeing to broadcast. But at the time he thought it was a good thing as he could get in some digs at the Nazis.

Beattie took the copy to an airfield, where an Air Force friend flew it to London and delivered it to Allied Command headquarters. "The plan worked, and my papers had the biggest scoop which had come out of Paris," Dawson wrote.[21]

* * *

Iris Carpenter and about a dozen other women correspondents missed the liberation because they were kept under custody in a hotel in Rennes by a public relations officer. Only Helen Kirkpatrick, Ann Stringer and Lee Carson of INS managed to escape this humiliation, attaching themselves to the troops. The other women were allowed in days later.[22]

Hemingway now had both his wife and lover in Paris. Martha Gellhorn was there for *Collier's* and Mary Welsh flew from London to be with him. Years later Kirkpatrick told a reporter: "First, I'd hear from Marty [Gellhorn] what an impossible man Hemingway was to live with, and then Mary would be saying how impossible Marty was being."[23]

Welsh and Hemingway now agreed to marry and she went to Noel Monks to break the news. He was deeply wounded. In his war memoir he made no mention of Welsh; the wife with whom he had escaped from Paris in 1940 had even been written out of that adventure. She later found he had withdrawn nearly all the funds from their joint bank account, including almost £500 of her earnings. He also removed all the furnishings from their London apartment, including her small library with some signed first editions. They were divorced on August 31, 1945, and she married Hemingway in Cuba in March 1946.[24]

Forced to play second fiddle to Hemingway as the *Collier's* correspondent, Gellhorn went in search of stories that would be of little interest to him. She visited a German prison inside the dank network of tunnels at Ivry, one of the old fortifications of Paris. The Germans locked prisoners in the tunnels until they died or until they decided to torture or shoot them. The central tunnel was underwater in places. "There was no light. It was so cold that within 10 minutes we were shivering; in half an hour one's clothes were damp and one was cold to the bone."

At Romainville, a Paris fortification used as a German barracks, Gellhorn found a small structure with brick ovens. At first the Germans had used heat from the ovens to disinfect wool cloth. Then they had another idea:

> to put human beings into these boxes and literally burn them alive. It would take quite a while to die in those closed, metal-lined boxes. First your feet burned, and when in agony you tried to raise yourself, you reached for red-hot hooks . . . After you had been burned enough, you would be brought out, cared for, questioned and, if recalcitrant, put back into the box.

In other rooms, the Germans placed a metal cap on prisoners' heads and pumped electricity into their bodies. Small bathtubs were filled with ice-cold water, in which prisoners were held head down until their pulses indicated they were near death. Then a German doctor would work on them so they would live and be nearly drowned again.[25]

Marguerite Higgins, 24, a *New York Herald-Tribune* correspondent who had arrived in Europe shortly before D-Day, came into Paris and wrote in her journal: "I, war correspondent Higgins, am a colleague of war correspondent Ernest Hemingway. How about that?" Higgins soon acquired a reputation as a hard-nosed reporter whose aggressive manner offended some of her colleagues. Janet Flanner of the *New Yorker*, who sailed with her to England, wrote: "She looked so sweet and innocent. I immediately thought of Goldilocks and wanted to protect her. If I'd known then what I know now I'd have thrown her overboard." The daughter of an Irish immigrant and a Frenchwoman who had met in a World War I bomb shelter, she was born in Hong Kong and learned Chinese and French as a child. She also spoke German.

While her newspaper's veteran correspondent Russell Hill covered the main story, she concentrated on the grumbling of the French over shortages, the arrest of American soldiers running black market operations and trials of French collaborators. A compulsive hard worker, she filed up to 3,000 words daily and many of her dispatches made the front page. In her spare time, she wrote fashion articles for *Mademoiselle*.[26]

Lee Miller returned to old haunts in Paris, and reunions with artist friends. "Picasso and I fell into each other's arms and between laughter and tears and having my bottom pinched and my hair mussed we exchanged news about friends and their work, incoherently. He has painted prodigiously during these four years, never accepting anything from the Germans." Likewise she and Jean Cocteau fell into each other's arms. She had starred in his 1930 film, *The Blood of a Poet*. "I am still a big girl in spite of having lost 24 pounds these last two weeks, so I could lift him off his feet." She also ran into Maurice Chevalier, who had "the tact to remember me," then interviewed and photographed Colette.[27]

* * *

Soon many correspondents, after their most enjoyable respite from war, would head back to battlefields. Ed Beattie of UP, John M. Mecklin of the *Chicago Sun* and Wright Bryan, managing editor of the *Atlanta Journal*, drove toward the Loire River on September 12 to cover a carefully arranged surrender of 20,000 German troops to American forces. They fell into a trap at a German roadblock and were captured after their Jeep was fired upon. Bryan was shot in the leg and a German army doctor removed the bullet.

The prisoners were separated and started on their way to German prison camps, but the next day troops holding Mecklin came under fire and released him. Back at the Third Army press camp, other correspondents gave him brandy, questioned him closely and one by one left the tent where he was holding forth to file their stories. Mecklin waited until the next day to file and received a stinging message from the *Chicago Sun*, informing him he had been scooped on his own story by every major U.S. newspaper.

Beattie and Bryan would remain in German captivity until the closing days of the war. A news report reaching Atlanta said Bryan had been "wounded in the fleshy part of the leg." A colleague, Sam Dull, called Bryan's wife and said: "I wouldn't worry yet, Ellen, because we both know there ain't no fleshy part of Wright Bryan. They must have captured someone else."

Beattie, 34, was shuttled from one camp to another in France for nearly a month and given only starvation rations, then was transferred to Limburg, Germany, on October 7. The camp there contained thousands of prisoners and Beattie wrote that conditions were so bad the camp was notorious even among Germans. "I spent less than 40 hours at Limburg and saw only enough of the place to convince me that it was a disgrace to the German army." He was transferred to a camp near Berlin and learned that Wright Bryan was in an American officers' camp near Poznan, Poland, still suffering from his wound.

On January 25, Beattie was transferred again, this time to a camp holding 17,000 men near Luckenwalde, south of Berlin. With the Red Army approaching on April 20, the guards deserted, handing over the camp to prisoners. On April 22, the Russians arrived. Prisoners and slave laborers flooded into Luckenwalde and went on a looting spree. "The Russians are more direct, more brutal and more thorough about looting," Beattie wrote. "They loot from everyone, including their friends. They like loot."

The camp population rose, with French and Italian prisoners and slave laborers coming in with carloads of loot. "They are a grafting, unscrupulous, unruly mob." On May 3, Beattie decided to strike out the next day toward Wittemberg to join American forces. But that evening Robert Vermillion of UP arrived in a Jeep to take him out. They drove to Magdeburg and flew to Paris, arriving on May 4, 1945.[28]

CHAPTER 16

THE WESTERN ALLIES DRIVE
TOWARD GERMANY

The Germans were in retreat, but the Allies suffered two major setbacks before establishing themselves firmly on Reich territory. The first was in the Netherlands in September 1944 when three airborne divisions landed near the German border to try to seize river and canal crossings and the Rhine bridge at Arnhem. The operation code-named Market Garden ended in failure and the withdrawal of those troops not taken prisoner. In December, Hitler surprised the Allies with an offensive in the Ardennes forest of Belgium, aimed at reaching Antwerp and splitting the Allied front. The Germans achieved an early break-through but the Battle of the Bulge, as it was called, ended in German defeat after clearing weather allowed Allied planes to wreak havoc among enemy tanks.

After the liberation of Paris, it was Brussels's turn on September 3. "I entered Brussels . . . and was immediately engulfed by a roaring crowd which surged over us in a tidal wave of joyful humanity," wrote John D'Arcy Dawson.

> I thought Paris could not be improved upon, but there was a quality about this welcome to Brussels which gripped the heart by its burning sincerity and thankfulness . . . I was kissed by old and young, by men and women . . . An old Jew with a long, grizzled beard hobbled up to me and, putting his arms round my neck, kissed me fervently on both cheeks, the tears coursing down his own.

People began singing the Belgian national anthem and "Tipperary", "which I am sure all Belgians thought was the British national anthem."[1]

Bill Downs reported: "I have been kissed so often that I almost wear a permanent blush of lipstick. I have refused enough wine to float a battleship. Never have I seen such joy."[2] Moorehead agreed. "Mad with excitement, the million people of Brussels rushed out into the open, screaming and shouting and waving flags . . . At one moment women would be spitting and kicking at the German prisoners; the next they would rush at the British soldiers with bottles of wine and cakes and flowers."

Correspondents checked into the Metropole Hotel and a British Army major charged with getting their dispatches to a censor and transmitter far behind the front had an extraordinary experience. Landing in a Piper Cub on a racecourse, he and the pilot came under crossfire. Civilians on bicycles took them to a tram shed in the city center. The director of trams, in a bowler hat, drove them to the hotel, speeding through districts still held by Germans. Having collected the dispatches, the major and his pilot took off under fire. They ran out of fuel before reaching their destination, but the plane landed safely and the intrepid major found another aircraft, flew to a filing point and saw that the dispatches were transmitted to London and New York.

Moorehead reported that German prisoners, Belgian traitors and the mistresses of Germans were put in cages at the Antwerp zoo. A Belgian officer explained that the Germans would be turned over to the British and the collaborators "will be shot this evening after a fair trial."[3]

* * *

In London, Walter Cronkite, summoned to press headquarters, was surprised to find Stanley Woodward, a star sports reporter for the *New York Herald-Tribune*, on hand. Woodward had been pleading for an overseas assignment and finally had one. But the overaged, overweight Woodward had come dressed for combat coverage in a khaki jacket, pink trousers and Oxford shoes. At division headquarters, he disappeared and Cronkite assumed the military had discouraged him from coming along.

Cronkite's glider landed without incident in a Dutch potato patch, then did a half flip, and his helmet flew off. He grabbed a helmet and slapped it on. Amid gunfire, he ran toward a drainage ditch, with several men following. One shouted: "Hey, lieutenant, are you sure we're going in the right direction?" Cronkite shouted back that he wasn't a lieutenant, he was a war correspondent. "With a full GI vocabulary of unrepeatable words, he advised me, rather strongly, that I was wearing a helmet with an officer's big white stripe down its back."

He was surprised to come upon Woodward, sitting on the edge of a ditch and holding his head in anguish. He had passed out from booze at the head-quarters bar and fellow drinkers had put him in a uniform several sizes too small and loaded him into a glider. "Nobody told me that it was going to be like this," he mumbled. His trousers wouldn't close at the fly and were held together by rope at the waist, and he had split the jacket at the shoulders. "Stan turned out to be a good sport and one terrific correspondent in the few days he was at the front," Cronkite wrote.

In Eindhoven a celebrating populace turned out to cheer them. During a German bombing attack, Downs and Cronkite became separated and Cronkite could not find his old friend. He began composing in his mind a letter to Downs's family about his death, then hitched a ride to Brussels to file. In the hotel bar was Downs, immaculate in a dress uniform. "My emotions seesawed from delight at his survival to anger," Cronkite wrote. Downs excused himself by saying he had feared the bombing would be followed by a ground attack so he fled. Later, back in the Netherlands, the two men ran into small arms and mortar fire and took refuge in a ditch. "Hey, just remember, Cronkite," Downs yelled. "These are the good old days."[4]

While Cronkite found Eindhoven welcoming, Dawson did not:

Eindhoven was more pro-German than pro-Allied. When the British turned the Germans out, the first thing the Dutch Church did was to issue an order that Dutch girls must not go about with British soldiers, as they wished to preserve the morals of the population. Such an insult to British troops had never been made in any other country through which we passed . . . The Dutch in this area . . . were sullen, suspicious and appeared to prefer Germans to British . . . In frontier towns many Dutch openly expressed the hope that the Germans would win, and women particularly appeared to favor the Germans.[5]

Frank Gillard broadcast an optimistic report to the BBC on September 19, telling listeners that British tanks were only 7 miles from Germany:

It's an incredible achievement; certainly one of the outstanding operations of the whole war. And now what is the result? The result is that the airborne and the Second Army troops between them have almost cut the whole of Holland south of the Rhine clean in two. Once we reach Nijmegen every German west of our new position will have to fight his way through our lines to get back to Germany, or somehow get across the river to the north.

On September 27, his optimism undimmed, he described the battle for Arnhem: "The Germans may try to crow, but looking at the picture as a whole the battle for Holland has so far gone very decidedly in our favor, and the glory of the men who fought this first battle of Arnhem against such odds will last forever."

That same day the British began a withdrawal and Stanley Maxted of the BBC reported:

After about 200 yards of silent trekking we knew we were among the enemy. It was difficult not to throw yourself flat when machine-gun tracers skinned your head or the scream of a shell or mortar bomb sounded very close . . . I felt as naked as if I were in Piccadilly Circus in my pyjamas because of the glow from fires across the river. The machine-gun and general bombardment had never let up.

He joined troops who crossed the Rhine by boat to get away.

The British military asked the BBC's Guy Byam, as a noncombatant, to contact the enemy to arrange evacuation of their wounded. Byam approached with a Red Cross flag and an SS lieutenant told him he was his prisoner, but he managed to get away and swam across the Rhine while Germans were machine-gunning those waiting for boats. He went on to praise beleaguered British airborne troops. "And how they fought! Their courage and their devotion are surely among the finest in the annals of the British race."[6]

Moorehead wrote of the despair that descended on correspondents: "We had lost our kit, we were cut off and consequently our messages were not getting through. We were cold and wet and dirty. One of our number had collapsed with malaria . . . Emotionally and physically we were fed up."[7]

Alan Wood volunteered to be dropped at Arnhem. *Daily Express* editor Arthur Christiansen, in his memoir, wrote: "Wood was a rangy, difficult sourpuss, a man with a permanent load of grievances, chief of which was that I did not pay him enough." Christiansen was surprised to get a radio message from the battlefield, which read: "How about a rise now, Mister Christiansen." When Wood returned to England, Christiansen gave him a raise, a long holiday and a four-day week. "But he never recovered from the ordeal of Arnhem and many years after the war he committed suicide." From the battlefield, Wood had also sent this message: "If ever you meet a man who was at Arnhem, buy him a drink." Christiansen wrote: "I salute the memory of this brave, awkward man."[8]

Jack Smyth, an Irish-born correspondent for Reuters, took part in the parachute drop at Arnhem. Most of the force he was covering was wiped out and he was among the injured and captured. For seventeen days the Gestapo tortured and interrogated him, threatening him with death. Nine months later, he came out of a prison camp and a friend quoted him in these terms: "Jaysus, they beat the shit out of me. There was I, in British Army officer's uniform, telling 'em I was a neutral and demanding to see the nearest Irish ambassador. Well, they were having none of that." Smyth went on to cover war in the Pacific but his postwar life was brief. On a stormy night in 1956, his car ran into the River Liffey in Ireland, drowning him and his wife.[9]

On September 28, 1944, Richard McMillan described in a long UP dispatch the rescue of survivors of the Arnhem battle:

> Struggling through a hurricane barrage of fire from 88mm guns, tank cannon and machine guns, the last survivors of the noble band of British Airborne troops who held the Arnhem bridgehead for nine days were ferried over to our lines . . . I saw the tragic but heroic cavalcade of bloody, mudstained, exhausted, hungry and bearded men flood up from the river bank into our lines after going through 230 hours of hell. Many were stretcher cases. Many were wrapped in blankets. Some hobbled with sticks. All were so completely exhausted that they could hardly keep their eyes open. They were beaten in body, but not in spirit. "Let us get back again; give us a few tanks and we will finish the job," they said.[10]

Martha Gellhorn went into Nijmegen even though she lacked accreditation. A military police officer stopped her and, finding she had no papers, suspected her of being a spy. He took her to Gen. James Gavin, his commander. Gavin laughed when he heard her story and told her that, if she was foolish enough to be there, he would pretend he had never seen her. His indulgence evidently owed something to her physical attractions. Over the next few months, he tried to find her again, and caught up with her in Paris. They started an affair.[11]

* * *

With the Luftwaffe now largely ineffective, or committed to the Russian front, the air war against Germany intensified. Richard Dimbleby was aboard a Lancaster bomber over Duisburg, a steel-making town in the Ruhr, and said in a broadcast:

> There must be men charged with the defense of the Reich whose hearts tonight are filled with dread and despair . . . The RAF has delivered its

greatest single attack against a German industrial target since the start of the war—more than a thousand heavy bombers, more than 4,500 tons of bombs—and it did it, this morning, in broad daylight . . . Duisburg lay underneath the shroud; and shroud, I think, is the right word.

The Americans drove toward the historic German city of Aachen, near the border with the Netherlands. Known in French and earlier in history as Aix-la-Chapelle, it had been the residence of Charlemagne and the city in which German kings were crowned. It took five weeks of pounding by bombs and ground assaults before the Americans were able to occupy its ruins. George Mucha, a Czech-born correspondent, described for the BBC on October 17 the capture of one group of Germans:

The doors opened . . . and out came the drabbest, filthiest inhabitants of the underworld I have ever seen. They came stumbling into the light, dazed. Then, catching a breath of fresh air, they started to jabber, push, scream and curse. Some rushed up to me brandishing their fists. "Where have you been so long?" they shouted. "Why don't you deliver us sooner from these devils?" It was a sight to stun you. There were the people of a German town . . . and they were weeping with hysterical joy amid the smoldering ruins of their homes . . . These people were all green with hate for the Nazis. It was no trick . . . It was the breakdown of a nation after having played the wrong cards for five years.[12]

Lee Miller was repulsed by the "arrogant and spoiled" people of Aachen.

The people lived in cellars and vaults, but wore fur coats, silk stockings and fiercely ugly hats. It was the crossroads of the looting of France . . . The "city of cathedrals and kings" had degenerated into a squalid desolation with a prideless population who hoarded selfishly, cheated in food queues and had more money than objects to buy.[13]

Three American correspondents took a shortcut through the town on the night of October 19. Engineers had marked the location of mines, but their driver hit a Teller mine. David Lardner, 25, of the *New Yorker*, son of the famed short-story writer Ring Lardner, was killed. Russell Hill suffered a broken arm and Richard Tregaskis, who had survived being shot in the head in Italy 11 months earlier, was wounded again. Lardner left a wife and two young children. Two years later his widow Frances married his brother Ring

Lardner Jr. Tregaskis was dogged by bad luck that continued after the war. In 1973, at age 56, he drowned while swimming near his home in Hawaii.[14]

Iris Carpenter, now fully accredited by the American First Army, took over INS coverage from Tregaskis as well as reporting for her usual two newspapers. Col. Flynn Andrews, press camp commander for the First Army, had a more enlightened view of women correspondents than some of his colleagues. "They can go wherever their reporter's conscience drives them—same as the men do—and if they get a beat on the story and scoop the pants off the men, it's all right with me," he told Carpenter.[15]

* * *

On November 28, Price Day stumbled upon what had been a German concentration camp, Natzweiler-Struthof. It was in the Vosges mountains southwest of Strasbourg and had housed mainly resistance fighters. The camp was evacuated two months before Day arrived and remaining prisoners sent on a death march to Dachau. A German laborer told Day that up to 6,000 people had been shot there in the last three years. On arrival, prisoners were forced to crawl through a three-foot steel door into unheated cubicles measuring four by four feet. Then, as they were ordered down steps to the crematorium, they were shot in the back of the head.[16]

In late 1944 the AP's Joseph Morton joined American Office of Strategic Services agents who went into Slovakia to try to find Allied prisoners of war. They were captured and it was not until July 1945 that another AP correspondent learned all had been executed at the Mauthausen concentration camp near Linz, Austria, on January 24. Morton was the only correspondent executed by the Axis powers during the war.[17]

* * *

The German offensive in the Ardennes was launched on December 16, 1944. The previous afternoon Montgomery had asserted that the Germans "cannot stage offensive operations" any more. But Mark Watson, the astute military writer of the *Baltimore Sun* who was to win a Pulitzer Prize for his war coverage, had earlier pointed to the German "reserves of tanks and infantry divisions," giving them the potential to stage a "really grand-scale counterattack" in a sector where the Allies were not strong.

He blamed the Allied Command for not detecting the strength of the German forces assembled, not recognizing the imminence of attack, not putting a sufficient defensive force in place and not protecting roads and mountain passes with enough anti-tank artillery, roadblocks or mines. He accused the Allied Command of spinning "fantastic clouds of optimism" while "concealing the grave aspects of the battle." Watson had been on the staff of Gen. John Pershing, the American commander in Europe in World War I. When Watson died after the war, the Pentagon press room in Washington was named for him.

His *Baltimore Sun* colleague Lee McCardell wrote of freezing cold in the Ardennes, with inadequately clad Allied troops sleeping in foxholes, their fingers numb and toes frostbitten. "I never return to my warm, lighted quarters at night without a deep sense of my own unworthiness and shame."[18]

On the fourth day of the German offensive, Lee Carson of INS reported that Germans had ambushed a supply and medical convoy near Saint-Vith, Belgium, disarmed GIs, marched them into a field and shot them dead. Carson also reported on a much larger massacre, involving field artillery and supply troops and medics near Malmedy. They were disarmed, robbed, marched to a clearing and searched again. Then the Germans opened fire. Eighty-six Americans were killed and four survived.[19]

On Christmas Eve, correspondents at Chaudfontaine discussed going to the front. Jack Frankish of UP said: "I don't think I'm going out tomorrow unless the picture clears. I've got a wife and a couple of kids. I guess I owe something to them as well as my paper." Carson replied: "Okay, that's right, if it's the way you feel. I guess that I'll go out, though. I figure if you got it comin', you get it." That night she returned to find the camp had been attacked by dive bombers and Frankish was dead. He was 30 years old.[20]

Cronkite joined the Third Army press camp and was caught briefly in a firefight south of Bastogne. Ducking into a doorway, he spotted a GI leaning out to take pot shots at Germans. "What's your name? What's your home-town?" Cronkite shouted. The GI shouted back the answers. "And what's your unit?" the reporter asked. The soldier turned and gave him a long look. "Hell, Mr. Cronkite. I'm your driver."

The 101st Airborne Division was surrounded at Bastogne and its commander, Gen. Maxwell Taylor, asked Cronkite if he wanted to go into the town with him. Cronkite declined, later describing his response as cowardly. He rationalized there was no communication link from Bastogne and other correspondents monitoring military communications on the outside would get a beat on the story. "I knew the truth—and I suspect he did: Taylor's drive to Bastogne could well have been a suicide mission."[21]

In one village, women told Richard McMillan of a German parachutist who got caught in a tree. He kept screaming for help and said he would freeze to death unless someone freed him. Villagers went out to watch, but no one offered to help. The next morning he was dead. "It made a good joke in the village," one woman told McMillan, who wrote: "Then, and only then, I began to appreciate the real depth of hatred of these people for the German."[22]

Andy Rooney was back in New York briefly and found himself "vaguely unsettled" at missing the battle. Ira Wolfert had pulled out earlier and wrote: "I'm bored with the war. A person gets bored with being afraid all the time. Fear is such a simple emotion that it fills your whole mind. It gets monotonous."[23]

* * *

The Army ordered Hemingway to Nancy in September to be interrogated about his activities around Rambouillet. Fellow correspondents had lodged several complaints: he had removed the C (for correspondent) insignia from his uniform to assume command of French partisans, had helped defend the town, had been a colonel or general officer with the partisans, had persistently run patrols, had kept weapons in his room where he maintained a "map room" and had told other correspondents he was no longer writing dispatches. The charges could cost him his accreditation and expulsion to the U.S.

Hemingway testified he may have taken off his tunic with the C insignia due to warm weather, but only briefly. He denied he had commanded troops and those who addressed him by military titles did so out of affection. Weapons were stored in his room only as a convenience to irregular troops under command of proper authorities. He owned maps and went on patrols only to gather material for magazine articles.

At the end of this perjury, the colonel conducting the inquiry advised him to set his mind at rest. The inquiry had been a charade; Hemingway had a lot of friends in the military and was fully exonerated. After spending more than six weeks back at the Ritz in Paris, he returned to the war as the Fourth Division prepared to do battle in the Hürtgen Forest near Aachen. He arrived with a Thompson submachine gun. On October 22, a German platoon attacked the command post of Col. Charles "Buck" Lanham. Hemingway moved in fast with his gun and the attack was repulsed. After the war Gen. Raymond Barton recommended he be awarded the Bronze Star for this action. The award was made on June 13, 1947.

Reunited in Paris with Mary Welsh, Hemingway got drunk, went into the bathroom of his hotel room and shot at a photograph of Welsh's husband

Noel Monks, destroying the toilet bowl and flooding the room in the process. (A harbinger of Hemingway's later breakdown?) Welsh was so angry she considered ending their relationship. On March 6, 1945, he flew back to the U.S.—and so ended the inglorious career of Ernest Hemingway, war correspondent. Mary Welsh Hemingway died in Idaho in November 1986, aged 78, twenty-five years after her husband's suicide. She never returned to journalism but arranged posthumous publication of several of his works, including *A Moveable Feast.*[24]

* * *

As German forces fell back in the east, the Russians launched a major offensive on June 22, 1944. Minsk fell on July 5 and the Russians pushed on toward Warsaw, East Prussia and Lithuania. In the south, they reached the Danube. Romania surrendered on August 23 and Bulgaria on September 9. A month later, the Germans began evacuating Greece. By February 1945 the Russians deployed 6.7 million men on a front ranging from the Baltic to the Adriatic.

With the success of Russian arms, Moscow-based correspondents were now allowed to cover some aspects of the offensive, the most extensive reports coming from Alexander Werth. Russian correspondents, of course, followed their troops all the way to Berlin, but were not permitted to report everything they saw—such as rapes committed by Russian soldiers. Alaric Jacob of the *Daily Express*, a Marxist, complained: "I have read more graphic reports about a cricket match at Lord's in peacetime than about some of the great battles in Russia."[25]

A large group of Western correspondents, accompanied by Averell Harriman's 25-year-old daughter Kathleen, were taken in January 1944 to view the scene of the Katyn Forest massacre outside Smolensk, after the Germans announced the discovery of thousands of graves there. Twenty-two thousand Polish officers and intellectuals had been massacred by Stalin's secret police in 1940. The Soviet government maintained the victims had been killed by the Germans and allowed correspondents to attend only one session of an enquiry it set up. They could not hint at criticism of the conduct of the enquiry. "The whole procedure had a distinctly prefabricated appearance," commented Werth.[26]

On the train to Smolensk, correspondents played card games and sang songs. But the mood changed abruptly at Katyn. "Here Smolenskites once came for berrying parties and picnics in the summer, here children came for sledding and snowball fights in the winter," Richard Lauterbach of *Time-Life* wrote. "Now from the bowels of the earth emerged a horrible stench and, one by one, we saw stiff, mildewed Poles in faded gray-blue uniforms. In one great trench . . . the Poles were neatly arranged like a seven-layer cake, row on row, black boots sticking through the dirt at one end and their bare skulls, with a fringe of snow, at the other end." All had been killed by a revolver shot passing from the base of the neck through the forehead.[27]

Details began to emerge of another massacre, carried out by Germans at Babi Yar, a ravine in Kiev, in September 1941. More than 100,000 people perished there, including 33,771 Jews, Soviet war prisoners, Communists and gypsies. Vasily Grossman's newspaper refused to publish his article on Babi Yar but it appeared in *Einikeit*, a journal of the Jewish Anti-Fascist Committee. "There are no Jews in the Ukraine," he wrote. "All is silence. Everything is still. A whole people has been brutally murdered."[28]

Werth was at Orel, more than 200 miles southwest of Moscow, in August 1943 after the Germans pulled out. Orel had been "a pleasant provincial backwater" but more than half the town was destroyed and ruins were still smoking. Just 30,000 of its 114,000 population remained. At a prison camp operated by the Germans, Russian soldiers "had been allowed to die like flies."

Outside Orel prison, Russian troops had exhumed 200 bodies and estimated there were at least 5,000 more. Townspeople said the Gestapo carried out their mass killings punctually on Tuesday and Friday mornings. The novelist Ivan Turgenev once lived in Orel, and his home had been made into a museum. The Germans took away 10,000 books from the Turgenev library and some exhibits, such as his shotgun.

On September 1, Werth traveled to Kharkov (Kharkiv) and, en route, one Jeep in his party struck a mine and two press officers and a captain were killed. Werth learned that the SS had murdered more than 200 Russian wounded in a Kharkov hospital.

Later he was in Klooga, near the Estonian capital of Tallinn, where he saw the charred remains of 2,000 Jews. They had been shot and then burned on bonfires they themselves had been ordered to build and light. One survivor told of a German soldier who addressed a weeping Jewish child: "My little one, don't cry like this; death will soon come."

In March 1944 Werth flew to the Ukrainian farming town of Uman. About one-fourth of its 43,000 population had been Jewish, but now there was "not a single Jewish face in the streets." Many had fled but 5,000 who remained were herded into a warehouse where all windows and doors were hermetically sealed. Within days, all had suffocated. In a field outside a prison were the fresh bodies of more than seventy civilians the Germans had shot before withdrawing. The mayor of a nearby village told Werth an SS officer would order a local official to supply him with girls every night, including girls of 13 or 14.

Werth talked to Valya, a woman of about 20, who had been deported for slave labor to Bavaria. After enduring brutal treatment and long working hours, she put her hand in a flax-cutting machine and all four fingers were cut off. The Germans waited four months before sending her home.

In April the Black Sea port of Odessa, which the Germans had turned over to Romanian control before taking it back for themselves, was liberated. Russian officers told Werth the Romanians had shot 40,000 Jews plus 10,000 Communist Party members or suspected Communists.[29]

Harrison Salisbury of UP was in the Crimea in June, after many Germans had escaped by ship from Sebastopol. In his memoir he wrote of seeing:

> corpses bobbing on the rocky shore of the slim peninsula where the last stand was made, and over the stony land the Limburger stench of putrescent bodies; heavy, it got into your clothes, it clogged your throat, it hung in the air like plague . . . I saw the pig-bellied bodies, eyes staring out of rotting heads, flaxen hair like wigs on a Kewpie doll, and the smell of piss-clotted uniforms, pants cruddy with excrement, with the pale worms of intestines, dirt, slime, paper, paper everywhere . . . War was the garbage heap of humanity. It was shit and piss and gas from the rump; terror and bowels that ran without control.[30]

With the start of Operation Bagration, the great Soviet offensive in 1944, Grossman wrote that in Belorussia "men are walking over [German] corpses . . . In some places, vehicles have to drive over the corpses, so densely do they lie upon the ground."[31]

Ilya Ehrenburg described atrocities in four Belorussian villages: After Germans set fire to a house, a woman threw her baby out the window, a German picked it up and threw it back into the blaze. A Catholic priest was tortured to death. All the people in one village were herded into an Orthodox church and burned to death. Two Catholic priests in another village were killed. Jews from Minsk and others brought from Prague were gassed in vans in yet another village, then their corpses dug up, doused with gasoline and burned. "There were charred bones all over the place," Ehrenburg wrote. "Unburned bodies were stacked like logs."[32]

Eddy Gilmore of the AP and Bill White of *Time* were at the Poltava airfield in Ukraine, where American planes were allowed to refuel after bombing runs over Germany. As German bombers began plastering the field, they sheltered in a slit trench, then returned to their tent. White's clothes were in shreds and Gilmore's pillow likewise. "I believe it was the closest I ever came to death," Gilmore wrote. Two Russian correspondents and an American officer were killed. The next day, with planes still burning, Soviet officers marched soldiers onto the airfield into nests of "butterfly bombs" that exploded when touched. Several men were killed. Of more than eighty American planes, fifty were destroyed and others so badly damaged that only four could still fly. The correspondents returned to Moscow, where censors blocked their stories. The news did not reach the American public until a year later.[33]

Canadian-born David M. Nichol of the *Chicago Daily News* reported on March 21, 1944, on the German retreat into Romania:

> I have never seen anything like this. Mile after muddy mile of Ukrainian highways are lined with every kind of conveyance in various stages of destruction . . . trucks and halftracks of every variety, staff cars and smaller automobiles, field kitchens, mobile radio stations, heavy guns . . . and immense Mark V and Mark VI tanks.

In Uman, streets were strewn with smashed sewing machines, torn feather quilts, pots and pans, household furniture. At the local airport, the Germans left behind 12,000 barrels of aviation fuel and the burned skeletons of big transport planes.[34]

* * *

Grossman went into Poland in July 1944. "There are no Jews in Poland. They have all been suffocated, killed, from elders to newborn babies. Their dead bodies have been burned in furnaces." He arrived at the Majdanek concentration camp but was not allowed by *Krasnaya Zvezda* to write about it; his rival, Konstantin Simonov, was brought in for this task.[35] Simonov, 28, had skyrocketed to fame on January 14, 1942, when *Pravda* published his war poem, "Wait for Me." In later years he wrote novels, short stories, plays, film scripts and poetry.

More than 79,000 people died at Majdanek, 59,000 of them Polish Jews. "Thousands not allowed to work from the fall of 1942 onward died of hunger and disease with horrifying speed." People were killed with iron bars, gassed, incinerated, drowned and hanged. After evening roll call, people were made to run for more than an hour and a half through mud, snow or summer heat. "In the morning the dead bodies were collected."

Simonov described how guards amused themselves by novel ways of killing prisoners. Some had their fingers put in the rollers of a washing machine; then a guard would turn a handle until half an arm or more had gone through the rollers. The mutilated prisoners would then be killed.

Women prisoners were guarded by SS women. A senior wardress carried a nine-foot-long whip, and at roll call would seek out the prettiest woman and strike her in the chest. When the woman collapsed, she would receive a second blow between the legs, then a kick from a steel-toed boot. "After one or two floggings the woman would become crippled and soon die."

The largest mass execution occurred on November 3, 1943. As 18,000 prisoners entered the camp, deafening music sounded from loudspeakers and all were shot in a field after being forced to strip and lie in ditches. Simonov did not mention the fact these 18,000 were Jews. Some reports gave the number as 20,000. He wrote that the camp included a brothel for soldiers. Women were taken from among the prisoners and when they became pregnant they were killed.[36]

William H. Lawrence, the *New York Times* Moscow correspondent, reached Majdanek on August 27, 1944. One captured German officer told him he had supervised the shipment of eighteen freight car-loads of clothing to Germany in two months, all from bodies of people killed. One survivor told of a Polish woman in her late twenties who refused an order to undress. A German soldier lost his temper, shouting, "I'll burn you alive." He directed attendants to bind her arms and legs, then threw her on an iron stretcher and pushed her into an oven.[37]

Werth visited Majdanek in August but the BBC refused to broadcast his detailed report. "They thought it was a Russian propaganda stunt," he wrote. He also reported that Western correspondents in Moscow largely ignored Simonov's account when it appeared in his newspaper. "My first reaction to Majdanek was a feeling of surprise," Werth wrote. "I had imagined something horrible and sinister beyond words. It was nothing like that. It looked singularly harmless from outside." Then he discovered the horrors inside.

At one end of the camp were enormous mounds of white ashes, small human bones scattered among them. Beyond that were acres of cabbages covered with white dust. The cabbages had been fertilized with human ashes. Some distance away was a long trench. "Looking down through the fearful stench, I could see hundreds of naked corpses, many with bullet holes at the back of their skulls. Most were men with shaved heads; it was said these had been Russian war prisoners."

A boy of about 11 told Werth he had seen ten prisoners beaten to death. He also had watched SS men use pickaxes to kill prisoners who collapsed while carrying stones, and heard an old man screaming while being chewed by police dogs.

Werth reported that clothing and other possessions taken from prisoners were kept in an enormous, barn-like structure. One long corridor contained thousands of women's dresses, another thousands of overcoats. "It was like being in a Woolworth store." Shelves were stacked with hundreds of safety razors and shaving brushes, thousands of pen knives and pencils, children's toys—all intended for shipment to Germany. Camp commanders had fled, but two Poles and four Germans who worked there were arrested and, after a trial, hanged.

"The press and radio in the West were still skeptical," Werth wrote. He quoted this comment from the *New York Herald-Tribune*:

> Maybe we should wait for further corroboration of the horror story that comes from Lublin. Even on top of all we have been taught of the maniacal Nazi ruthlessness, this example sounds inconceivable ... The picture presented by American correspondents requires no comment except that, if authentic, the regime capable of such crimes deserves annihilation.[38]

Grossman reported on the Treblinka camp further north. The SS had tried to destroy all traces of its existence, but the Russians found about forty survivors hiding in nearby forests. Grossman interviewed them as well as Polish peasants. His article on the experience of 800,000 victims there was published in November 1944 in *Znamya* under the title "The Hell Called Treblinka," and was quoted at the Nuremberg trials:

> Thrift, thoroughness and pedantic cleanliness—all these are good qualities typical of many Germans ... But Hitler has put these qualities of the German character to work committing crimes against humanity. In the labor camps in Poland, the SS acted as if it was all about growing cauliflowers and potatoes ... In the early morning on July 23, guards and SS soldiers drank some schnapps for courage and began the liquidation of the camp. By the evening, all prisoners at the camps were killed and buried.

Returning to Moscow in August 1944, Grossman collapsed from nervous exhaustion, stress and nausea. Then in mid-January 1945 he became one of the first journalists to enter Warsaw with Soviet troops. In the ghetto, "there isn't a single wall intact . . . The beast's anger was terrible."

At Łódź, he wrote of how famine had reduced the ghetto population by 150 people a day. By January 1943, a Jewish population of 250,000 was down to 74,000 and after the final annihilation just 850 remained.

In his notebooks, Grossman wrote: "The front-line soldiers advance by day and night in fire, holy and pure. The rear soldiers who follow them rape, drink, loot and rob." Russian girls working at a Focke-Wulf plant in Poland "had been clean and well dressed until our soldiers came and robbed them blind and took their watches. Liberated Soviet girls often complain about being raped by our soldiers." He described the girls as lice-infested, swollen from hunger and having no clothes.

In his notebook after arriving in Poznan: "Horrifying things are happening to German women." A German explained that his wife already had been raped by ten men that day. Some liberated Soviet girls hid in correspondents' rooms, but in the night journalists were awakened by screams. "One of the correspondents couldn't resist the temptation." Grossman told of a breast-feeding woman being raped in a barn; her relatives asked her attackers to let her have a break because her baby was crying with hunger.

Going into Germany, he wrote: "Huge crowds on the roads. Prisoners of war of all nationalities: French, Belgian, Dutch, all loaded with looted things. Only Americans are walking light, without even hats. They don't need anything except alcohol."[39]

The Russians liberated Auschwitz on January 27, 1945, but I have found no evidence that any journalist was present for that momentous event. Initial reports in the Western press were sketchy but on May 8, 1945, a Soviet state commission revealed the full horrors after interviewing nearly 3,000 survivors: 4 million people died there from 1941 to 1945, by its estimate. The Auschwitz Museum later revised the toll to between 1 million and 1.5 million, of whom almost 1 million were Jews.

CHAPTER 17

GERMANY INVADED

While Allied bombers pounded German cities, ground forces punched into the Reich. The Americans secured a railway bridge over the Rhine at Remagen on March 7, 1945, while, further south, Patton seized his own bridgehead at Oppenheim on March 22. In places the Allies still met fanatical resistance. The historic link-up between Western and Russian forces would take longer than expected. It was mid-April before the Russians crossed into Germany.

The newly widowed Ann Stringer of UP was determined to disobey Army regulations barring women correspondents from frontline reporting. "I was there to get a story, and I wasn't going to get it from some Paris bar." In mid-February 1945, she and another correspondent crossed the Rur River into the German town of Jülich. The Germans had blown the bridges but they crossed in a rowboat and went to the sixteenth-century citadel, a fortress surrounded by a moat. Three guards let them in, but she never understood why. When they came out, a few frightened, mud-caked GIs had arrived, only to find the Germans had fled.

The Army was not happy with the Jülich dateline. When Stringer returned to the press camp at Maastricht in the Netherlands, the Army public relations officer, Barney Oldfield, chewed her out in front of other correspondents for an unauthorized trip, reducing her to tears. She went for a drink with her UP colleague Jim McGlincy, and he escorted her back to the house of a Dutch family where she was staying. Smitten by the beautiful Stringer and fueled by too many drinks, McGlincy awakened Oldfield at midnight and told him the Dutchman with whom she was staying had pushed him into the street, slammed the door and locked it. Swearing he would get Stringer out and give her his hotel room, he returned to the house, pounding on the door, and the Dutchman came out, threatening to call police. He slammed the door again and McGlincy fired a shot through it. Stringer emerged and McGlincy took her to his hotel room. She went in, locked the door and he slept in the lobby. Police were called, but McGlincy escaped arrest. UP soon recalled him to Paris.[1]

It was not his first such incident. In the summer of 1944, he had come into a press tent one night, fortified by Calvados and waving a souvenir German pistol, declaring that he was looking for "the enemy." His colleagues fled until one of them disarmed him.[2]

* * *

BBC correspondent Guy Byam, 26, was killed on February 3, 1945, during a bombing raid on Berlin with the U.S. Eighth Air Force. Damaged by anti-aircraft fire over Berlin, the plane disappeared over the North Sea. Earlier in the war, Byam had served with the Royal Naval Volunteer Reserve and Combined Operations but was wounded and invalided out. He joined the BBC war reporting unit in April 1944 and parachuted into Normandy on D-Day.[3]

* * *

Austen Lake drove for the French ambulance corps in World War I and later joined the U.S. Tank Corps. Afterward he was a pro football player in Buffalo and Philadelphia, then a sportswriter for the *Boston Transcript*. On March 19, 1945, he was the *Boston Evening American*'s man in Coblenz, which he had last seen twenty-six years earlier. "This ancient Prussian capital resembles a prehistoric ruin of cliff dwellers. It is a smoking shell with scarcely a habitable house." In Fort Konstantine, "a handful of suicidal Nazis were making silly theatrics." The townspeople struck him as unrepentant Nazi supporters:

> I have seen hate in the eyes of many of these German townsmen, sullen smoldering accusation from under heavy brows, phlegmatic, stolid animosity from eyes that burn like sealing wax. There is no joy of deliverance from Hitler's philosophies. They are unreconstructed and full of potential menace . . . Only the moon, owls and slinking alley cats provide our soldiers with nighttime society. Coblenz is a corpse.[4]

But Richard McMillan, going into Germany, was struck to find people cringing, servile and polite. "It was a surprise to find so many unaware of any guilt or wrong committed by Germany . . . The German conscious of guilt wanted to escape the consequences. At heart he was still . . . the would-be ruler of humanity, the man with the lash and the jackboot and worse." Germany was "like an ocean of whitecaps," with surrender flags flying everywhere.[5]

* * *

Ann Stringer, Iris Carpenter and Lee Miller filed so many stories from inside Germany that the Army labeled them "the Rhine Maidens" and *Newsweek* carried an article with that title. On March 7, Stringer entered shattered Cologne with the first American troops. A sobbing, middle-aged Frenchman threw his arms around a GI, crying with joy at being released from slave labor. Few civilians were on the street.[6]

Moorehead arrived in Cologne unprepared for the scale of its destruction:

> There was something awesome about the ruins of Cologne, something the mind was unwilling to grasp, and the cathedral spires still soaring miraculously to the sky only made the debacle below more difficult to accept and comprehend. A city means movement and noise and people; not silence and emptiness and stillness, a kind of cemetery stillness.[7]

Miller found Germans in Cologne:

> repugnant in their servility, hypocrisy and amiability. The underground network of inhabited cellars vomited out more worms, palely clean and well nourished on the stored and stolen fats of Normandy and Belgium. I was constantly irritated and insulted by slimy invitations to dine in German underground homes and amazed by the audacity of Germans to beg a ride in a military vehicle, try to cadge cigarettes, chewing gum or soap like the kids we spoiled in France. How dared they? . . . From what kind of escape zones in the unventilated alleys of their brains are they able to conjure up the idea that they are liberated instead of conquered people?[8]

Andy Rooney saw a German Tiger tank fire into a Sherman tank. Two crewmen pulled themselves out. The tank commander, a major, had to be helped out because his left leg was missing. "They lifted him to a protected place by a doorway and put him down. He died. I had never been present before at the moment someone died. I didn't know whether to cry or throw up."[9]

Gellhorn toured the area around Cologne and wrote of Germans who denied having supported the regime:

> No one is a Nazi. No one ever was. There may have been some Nazis in the next village, and as a matter of fact, that town about 20 kilometers away was a veritable hotbed of Nazidom . . . Oh, the Jews? Well, there weren't really many Jews in this neighborhood. Two maybe, maybe six. They were taken away. I hid a Jew for six weeks. I hid a Jew for eight weeks. (I hid a Jew, he hid a Jew, all God's chillun hid Jews.)

* * *

Stringer heard rumors that the Americans were moving toward the intact Rhine railway bridge at Remagen. On March 10, her Jeep driver took her there but he refused to cross because of heavy firing. Stringer got out and walked across. Gene Gillette of UP watched her return and told her he nearly fainted at the sight. Stringer's driver was now emboldened and they drove across. American anti-aircraft guns opened up on a German fighter plane, it caught fire and crashed nearby.

Stringer wrote that some people thought her action showed she had a death wish, but that was not true. "I preferred to stay alive and get the story. Bill [her husband, killed in France] hadn't been afraid of dangerous situations. Why should I have been?"[10]

Carpenter was taken to the bridge, but her driver turned and sped to safety when Germans began firing 88mm artillery in their direction. The Army allowed correspondents to report that the First Army was across the Rhine, but wouldn't allow them to say how it got there. As though this was unknown to the Germans.

On March 11, Peter Lawless, 55, of the *Daily Telegraph* was killed by German artillery fire while he and two colleagues stood near the bridge. Walter Farr of the *Daily Mail* and Bill Troughton of the *Daily Express* were slightly wounded.[11]

Two weeks later, Stanley Maxted of the BBC was wounded when the glider in which he was crossing the Rhine was hit by machine-gun fire. "There was an explosion that appeared to be inside my head, the smell of burnt cordite," he said in a broadcast. "Something hot and sickly was dropping over my right eye and off my chin and all over my clothes." Once the glider was down, a doctor helped him and a wounded officer to a dressing station. "On the way, I saw burning gliders, crashed gliders and the great courage of men going in to fight almost before they had finished touching down." Hospitalized in London, he came out to find the BBC accounting department urgently requesting he settle a phone bill of one shilling six pence for a call to Birmingham, "in arrears for some time."[12]

A Richard Dimbleby broadcast described what he saw while aboard a plane towing a glider at the Rhine:

> The whole of this mighty airborne army is now crossing and filling the whole sky. On our right hand a Dakota has just gone down in flames . . . Ahead of us, another pillar of black smoke marks the spot where an aircraft has gone down and yet another one; it's a Stirling—a British Stirling . . . four parachutes are coming out—one, two, three, four—four parachutes have come out of the Stirling . . . We're on the east bank of the river . . . We've cast off our glider . . . We've turned hard away, hard away in a tight circle to port to get out of this area. I'm sorry if I'm shouting—it is a very tremendous sight.[13]

Robert Vermillion of UP had entrusted his typewriter to Geoffrey Bocca of the *Daily Express*, aboard another glider. A British officer told Vermillion the glider had crashed and Bocca was dead. Two years after the war, Vermillion was working for UP in New York and received a phone call from the man he thought was dead. Bocca explained he had been shot five times, captured, escaped and recaptured. "I did try, but really, Bob, it [the typewriter] simply was full of holes."[14]

Seaghan Maynes of Reuters took part in a parachute drop across the Rhine in March. He and British Captain Gus Moore found themselves within yards of a German machine-gun nest. While Moore covered him with a Sten gun, Maynes yelled, "Hands up!" and jumped behind a tree. "The trick worked," Maynes wrote. "Five Germans with a machine gun marched out, their hands in the air, while we shouted orders to imaginary paratroopers in case the Germans should change their minds and fire on us."[15]

Richard C. Hottelet was aboard a B-17 covering the drop of paratroopers east of the Rhine in March. His plane was hit by anti-aircraft fire and the left wing caught fire, but the pilot kept the plane aloft until it was back over the west side of the river. Then everyone bailed out and Hottelet landed in a cow pasture.[16]

* * *

Near Kalkar, a town close to the Rhine in north Germany, John D'Arcy
Dawson came across a woodland hospital housing German refugees and
newly freed displaced persons (DPs). The Germans refused to share food with
the DPs. After British soldiers arrived, the Germans were made to carry food
to the DPs and wash the dishes afterward. "I hate the sentimentality which
tries to make out that only the Nazis were guilty of atrocious behavior. All the
Germans were equally guilty . . . The Germans are beasts, and we must never
forget their fundamental beastliness."

He went on to Ibbenbüren, where Russian prisoners were forced to work
in coal mines and "treated with abominable cruelty." Contrary to the Geneva
conventions, Russian officers were made to dig coal, and prisoners injured at
work were beaten by doctors when taken to a hospital. Dawson also reported
the Gestapo singled out Russians suspected of being Communist leaders and
put their legs through sheep hurdles (frames for sheep pens) and slowly broke
each leg. Then the victims were taken to hospital and beaten.

Later Dawson came upon a liberated slave labor camp outside Celle. Four
thousand prisoners from Russia had been herded onto a train which was
bombed as it neared the town. Survivors fled into the woods and were hunted
down. A Scots unit that liberated the camp ordered 400 civilians to take
stretchers and carry sick and wounded to a hospital. The Scots learned that
the camp hangman had just returned to Celle. Dawson went to his house with
soldiers. "I was standing outside when a man came flying through the door,
pulling up when my Mauser dented his stomach." The hangman was sent to
a prison camp.[17]

* * *

Osmar White, returning to war coverage in November 1944 after recovering
from the wounds he suffered on New Georgia Island in August 1943, followed
Patton's Third Army. He referred to Patton as "neurotic and bloodthirsty" but
the most brilliant of Allied generals. At one point Patton had been expected to
cross the Rhine but instead wheeled about and crossed the Mosel (which joins
the Rhine at Coblenz) and encircled a southern group of German armies in
what White called "a brilliant, decisive move."

Patton was still the only Allied general in the field with a full realization
of what speed blitzkrieg could achieve. Patton took great risks to force

the pace. Montgomery's British and Canadians . . . were cautious, unin-
spired . . . Disliking Patton as much as I did—his childish love of notoriety, his foul mouth, his preoccupation . . . with corpses—it was distasteful
to admit that the man's genius as a commander in the field overshadowed
that of his fellow generals . . .

Coblenz was the first large ruined city that White saw. "Smell was the
insistent sense. A city under bombardment has a subtle, terrifying odor . . . It
is not unpleasant, just terrifying . . . Only later, when the city has stopped
burning, does this perfume of destruction become a stink . . ." A Wehrmacht
colonel waiting for someone to accept his surrender and that of eighty men
with him told White: "This is not war. You do not need tanks and guns any
longer. Your airplanes alone could finish us."

The aerial slaughter reached a climax near Bad Kreuznach between March
18 and 23. Hundreds of German trucks, armored vehicles and horse-drawn
artillery made a dash for the Rhine but P-51 Mustang fighters "piled up hill-
ocks of dead and wounded horses and smashed limbers into which traffic
speeding behind crashed." White quoted an American pilot as likening it to a
rat hunt: "You beat the ground. You flushed the vermin. Then you killed it."

On the night of March 22–3 Patton sent his Fifth Division over the Rhine
at Oppenheim, 15 miles west of Darmstadt. "He thrust like a dagger into the
very vitals of central Germany . . . Even with opposition broken, it was a
supremely daring maneuver and I believe it contributed substantially to short-
ening the war."

White often had to peel off from coverage and make round trips of more
than 200 miles to reach Army headquarters for transmission of his dispatches.
He drove long distances without seeing an American soldier and expected
German civilians would "snap out of their stunned docility" and attack him.
But nothing happened.

After the battle of the Rhineland, the enemy no longer had the will to fight
on . . . German civilian morale collapsed totally . . . It used to sicken me to
hear the eagerness with which the people who had made a god of Hitler
and a religion of his words now denied him. If Hitler had been the Devil
himself, it would still have been distasteful.

Only in Mainz did he find what he regarded as an amusing example of a
German's eagerness to ingratiate herself with the Allies. Snipers were holding
up an advance until a massive woman, waving a white flag on a broomstick,

emerged from a house opposite the one from which sniping was coming. She crossed the road and disappeared inside. Minutes later she emerged, leading the snipers by their ears. They were her sons, aged 12 and 14.

Later, White went to Hitler's Eagle's Nest retreat near the Austrian border. "The Führer's fabulous pimple on the Bavarian peak was less impressive than many a public lavatory! I came down . . . profoundly flat in spirit. The evil Colossus who had bestridden Europe was a little man—the kind of man who, failing all else, carves his name on glacial boulders to make sure he will be remembered."

American forces in central and southern Germany unearthed fifty-three deposits of Nazi loot in April and May. This included the entire Reichsbank reserve of gold bullion and most of the Hungarian Treasury's silver, as well as precious stones, silver and gold watches, art treasures, wedding rings taken from women in concentration camps and gold and silver fillings from the teeth of camp victims.

White went into a salt mine 2,000 feet deep near Merkers where the Reichsbank gold was sealed in a chamber. Also hidden were crates of Greek, Chinese and Egyptian ceramics, and paintings by German, French, English and Italian masters. Another morning White went to see Hermann Göring's art collection in a mine near Berchtesgaden. One room contained seven Rubens paintings, including his most famous crucifixion scene. "I looked, and felt a wave of nausea. Rubens must have seen torture. No one who had not seen torture could have painted that crucifixion."[18]

* * *

Near Kirchhain, north of Frankfurt, a woman begged Iris Carpenter for help and she heard a girl screaming behind a locked door. A GI shouted, "Stop clawing, you little bitch, or I'm gonna break your bloody neck." Carpenter, banging on the door and kicking it, yelled: "Hey, quit that and open the door!" The GI came to the door and said, "I've got a pistol and there ain't nobody going to stop me having her or any other German gal I want. And why not? We won'em, didn't we? What the hell can they expect of an army that licked 'em?" He slammed the door. Carpenter found an American officer who set off to rescue the girl, exclaiming: "Hell! The most stinking part of this whole stinking war business is that there should be women anywhere near it."[19]

* * *

American troops came upon a camp at Nordhausen in the Harz mountains of Thuringia, where 10,000 political prisoners had been used as slave labor in building V-2 rockets. Stringer arrived on April 11. Half the prisoners were dead and the rest dying in a dozen bomb-wrecked buildings. The living were too weak from hunger to move.

"It was beyond human conception. I saw hundreds of shrunken bodies stacked like cordwood. Some had been in the building for 18 months." There were no sanitary facilities and prisoners received 3 ounces of bread and a bowl of grass soup daily. After the Allies began bombing the facility, none had been fed.

Survivors said guards had fled fifteen days before American troops arrived. Gen. J. Lawton Collins ordered leading citizens of Nordhausen to bury the dead. The burgomeister objected that the ground chosen was private property. A major threatened to bury him with the rest if he didn't get on with it. Local people were repulsed at having to handle the dead but Collins ruled they had to carry them with their bare hands in a procession to the cemetery. They buried 2,017 victims of various nationalities.[20]

Carpenter was greeted by a stench at the camp hospital. She found eighty people lying on straw mattresses, given no medical care by doctors who were themselves prisoners and had no medicine. All were in the final stages of starvation. The prisoners told of wives and children who had been raped, shot and tortured before their eyes. A Polish doctor described how eight men raped his wife and small daughter in front of him, then beat them to death. His right hand had been amputated because of frostbite during an eleven-day journey to the camp in an open cattle truck. Of forty men in his room, all had lost either a hand or foot in the same way.[21]

* * *

Matthew Halton of the Canadian Broadcasting Corporation encountered a German eagerness to cooperate and said in a broadcast:

> Your hate rises of course against everything German when you see, as I saw the other day, Dutchmen who had been tortured to death. And it rises again when you see the streams of freed slaves thronging down the roads . . . In the areas we've already overrun in Germany we've liberated over two million of these slaves . . . It makes you hate all right when . . . women tell you how they were brought from Russia, put up on auction blocks, pawed and mauled by lecherous fat Germans and sold into slavery. I've seen women on

their knees, tears running down their cheeks, as British tanks rolled past and they knew they were free . . . Is there any measure for the rivers and tides of sorrows and tears that the Nazis have set flowing in Europe?[22]

Eric Sevareid came upon 400 Italian slave workers stumbling toward American lines and saw "deep, fixed indignation" in the faces of German civilians. "I could not avoid a sudden feeling of detestation and incredulity. One could tell at once . . . that they had not the faintest sense of having done anything wrong . . ."[23]

* * *

Osmar White observed that the farther he went into Germany, the more the appearance of liberated slaves began to change. Instead of the vigorous men he had initially seen, some limped and were ill and half-starved. Farm workers had been relatively well treated, but in factories there had been merciless slave driving, 80-hour work weeks, starvation, bitter cold and other indignities. Near Besingham, one old peasant woman begged an American commander to stop her Russian slave from running away. There would be nobody left to do the heavy farm work and her family would starve. The American's reply, White wrote, was unprintable.

More than most correspondents, he was critical of the conduct of some Allied soldiers. "Conquest tacitly implied the right to booty. The victorious troops appropriated whatever portable enemy property they fancied—liquor and cigars, cameras, binoculars, shotguns and sporting rifles, ceremonial swords and daggers, silver ornaments and plate, and fur garments." Military police looked the other way until some troops began to steal expensive cars, antique furniture, radios and industrial equipment, and devise ways to smuggle the loot to England.

White reported there was "a good deal" of rape by combat troops. "For brutal or perverted sexual offenses against German women, some soldiers were shot—particularly if they happened to be Negroes. Yet I know for a fact that many women were raped by white Americans. No action was taken against the culprits." The Allies had a policy of no fraternization between troops and German civilians. White quoted one distinguished army commander, whom he did not name, as wisecracking: "Copulation without conversation does not constitute fraternization." Later, when he got into Berlin, he reported on the more widespread rape of German women by Russian troops.[24]

* * *

At a bivouac in Germany, John MacVane encountered a freed war prisoner he knew. He was Edward Ward of the BBC, taken prisoner in North Africa in 1942 and freed when his camp was liberated. "Eddy was haggard and gaunt from undernourishment. But there was a gleam in his eye when he shook hands," MacVane wrote. Ward returned to England to recover but was back in Germany to cover the battle for Leipzig.[25]

He and Harold Denny of the *New York Times*, another former prisoner who had been released much earlier, went into the Leipzig Town Hall just as the last defenders were coming out with their hands up. People in a nearby shelter told them Mayor Freyburg and his wife and daughter had killed themselves. Beside the door to the mayor's office a member of the Volkssturm—Hitler's home guard, recruited near the end of the war—lay dead, 20- and 50-mark notes scattered around him. He had poisoned himself. Ward and Denny stepped into a luxuriously furnished, oak-paneled room.

The fat, middle-aged mayor was seated at a large desk, his shaven head slightly tilted back. Opposite him in an armchair was his wife and, in another armchair, their daughter, a flaxen-haired young woman of 18. All were dead. A phial that had contained poison lay on the desk. A pocket volume of Schiller's poems was beside the mayor's hands and on the wall was an oil painting of Hitler. "The caretaker seemed entirely unmoved by this terrible spectacle," Ward said in a BBC broadcast.[26]

Carpenter arrived later and, in another room, city treasurer Droto Liss lay slumped on a desk. His daughter, wearing a nurse's uniform, was on a sofa opposite and in an armchair sat his wife in a tailored black suit. Another phial lay on the desk. The daughter, Carpenter wrote, "was exquisite as a Dresden doll."[27]

Lee Carson, Don Whitehead and Bill Walton of *Time*, accompanied by the photographer Margaret Bourke-White, arrived on April 23 at the Erla work camp near Leipzig. Driving down a country road, they detected a strange odor, then saw a high barbed-wire fence. Along the fence were charred bodies of inmates.

"We stood frozen with horror," Carson reported. Walton threw up. Then skeletal figures appeared. They were among 350 original workers at an aircraft factory on the grounds. SS guards had told them the Americans would arrive soon, and carried a large vat of soup into the barracks to entice them inside. Then they locked the doors and windows and set the barracks on fire. A few men somehow fought their way outside, and were killed at the barbed wire.

The survivors were eighteen men who had been outside the barracks when the others were locked in.[28]

MacVane arrived at a women's camp near Leipzig and found a white-haired Massachusetts woman with a lined face. "I married a Frenchman," she told him. "I am the Countess Henri de Mauduit." A surprised MacVane told her he had dined in Paris a month earlier with her husband. He was the brother-in-law of Jacqueline de Mauduit, the secretary of the INS bureau in Paris when MacVane worked there before the war. The American woman "swayed on her bunk as though she had been hit by a rifle bullet." Then she broke into uncontrollable weeping, explaining that she hadn't known since 1940 if her husband were alive or dead.

She had gone to the family chateau in Brittany after the fall of France, and helped downed American pilots to escape. The Gestapo suspected she was hiding some of them and, when they could find none, they took her to a concentration camp at Ravensbrück, then Leipzig.[29]

* * *

At Landsberg, near the Austrian border, Eleanor Packard of UP watched as people from nearby villages uncovered the bodies of about 500 men, mostly Jews, who had been used as slave labor until they became ill and were no longer fed. "Most were naked. Their gaunt skeleton frameworks looked more like gruesome waxworks from a horror museum than human beings." Another 600 were barely alive.

Virginia Irwin of the *St. Louis Post-Dispatch* visited an "abortion camp" in a forest near Niederaula, north of Kassel. She reported that pregnant Russian and Polish women slaves underwent "operations" that were less often abortions than induced deliveries in which the baby always died. The process was "too barbaric for print." Sixty per cent of the mothers died.[30]

Carpenter and two colleagues arrived at a camp for American and British prisoners near Duderstadt. Originally housing several thousand men, it was reduced to a few hundred—all too sick with dysentery and starvation to move. "All had *walked* to this camp from Silesia. The place crawled with lice." The men slept on straw and had been given one meal a day of watery soup. When they became too sick to stay in the main building, they were moved to a shed and died there at the rate of several dozen a day. "What we had seen had badly shaken us."[31]

Lee Miller visited a hospital where several hundred American soldiers liberated from a prison camp were treated. "They were very badly cared for and practically starved to death. Their diet consisted of horse-turnip soup and a square inch of black bread daily."[32] Thoburn "Toby" Wiant of the AP reported on April 20, 1945, that some prisoners had been forced to walk a hundred miles or more to camps, assigned filthy quarters that were unheated in winter, given barely enough food to stay alive and, in at least one camp, beaten with rifle butts. Army censors at first refused to allow correspondents to report fully on the severe cruelty found in these camps, worried that "unfounded exaggerations might be printed, provoking the Germans to retaliate."[33]

Sandborstel, built on swampy ground north of Bremen, was originally a prisoner-of-war camp that, over a six-year period, held a million prisoners of forty-six nations. After it was liberated on April 29, 1945, by the British Army, Larry Solon of the *News Chronicle* focused on child inmates: "Their starved bodies and their eyes like coals burning in their starved, gray faces bear witness to the greatest mass horror the world has seen."[34]

* * *

For Alan Moorehead and Alexander Clifford, the approaching end of the war induced caution after all they had endured in North Africa and Europe. "We lived in comfortable safe billets behind the line," Moorehead wrote. "We had sessions of reading poetry and plays aloud . . . Skirmishes at the front which once would have filled our day's horizon now often seemed to us repetitive and useless folly."

For Clifford, there was an additional reason for caution: he had fallen in love. Jenny Nicholson, an actress and journalist and daughter of poet Robert Graves, had come to Normandy as an officer on the women's side of the RAF and met Clifford. They took a break from war to marry in London on February 22, 1945. "She stimulated him as he had never been before," Moorehead wrote.[35]

* * *

Scottish-born Evelyn Irons, 45, of the *Evening Standard* had achieved some notoriety in 1931 when she was briefly the lover of writer Vita Sackville-West (later the lover of Virginia Woolf). The romance between Irons and Sackville-West ended when Irons met fellow journalist Joy McSweeney, with whom she lived until McSweeney's death in 1978. In 1945, Irons was accredited to the Free French Army and preceded it into a village in Bavaria. She boasted afterward of how she and fellow correspondents used guns to intimidate local people and steal from them. "We were armed—the French would have none of this nonsense about war correspondents not carrying weapons—so we held up everyone at gunpoint . . . Then we helped ourselves to all the radios, cameras and binoculars we could find and drove off."[36]

* * *

In Germany, the gun-toting Holbrook Bradley of the *Baltimore Sun*, by his own account, committed his most blatant violation of the Geneva conventions. Near Bielefeld, he was offered a ride in a tank, and sat next to the commander. A lieutenant instructed him on how to fire a .50-caliber machine gun. Soon a German staff car appeared and the tank commander ordered Bradley to fire.

"I squeezed the heavy trigger, watching the stream of tracers that seemed to flow like water. Then, as bullets hit the staff car, I could spot a driver and another man in the front, along with three officers in the rear, as the vehicle disintegrated in a blast of flame, smoke and flying parts—both steel and flesh."

This account leaves questions unanswered that might cause some to doubt Bradley's veracity. Why was the seat next to the tank commander empty, leaving no one to man the machine gun before Bradley entered? Why would a commander entrust firing of the gun to an untrained correspondent instead of using one of his own crew?

Later, as Bradley approached a POW camp near Hanover, a colonel handed him a carbine in case they ran into German resistance. Soon after, in a wooded area near Wolfsburg, Bradley was brandishing the Walther pistol he had picked up in Normandy when he came upon a German colonel who wanted to give himself up. The colonel handed over his Luger, and Bradley turned him over to two GIs.

After the war, Bradley joined the Washington bureau of *Life* magazine but was fired after two years. He went to work for the American military government in occupied Germany, later serving as editorial director of the Asian Foundation, then the Voice of America as an editorial writer for Asia. He died in July 2010 at age 93.[37]

* * *

Toby Wiant had a problem he couldn't overcome while covering Patton's charge through Germany. He began drinking heavily, and missed stories.

When Patton reached the Rhine, Wiant "ran into a bottle of booze and didn't come back for days," his AP colleague Ed Ball wrote in a letter home.

Wiant had had a drink problem earlier in life and his experience in covering German atrocities may have contributed to his descent into alcoholism. He wrote of the liberation of 900 Hungarian Jewish females who had been forced to work in gas and arms factories. "Whenever a girl became ill, she was stripped naked, thrown onto a truck containing the bodies of dead girls and carted off for cremation." In a letter he wrote: "I've seen a lot of war in the past five months on the Western Front and will admit I'm fed up with the awfulness of it all. I've seen concentration and prison camps unbelievably inhuman, and come away wondering what, if anything, even could be done with such bestial people."

He told Wes Gallagher, the AP's Paris bureau chief, that he was on the verge of a nervous breakdown and would resign if there were no other way to get home. Gallagher reported his behavior was increasingly erratic. "One evening Toby decided he was a werewolf and tore up a night club." The AP informed him he would have to resign or be fired. Back home, he resigned and joined an advertising agency in Detroit. Police found him unconscious on a downtown sidewalk after a week-long binge. Threatened with divorce, he entered Alcoholics Anonymous.

He was also a heavy smoker and in 1949 suffered two heart attacks. Four years later, he developed the first of three cancers that were to plague his last years. On February 5, 1963, he died at age 52. The sad story of Toby Wiant was told forty-seven years later in an unsparing book by his journalist daughter, Susan.[38]

CHAPTER 18

THE CAMPS INSIDE GERMANY

With the end finally in sight in Europe in the heady spring days of 1945, many correspondents were exhausted, mentally and physically. Some had been covering the war only since D-Day in Normandy, but a few had endured for six mind-shattering and bone-wearying years the eternal presence of death and the threat of death, impersonal death as well as the loss of friends and colleagues; destruction on a scale too vast for the mind to encompass; lack of sleep and proper food; constant problems of transportation and battles with censors; the draining effect of witnessing suffering and loss. They thought they had seen it all.

None of them was fully prepared for the horrors that war would spew forth in those last weeks, horrors in a form outside almost any previous human experience. They had known there were German concentration camps but the degree of depravity found within was beyond their imagination. When the secrets of the camps finally were revealed, it was the single most stunning development of the war for correspondents—and for most of their readers and listeners as well. This was the ultimate expression of a new kind of warfare not fought on battlefields. But correspondents put aside its shattering personal effects and produced some of the most graphic reporting of the entire conflict. In some instances, the truth they revealed was, as in Poland, too shocking for their editors to accept; surely there was exaggeration in the accounts, something disturbingly overwrought? There was not.

There had been abundant but little-noticed evidence beforehand that genocide was taking place in Europe. On June 28, 1942, a UP report quoted the World Jewish Congress as saying the Germans had massacred more than a million Jews since the beginning of the war. Three days later, the *New York*

Times reported the Polish government-in-exile in London had evidence that 700,000 Jews in German-occupied territories had been slaughtered. Edward R. Murrow told his listeners in a 1942 broadcast:

> One is almost stunned into silence by some of the information reaching London. Some of it is months old, but it's eyewitness stuff supported by a wealth of detail and vouched for by responsible governments. What is happening is this: Millions of human beings, most of them Jews, are being gathered up with ruthless efficiency and murdered . . . When you piece it all together . . . you have a picture of mass murder and moral depravity unequaled in the history of the world.[1]

But a horror confined to numbers, even such staggering numbers, remained something of an abstraction. Many people also were mindful of the fact that stories of German atrocities in Belgium in World War I proved to be pure propaganda. Others, while fully accepting the evil nature of the Hitler regime, could not bring themselves to believe a nation with a rich history of high culture had descended to such degeneracy.

On April 4, 1945, the American Army liberated the first camp to be found on German territory. It was near Ohrdruf in Thuringia, and prisoners had been used for slave labor on a rail line. Ohrdruf had contained 11,700 prisoners but the SS had shot those too ill to move and evacuated the rest to Buchenwald. Three days after it was liberated, Lee McCardell of the *Baltimore Sun* found the bodies of thirty-one men on the ground, each with a bullet in the back of the head. More naked bodies than he could count lay in two barracks. The camp had been swept by a typhus epidemic that killed an average of thirty per day. Trucks hauled the bodies—an estimated 3,000 to 5,000—to a pit in the woods, where they were burned.[2]

The Australian correspondent Osmar White reported that on April 8 Col. Hayden Sears ordered every able-bodied male in Ohrdruf to go to the camp and view the remains of victims. "A stench of roasted flesh and putrefaction filled the air," White wrote. Sears observed the hesitancy of villagers and ordered his troops: "Make them stand closer and look!" The burgomeister had been charged with assembling the male population; afterward, he and his wife were found hanged in their bedroom, their wrists slashed with razor blades.[3]

Later that month, the SS began moving Jewish prisoners east from Buchenwald and Flossenberg, but a half mile west of Neunburg the march was halted and most prisoners were shot. McCardell wrote that others appeared to have been brained by clubs and rifle butts, and some had their eyes gouged out. The U.S. Army forced every man, woman and child above the age of five from the village to file past the bodies lying in open coffins. Some accepted the task stoically, but McCardell wrote that "several women faltered and wept and one fainted with hysteria."[4]

John R. Wilhelm of the *Chicago Sun* reported that 11,000 prisoners took part in the evacuation from Buchenwald, and only 6,000 survived. "One man was left for dead every ten yards of the 125-mile march from Buchenwald." Bodies of victims formed "a line of grisly, shrunken corpses sprawled in ditches and hedges along the highway. They were shot and killed as, starved and unable to keep up, they fell by the wayside." At the funeral service, he wrote, "several women were weeping. Many shuddered. Others turned away in a faint. But the burial went on . . . There was shame in most of their eyes and they were silent. There was one exception, a woman who giggled." An American soldier walked over and rebuked her.[5]

* * *

The U.S. Third Army under Patton liberated Buchenwald on April 11, 1945. Located on a hill outside Weimar, Buchenwald—it means Beech Wood, suggesting a pleasant sylvan retreat—had contained 238,380 prisoners, of whom 56,000 died. The irony of the camp's location was that Weimar was historically associated with high German culture. Johann Wolfgang von Goethe, Friedrich Schiller and Johann Sebastian Bach had lived there. Franz Liszt had his greatest period of creativity in Weimar and Friedrich Nietzsche died there. But in the 1930s Weimar had become a narrow, provincial town noted for anti-Semitism, right-wing extremism and nationalism.

Murrow, reporting from the camp on April 15, said: "As we walked out into the courtyard, a man fell dead. Two others . . . were crawling toward the latrine. Children clung to my hands and stared." In a courtyard, he found stacks of bodies, all but two of them naked. He estimated there were more than 500 men and boys, most of whom had apparently died of starvation. "I pray you to believe what I have said about Buchenwald," he told CBS listeners. "I have reported what I saw and heard, but only part of it. For most of it I have no words."[6]

Murrow's CBS colleague Charles Collingwood wrote later: "He felt inadequate, defeated by his inability to handle what he saw. He wandered giddy with incomprehension through Buchenwald, pressing a small fortune in dollar bills—winnings from poker games—to living skeletons."[7]

Don Whitehead visited 800 children in a barracks that formerly housed SS troops. Most had been evacuated from Auschwitz:

The youngest of them was a boy who had spent four of his eight years as a prisoner of the Nazis. He remembers nothing but prison life. He has no recollection of his father or mother or any life except that within Buchenwald. There was another nine-year-old who had been a prisoner for three years. He has the face of a 16-year-old . . . Most of them are Polish Jews . . . None of them knew what had become of their families. Some had a faint remembrance of their mothers and fathers.[8]

Marguerite Higgins of the *New York Herald-Tribune* arrived just hours after Buchenwald was liberated. Suspecting the camp's reputation for horrors was part of a propaganda campaign, she began interrogating inmates relentlessly. Her biographer, Antoinette May, wrote: "Sick with shame, she realized how insensitive she had been to the first prisoners she interviewed. She saw rigid bodies of thousands murdered in the last days."

Bodies had spilled out of trucks and carts, others were piled in corners or propped against buildings. Higgins wrote: "As if to emphasize the horror, the frosty spring nights had frozen into ghastly stalactites the trickles of blood and yellow bubbles of mucus that oozed from the eyes and noses of the many who had been bludgeoned or otherwise tortured to death."

Civilians from Weimar were ordered to witness the result of atrocities committed at Buchenwald. Higgins accompanied them and her account was published in the army newspaper *Stars and Stripes* on April 20:

The men and women were marched past heaps of stiff and naked bodies of people who, through starvation, beatings and torture, had died in such great numbers that the Gestapo had not had the opportunity to dispose of them before the American conquest of the camp. At the crematorium where some 200 prisoners were disposed of daily, several women fainted at the sight of half-burned humans still in the oven. Others attempted to put their hands over their eyes. But one of the government officials immediately stepped forward and ordered them to look . . . The odor of excrement, vomit and the smell of death still lay heavy over the camp. Two of the men died this afternoon, quietly and without a second glance from their desperately ill companions.[9]

A French-speaking prisoner told Osmar White that more than 35,000 prisoners had died or been killed. The surviving prisoners "stank with the thin, sour smell of starvation." White was taken to the crematorium. "Piled neatly against one wall were 103 blue-white human corpses. They were naked

. . . Many had been beaten. There were whip cuts on the skin of their backs and some were mottled purple with bruises. The bodies were spattered with dried blood and pus." There was a garrotting room, where window sash cords were tied around prisoners' necks so they could be suspended from hooks and strangled. White's guide told him that sometimes other prisoners were forced to grab victims around their knees and bear them down with their weight. Anyone who survived was clubbed to death. The guide said he believed 20 to 30 British and American airmen had been killed in this room a few months earlier.

In the barracks, White began to walk between tiers of bunks and heard a low, growling noise:

> I did not recognize it as applause until someone started handclapping. A man crawled weakly out into the passage and stood at attention, saluting. "English . . . ah, English, English!" . . . The voices were like the sound of wind in a dark, deep place . . . The image of their eyes and their teeth as they smiled will, until the day I die, remain life's most terrible recollection.

Leaving the barracks, White vomited.

He spent two weeks in various camps. A Belgian girl who had been in Auschwitz told him newborn infants there were thrown alive into crematorium furnaces, including her own child, conceived in rape by a German officer. A Polish officer from Auschwitz said his best friend fell into a latrine pit in a barracks hut and smothered to death, other inmates too weak to pull him out.[10]

Ann Stringer of UP reported that Ilse Koch, wife of the commandant and known to inmates as the beast of Buchenwald, showed correspondents her tattooed "art treasures" made from human skin. "She displayed them with great pride."[11]

Lee Miller adopted a sardonic tone in writing of the camp:

> My fine Baedeker tour of Germany includes many such places as Buchenwald which were not mentioned in my 1913 edition, and if there is a later one I doubt if they were mentioned there either, because no one in Germany has ever heard of a concentration camp, and I guess they didn't want any tourist business either. Visitors took one-way tickets only, in any case, and if they lived long enough they had plenty of time to learn the places of interest, both historic and modern, by personal and practical experimentation. Now, in spite of the fact that the local Gestapo Rotary

Club did no advertising, a constant stream of tourists arrives in this camp to see the horrors.

This was a reference to the Weimar citizens forced to come to the camp. "The tourists . . . fainted all over the place, although some remained arrogant. Even after the place was 95 per cent cleaned up, soldiers . . . are sick and miserable at what they see here." She wrote that one SS man hanged himself. "He was taken out on a stretcher, stripped and thrown on a heap of bony cadavers where he looked shockingly big, the well-fed bastard."[12]

Edward Ward of the BBC saw prisoners too weak to move. "With ghost-like voices they tried to speak but scarcely a sound came from their shrunken, rope-like throats. I could have made the fingers of one hand meet round the thighs of most of them. It simply didn't seem possible that human beings could be in such a condition and still be alive." A French guide told him that all would die.[13]

Robert Reid of the BBC interviewed British Captain C. A. G. Burney, who had been a prisoner for 15 months. Burney told him the Germans executed escapees who were recaptured. "They hanged; they shot, they had patent traps where you stood on a trapdoor which let off a bullet into your neck; they electrocuted; they injected with phenol, they injected with air, they injected with milk." Reid asked if there had been any community spirit among prisoners. Burney replied: "I can't say there was, frankly. If you wanted to be disgusted with humanity, all you had to do was to come and live in this camp. People were stealing, they were killing each other for a slice of bread, they were always quarrelling, there was always a lot of political intrigue. One group hated another and the other group hated the next and so forth."[14]

Denis Johnston, an Irish playwright now working for the BBC, was shown around Buchenwald by two Channel Island former prisoners. They stripped a tarpaulin from a truck and revealed an interior piled high with emaciated, yellow, naked corpses. In a cellar beneath the crematorium, somebody had tried to whitewash the walls but they still bore bloodstains. "They beat us and hanged us here," said James Quick, one of the former prisoners. Some charred bones lay in furnaces. Johnston went into one hut where prisoners were lying on bunks, "packed tightly side by side, like knives and forks in a drawer . . . all of them skeletons." A stench hit him and he heard a "queer wailing," which he realized was a pitiful attempt at cheering by the men when they saw his British uniform.

A half-dead Polish Jew spoke of another camp in which prisoners had been forced to stand under a hose for a half hour in midwinter, and many had frozen to death. A Czech doctor said many Jews brought to Buchenwald had been castrated.[15]

*   *   *

Further north, in the British zone of operations, Wynford Vaughan-Thomas of the BBC heard of a camp where typhus had broken out. He thought it would be another of many prisoner-of-war camps and declined to go, but his colleague Richard Dimbleby did not. The camp was Bergen-Belsen and its name soon became, like so many others, a byword for the unspeakable barbarity of the Hitler regime. Twenty thousand Russian war prisoners and 50,000 other inmates, mostly Jews, died there. Up to 35,000 died in the first months of 1945 from typhus, among them Anne Frank. When British troops liberated the camp on April 15, there were 53,000 survivors, most half-starved and seriously ill. Thirteen thousand corpses lay unburied.

Dimbleby heard the voice of a girl, "a living skeleton," who was stretching out her stick of an arm and gasping, "English, English, medicine, medicine." Bodies lay under trees, all naked. "They were like polished skeletons, the skeletons that medical students like to play practical jokes with." One woman, who had gone mad, flung herself at a British soldier and begged him to give her milk for the baby she held in her arms. She threw herself at his feet and kissed his boots. When she got up, she put the baby in his arms and ran off crying that she would find milk for it. The soldier opened the bundle of rags and looked at the child. It had been dead for days.

Dimbleby returned from his visit "a changed man," according to Vaughan-Thomas:

> Richard . . . said to me at once, "It's horrible. Human beings have no right to do this to each other. You must go and see it, but you'll never wash the smell of it off your hands, never get the filth of it out of your mind. I've just made a decision . . . I must tell the exact truth, every detail of it, even if people don't believe me, even if they feel these things should not be told. This is an outrage . . . an outrage."

The BBC refused to believe Dimbleby's report or broadcast it, insisting on confirmation from other sources. In a rage, Dimbleby phoned London and warned that, unless the report went through, he would never broadcast again. His report, originally running to 14 minutes, eventually went on the air in an abbreviated but still horrifying form. The following month he revisited the camp and commented that what shocked British doctors and soldiers was "to see, for the first time in their lives, human beings who had been deliberately degraded to the level of animals."

Returning to Belsen in 1965, Dimbleby wrote:

The report which I sent back from here caused a lot of worry at Broadcasting House. When they heard it, some people wondered if Dimbleby had gone off his head or something. I think it was only the fact that I'd been fairly reliable up to then that they believed the story. I broke down five times while I was recording it.

The camp guards expected to be shot at once and couldn't understand the idea of a trial. "One of them asked me if anything would happen to him. I was so angry that I turned on him and told him that he would be tried and I hoped hanged."[16]

On entering Belsen, John D'Arcy Dawson was taken to the office of commandant Josef Kramer. "He was as massive as a giant oak, but not so wholesome." Kramer had a large head with shaven skull and fat cheeks, with two hard eyes "looking at us from deep pits of fat, expressionless as a lizard." Dawson found 500 prisoners lying dead or dying near a potato patch. Desperate for food, they had rushed to collect rotting potatoes and the Germans had shot them. "The Nazis were amused that we should be so angry," he wrote.

Two Jewish women told how they were marched from Auschwitz to Belsen. At the Polish camp, they had been forced to watch their parents thrust into a furnace while still alive. Dawson wrote: "We were surrounded by a horde of verminous creatures, covered with running sores, mouths a mass of ulcers, their breasts running with lice, the pus coursing down the dirt-encrusted skin." In the corner of one barracks, fifty naked bodies lay in a pile. No one had had the strength to take them away, "so they rotted there while the living sat and slept and ignored death." At a large open space, nearly 3,000 bodies were piled up in a pit. Kramer looked down, expressionless.

A young French prisoner who had been put in charge of crematorium records told Dawson that 17,337 people had passed through the furnaces just in March. Then the coal gave out and the dead were thrown into pits or piled up. Kramer, who had been in charge of the gas chambers at Auschwitz before coming to Belsen in December 1944, was hanged by the British as a war criminal on December 13, 1945.

"Belsen will live in my memory as the most horrible sight I have ever seen," Dawson wrote. Already a confirmed German-hater, he added: "'Carnivorous sheep' is the finest description I have ever read of this disgusting race." He contracted a fever after visiting Belsen, and thus ended his war coverage. On Victory in Europe Day, he was still recuperating in a hospital.[17]

* * *

Alan Moorehead arrived at the camp to find some inmates lying on the earth partly covered in rags. "It was not possible to say whether they were alive or dead or simply in the process of dying. It would be a day or two before the doctors got round to them for a diagnosis." Moorehead entered a room where women guards in detention got up and stood at attention. "Thin ones, fat ones, scraggy ones and muscular ones; all of them ugly and one or two of them distinctly cretinous." SS male guards had undergone interrogation that morning and had been beaten by British soldiers. "There were half a dozen men lying or half-lying on the floor. The man nearest me, his shirt and face spattered with blood, made two attempts before he got onto his knees and then gradually onto his feet."

A British captain told Moorehead that a camp doctor had invented some of the tortures practiced there, including injecting prisoners' veins with creosote and gasoline. The doctor was now lying in his blood on the floor. Finally he stood up and whispered to the men who had beaten him: "Why don't you kill me? Why don't you kill me? I can't stand any more."[18]

Richard McMillan of UP wrote of entering Belsen: "The stench of the charnel-house gripped us, chilled us, choked us . . . It was nausea beyond conception or toleration." A rabbi who was a prisoner told him: "If the heavens were paper and all the water in the world were ink, and all the trees were turned into pens, you could not even then record the sufferings and horrors." For several days after liberation, 300 people died every night.

> Men and women and children lay there in huge piles, heaped upon one another, emaciated, deformed, naked, decayed . . . I wanted to scream. What communion with the power of evil had found its fountainhead in this majestic murder! . . . I made an effort to enter a hut. I staggered back. Revulsion, nausea, something near a mental blackout drove me from the place. I could sense rather than discern that the vague shadows in the dark corners were more—more what? Dead, dead, everywhere dead. I tried again to enter. I could not.

McMillan wrote that SS guards were forced to load bodies onto trucks, but three of them could stand it only a short time and ran screaming. British guards cut them down with Sten guns. "Not a murmur of pity was heard." Camp doctors told McMillan some prisoners were so desperate they had eaten the hearts and kidneys of the dead. He was taken to see SS women guards. "They were in cells, husky, upstanding, revolting specimens of the race . . . I talked with them until I felt I could not stay any longer in the presence of such loathsome specimens of womanhood." He learned that one SS woman had once tied a living woman to the corpse of a dead one, poured gasoline over them and burned the living and dead together. Before doing so, she cut off one of the living woman's fingers.[19]

Ronald Monson, writing for the Sydney *Daily Telegraph*, the *Melbourne Age* and London's *Daily Express*, was so angered when he entered Belsen that he punched the first German he saw. Leaving the camp, still in a rage, "I drove my car into a column of German prisoners. My God, did they scream!"[20]

Reginald W. Thompson had previously been an Intelligence Corps captain working as a censor, but was released in July 1944 to become a correspondent for *The Sunday Times* and the Kemsley Newspapers. Josef Kramer and his guards "are actually proud of this camp," he wrote. "They do not see anything wrong about it. In fact these Germans are without hope. They are not as other men. The thing is satanic."

"There is no sanitation," Thompson wrote. "People just excrete when they must where they are." In one hut, he found human excrement mixed with clothing, straw and bedding on the floor. "These are things beyond the conception of the human race . . . a kind of missing-link atrocity committed against mankind."

Thompson wrote that middle-class Germans bombarded officers with petty complaints. One woman groused that freed Polish prisoners were stealing her chickens. An outraged American soldier said to her: "Don't you know about the thousand Polish civilians burned in barns! Don't you know about the way you have treated these people in your filthy horror camps!" The woman replied: "Yes. But they still go on stealing my chickens."[21]

* * *

Dachau, 9 miles northwest of Munich, was liberated by the American Army on April 29. Established in 1933, it was the oldest of the camps and was set up to house political prisoners but later included many Jews. At various times it contained 200,000 prisoners, two-thirds of them political, and 25,613 died. There were 32,000 survivors.

Marguerite Higgins was 6 miles from Dachau, in an area yet to be secured by the Allies. She and her army driver, Peter Furst, passed Wehrmacht soldiers in a village strewn with white flags. The soldiers handed over rifles, pistols and grenades until their Jeep could hold no more. As Higgins and Furst approached the camp, she wrote, "I became aware of a strange smell, at first sweet and cloying, then heavy with decay." Near a string of boxcars, she was convulsed with nausea; they were full of rotting corpses. The prisoners had been brought from Buchenwald, and some who survived walked or crawled out of the cars. Some were shot, others beaten to death, others left locked in until they died. Higgins turned away to be sick.

When they reached the main gate, she wrote, an SS general was holding a large white flag while, above her, a watchtower was filled with men whose rifles and machine guns were trained on her. She said she called out: "Kommen Sie hier, bitte. Wir sind Amerikaner." Twenty-two guards walked out with hands up. By her account, Furst shoved an SS officer onto the hood of his Jeep, cocked a pistol and handed it to her to keep him from running away, then drove through the gate. Prisoners rushed out screaming with joy. A Polish priest began kissing Higgins, then apologized profusely when he found this uniformed figure was not a man as he supposed.

Higgins related that she addressed prisoners in French, English and German, telling them they were free. Then, she went on, an American officer grabbed her, told her the camp was raging with typhus and ordered her out. "Goddammit to hell!" she shouted. "I've had my typhus shots! Lay off me! I'm doing my job!" Prisoners began rioting when told they would have to be screened for typhus before they could leave. Higgins wrote that she got on a loudspeaker and explained the dangers of prisoners hurling themselves on the electrified fence. But six did so in a suicidal protest.[22]

This is a remarkable tale of bravado, one of the most striking such accounts of the war, but how much of it is true? That Higgins and Furst were the first reporters on the scene, and that Higgins was a notably hard-driving, enterprising correspondent, are not in doubt. But testimony from a number of Army officers and prisoners who were present alongside Higgins does not support her account. The most detailed version of events was provided in an official report by Lt. William Cowling III, an aide to Brig. Gen. Henning Linden. Linden accepted the surrender of the camp—not by an SS general but a lieutenant. Cowling wrote that he, not Higgins, spoke in German to the guards in the tower and ordered them to come down. Twelve, not twenty-two, did so. In a letter to his parents, giving a more colorful account, Cowling said Higgins and Furst told him they were going into the camp so he climbed onto the front of their Jeep and led them inside. He made no mention of any officer attempting to stop Higgins, or of her supposed heated rejoinder. Inside the camp, prisoners rushed to them, attempting to shake their hands, kiss them or just touch them. They grabbed Cowling and the two correspondents and threw them into the air. Then some prisoners flung themselves across a ditch onto the electrified fence and died immediately. Cowling did not support Higgins's claim that these were suicides, nor did he refer to her addressing prisoners through a loudspeaker. Did Higgins indulge in unwarranted and unprofessional self-dramatization? The accounts by Cowling and others indirectly suggest that she did.[23]

Ann Stringer, who arrived later, saw bodies still lying in ovens. The commandant apologized because he had run out of fuel to keep the ovens running. "After seeing all this, I had hated a lot of Germans for a long time," she wrote later. "When I recall scenes like these even now . . . I always think it is a wonder that any of us who were there came out of it with our sanity intact."[24]

When news of Dachau broke, the New York newspaper *PM* cabled its correspondent Raymond Davies: JEWISH ATROCITY STORIES NOT ACCEPTABLE NEWS MATERIAL. The reason for that is unclear today. *PM* was a left-wing newspaper and sympathetic to Jews.[25]

Martha Gellhorn arrived to find liberated prisoners were sitting in the sun and searching themselves for lice. "They have no age and no faces; they all look alike and like nothing you will ever see if you are lucky." A Polish doctor told her of barbaric experiments carried out in the camp. The Germans wished to see how long an aviator could go without oxygen, so they put prisoners inside closed cars from which they pumped the oxygen. "Death doesn't take more than 15 minutes, but it is a hard death," she wrote. All 800 victims of that experiment died. Another one was intended to find out how long pilots could survive when shot down over water. Prisoners were made to stand in vats of water up to their necks. At 8 degrees below zero, a person can resist for two and a half hours. Six hundred died in this experiment.

A German doctor inoculated 11,000 prisoners with tertiary malaria, seeking a way of immunizing soldiers against it. "The death rate was not too heavy, but it meant they died more quickly afterward from hunger." Gellhorn also wrote that Jews and gypsies were castrated and any foreign slave laborer who had had relations with a German woman was sterilized. In another experiment, Polish priests were injected with streptococci germs in the upper leg. Abscesses formed, accompanied by fever and extreme pain. At least thirty-one died. Gellhorn found piles of bodies in the crematorium, all naked. "The bodies were dumped like garbage, rotting in the sun, yellow and nothing but bones, bones grown huge because there was no flesh to cover them, hideous, terrible, agonizing bones, and the unendurable smell of death."[26]

Lee Miller wrote that a small canal bounding the camp was "a floating mess of SS, in their spotted camouflage suits and nail-studded boots. They slithered along in the current, along with a dead dog or two and smashed rifles."

The prisoners included a number of journalists, among them Philippe Brundt of Brussels's *Le Peuple* and *Le Soir*, and Leurs Vancoeverde, a Dutch UP correspondent. In a letter to a friend, Miller wrote: "The sight of the blue and white striped tatters shrouding the bestial death of the hundreds of starved and maimed men and women had left us gulping for air and for violence."[27]

On May 1, Ian Wilson reported in a BBC broadcast that 2,000 prisoners had been murdered by machine-gun fire a few hours before liberation. He observed this notice in German on walls of the crematorium: "Cleanliness is a duty here so don't forget to wipe your hands."[28]

* * *

Last to be liberated was Ravensbrück, a women's camp 55 miles north of Berlin. In its six-year existence, 130,000 women had been held there, and estimates on the number of survivors ranged from 15,000 to 32,000. As Russian troops approached, German guards took 20,000 women on a death march toward Mecklenburg, and the Russians arrived on April 30 to find 3,500 women and 300 men still in the camp. Russians soon liberated the women on the death march.

Sigrid Schultz, a former Berlin-based correspondent of the *Chicago Tribune* and now a broadcaster for the Mutual network, reported that SS women guards carried whips with leather clods and used them freely. One officer trampled on a woman who fainted from exhaustion. Schultz reported that all women, upon arrival in the camp, were given sterility shots and now feared they would remain sterile for life. "The healthiest and most beautiful women ... were segregated in an experimental station where veins were removed from their legs and grafted on other bodies, while the wounds were infected with diseases which the Germans wanted to study."[29]

CHAPTER 19

THE END OF THE WAR IN EUROPE

Russian and American forces met beside the Elbe River at Torgau on April 24, 1945. The next day, Berlin was surrounded by two Russian armies. In Italy, Mussolini was captured and shot by partisans on April 28, and the next day German forces in Italy surrendered. Hitler and his bride Eva Braun committed suicide on April 30. German troops in northwest Germany, the Netherlands and Denmark surrendered to the British on May 4; resistance on the American fronts ended two days later. The Germans hoped for an exclusive final surrender to the Americans, but Eisenhower demanded that it apply on all fronts. General Alfred Jodl signed it on May 7, but Stalin insisted on a further surrender ceremony in Berlin on May 8.

Ann Stringer was in Leipzig when she got word on April 25 of the Torgau link-up. The army provided two Piper Cubs and pilots to fly her and INS photographer Allan Jackson there the next day. The planes landed in a field just outside Torgau. A young Russian ran down the street wearing only shorts and a gray cap with a red star and hammer and sickle on it. He had just swum the Elbe to greet them.

"Bravo, Amerikanski! Bravo, comrades!" he shouted. Giving his red star to Stringer, he led them to a river bank where they found two racing shells and rowed across. More Russians ran up shouting, "Vive Roosevelt!" and "Vive Stalin!" They had not been told that Roosevelt had died two weeks earlier. Stringer and Jackson were driven to nearby Werdau to meet the regimental commander, Maj. Gen. Vladimir Rusakov, who invited them to lunch. He told Stringer she was the first American woman he and his troops had ever seen.

Lunch included traditional toasts, not just in vodka but cognac, wine, schnapps and other drinks. Stringer, while reluctant to leave, was mindful of the fact Jack Thompson of the *Chicago Tribune* was present and she was determined to file first. "I knew I just *had* to head back for Paris, and quickly." The Russians helped her into the racing shell and gave it a push—too hard. It overturned and she went into the river. Soaking wet and with her notes blurred, she found her pilot waiting but he told her there was no way a Piper Cub could fly to Paris. Nonetheless, they started out and soon saw a C-47 transport landing in a field. They put down alongside it and Stringer rushed up to two airmen, explaining she had just met the Russians and had to get to Paris to file. They smiled but refused to believe her. Instead of arguing, she sat down on the grass and started typing. The airmen read over her shoulder and one exclaimed: "Hey! She met the Russians! She *did* meet the Russians! Let's go!"

In Paris she filed her story at the Hotel Scribe press center, along with Jackson's photos, then happened upon other correspondents who had heard of the meeting with the Russians. Before she had the chance to tell them she had just some from Torgau, they commiserated with her for having missed a good story.

Stringer later learned fresh details of the Torgau meeting. German guards had deserted a nearby prison camp and an Irish sergeant in the British Army found a bottle of cognac, drained it and decided to walk into Torgau to buy his wife a present. As he staggered down the street in British uniform, inhabitants thought the Allies had arrived and put out white flags. One American prisoner told Stringer that seventy-six German officers, including five generals, had been held at the camp, most suspected of involvement in the plot on Hitler's life in 1944. "The Germans had been executing them at the rate of five and six daily," he said. Six Americans were under sentence of death and five others on trial for "planning treason against the Reich."[1]

Other correspondents reached Torgau. Edward Ward reported in a BBC broadcast on April 27: "In the picturesque medieval town of Torgau I saw soldiers of the First American and the Red Armies throw their arms round each other's neck and kiss each other on the cheeks. I even had to undergo this greeting myself from a burly Ukrainian soldier."[2]

Richard Hottelet of CBS reconstructed the initial meeting, which he had not witnessed:

There were no brass bands, no sign of the titanic strength of both these armies. The Americans who met the Red Army were a couple of dust-covered lieutenants and a handful of enlisted men in their Jeeps on reconnaissance . . . That's just the way it was, as simple and untheatrical as that. Just some men meeting, shaking hands.[3]

Virginia Irwin of the *St. Louis Post-Dispatch* and Andrew Tully of the *Boston Traveler* attended Russian celebrations, then decided on impulse to head for Berlin. They persuaded the 26th Infantry to turn over a Jeep to them, along with driver Sgt. Johnny Wilson, even though Berlin was out of bounds to the American press. Lee Carson and Don Whitehead had the same idea, but their car broke down and by the time it was fixed the fighting was too heavy for them to continue.

Irwin and Tully came upon highways clogged with Russian vehicles. "The fierce fighting men of the Red Army in their tunics and great boots, shabby and ragged after their long war . . . were like so many holiday-makers going on a picnic," Irwin wrote. In Berlin, bodies lay all about, horses ran loose. "The Russians were walking on a carpet of dead Germans." Russian soldiers suspected the correspondents were spies and took them to a command post. There an officer cleared them of suspicion and laid on a sumptuous dinner, with dancing afterward.

On the evening of their second day in Berlin, Irwin and Tully thought it was time to get back to American lines and file. They reached the Elbe but the Russians refused to take them across, so Irwin stood on the river bank and shouted: "I'm an American woman, come and get me away from these Russians." Two assault boats put out and brought them across.

At a press camp in Weimar, censors refused to clear their stories and the Allied Command suspended their credentials. Eventually their dispatches were allowed to go out, but too late to have the impact they had expected. Tully reported he had seen "desperate fear" in the eyes of German civilians when he told them American troops would not be coming to Berlin. "The man in the street in Berlin is well aware of his crimes against the Russian people and he is horrified by the fact that retribution is at hand." In 1936, Tully had become the youngest newspaper publisher in the U.S. when he bought the *Southbridge Press* in Massachusetts at age 21.[4]

Seymour Freidin of the *New York Herald-Tribune* got into Berlin and reported that he saw Russian soldiers sweep into the Tiergarten and subdue the last defenders. "This once great capital . . . is a charred, twisted, unrecognizable graveyard. Nothing is left in Berlin. There are no homes, no shops, no transportation, no government buildings. Only a few walls—and even these are riddled with shellfire . . ."[5]

Other correspondents headed for Berlin—MacVane, Hottelet, Victor
Bernstein of *PM* and Bob Reuben of Reuters. Accompanied by press officer
Jack Hansen, they arrived on May 4. The Propaganda Ministry was burning
and they saw the ruins of Hitler's Chancellery. On May 8, they returned to their
press camp and were warned that, if word of their trip got out, Hansen would
be court-martialed and they would be disaccredited and sent home. They agreed
to report they had been with the Red Army but to make no mention of Berlin.
The secret remained intact until MacVane revealed it in a book in 1979.[6]

* * *

On April 27, partisans in northern Italy captured Benito Mussolini beside
Lake Como and executed him the next day. The *Baltimore Sun* claimed this
story as its biggest war scoop. *Sun* correspondent Howard Norton and several
colleagues were in Verona when they heard rumors of Mussolini's capture.
They rushed to Milan, saw the bodies of Mussolini, his mistress Clara Petacci
and his Fascist minions, interviewed partisans, then drew straws to see who
would file first. Norton drew the long straw, but those who filed ahead of him
only sent four-word flashes: Mussolini Killed by Partisans. He sent a far longer
piece—then sun spots disrupted radio communication with the rest of
Europe. So his competitors could not flesh out their copy until later, giving
the *Sun* a world beat.[7]

Milton Bracker of the *New York Times*, who was with Norton, described
his own coverage of this story as "the greatest moment of my professional
life . . . That moment . . . roared into and possessed my spirit." Bracker
described how Mussolini's yellowing face was propped up with a rifle butt to
turn it into the sun for the only two Allied cameramen present. "I crouched
over the body to the left in order not to cut off the sun from his turned face.
A group of us had been thrust by the enthusiastic Milanese . . . right into the
circle of death. It was naturally one of the grimmest moments of our lives . . ."

The *New York Times* got the first photos of Mussolini's body, taken by an
Italian photographer. *Times* publisher Arthur Hays Sulzberger received offers
as high as $5,000 for republication rights but released the photos free to
anyone who wanted them.[8]

* * *

A Soviet war correspondent, who did not give his name, described for the
BBC on April 30 the Red Army's approach to Berlin:

One of Hitler's warriors has a beard to his waist; another, in dark glasses, steps high like a blind pony. A third stumps along on a wooden leg . . . The streets are strewn with SS badges, ribbons stamped with the swastika, torn-up Nazi Party cards, officers' shoulder straps ripped out . . . Berliners . . . say that in the area still uncaptured mobs of people are looting the food stores and neither the police nor SS can stop them. A police battalion, sent to round up deserters, itself deserted almost to a man on the road.[9]

Ian Monks was with an American unit that liberated a Russian prisoner-of-war camp near Magdeburg holding 10,000 men. Gen. W. S. Simpson met Russian officers and asked for help in feeding the men. An officer replied: "If they are prisoners, they are not Russians. We don't want them. We won't have them." Simpson sent them to Russian lines anyway. The usual fate of Russians who had surrendered was to be sent to Siberian labor camps on Stalin's orders.[10]

* * *

In the Bavarian town of Lichtenfels, Marguerite Higgins ran across a bizarre story. The secret correspondence of Dr. Alfred Rosenberg, the Nazi philosopher and formulator of Nazi racial history, was found in a cellar five stories below the sixteenth-century Lichtenfels Castle. Rosenberg's right-hand man, Baron Kurt von Behr, offered to reveal the hiding place in exchange for some space in the castle for himself and his wife. The terms were agreed, and the couple were later found dead in a luxurious room to which they had been assigned. They had washed down phials of poison with champagne.[11]

On May 1, the day Hitler's death was announced, Lee Miller enjoyed the singular experience of living in Hitler's private apartment at Prinzregentenplatz 16 in Munich. It had become a command post of the 179th Regiment of the U.S. 45th Division. Miller wrote there was no indication that "anyone more pretentious than merchants or retired clergy had lived there . . . It lacked grace and charm, it lacked intimacy . . . The art work . . . was mediocre as were the paintings on all the walls." All the crystal, china, linen and silver bore a swastika and the initials A. H.

In the 1920s Hitler had been a lodger in the apartment, owned by Rhineland manufacturers who had gone bankrupt. By 1929 Hitler had taken it over and installed a couple as housekeepers. He bought the entire building in 1935. Three blocks away, at Wasserburgerstrasse 12, was the villa of his lover, Eva Braun. "Portraits of Hitler tenderly autographed to Eva and to her sister Gretl, who lived with her, were in plain view," Miller wrote. "I took a nap on Eva's bed."[12]

* * *

Chester Wilmot covered the German surrender to Field Marshal Montgomery on May 4 at Lüneburg Heath near the River Elbe. "The triumph of the British armies in Europe is complete," he said in a BBC broadcast. "Tomorrow morning at eight o'clock the war will be over for the British and Canadian troops, and for the airmen of Britain and the Commonwealth . . ." Wilmot interviewed a British sergeant-major who was present after the suicide of Heinrich Himmler, the SS chief. The soldier had difficulty expressing himself and had to be encouraged with coffee and brandy. Censors cut out his last words: "And I spat in his eye, the dirty bastard."[13]

Moorehead witnessed the surrender, then flew with other correspondents to Copenhagen. "Unwisely one or two of us ventured out of the hotel, hoping to see something of the town. We were seized by the crowd and hoisted shoulder-high around the square. When we pleaded to be put down they dumped us on the roof of a car and began to parade us round the streets." The press contingent continued to Oslo. At the Grand Hotel, correspondents were pushed onto a balcony overlooking the central square. It was filled with a crowd extending into side streets, "a great pink carpet of upturned faces and waving red flags. They hung from the roofs and windowsills. They shouted across from the neighboring buildings." Then the crowd began to sing the national anthem.

Two men pushed their way into the hotel room, one the lame leader of the Resistance movement, the other his lieutenant. They had just broken out of jail and now, overcome with emotion, could not speak. They stood holding correspondents' hands. Moorehead commented on how an ordinary man can grow in stature during conflict, as the Resistance leader did:

> He was suddenly projected out of a shallow and material world into an atmosphere where there really were possibilities of touching the heights, and here and there a man found greatness in himself . . . Five years of watching war have made me personally hate and loathe war, especially the childish wastage of it. But this thing—the brief ennoblement inside himself of the otherwise dreary and materialistic man—kept recurring again and again up to the very end, and it refreshed and lighted the whole heroic and sordid story.[14]

* * *

In Moscow, Duncan Hooper of Reuters learned of the suicide of Nazi propaganda chief Joseph Goebbels in Hitler's bunker. A Soviet official approached
him at a party and said: "It is very sad about Dr. Goebbels." Not knowing
what he was talking about, Hooper replied: "Very sad." Then the official said:
"You know they killed all the family. They killed the children in the bunker
and then killed themselves."[15]

Vasily Grossman arrived in Berlin when Soviet troops entered on May 2.
He wrote of "a monstrous concentration of impressions. Fires and fires,
smoke, smoke, smoke. Enormous crowds of prisoners . . . This overcast, cold
and rainy day is undoubtedly the day of Germany's ruin." Grossman entered
Hitler's office and opened a desk drawer. Inside were official stamps saying
"The Führer has confirmed," "The Führer has agreed," etc. He took several
and they now reside in the same Moscow archive as his papers.[16]

* * *

The German surrender was scheduled for May 7 at Eisenhower's headquarters, a schoolhouse in Reims. Unbelievably, Lt. Gen. Walter Bedell Smith,
Ike's chief of staff, had decided there would be no press coverage. On May 4,
Charles Wertenbaker of Life magazine showed up, but was lured outside and
left there. Knowing something big was about to break, he waited and saw two
German officers arrive in uniform. Wertenbaker drove to Paris, where Allied
press headquarters was located. Back at Reims, a captain on Eisenhower's staff
decided to override Smith. He phoned Brig. Gen. Frank Allen, the public
relations chief in Paris, and instructed him to bring a minimum press party.

On May 6, Ed Kennedy, now Paris bureau chief for the AP, was awakened
by a phone call. The AP could send a single correspondent to report an event
that could not be disclosed. Convinced it was the German surrender, Kennedy
decided to cover it himself. What followed would touch off the most highly
publicized and long-lasting journalistic controversy of the entire war.

Allen selected seventeen correspondents from news agencies, radio
networks and newspapers that included Army publications. On board the
flight to Reims, reporters were told it was the surrender. A public relations
officer said the story would be held for release at a time to be set by Eisenhower's
headquarters, and asked if they understood that. All said yes. In Reims,
correspondents had to wait nine hours in the school. About twenty others
who had not been invited but had learned the surrender was imminent arrived

to express their indignation at being excluded. Allen barred them from the building.

Finally at 2:41 a.m. on May 7, Gen. Alfred Jodl, chief of the operations staff of the German Armed Forces High Command, signed the document of surrender, and it was countersigned by U.S., Russian and French generals. Osmar White wrote: "Jodl's eyes were suffused with tears and his face was etched with lines of bitter humiliation and despair." After the ceremony, Allen allowed the correspondents who had been left outside to enter the headquarters and look at the signing room.

Then the press pool watched as the Germans called on Eisenhower, who had not attended the ceremony and was in his office. "We heard him record his short victory speech in a quiet, clear, tired voice," White wrote. "His eyes, too, were purple-shadowed and his cheeks hung slackly. That was how they made peace in Europe."

Kennedy wrote a dispatch and a censor approved it, then asked for it back and crossed out his "okay" because the release time was still uncertain. Allen told correspondents that Eisenhower wanted the news announced immediately, but his hands were tied politically and the release was set for 3 p.m. Paris time on May 8. "I knew from experience that one might as well try to censor the rising of the sun," Kennedy later wrote. After correspondents were back in Paris, he learned that Washington and London had ordered the delay at the request of the Russians, who wanted another "and more formal" surrender ceremony in Berlin. "It was apparent that any second surrender in Berlin would be wholly meaningless and staged for Soviet propaganda purposes," Kennedy wrote.

At 2:03 p.m. on May 7, Count Johann Ludwig von Krosigk, foreign minister of the new German government of Adm. Karl Dönitz, spoke over the radio at Flensburg to announce the surrender for the benefit of German troops. The British Ministry of Information picked up the broadcast and made it available to the press in London. Still, the Reims embargo remained in effect. Kennedy went to Lt. Col. Richard H. Merrick, the chief American censor, and told him that, since Eisenhower's headquarters had plainly authorized release of the story in London, he felt himself under no further obligation to observe censorship. "I give you warning now that I am going to release the story," he said. With a shrug, Merrick replied: "Do as you please."

Kennedy went to his hotel bedroom and debated with himself. After 15 minutes he decided to send the news, knowing he could reach the AP office in London through a military telephone. He asked Morton Gudebrod of the AP to put in a call to London, then dictated his story, giving all the essential details, before the connection failed. When the story reached New York, executives were hesitant because UP and INS had carried nothing and no world capital had confirmed the Flensburg report. Finally, at 9:35 a.m. Eastern War Time, May 7, the AP put the story on its wires. In Paris, Kennedy told his staff: "Well, now let's see what happens. I may not be around here much longer."

Later he wrote: "The storm broke quickly." Allen suspended AP operations throughout Europe, and the hotel room phones of AP correspondents were cut off. Six hours later the suspension of AP operations was lifted but the ban on Kennedy and Gudebrod remained. Allen's inquiry concluded that Kennedy's action was a violation of security "definitely involving possible loss of American and Allied lives." Kennedy commented in his memoir: "Lives are not lost by announcing the end of a war; they may be lost by withholding an announcement of it."

Back in Paris, Marshall Yarrow of Reuters and Drew Middleton of the *New York Times* resented the renewal of AP privileges, and fifty-four correspondents drafted a letter to Eisenhower, in Kennedy's words, "condemning me in language of an extravagance worthy of the frenzied mood of the assemblage." He wrote that correspondents who argued against sending the letter were shouted down. The letter stated: "We have respected the confidence placed in us by SHAEF [Supreme Headquarters Allied Expeditionary Force] and as a result have suffered the most disgraceful, deliberate and unethical doublecross in the history of journalism."

But that was not the reaction at home. The U.S. War Department cabled Eisenhower that the American press and radio "is featuring Associated Press story as great scoop and making martyr out of Kennedy as victim of unjustified withholding of news by your headquarters." It suggested any statement should come from him. Eisenhower issued a statement denouncing "a self-admitted, deliberate breach of confidence" and accusing the AP of a "clear violation of its word of honor to me as Supreme Commander of the Allied Forces in Europe." He added: "It has been one of the very few unfortunate experiences I have had with the press during my service as a commander. Up to now I have felt free to take all correspondents into my confidence."

The AP retreated. AP President Robert McLean, publisher of the *Philadelphia Bulletin*, said: "The Associated Press profoundly regrets the distribution on Monday of the report of the total surrender in Europe which investigation now clearly discloses was distributed in advance of authorization by Supreme Allied Headquarters." AP General Manager Kent Cooper said he was "reserving judgment" until he had talked to Kennedy. Wes Gallagher was chosen to replace Kennedy as manager in Paris, and went to Eisenhower to ask him to "get the Army off the AP's back." Gallagher said he would have done the same as Kennedy and Eisenhower, laughing, replied: "I would have thrown you in jail." Then they had lunch.

Kennedy returned to New York and held an impromptu press conference on a pier when his ship docked. He admitted he would "do it again" under the same circumstances. He met Cooper and offered to resign, but Cooper urged him to do nothing hasty and suggested he take a vacation. Kennedy did so, then returned to meet with McLean and Cooper. He offered his resignation but Cooper declined to accept it. Kennedy suggested that, if Cooper was not going to support him, he should fire him. Cooper declined and advised him to take a job being offered in the *New York Daily News* Washington bureau. On August 18, having turned down various offers to write magazine articles or a book, Kennedy resigned. The AP initially demurred but on October 20 made a $4,986.80 severance payment into his bank account, thus accepting the resignation.

Eisenhower subsequently agreed to review Kennedy's case. Afterward he said he had not been aware of all the facts and restored Kennedy's credentials and wished him well. But, loyal to his subordinates, he decreed that the order disaccrediting Kennedy had been "fully justified."

Kennedy took a job as managing editor of the *News-Press* in Santa Barbara and later became assistant editor and publisher of another California news-paper, the *Monterey Peninsula Herald*. He married AP correspondent Lyn Crost in New York in 1946 but they were divorced in 1951. In 1960 a number of correspondents covering John F. Kennedy's presidential campaign met in California. James Reston of the *New York Times* greeted Ed Kennedy affectionately. Walter Cronkite and others were barely civil. On November 29, 1963, a week after President Kennedy's assassination, Ed Kennedy was fatally injured when he was struck by a sports car while walking home on a rainy night. He had been expected to recover but a coroner's report listed his cause of death as cancer of the throat complicated by the accident injuries. He was 58.[17]

The controversy he unleashed outlived him by almost five decades. Then, on May 4, 2012, Kennedy won a posthumous apology from his former employer as his memoirs were published by Louisiana State University Press. Tom Curley, chief executive of the AP, acknowledged: "It was a terrible day for the AP. It was handled in the worst possible way." Kennedy's dismissal was a "great tragedy" for he had done "the right thing" and "stood up to power."[18]

Most people today undoubtedly would agree. Wartime censorship was supposed to be limited to questions of military security, and that plainly was not involved. President Truman acceded to Stalin's request to delay the announcement and Churchill went along reluctantly. News events by right become public information when they occur, not thirty-six hours later, and the German surrender made the reasons for maintaining censorship disappear. General Allen's suggestion that early release endangered lives was spurious and an unworthy smear on Kennedy.

On the other hand, a vital question remains. Some of Kennedy's critics insisted he had an obligation to inform fellow correspondents before filing. His response was that there were a hundred or so correspondents in Paris and he had no way of reaching them all immediately. But should he have informed his direct competitors at UP, INS and Reuters? A more pertinent question that he did not address. If the news agencies had collectively agreed to break the embargo, he could not have been accused of having engineered a scoop by underhanded means. And, even if his competitors had decided to abide by the embargo, his behavior, in my view, would have been more honorable by his not having kept them in the dark.

There is a plaque in a California park dedicated to the memory of Ed Kennedy. It reads: "He gave the world 24 hours more of happiness."[19]

CHAPTER 20

FINAL BATTLES IN THE PACIFIC

The capture of Tarawa in late 1943 cleared the way for the 1944 seizure of the Marshall Islands and the Marianas islands of Saipan, Tinian and Guam. The Japanese Combined Fleet sailed to meet the invaders in the Marianas. Three Japanese carriers were sunk and two others damaged. Saipan, with a garrison of 32,000 men, was attacked by 77,000 Marines on June 15. The Japanese suffered 4,000 casualties in the first forty-eight hours but it took three weeks to capture the island. The Americans began landing on Guam, which had a 19,000-man garrison, on July 21, and on Tinian on July 24. Most opposition ended after twelve days. The liberation of the Philippines and final battles of the Pacific lay ahead.

A victory in Saipan would give the United States its first B-29 base within range of Japan, 1,500 miles away. Robert Sherrod, the *Time* and *Life* correspondent, described the island as looking in profile like a low-lying prehistoric monster with a spine rising in the center to 1,554-foot Mount Tapotchau. For two days prior to the invasion, American ships pounded the island and air strikes followed. Sherrod wrote in his notebook: "I fear all this smoke and noise does not mean many Japs been killed." He was right about that. The early waves of Marines got ashore without much difficulty, then met heavy machine-gun and mortar fire.[1]

Howard Norton of the *Baltimore Sun* waded ashore on the opening day of battle and reported a stench of death hanging over the beach. "Bodies of Marines . . . lay where they had fallen along the water's edge. Swollen bodies of dead Japs lay farther inland among the trees and along the embankment of a narrow-gauge sugar cane railway." At this stage, Marines had not yet met the main enemy force. "All are convinced that they're watching a battle which will take a place in history beside Guadalcanal as one of the war's turning points," Norton wrote.[2]

American pilots flying from aircraft carriers sank four large Japanese ships 3 miles north of the landing area, and three smaller ones turned over on their sides. Sherrod went ashore with a Marine brigadier general and they sheltered in a Japanese-built tank trap as shells landed near them every 3 seconds for the first 20 minutes. "The Japs had not learned much about the proper use of artillery; most shots went into the water," Sherrod wrote. As he dug a foxhole, he estimated he had seen 100 dead Marines and only about 20 dead Japanese.

Heavy shelling by artillery and mortars, one every five seconds, continued through the night but for Sherrod there was none of the terror he had experienced on Tarawa. He had got used to being shot at, but he also knew he didn't have to fear Japanese counterattacks at night; front lines were lighted up constantly with star shells. Further, the front lines were 500 yards away, not 20 feet as on Tarawa. A Japanese counterattack left about 700 of the enemy dead, but Marine casualties were much heavier than expected. They were facing Japanese hidden in mountainside dugouts, "looking down our throats."

Sherrod returned to his ship that day to write his first story, thus missing a large-scale Japanese tank attack against the Marines that began at 3:30 a.m. Marines firing bazookas from foxholes knocked out twenty-nine tanks. At 7:35 a.m., Marines attacked up the slopes of Mount Tapotchau and found one Japanese civilian had cut the throats of his wife and child. Some Marines attacking a cave called for a flamethrower, and when the six Japanese soldiers inside heard the word they blew themselves up with grenades.

Sherrod wrote two more stories before he discovered no news had been transmitted except for a pooled news agency dispatch on the first day. The ships offshore had pulled out, and seaplanes that were supposed to fly dispatches to Kwajalein or Pearl Harbor for radio transmission had been kept on Saipan to serve as search patrols.[3]

In late June, Marine Lt. Gen. Holland Smith, directing the operation, relieved an army commander, Maj. Gen. Ralph Smith, for holding his men back when he had been ordered to attack in support of Marines. Sherrod wrote that no correspondent was disposed to write about this, partly because they knew censors would never pass a story about friction among commanders. But, on July 8, the Hearst-owned *San Francisco Examiner* carried a Washington-datelined story, and Hearst's *New York Journal-American* editorialized in Ralph Smith's favor on July 17.

Throughout the war, battlefield commanders had been relieved on various fronts and this had attracted no publicity. But the Hearst papers unleashed a public controversy that was fanned that September when Holland Smith confirmed at a Pentagon news conference that he had relieved the Army general. Sherrod, then back in New York, wrote an article for *Time* that fully supported Holland Smith's version of events, igniting a further uproar. As Holland Smith later wrote, "You would have thought the skies were falling."

In his article Sherrod accused the third regiment of the Army's 27th Division of having "failed dismally" and said the troops "froze in their foxholes." Sherrod wrote that Ralph Smith's chief fault was that he had earlier failed to get tough enough to remove incompetent subordinate officers. Lt. Gen. Robert C. Richardson, who commanded Army troops in the Central Pacific and bitterly resented the removal of an Army general, demanded that Sherrod's press credentials be revoked.

The issue finally went before Adm. Ernest J. King, chief of naval operations in Washington, who concluded that Richardson had acted improperly. Sherrod's credentials were not revoked and he soon returned to reporting from the Pacific theater. It is noteworthy that, in his book about the Saipan battle, Sherrod made no mention of his article and the ensuing uproar, strongly suggesting he had had second thoughts about his role in the matter. Indeed, forty-five years later in 1990, he admitted he had gone "too far in questioning the courage of the 27th Division soldiers" when he wrote that they "froze in their foxholes." He added: "I should not have done it and I'm sorry."[4]

Sherrod, incidentally, was one of the few war correspondents who had anything good to say about military censorship:

> In the Central Pacific I found most censors men of goodwill . . . Working . . . was never made excessively difficult by the restriction of censorship, even if some of those restrictions seemed absurd at times . . . Whatever a correspondent wrote had to be held within the broad outlines of the communique, but the communique, if sometimes slow, was nearly always honest and reasonable.[5]

On July 9, after a final Japanese banzai attack in which 2,000 were killed, Saipan was declared secure. But mopping-up operations against Japanese entrenched in caves went on for more than a year. In the aftermath of fighting, Keith Wheeler of the *Chicago Times* and Frank Kelly of the *New York Herald-Tribune* returned from Marpi Point on the northern tip of the island to report that whole families of Japanese civilians were wading out to sea and drowning themselves rather than surrender. Fathers were throwing children off cliffs and some families clustered together, pulling pins out of grenades in mass suicides.

Sherrod then went to Marpi Point. On the edge of rocks by the sea, a Japanese boy about 13 years old walked back and forth, then sat on a rock and let a wave sweep him out to sea. He lay inert on the surface, then some instinct for survival caused him to flail frantically with his arms before he died. Marines told Sherrod they had seen parents blow their children's heads off with grenades, then jump off cliffs into the sea.

One Japanese sniper spotted a couple and their four children, preparing to drown themselves but evidently becoming undecided. He shot the parents and would have shot the children if a Japanese woman had not carried them out of range. The sniper then walked proudly out of his cave and met a fusillade of bullets.

Marines told of watching three women sitting on rocks, leisurely combing their long, black hair. Finally they joined hands and walked slowly into the sea. About a hundred Japanese on seaside rocks bowed to Marines watching from a cliff, stripped off their clothes, bathed in the sea, put on new clothes and spread a huge Japanese flag on a rock. Their leader distributed grenades and they killed themselves. Fifty other civilians were watched by six Japanese soldiers who dashed out of a cave and blew themselves up. Thus shamed, the civilians did likewise. A Marine told Sherrod of a woman who drowned herself while giving birth; the baby's head had just appeared when she went under water.

A Marine lieutenant took amphibious tractors to try to fetch Japanese soldiers who had fled to a reef. As he approached, an officer drew his sword and six men knelt on coral rocks. The officer sliced off four heads, which rolled into the sea, as the amphtracs (amtraks in later wars) drew near. Then, sword in hand, he charged the amphtracs. The Marines shot him and the two remaining men.

Sherrod remained on Saipan until July 13. He reported that 15,000 soldiers and Marines had been killed or wounded, but the Americans had acquired their first B-29 base in the Central Pacific.[6]

Guam was invaded after Saipan. On July 21, 1944, Howard Norton was aboard a submarine chaser that received a direct hit. Standing on the exposed forward deck, he ran back toward the main cabin and crouched down between two men blocking a door. "I hardly hit the deck when a third shell burst with a terrific roar, smack on the forward guns' ammunition cases, about 10 feet from where the three of us were crouching." Three men handling ammunition were killed and the steward's mate, beheaded and dismembered, lay beneath a gun. Thirteen men were wounded and Norton found the metal visor of his helmet had deflected shrapnel. "So much blood spilled over me from injured shipmates that I had difficulty convincing the skipper I was not injured."

Norton wrote that troops were bitter over a lack of interest at home in the Pacific war. Nothing happening in Europe, in his view, compared with what he had seen on Saipan. "The world was amazed by the Russian army's advance of more than 900 miles. But in the last nine months our forces in the Central Pacific advanced 3,000 and in the Southwest Pacific nearly 1,000. They recaptured more than eight million square miles."[7]

Wilfred Burchett of the *Daily Express* observed the opening of the Guam invasion from the destroyer *Ringgold*. "After covering defeats and retreats, I found it exhilarating to be in the theater of victories and advances." As dive bombers dropped their payloads and Hellcat fighters strafed beaches, "it looked and sounded like an overkill of absurd dimensions. No enemy positions or living beings could possibly have survived . . . Not even the hermit crabs could still be alive. But some defenders were incredibly alive and active."

Two landing craft were soon dead in the water. Three more were burning. But Alligators hauling supplies reached shore safely. Burchett and other correspondents went ashore in late morning, stayed for two hours and returned to the ship to file. That night, they were back on shore and in foxholes. Japanese artillery began spraying the beaches and broke through to within 20 yards of field headquarters. Burchett reported that 950 of them died that night, 600 in a banzai charge in which they attached bayonets to long bamboo poles and jabbed them into foxholes. About sixty Marines died.

"For the first five nights we didn't sleep. We were kept awake by U.S. artillery or Jap counterfire with mortars and heavy machine guns." He went along with Marines moving toward an airfield and, as they reached the top of a quarry, a machine gun opened up. Three men fell. Burchett peered over a coconut log and saw a Japanese sniper firing from a platform near the top of a coconut palm. Grabbing a carbine dropped by one of the wounded, he fired at the sniper. "The whole top of the palm was blown off. I thought I had touched off a hand grenade, but I saw smoke trailing out of the barrel of a tank-mounted artillery piece. That was the only shot I fired in the war."

The Japanese had prepared their defenses in shelters reinforced by coconut logs underneath grassy mounds. The firing slits were too small to allow Marines to toss in grenades or demolition charges, so they fitted bulldozer blades to tanks and scooped off the tops of the mounds. The Japanese inside were then killed with grenades and flamethrowers. The Marines pulled out for a rest and Burchett described them as looking as though they had fought to the limits of human endurance.[8]

* * *

On February 29, 1944, Frank Legg of the Australian Broadcasting Commission joined American troops in an invasion of Los Negros, in the Admiralties Group north of Papua New Guinea, to seize a harbor and airstrip. He found the aim of Japanese artillery and machine-gun fire on the landing craft was "incredibly bad." As troops reached the edge of the airstrip, there was no sign of Japanese but soldiers were reluctant to move. Legg, a soldier before becoming a correspondent, thought the Americans were suffering from inexperienced leadership. He and a cameraman, "our carbines slung on our shoulders," led the way across the airstrip and "captured" it while the troops still hesitated. A week later, Allied planes were using the strip.[9]

* * *

The American campaign to regain the Philippines began in September 1944 with carrier-based planes destroying hundreds of Japanese aircraft on the ground and in the air. Four army divisions began landing on Leyte Island on October 20, against light opposition. The scene was now set for the greatest naval battle in history, involving two Japanese and two American fleets. In one battle, nine Japanese ships were sunk and the survivors turned for home. Another Japanese fleet headed undetected toward Leyte Gulf, inflicting a number of losses on the Americans. Adm. Halsey's aircraft then sank seven ships. Eleven thousand Japanese died in the naval battles, to 2,803 Americans. On January 9, 1945, U.S. forces landed on Luzon. Manila was razed and up to 100,000 Filipinos died in its ruins, along with 1,000 Americans and 16,000 Japanese. Altogether, nearly half a million Filipinos died in the war from combat, massacre, famine and disease.

Bill Dickinson of UP, assigned to write a pool report for all media outlets, waded ashore alongside MacArthur. The general went to a hastily set up radio station and broadcast to the Filipino people: "I have returned." A few days later, a group of correspondents came under bombing attack while trying to get back to their ship to file. One bomb killed Asahel "Ace" Bush of the AP and Stanley Gunn, a newcomer from the *Fort Worth Star-Telegram.* Clete Roberts of the Blue Network was slightly wounded.[10]

When Marines went ashore on Peleliu, east of the Philippines, in September, Wilfred Burchett was overhead in a Helldiver plane. The pilot agreed to "dive bomb" his dispatch onto a transmission ship. "The islands in the Palau group were like clumps of dung dropped by some prehistoric monster," Burchett wrote. "The plane turned down in a totally vertical dive. I thought: I can never stand it . . . We pulled out over the tops of palm trees, causing a sickening rush of blood to my head that made me vomit . . . I finished off a handwritten dispatch, sealed it in a tube with a smoke signal attached and dropped it alongside the transmission ship."

In Philippine waters later, he watched *Hancock* dive bombers take off to attack Japanese ships, but only 3 of 12 returned. Short of fuel, several landed in the water and the crews were rescued; others landed on smaller escort carriers. "The return of the second wave was different. In heavy rain and fog, planes ran out of fuel and plunged into the sea or crashed into battleships and cruisers, thinking they were carriers. Losses were heavy."[11]

George E. Jones of UP, aboard the carrier *Lexington* (a replacement for the one sunk in the Coral Sea), wrote an account of the battle that had to be taken by courier plane to Guam. Jones gave one copy to the pilot and kept two others in his pocket. On October 27, Harold Stassen, flag secretary to Adm. Halsey, former governor of Minnesota and perennial candidate for president after the war, flew to the *Lexington* to confer with its commander. Stassen agreed to deliver Jones's copy in Guam and he arrived ahead of the courier plane. Thus Jones had an exclusive story on the greatest battle in naval history.[12]

* * *

John Graham Dowling of the *Chicago Sun* was aboard a destroyer in the Mindanao Sea on December 13 when a crippled Japanese plane began diving toward it. "He still had the plane under control . . . Then came the horrible certainty that he had chosen his target and you were it . . . The Jap was no more than 75 yards off and still coming . . . You were feeling wobbly. 'Well, well—so this is how you go out.' Then, in an instant, the Jap wavered." The destroyer's guns were "simply putting so much fire into it that even a mouse in it could not stay alive." The plane crashed into the sea. "You, the observer, went down to the captain's cabin to the captain's washroom and threw up your lunch."[13]

* * *

On December 20, Homer Bigart was aboard a PT boat off Cebu when he and the crew spotted a flashing light from shore. They feared it might be Japanese trying to lure them in. "You do not have to be psychic to feel clammy apprehension, such as comes from finding a letter from the Bureau of Internal Revenue," Bigart wrote. But the light came from Americans who had been hiding from the Japanese—for more than three years in one case. The men who were rescued included an oil-well driller from California, a sugar plantation manager from Hawaii and nine members of a B-24 crew who had been shot down nineteen days earlier.

Later Bigart was on a boat off Corregidor when U.S. troops began attacking Japanese emplacements. From the mouth of a clifftop cave, a Japanese opened fire with a machine gun. "Our boat was nearest shore and we caught the first fusillade . . . We groveled in the slimy bottom near the ramp . . . On my right a doughboy suddenly raised the bloody stump of his right hand. An instant later, a soldier squatting next to him toppled dead." Bigart's craft came ashore and the men scrambled for cover. Then a mortar shell fragment sailing over Bigart's foxhole killed a soldier lying to his right. Troops stormed the hill and cleared snipers from the crest.[14]

* * *

On January 6, 1945, one of the first fierce Japanese kamikaze attacks occurred in the Lingayen Gulf west of Luzon. William Chickering, 28, of *Time-Life* was killed when a plane crashed onto the bridge of the battleship *New Mexico*. He left a wife and young son and, ten days after his death, a second son, William Henry Chickering III, was born. A tall, handsome Californian and Yale graduate, Chickering had been at his home in Honolulu when Pearl Harbor was attacked. In the next three years, he covered fighting on several Pacific islands. On the day before his death, he wrote to his wife Audrey, describing an attack on his ship by swarms of Japanese planes. "The planes came in swiftly, low, over the water, and we shot them, our bursts seeming to spray our own ships they were so low. Some of our ships were hit, but none seriously . . . We go into Lingayen tomorrow morning to start bombarding. Whew!"[15]

* * *

At Cabanatuan, due north of Manila, U.S. Rangers marched 30 miles behind enemy lines on January 30, 1945, to rescue 511 Americans. MacArthur then decided on a thrust of 60 miles through Japanese lines into Manila, where 4,000 prisoners were held at Santo Tomas University. This operation was of special interest to correspondents because some of their colleagues and spouses were there, as recounted in Chapter 8. Perhaps none was more anxious to reach Santo Tomas than Frank Hewlett of UP, whose wife Virginia was a prisoner.

U.S. Cavalry troops moved in on February 3, 1945, with four correspondents following. Near the university, they came under fire and hit the ground. An American colonel, wounded in the leg, ordered a tank to go in. Hewlett and Mydans ran toward the entrance and saw the lobby and stairway filled with people. "Who are you?" an unfriendly voice called loudly.

"Americans," they replied. "If you're Americans, put that flashlight on yourself." Mydans turned a flashlight on himself and said, "I'm Carl Mydans." There was a moment of silence, then yells and screams. Betty Wellborn threw her arms around him. "We thought you were Japs," she said, laughing. "We thought you were Japs." She began to sob.

Virginia Hewlett was nowhere to be seen. Frank asked a young girl, who motioned him outside. In the hospital building, a woman weighing no more than 80 pounds was coming down the stairs. Hewlett didn't recognize her at first. Then he threw his arms around her. Back in the main building, they came toward Mydans, holding hands and smiling. "She's just fine," Hewlett kept repeating. "She's completely recovered and she's just fine."

The prison wasn't yet entirely liberated. Sixty-five Japanese soldiers in one building were holding 220 hostages. The Japanese wanted, in exchange for freeing the hostages, to return to their own lines with full arms and ammunition. An American colonel agreed to side arms and rifles only. The Japanese accepted and came out the next day.[16]

The Australian correspondent Jack Percival had gone into Santo Tomas weighing 152 pounds and came out at 92. He immediately resumed filing for his Australian and British newspapers.[17]

Mydan's wife Shelley Smith was now reporting from Guam. After Manila fell, Mydans flew there to join her. MacArthur lifted his ban on women correspondents and they flew back to the Philippines. "The remnants of the Jap army was scattered in the mountains of central Luzon, starving, bug-ridden, sick and bewildered," Mydans wrote.[18]

H. D. "Doc" Quigg of UP followed the Cavalry when it liberated Santo Tomas. His UP colleague Robert Crabb was there, with his wife and two small children, and so was Vivian Weissblatt, whose husband Franz had been captured on Bataan in 1942. The next day Quigg followed an infantry division to Bilibid Prison in Manila. Quigg heard what sounded like American voices from inside. "Even as Stanley did in darkest Africa those many years ago, I said, 'I'm Quigg, United Press.' The Dr. Livingstone of Bilibid Prison grasped my hand firmly. 'I'm Weissblatt, United Press.' " Neither Weissblatt nor his wife had known anything of each other's fate for three years.[19]

On February 23, the Americans struck at dawn 25 miles behind Japanese lines at Los Baños, southeast of Manila, and rescued 2,100 internees. The entire garrison of 243 Japanese guards was killed. Gordon Walker of the *Christian Science Monitor* reported that the battle was "packed with all the drama and suspense of a Wild West dime thriller."[20]

* * *

American forces turned their attention to islands closer to Japan—Iwo Jima in February–March 1945, then Okinawa from April to mid-June, making the Japanese mainland subject to more air attacks. An invasion of Japan was being considered for November 1945.

Philip Heisler, 29, of the *Baltimore Sun* would cover Iwo Jima. But first he had to ride out a typhoon in a small escort carrier. His account was published on February 18, 1945:

> In the ready room, the pilots were huddled around the radio speaker. As the ship rolled to the starboard the heavy cabinet, chairs and tables slid across the steel deck, crashing into the men and pinning them to the bulk-head . . . Suddenly one plane tore loose. It thrashed into three other planes until all four crashed over the side of the ship. Other planes began tearing loose . . . Somebody told me the ship was built in less than a month by women war workers. It was not a comforting thought . . . Now a torpedo plane was thrown back on deck and crashed through an open elevator pit, landing on top of a fighter plane. From then on, after seven hours of being buffeted, things got better.[21]

Iwo Jima is 660 miles south of Japan and the U.S. Air Force needed it to shorten the distance for bomb runs and to rescue B-29 crews that went down near the Japanese coast. Robert Sherrod was aboard a ship off Iwo Jima for the heaviest naval and air bombardment of an island he had ever seen. In his notebook he wrote: "Though I've seen this many times, I can't help thinking, 'Nobody can live through this.' But I know better."

Despite the fear he often felt in covering battle, Sherrod now concluded that, of the millions of Americans involved in the war, none was more fortunate than the war correspondents, "privileged to witness history in the making . . . men who could come and go with a freedom barely restricted by military orders."

Keith Wheeler of the *Chicago Times* went in with the first Marine landing parties on February 19, 1945, and, when Sherrod arrived later, Wheeler was on his way back to the ship to file. He told Sherrod the beaches were blanketed with Japanese mortars, dead Marines were everywhere and landing craft were being smashed before they could pull out. He urged Sherrod not to attempt to go in. But Sherrod looked at the Marines in his patrol craft and "saw the same fear that gripped at my guts. I knew I couldn't stay aboard . . . I was mighty scared." But he knew the men on the boat and didn't want them to know he was afraid to face something they had to face. He also remembered that he had always felt contempt for "communique commandos" who reported from rear areas and never knew "what gunpowder actually smelled like.[22]

Philip Heisler reported:

The beach where the Marines landed reaches to a ridge . . . some 500 yards inland. Black sand churned by constant shelling formed a black fog that covered the entire area and obscured the sun, so that one did not know when daylight ended and night began . . . Frontline positions could be determined only by a line of twinkling flashes from enemy fire, or by occasional sheets of flame when Marines succeeded in crawling up to a pillbox and frying the enemy position.[23]

Onshore, Sherrod saw about twenty dead Marines. He began digging a foxhole, a difficult task in a beach composed of volcanic ash, and settled down for the night. At 4 a.m., mortar shells were raining down near him, but naval fire put a stop to that. At daybreak, dead Americans lay everywhere. There were fewer dead Japanese. That evening Sherrod wanted to go back to the ship to file but too many wounded Americans were waiting for evacuation so he stayed on the island. By evening the Marine position was more secure and the troops had captured one of two airfields. But Wheeler was wounded by a sniper on the airfield. He was hit in the neck, and fell into the arms of two Marine doctors.

Much later Sherrod learned that the aircraft carrier *Saratoga*, 50 miles off Iwo Jima, had been struck by seven kamikaze planes, with the loss of 123 men and 196 wounded. The escort carrier *Bismarck Sea* sank after a kamikaze attack, going down with 312 men. At the time, censors forbade correspondents from writing about suicide attacks. Adm. Chester Nimitz did not remove the restriction until April 13 Pacific time, a half hour before the death of President Roosevelt was announced. With the news now focused on Washington, kamikaze attacks got little space in newspapers.[24]

On February 23, Marines staged the historic raising of the American flag on the peak of Mount Suribachi. Heisler witnessed the flag raising from offshore and filed a report before correspondents on the island could return to the ship. Describing how Marines fought their way up to the volcano, he wrote: "They can talk about the flea-eye accuracy of Navy gunfire and pinpoint bombing, but there is nothing so accurate as a stick of dynamite placed next to the enemy you want to get. There is also nothing so dangerous to the guy who is doing it."[25]

Later Sherrod was on the captured airfield with *Newsweek*'s John Lardner when a sniper opened up. Lardner, a sports columnist turned war correspondent and son of the short-story writer Ring Lardner, was hit. "The thud sounded as though an ox had been hit on the head with an axe," Sherrod wrote. Lardner told Sherrod: "That felt like no bullet; that felt like a rock." The welt on his leg suggested it was a rock; the bullet must have hit a rock that ricocheted into his leg. "That's what I get for writing that the Japs are suckers for a fast curve," Lardner joked.[26]

On March 2, Heisler suggested the end of the battle was near:

Advance Marine patrols probing on this forsaken island today reported finding the bodies of Japanese women who had apparently committed suicide when the Jap troops were forced to retreat or face annihilation . . . The women were dressed in ceremonial kimonos, with fatal knife wounds in their bodies. Other patrols . . . reported finding an increasing number of Jap officers who had apparently committed hari-kiri . . . The officers' bodies were found in clean fancy uniforms with full gold braid and wearing ceremonial swords and decorations . . . The certainty of victory in the Iwo Jima campaign was typified today by the arrival on the scarred beach of a landing craft loaded with shining band instruments and bundles of brooms.

The battle lasted for twenty-six days. The Americans lost 20,000 men.[27]

The Okinawa landing took place on April 1, Easter Sunday. As correspondents were boarding ships, someone shouted, "Keep your head down, Ernie." Ernie Pyle turned to his colleagues and said: "Listen, you bastards, I'll take a drink over every one of your graves." Pyle had returned to the war in mid-February 1945.[28]

On the day of the Okinawa landing, a friend of Pyle's, Frederick C. Painton of *Reader's Digest*, was standing on a Guam airstrip, seeing off B-29 crews heading for Japan, when he fell dead of a heart attack at age 49. In his last column, published posthumously, Pyle paid tribute to his friend who had been an air service sergeant in World War I:

> He was just about to start back to America when he died. He had grown pretty weary of war . . . I have no idea how Fred Painton would have liked to die. But somehow I'm glad he didn't have to go through the unnatural terror of dying on the battlefield. For he was one of my dear friends and I know that he, like myself, had come to feel that terror.[29]

The Okinawa landing was unopposed, and civilians were soon streaming into American lines. "These were the most miserable people, I thought, who inhabited the earth," Sherrod wrote. "They averaged no more than five feet in height. They were undernourished beyond description . . . Many Okinawans had leprosy, and many others suffered from lifelong malnutritional diseases."

Sherrod told Pyle he had decided to go home after a few more days. Pyle replied: "I'm getting too old to stay in combat with these kids, and I'm going to go home, too, in about a month." Earlier, Sherrod had met Pyle on Guam after its capture, and Sherrod talked of their getting together after the war. But Pyle shook his head. "I'm not coming back from this one." Sherrod tried to laugh it off, telling him: "You said that about Sicily [and] Normandy and every other operation, and you're still here and doing fine." Pyle replied: "I always believed it when I said it, and I believe it now, and sometime I have got to be right."[30]

While the Okinawa landings were unopposed, U.S. forces met heavy resistance when they moved inland. The battle produced 47,000 U.S. casualties, among them John Cashman of INS. While serving in the Navy earlier, he lost an arm and then joined INS. He was killed in a plane crash on July 31.[31]

Just after 10 a.m. on April 18, Pyle accompanied troops ashore on Ie Shima, a 10-square-mile island west of Okinawa. He set off by Jeep with four soldiers to find a command-post site for the 305th Regiment of the 77th Infantry Division. The Jeep was fired on near the village of Ie, and the men took cover in ditches. Pyle raised his head to look for a companion and died instantly when a bullet pierced his left temple. He was 44.

Infantrymen who recovered the body under fire found in Pyle's pocket the draft of an unfinished column he had intended for release upon the end of the war in Europe. The column began: "My heart is still in Europe, and that's why I'm writing this column. It is to the boys who were my friends for so long. My one great regret of the war is that I am not with them when it has ended. For the companionship of two and a half years of death and misery is a spouse that tolerates no divorce." Scripps-Howard editors chose not to release the column but it later appeared in books and articles. In Leipzig, Hal Boyle read a wire-service report of Pyle's death and woke up his colleagues, crying: "Ernie got it!" They got out of bed and drank themselves into a stupor.

Pyle was buried on Ie Shima in a crude wooden coffin that a soldier built. At the site of his death, soldiers put up a sign, later turned into a permanent monument, that read: "At this point the 77th Infantry Division lost a buddy, Ernie Pyle. 18 April 1945." Later he was buried, with his helmet on, in the National Memorial Cemetery of the Pacific in Honolulu.

Pyle's death came as a shock to the public greater than that of any other correspondent. President Truman compared the reaction to that of the death of President Roosevelt six days earlier: "The nation is quickly saddened again by the death of Ernie Pyle." Pyle's mentally unstable wife Jerry died seven months later, on November 23, 1945, in Albuquerque, New Mexico, of uremic poisoning.[32]

CHAPTER 21

VICTORY OVER JAPAN

Maj. Gen. Curtis LeMay organized the first of the great fire-raising raids on Tokyo on the night of March 9–10, 1945. Flying at low level, 325 B-29 bombers rained incendiary bombs and napalm on the capital, killing 100,000 civilians, making a million people homeless and reducing a quarter of the city to ashes. In fourteen months, the U.S. dropped 170,000 tons of bombs on Japan and virtually destroyed sixty-five cities.

On July 10, Admiral Halsey's fleet began carrier strikes against the mainland. A B-29 flying from Tinian dropped an atomic bomb on Hiroshima on August 6, killing at least 70,000 people. Nagasaki was the target of another atomic bomb on August 9 and at least 30,000 died. The Soviet Union declared war on Japan and captured Japanese-held Manchuria and northern Korea after eleven days. Japan agreed to unconditional surrender on August 14 and World War II ended on September 1 with the signing of surrender documents on the battleship Missouri in Tokyo Bay.

Homer Bigart went aboard a B-29 on July 29 for a raid on Aomori on Honshu Island. The planes encountered no opposition on their 3,700-mile roundtrip flight, and the raid left a square mile of the city in flames:

It is no use pretending that B-29 raids on smaller empire cities are exceptionally thrilling. Apart from the uneasiness that comes with going over enemy territory, and a moment of tension during the bomb run, there is seldom anything to alter the brutal monotony of those 1,500-mile missions over water. A conflagration seen from 14,000 feet has the same fascination as a pile of burning leaves to a small boy.[1]

On August 5, William L. Laurence of the *New York Times* arrived on Tinian as planes were being loaded. "I had a fairly good notion that I was to be privileged to be an eyewitness of the dropping of the first atomic bomb, just as I had witnessed the first test in New Mexico." Laurence, 57 at the time, was a Lithuanian-born science writer and Harvard graduate who had emigrated to the U.S. in 1905 at age 17 (and changed his birth name, Leib Wolf Siew). In April 1945 he was approached by Gen. Leslie Groves, director of the Manhattan Project to build the A-bomb, to serve as the project's official historian. In that capacity, he wrote official papers and became the only reporter allowed to witness the first atomic bomb explosion in New Mexico in July. The *New York Times* knew of his official role but did not object.

Arriving on Tinian three days behind schedule, he was told it was too late to put him on the Hiroshima mission. He was assigned to the next one, scheduled for August 11, but thought there might not be a next one; Hiroshima could force Japan's surrender. He was present, however, for the briefing of the *Enola Gay* crew by its commander, Col. Paul Tibbets, 30. Tibbets told his men they would drop a bomb unlike any before, having a destructive force equivalent to 20,000 tons of TNT and their mission could make history. Laurence described "a look of amazement and incredulity on every face."

Three planes would take off one hour before the *Enola Gay*, acting as weather reporters and covering three previously selected targets. The target could be changed if weather made that necessary. A second three B-29s, including the *Enola Gay* (named for Tibbets's mother), would assemble over Iwo Jima at 15 minutes after daybreak and enter the target area together. At 2:45 a.m. on August 6, three B-29s took off from three parallel runways. Well-wishers waved goodbye to Tibbets and wished him luck. "He waved back and smiled, a tired smile."

"It was a night in purgatory" for those waiting for results of the mission. The *Enola Gay* was scheduled to drop the bomb at 9:15 a.m. At exactly 9:30 Capt. William Parsons, aboard the plane, messaged: "Mission successful!" At 3 p.m. Tibbets brought the plane in. He was greeted by Gen. Carl Spaatz, commander of U.S. Strategic Air Forces in the Pacific, who pinned the Distinguished Service Cross on his flying overalls.

"As the fliers were questioned one by one, the story sounded more and more fantastic and awesome, more terrifying than any horror tale in fiction, more like something out of the pages of Dante," Laurence wrote. He took copious notes, then rushed to a typewriter and had his dispatch approved by a censor. He gave it to Groves to be kept in his locked safe until President

Truman, attending a conference in Potsdam with Churchill and Stalin, announced the news to the world. Laurence's report began:

> The first atomic bomb ever used in warfare, a small, man-made fireball exploding with the force of 20,000 tons of TNT, dropped from a B-29 today wiped out the great Japanese industrial and military center of Hiroshima. At exactly 9:15 this morning Hiroshima stood out under the clear blue sky. One-tenth of a millionth of a second later, a time imperceptible by any clock, it had been swallowed by a cloud of swirling fire as though it had never existed.

Laurence reported the plane encountered no flak or alarm of any kind. A mushroom cloud rose to 45,000–50,000 feet. Laurence had asked co-pilot Capt. Robert A. Lewis to keep a log of the flight and, when the plane was over Hiroshima, he wrote: "There will be a short intermission while we bomb our target." The next entry read: "My God!" Laurence's story, which should have been exclusive, was never published. "It was no little shock to me, on returning to Washington a month later, to learn that neither that story nor subsequent stories I had written about Hiroshima had ever reached their destination. What happened I do not know to this day."

Truman announced the bombing on August 7. Laurence noted that he had had "the honor, unique in the history of journalism, of preparing the War Department's official press release for worldwide distribution. No greater honor could have come to any newspaperman." The fact he was writing a government handout while employed by the *New York Times* clearly did not trouble him—or his newspaper.

The bombing of Nagasaki had been scheduled for August 11 but bad weather was expected and the date was advanced to August 9. Laurence was informed he would go along as the official reporter, but not in the plane carrying the bomb. At 3:50 a.m. the strike plane, the *Great Artiste*, took off. "Does one feel any pity or compassion for the poor devils about to die?" Laurence wrote in his notebook. "Not when one thinks of Pearl Harbor and the Death March on Bataan."

The three planes in the group ran into flak after they crossed the coastline, with Nagasaki a hundred miles west. When they arrived, the city was under thick clouds. The strike plane needed to make a visual drop, so they circled while waiting for a break in the clouds. The Japanese opened fire and the pilot of Laurence's plane took it up out of flak range. Then a squadron of twenty-one fighter planes emerged from the clouds but soon disappeared.

When the clouds parted at 12:01 p.m., the bomb fell and there was a giant flash. "Then a tremendous blast wave struck the ship and made it tremble." There were four more blasts in rapid succession. As the plane turned in the direction of the explosion, a pillar of purple fire reached it. The bottom of the cloud was brown, its center amber, its top white:

> It was a living totem pole. Just when it appeared to have settled down into a state of permanence, there came shooting out of the top a giant mushroom that increased the height of the pillar to 45,000 feet. Momentum carried it to about 60,000 feet. Then another mushroom, smaller, began emerging out of the pillar. The first mushroom changed shape into a flowerlike form, giant petals curving downward, creamy white outside, rose colored inside.

The planes were now so short on fuel that it appeared likely everyone would have to bail out before they reached Okinawa. But they made it— just. When the *Great Artiste* touched down, two motors stopped dead halfway down the runway for lack of fuel. The planes returned to Tinian at 10:25 p.m.[2]

* * *

Bigart filed what is widely regarded as the last combat dispatch of World War II on the day Japan surrendered, August 15 Tokyo time (August 14 in the U.S.). Bigart was aboard one of about 400 B-29s that attacked three targets. "The radio tells us that the war is over, but from where I sit it looks suspiciously like a rumor. A few minutes ago—at 1:32 a.m.—we fire-bombed Kumagaya, a small industrial city behind Tokyo."[3]

Correspondents began preparing to enter the country. Frank Legg of the Australian Broadcasting Commission drew a pistol from the quartermaster's store in Manila—"even war correspondents were to be armed for the entry into Japan." He was aboard a ship en route when the surrender came, and the U.S. Navy short-waved his broadcast to Sydney. ABC failed to monitor the transmission and Legg's report was never broadcast.[4]

After sixteen correspondents flew into Yokohama, Gordon Walker of the *Christian Science Monitor* and Australian Jack Percival got on a train to Tokyo. Japanese passengers stared at them in awe. They went into the Imperial Hotel and consumed a five-course dinner at the expense of the Japanese government. At the radio center in Tokyo, Percival produced a pistol and told the operator: "London, London." The operator sent their dispatches. The next day, American troops arrested them and took them to MacArthur's headquarters, where they were lectured about going out of bounds and evading censorship.[5]

George H. Johnston of Melbourne's *Argus* flew into Yokohama and rode in a bus with other correspondents along a route guarded by Japanese policemen, their backs turned away from the road:

> It was difficult to capture any feeling of reality as we drove through lines of propellerless fighter planes, angrily staring soldiers and naval ensigns, children hiding their eyes or fleeing in panic, girls turning their backs and cringing as if expecting blows, men just looking at us without expression. Sometimes a little boy would poke out his tongue and then flee wildly across the fields. In most of the faces there was a dull apathy, in some dismay, in some bewilderment, in many a sullen hostility.

Yokohama presented a picture of "a rust-red desert of crumpled iron and broken timber and torn earth in which families had burrowed like rabbits." The correspondents traveled to the industrial city of Kawasaki:

> every building . . . a tangle of ruin . . . All the way to Tokyo there was no break in the frightful pattern of destruction . . . Already we knew that even without the atom Japan had been defeated. Behind the bold facade of saber-rattling arrogance there had been a shattered economy and a miserable, impoverished populace . . . it is doubtful if Japan could have survived another three months. Many of the people were starving and diseased.[6]

* * *

Two B-17s flew correspondents over Nagasaki and Hiroshima on August 27. Bigart reported that little remained of Nagasaki but twisted frames of foundries and ships, scorched trees and blackened buildings for at least a mile from the center of impact. "Although we make more than a score of runs over Nagasaki, we do not see a single motor vehicle. But streetcars are running in the main part of town."[7]

On August 31, George Weller filed from Tokyo the first report of radiation sickness that was killing people from Hiroshima. The article was stamped "Passed by Censors" but, for reasons now unknown, was never published.

Weller wrote of an actor and actress who had been living in Hiroshima. The actor came to Tokyo and soon complained of excessive warmth in his stomach. This turned to burning and he died within days. An autopsy showed his entrails had been eaten away. The actress died from a swelling that soon covered her entire body.[8]

* * *

The surrender ceremony in Tokyo Bay was the biggest story to be covered as far as most correspondents were concerned. Bigart witnessed it and wrote:

> Japan, paying for her desperate throw of the dice at Pearl Harbor, passed from the ranks of the major powers at 9:05 a.m. today when Foreign Minister Mamoru Shigemitsu signed the documents of unconditional surrender . . . If memories of the bestialities of the Japanese prison camps were not so fresh in mind, one might have felt sorry for Shigemitsu as he hobbled on his wooden leg toward the green baize-covered table where the papers lay waiting.[9]

Wilfred Burchett sailed from Okinawa and arrived at Yokosuka naval base a few days after the surrender. He and Bill McGaffin of the *Chicago Daily News* went straight to the railway station and jumped aboard a Tokyo-bound train. "We created something of a sensation," Burchett wrote. "Although the train was packed, passengers cleared a space around us, gazing at us with a mixture of fear and curiosity."

They traveled "through miles of devastation we thought must be without parallel in modern times . . . Nothing was left but flat acres." At the Dai Ichi Hotel in Tokyo, the manager pointed out they would be the only foreigners in a hotel full of Japanese, many of them "hotheads." They left for Yokohama, where an Allied press center had been set up.

McGaffin was intent on covering the surrender ceremony, but Burchett was determined to get to Hiroshima. "I found a train still went to where Hiroshima used to be." He visited the offices of Domei, the Japanese news agency, and its editors gave him a letter addressed to their Hiroshima correspondent, asking him to show Burchett around and transmit his messages to the Tokyo office. Burchett's *Daily Express* colleague, Henry Keys, gave him his .45 pistol and wished him luck. On September 2, while 600 correspondents were on their way to the surrender ceremony, Burchett headed to Tokyo to board a 6 a.m. train to Hiroshima.

The train carried Japanese troops. They were sullen at first but brightened up when he handed around cigarettes. Several soldiers offered him bits of dried fish or hard-boiled eggs. Burchett showed off a large scar on his leg, trying to convey to them it was caused by a Japanese plane in Burma and that he was a journalist. "From then on it was smiles and friendship." After six hours he found a seat among officers and "here the hostility was total." An American priest warned him any false move might cost them their lives—the officers were furious and humiliated at their defeat. The priest had been brought to Tokyo from an internment camp to broadcast to American troops on how to behave to avoid friction with local people. He was escorted off the train at Kyoto.

The train arrived at Hiroshima at 2 a.m. after a twenty-hour journey. Two guards grabbed Burchett, presumably thinking he was a runaway war prisoner, and he tried to explain he was a journalist. The guards took him to a shelter and gave him to understand he was "locked up."

Burchett produced the letter from Domei and the guards released him. Just then the Domei man, Nakamura, arrived, together with a Canadian-born Japanese girl who spoke excellent English. They drove into the devastated city:

Vapors drifted up from fissures in the ground, an acrid sulphurous smell. The few people about hurried past, white masks covering mouths and nostrils. Buildings had dissolved into gray and reddish dust . . . Trees lay on their sides. Younger trees were still standing, leaves and smaller branches stripped off.

Nakamura told him that, when the bomb went off, he was just wheeling out his bicycle to ride to his office. There was a blinding flash and he felt a scorching heat on his face and a blast of wind like a tornado. He was knocked to the ground and his house collapsed.

Burchett went to police headquarters. "The atmosphere was very tense and the police looked at me with cold hostility." Thirty-five years later, when he returned, Nakamura revealed that some policemen had wanted both of them summarily shot. But the head of the Thought Control police accepted Burchett's explanation that he wanted to tell the world what had happened, and arranged a police car to drive him to the only hospital still functioning.

It contained patients "in various stages of physical disintegration . . . The patients were terribly emaciated and gave off a nauseating odor." A Dr. Katsube said he did not know how to treat them. Some bore no sign of injury but fell sick and died. "Every person carried in here as a patient is carried out as a corpse," he said, adding that the hospital had no nurses; some were killed immediately, some died after handling patients, others left. Katsube asked Burchett to leave, saying he could not guarantee his safety. As for himself, he was resigned to death. "I can't understand it," he said. "I was trained in the United States; I believed in Western civilization. I'm a Christian. But how can Christians do what you have done here?" Burchett sat on a rock in the city center and typed a story that began:

> In Hiroshima, 30 days after the first atomic bomb destroyed the city and shook the world, people are still dying, mysteriously and horribly—people who were uninjured by the cataclysm—from an unknown something which I can only describe as atomic plague. Hiroshima does not look like a bombed city. It looks as if a monster steamroller had passed over it and squashed it out of existence . . . I have seen the most terrible and frightening desolation in four years of war that makes a blitzed Pacific Island look like an Eden . . . Hundreds upon hundreds were so badly burned in the terrific heat generated by the bomb that it was not even possible to tell whether they were men or women, old or young . . . The doctors gave their patients Vitamin A injections. The results were horrible. The flesh started rotting away from the hole caused by the injection of the needle . . .

Nakamura used a hand-operated Morse set to relay the dispatch to Tokyo. Burchett's colleague Henry Keys had hired a Japanese courier to sit in the Domei office there and rush any message from Burchett to him in Yokohama. Keys took it to censors, who tried to kill it. But he insisted censorship had ended when the war ended, and they yielded. The dispatch appeared in the *Daily Express* of September 6 under a mistaken byline, Peter Burchett. It caused a worldwide sensation.

On his trip back, Burchett found some Australian war prisoners at the Kyoto station, and they insisted he visit their camps to persuade inmates the war was over. Some, they said, were dying every hour. Burchett spent several days touring prison camps and persuading Japanese authorities to improve food and other conditions.

When he reached Tokyo, American officers were holding a news conference. He walked in, "grimy, unshaved and disheveled," and it was at once clear to him that the main purpose was to deny his Hiroshima dispatch. Brig. Gen. Thomas Farrell, deputy chief of the Manhattan Project and a scientist, explained there could be no question of atomic radiation because the bombs were exploded at such a height as to obviate any such risk. Burchett asked if he had been to Hiroshima. He had not. Burchett described what he had seen and asked for explanations. Farrell said those he saw in the hospital were victims of blast and burn and Japanese doctors were incompetent to handle them or lacked the right medications. Burchett kept pressing and a spokesman said: "I'm afraid you've fallen victim to Japanese propaganda."

Burchett was then whisked to a U.S. Army hospital, where tests showed his white corpuscle count was down. He was also told that MacArthur was expelling him for violation of occupation rules. Doctors decided his blood count was due to antibiotics given to him earlier for a knee infection. His camera with photos of Hiroshima disappeared while he was in hospital. "The expulsion was rescinded because I was able to prove—with hilarious support by the Navy—I had landed as an accredited correspondent to the Pacific Fleet and it had set no restrictions on correspondents' movements," he wrote.[10]

Support for Burchett's reporting came from other correspondents who were taken to Hiroshima. William H. Lawrence, who had been the *New York Times* bureau chief in Moscow before moving to Asia, wrote of the deadly effects of radiation and quoted worries by Japanese doctors that "all who had been in Hiroshima that day would die as a result of the bomb's lingering effects." He described how "persons who had been only slightly injured on the day of the blast lost 86 per cent of their white blood corpuscles, developed temperatures of 104 degrees Fahrenheit, their hair began to drop out, they lost their appetites, vomited blood and finally died." Then he added: "I am convinced that, horrible as the bomb undoubtedly is, the Japanese are exaggerating its effects."

A week later, in an article headlined NO RADIOACTIVITY IN HIROSHIMA RUIN, he contradicted his own reporting. He wrote that General Farrell "denied categorically that [the bomb] produced a dangerous, lingering radioactivity." He offered no qualifying remarks about his visit to Hiroshima.

Bigart was part of the contingent that visited Hiroshima. "We walked today through Hiroshima, where survivors . . . are still dying at the rate of about 100 daily from burns and infections which the Japanese doctors seem unable to cure." Bigart found hatred in the glances of some people, but generally more curiosity than hatred. "We were representatives of an enemy power that had employed a weapon far more terrible and deadly than poison gas, yet in the four hours we spent in Hiroshima none so much as spat at us, nor threw a stone."

On September 9, General Groves invited thirty reporters, including William L. Laurence, to the New Mexico test site to demonstrate that no radiation lingered there. Laurence obliged in an article published in the *New York Times* on September 12: "This historic ground in New Mexico . . . gave the most effective answer today to Japanese propaganda that radiations [sic] were responsible for deaths even after the day of the explosion, August 6, and that persons entering Hiroshima had contracted mysterious maladies due to persistent radioactivity."

Laurence wrote that Japanese propaganda was aimed at creating the impression the Allies won the war unfairly, and had "described 'symptoms' that did not ring true." He wrote ten articles about the nuclear program and won the Pulitzer Prize. In 2004, U.S. journalists Amy and David Goodman accused him of having withheld what he knew about radioactive fallout that poisoned local residents and livestock in New Mexico and about Geiger counter readings around the test site. They urged that he be stripped of his Pulitzer. That never happened.[11]

Weller, who described Tokyo in a dispatch as "an ashtray filled with the cigarette butts of buildings," covered the surrender ceremony on September 2, then slipped off the next day to an island kamikaze base near the southern tip of Kyushu. He went ostensibly to cover the landing of American forces and, after filing two pieces, crossed to the mainland on September 5 and traveled by train to Nagasaki, which MacArthur had placed off limits to correspondents. Weller felt he had a right to be there; censorship was being prolonged well after the slightest pretext for it existed. He remembered that MacArthur's censors had earlier killed a dispatch he wrote criticizing Roosevelt's defeat by Stalin at the Yalta conference. "With security no longer in question, I was not going to be stifled again."

Much later he wrote:

> When I walked out of Nagasaki's roofless railroad station I saw a city friz-zled like a baked apple, crusted black at the open core where the searing sun born at Alamogordo [New Mexico] had split open the blue sky of midday . . . Along the blistered boulevards the shadows of fallen telegraph poles were branded upright on buildings, the signature of the ray stamped in huge ideograms. I can never forget the hospitals where I heard from X-ray specialists the devouring effects of the ray on the human blood-stream and viscera. I felt pity, but no remorse. The Japanese military had cured me of that.

Posing as an American colonel, he spent four days in the city, guided by a Japanese lieutenant. From the lieutenant he learned the bomb fell almost at the noontime factory break, producing a blast wave that caused ceilings to crash and buildings to collapse. Firemen couldn't get to the source of some blazes because fallen buildings blocked the streets. Doctors told Weller that survivors were now dying because platelets in their blood were being destroyed, and they were helpless to treat them. They said the victims were suffering the delayed effect of beta, gamma or neutron rays, resulting in a reduction in white corpuscles, constriction in the throat, vomiting, diarrhea and small hemorrhages just below the skin.

Weller spent three hours each night writing dispatches that finally ran to 25,000 words. Each article was sent to the chief censor in Tokyo. Later he wrote that he could have smuggled out the dispatches but wanted to give MacArthur's command the least possible excuse to hold up his reporting. All of the stories were blocked by censors.

In a September 8 dispatch, Weller wrote: "The Japanese have heard the legend from American radio that the ground preserves deadly irradiation. But hours of walking amid ruins where the odor of decaying flesh is still strong produces in this writer nausea, but no signs of burns or debilitation." The next day he wrote:

> The atomic bomb's peculiar "disease," uncured because it is untreated and untreated because it is undiagnosed, is still snatching away lives here. Men, women and children with no outward marks of injury are dying daily in hospitals, some after having walked around for three or four weeks thinking they have escaped.

While he was in the city, a "traveling circus" of reporters from Washington landed for a brief visit, and their leader offered to take carbon copies of Weller's articles and file them from the plane when it took off. But Weller stubbornly refused, determined to see through his fight with MacArthur. This decision haunted him for the rest of his life. "I threw away my one good chance to communicate, trying for a fuller, more perfect story. Oh Nagasaki! What a way to lose a war!"

From Nagasaki, he traveled 40 miles to Omuta and the largest prison camp in Japan, holding 1,700 American, British, Dutch and Australians who had been forced to work in coal mines. His articles never again got past censors. Later he wrote a 5,000-word short story about a fictional prison camp evidently modeled on Omuta, and sold it to the *Saturday Evening Post*. Chinese prisoners, also forced to work in coal mines, were housed near the Allied camp but neither group knew of each other's existence. At the end of the war, Japanese guards fled the Chinese camp and the prisoners went hungry until September 12 when B-29 bombers dropped food to them.[12]

* * *

On September 6, SS Col. Josef Albert Meisinger, 46, known as the Butcher of Warsaw, surrendered to Clark Lee of INS and Robert Brumby of Mutual Broadcasting at the Fujiya Hotel in Hakone, Kanagawa. The reporters drove him to Yokohama and handed him over to the U.S. Counter-Intelligence Corps. Meisinger served as commander of state police in the Warsaw District after Poland fell in 1939, and subsequently ordered reprisal killings of Jews. His crimes appalled even some of his superiors, and SS leaders sent him to Tokyo by submarine when it appeared he would be court-martialed. He served as liaison to Japanese authorities, and in 1941 tried to persuade the Japanese to exterminate more than 18,000 Jews in Shanghai who had escaped from Austria and Germany. He was handed over to Polish authorities in 1946. A Warsaw tribunal condemned him to death and he was executed on March 7, 1947.[13]

The day after Meisinger's surrender, a Japanese friend took Clark Lee to interview Gen. Hideki Tojo, 61, at his home just outside Tokyo. Tojo had been prime minister from 1941 to 1944 and bore direct responsibility for Pearl Harbor. After the fall of Saipan, he had been forced to resign on July 18, 1944. Tojo told Lee he was now a farmer. He accepted full responsibility for the war but denied that made him a war criminal. The next day, Lee learned that MacArthur had ordered Tojo's arrest. He returned and offered to give Tojo a ride to MacArthur's headquarters. Tojo, wearing shorts and a green shirt, exclaimed: "No! I will wait for the authorities!" Meantime two carloads of correspondents showed up. In the next hour and a half, most wandered off or drove back to Tokyo. Unknown to Lee, Tojo was busy writing his last will and testament.

Two Jeeps arrived, carrying about twenty Americans. Tojo looked out a side window and said brusquely in English, "This Tojo." A Major Kraus asked him to open the door and he replied in Japanese: "Unless this is an official order, I will not discuss it." Kraus instructed an interpreter to tell him to open the door. As the Americans reached the entrance, Tojo shot himself while seated. Then he partially rose. Half on his feet and wavering, he held a .32 Colt revolver. "Don't shoot!" Kraus shouted. Tojo looked up, let the gun drop and slumped back into his chair.

"I pushed into the room," Lee wrote. "Tojo lay back in a small armchair, his eyes closed and sweat standing out on his forehead. Blood oozed slowly from a wound just above his heart." An excited voice panted into Lee's ear: "The bastard has killed himself." Then: "No. The son of a bitch is still breathing. Look at his belly going up and down." Tojo's chauffeur leaned over him, sobbing and patting his shoulder. Some Japanese policemen came in, then walked out laughing. Before shooting himself, Tojo had changed out of his shorts and put on army trousers, polished brown boots and a clean white shirt.

Lee raced to a nearby lumber yard where a phone was available and called the press hotel. Bill Dunn of CBS answered. Then a Japanese friend ran down the lane and told Lee that Tojo was dead. Lee dictated a flash to Dunn before running back to the house. Harry Brundidge of *Cosmpolitan* magazine told him Tojo was not dead and was still sitting in his chair, groaning a little. He began to speak.

"The war in the greater East Asia region started right," he said. "It was a just war. That is my conviction. But with all our strength gone, we finally fell." Again he shouldered full responsibility for the war, said he didn't want to be tried by the victors and expressed regret he had failed to shoot himself in the heart. A doctor arrived and said he had but a short time to live. Russell Brines of the AP picked up Tojo's phone and dictated a story to his office. Then he passed the phone to Lee, who did the same. Tojo began bleeding heavily, but an American doctor sewed up his wound. Tojo recovered and was executed as a war criminal on December 23, 1948.[14]

Another wanted war criminal, Gen. Masaharu Homma, who led the invasion of the Philippines, fell into the hands of Al Dopking of the AP. A friendly Japanese tipped Dopking that Homma would appear at a suburban Tokyo rail station while the army was searching for him. The AP kept Homma at its offices for twenty-four hours to interview him before he turned himself in on September 14. Homma had been forced into retirement in August 1943. He was tried for war crimes, and specifically the Bataan death march. On April 3, 1946, he was shot by a Filipino and American firing squad. He was 58.[15]

The arrest of Homma was one of the last footnotes of the war before correspondents began packing and going their separate ways. In journalistic terms, had it been a good war? The columnist Marquis Childs had this to say about the war correspondents in a *Look* magazine article in 1945:

If there is anything a fighting man has done in this war that a war correspondent has failed to do, I do not know what it is . . . The number of war correspondents killed is far greater in proportion than the number of deaths among combat troops. That is because their own zeal to see it themselves, to be there when it happens, drives them into the face of danger . . . Battle reporters on the job have the hardboiled nonchalance of the fighting man. Outwardly they take themselves and their work with the utmost casualness. That, however, is largely a facade. They are adventure-loving, deeply sentimental and insatiably curious. If they weren't, of course, they would be writing about something a lot quieter and safer than war.

The zeal and courage of most war correspondents might have been amply demonstrated, but a question remains of how well they covered the war and particularly the mistakes of war. I have quoted one journalistic critic in the Introduction to this book, suggesting the correspondents were basically cheer-leaders for the Allied campaign. There was evidently truth in that observation, but to what extent did the demands of war—of Western survival—justify such a role? When the Germans sank the British battleship *Royal Oak* off the Scottish coast six weeks after the outset of war in 1939, the *New York Times*'s James Reston noted that London-based correspondents complained about British suppression of the news but conceded that reporting the loss would have under-mined British morale. Maintaining public morale was rightly seen by Allied leaders as a vital necessity and, in any case, they and not the correspondents suppressed the news. Whether that and later acts of suppression were always correct may be doubted. But any attempts at evading censorship on such matters could have opened correspondents to charges of undermining the war effort. Many of their readers no doubt would have equated that with treason.

But in Norway Leland Stowe, writing outside the constraints of British censorship, did manage to reveal the disastrous mistakes of British interven-tion and help bring about the downfall of the Chamberlain government, an act that produced the beneficial effect of bringing Churchill to power. This book is replete with examples of political and military mistakes that corre-spondents on the spot were not allowed to report but, in some instances, were readily apparent to the public afterward. For example, Moscow correspon-dents could not report or comment on Stalin's lack of preparedness for the German invasion of the Soviet Union but these failings were self-evident as German forces rapidly swept almost to the gates of Moscow before being turned back. Likewise, the firing of two successive British commanders in North Africa made it abundantly clear that the war there was not going well, even if correspondents were not allowed to comment on the reasons and British communiqués often lied about the course of fighting.

American military authorities were remiss in failing to go on the alert at Pearl Harbor and throughout the Pacific as a diplomatic dispute with Japan reached crisis point. General MacArthur was signally at fault in failing to get planes in the air as hostilities loomed in the Philippines. Allied intelligence badly failed to anticipate the hostile reaction of the Vichy French at the time of the North African landings. An American general's timidity at Anzio cost thousands of lives and delayed the liberation of Italy. The Market Garden operation in the Netherlands was a disastrous mistake in planning and execution, and the subsequent surprise attack in the Ardennes—the Battle of the Bulge—was yet another Allied intelligence failure. In Naples, Paris and elsewhere, there were significant desertions by Allied troops who engaged in black marketeering, and rapes were sometimes committed by these or other soldiers.

None of these debacles and crimes was reported by correspondents in the countries concerned, for the very clear reason that any attempt to do so would have been suppressed by Allied censors. To that extent, World War II stands out, by comparison with later wars, as one that was not properly covered. Correspondents generally accepted the necessity of censorship, even as they fought stubborn battles against some of the more ludicrous misjudgements of overly zealous and often untrained censors.

The self-censorship of correspondents who declined to report General Patton's abuse of soldiers suffering from post-traumatic stress syndrome was another matter. Eisenhower, while reluctant to see the incidents reported, informed them there was no question of censorship. But the correspondents took it upon themselves to judge the effects on the war effort of revealing Patton's behavior, failing at the same time to anticipate that the story was bound to leak elsewhere. A judgment as to whether their self-censorship was correct is not easily rendered. There are times, not always during war, when correspondents or the media they represent withhold information that they possess for reasons of national security, either voluntarily or at government request. Had Patton's behavior been reported, and had this led to his being called home, his brilliant achievements in Europe in 1944–5 would never have occurred and it is even conceivable the war might not have ended as early as it did. In short, self-censorship can sometimes be appropriate but will always provoke doubts and controversy.

The most serious question about the integrity of World War II reporting involved the AP and arose only in March 2016 when a German historian, Harriet Scharnberg, discovered that the AP had entered into a mutually beneficial cooperation agreement with the Nazi regime. The AP, she reported, signed up to the so-called *Schriftleitergesetz* (editor's law), promising not to publish material "calculated to weaken the strength of the Reich abroad or at home." The AP employed a photographer who was a member of an SS paramilitary unit and allowed the regime to use its photo archives for its anti-Semitic propaganda. In Chapter 1, I noted that the AP reported a German–Polish agreement was at hand to avert war in 1939, just days before Germany invaded Poland. In 1940 (Chapter 4), the AP reported imminent German plans for an invasion of Britain. In both instances the AP was wrong, its reports served German interests and the rival UP resisted pressure to match those reports.

Did the AP report on the basis of tips from the German propaganda machine designed to further German aims? We will never know for certain. But Joseph C. Harsch, who had been in Berlin for the *Christian Science Monitor,* wrote after the war of instances in which the Germans favored three correspondents: Louis Lochner of the AP, Pierre J. Huss of the INS and Guido Enderis of the *New York Times.* "Those who refused favors felt that the others were being unduly pro-German," he wrote. William Shirer wrote: "Pierre, it seemed to me, had always played the Nazi game a little. Louis too, if only to get a beat, a scoop."

Lochner won a Pulitzer Prize in 1939 for reporting from Germany. The articles that comprised his Pulitzer entry, made available to me by prize officials at Columbia University, contained no outright criticism of Nazi policies. But one, while referring at the outset to the "seeming economic miracle" wrought by Hitler, carefully noted deeper into the article that the Nazi leader achieved full employment largely by military conscription, compulsory labor service and expansion of security organs. Some articles gave a detailed account of Nazi measures against Jews but were based almost entirely on official decrees. In one article, Lochner suggested that Hitler would have been justified in intervening on behalf of Sudeten Germans in Czechoslovakia earlier than he did, ignoring the fact that intervention was a violation of international law. In another Lochner wrote of the "just claims" of the many nationalities in Czechoslovakia, thus suggesting that pro-Nazi Sudeten Germans were justified in seeking to secede. Reading his otherwise mostly anodyne Pulitzer entries today, it is difficult to see how they qualified for such a prestigious award. It is worth noting that correspondents whose reporting incurred German wrath were routinely expelled. Lochner was not.

The restrictions placed on war reporting by Allied authorities were another matter, and they went unexamined when the conflict was over. Both correspondents and the media they represented simply ignored a responsibility to investigate the mistakes that occurred, to fix the blame where it lay and to examine the serious flaws in the censorship system. This was vital to ensuring that future wars would be covered in a different way. But evidently the heady achievement of victory produced no appetite for rehashing mistakes of the past. This role was left to later historians. No war since then has been followed by such an uncritical approach by the news media.

The experience of the Australian correspondent Osmar White is illustrative of the mood that followed World War II. In 1945 his account of the war in Europe, *Conquerors' Road*, met with initial enthusiasm from his American and British publishers. Then they declined to publish it. White suspected pressure had been brought to bear on them because the book dealt candidly with the misbehavior of some Allied troops in Germany, questioned the wisdom of military government policies and was critical of the Nuremberg trials. The book certainly could not have been rejected for lack of merit; it is one of the best by any correspondent on that phase of the war. Nearly forty years later, White dug out the manuscript and got it published.

Other correspondents might well have followed White's example in their own postwar histories and memoirs in making a critical examination of how the war was reported. Almost uniformly they did report on their battles with censors but only superficially, if at all, did they go beyond that in assessing the effect of news that was withheld or deliberately distorted by military communiqués. That was a failing, but not the whole story. In the reporting of Allied victories, in telling the individual stories of fighting men, in revealing the horrors of the concentration camps, in describing the slaughter on the beaches, in explaining what it was like to be in a bomber over Berlin and being attacked by fighter planes, they were often superb. It bears repeating that they did all this while putting their lives on the line, and sometimes losing them. It was no small achievement.[16]

CHAPTER 22

AFTER THE WAR

While crowds across Europe celebrated the end of the war on May 8, Ed Murrow spoke in a broadcast of the debris of war: the homeless, the hungry and poorly clothed, of economies in shreds. "Perhaps we should remember, even tonight in the midst of the celebration, that the suffering will continue for many years."[1]

The coterie of correspondents who had covered the war began to break up. Some remained in Europe to report on the continent's recovery and the Nuremberg trials of war criminals, some returned home, a few moved on to the Pacific war.

Murrow reluctantly left London to become head of CBS News. His simmering feud with William Shirer, whom he resented for having left the war early, ended in 1947 when Shirer was fired, ostensibly for failing to research topics on which he commented. Shortly after his return to the U.S., Murrow broke off an affair with Pamela Churchill, the former wife of Randolph Churchill, just as it appeared he might leave his wife Janet and marry her. The birth of the Murrows' son Casey in 1945 decided the matter.

Murrow returned to the air in September 1947 as anchor of *CBS Evening News*. He later inaugurated a program called *Hear It Now*, transmuted in the television age to *See It Now*, and used it to expose the demagoguery of Sen. Joseph McCarthy, who had plunged America into postwar hysteria about alleged Communists in government. Such was Murrow's immense authority with the American public, he was credited with having been partly responsible for Congress's censure of McCarthy. Murrow and William Paley, the founder and president of CBS, had differences over *See It Now*, and the broadcaster resigned in 1961 to accept President Kennedy's appointment to head the

United States Information Agency. A lifelong chain smoker—he was reputed to smoke sixty to sixty-five cigarettes a day—he developed cancer and died in 1965, two days after his 57th birthday, the most famous and respected broadcaster in America.[2]

That role later went to Walter Cronkite. He was not one of the original "Murrow Boys"—the correspondents hired during the war—but Murrow did persuade him to join CBS in 1950. He anchored *CBS Evening News* from 1962 until his retirement in 1981 and a poll once named him "the most trusted man in America." After he returned from Vietnam to report the war unwinnable, President Lyndon Johnson was reported to have said: "If I've lost Cronkite, I've lost Middle America." That has been disputed, but weeks later Johnson announced he would not seek re-election in 1968. Cronkite continued doing occasional reports for CBS and the Public Broadcasting Service after retirement. He died on July 17, 2009, aged 92. He sometimes winced at being described as a courageous war correspondent, telling *Playboy* magazine in 1973: "I feel I was an overweening coward in the war . . . I was scared to death all the time. I did everything possible to avoid getting into combat. Except the ultimate thing of not doing it."[3]

For one Murrow Boy, the postwar era led to the uncovering of a secret past. Given the Rome bureau of CBS, Winston Burdett in 1950 was faced with a loyalty questionnaire, asking whether he had ever been a member of the Communist Party or any Communist organization. Burdett decided to come clean: from 1940 to 1942 he had been a paid spy for the Soviet Union, then had renounced Communism. When his questionnaire reached New York, he was ordered to return. He apparently persuaded CBS he had never been disloyal to the United States; CBS kept him on, kept his secret and named him United Nations correspondent.

But in 1955 Burdett decided to go public because of a desire to educate the public about the evils of Communism. He volunteered to testify before the Senate Internal Security Committee, and admitted he had been a Communist from 1937 to 1942 and had engaged in espionage. He claimed his Italian wife Lea Schiavi had been killed in Iran by Russian soldiers in revenge for his refusal to continue as a Soviet spy. Other accounts said she was shot dead by bandits.

A Harvard *summa cum laude* graduate, Burdett had been on the staff of the *Brooklyn Eagle* when he and others there joined the party. At the insistence of the Senate committee, Burdett named twenty-three people who had been Communists, saying he was sure most had left the party. Twenty-two people summoned by the committee took the Fifth Amendment and six, including three from the *New York Times*, were fired. The committee's aim had been to discredit the liberal press (right-wingers referred to CBS as the Communist Broadcasting System). Some of Burdett's colleagues never forgave him for naming names. CBS sent him back to Rome in 1956, a post he held for twenty-two years. He died in 1993, aged 79.[4]

Eric Sevareid produced a widely acclaimed memoir, *Not So Wild a Dream*, and remained a CBS broadcaster for the rest of his life. He headed the Washington bureau from 1946 to 1954 and was an early critic of McCarthyism. He became a secret target of FBI investigations because of suspected Communist sympathies, but the agency dropped its inquiries in 1953. From 1959 to 1961 he was CBS's roving European correspondent, then a news analyst on *CBS Evening News*. A critic of the Vietnam War, he retired in 1977 and died of stomach cancer in July 1992, aged 79.[5]

William L. Shirer forged an illustrious and highly lucrative career as broadcaster, author and public speaker. After CBS fired him he served briefly as an analyst for Mutual, then was unable to find regular radio work. In 1960 his *The Rise and Fall of the Third Reich* became a worldwide bestseller. The author of fourteen non-fiction books and three novels, Shirer died in 1993, aged 89.[6]

Larry LeSueur covered the White House and then the UN for CBS. In 1963 he joined Voice of America as White House correspondent and retired in 1984. After a long battle with Parkinson's disease, he succumbed in February 2003 at age 93.[7]

Charles Collingwood became chief correspondent of CBS, and reported from Vietnam and the White House. In the 1960s he was the first U.S. correspondent allowed into North Vietnam. He married actress Louise Albritton in 1946 and, following her death in 1979, the singer Tatiana Jolin. In 1985 he died of cancer, aged 68.[8]

Richard C. Hottelet, the youngest of the Murrow Boys when he was hired at age 26, outlived all of them, dying on December 16, 2014, at the age of 97. He retired from CBS in 1985 after stints in Moscow, Bonn and the United Nations.

Richard Dimbleby entered Berlin with the first Western troops and broadcast from Hitler's bombed study. "I found his chair and I am sitting in that chair now . . . in the filth and the rubble that is found in every corner of this huge building," he told listeners. He pocketed some tableware with the initials A. H., and later used them at dinner parties for people he didn't like. A Red Army patrol arrested him but he was released when he persuaded the Russians he was a member of the Churchill family.

Dimbleby was the commentator when Churchill presided at a victory parade in Berlin. After the war, when the BBC was putting together a team of foreign correspondents, he was told the network had nothing to offer but could put him in a pool of twenty-five reporters on the home front. Dimbleby resigned in anger, returned to management of his family's London suburban newspaper and afterward did freelance work for the BBC, achieving his greatest fame as the commentator at the queen's coronation and the funerals of King George VI, John F. Kennedy and Churchill. In his last five years, he suffered from testicular cancer, which he attributed to smoking. He died on December 22, 1965, aged 52. His sons David and Jonathan followed him as leading BBC news and current affairs broadcasters.[9]

Duncan Hooper of Reuters' Moscow bureau reached Berlin after the German surrender and scored a major scoop on the discovery of Hitler's body outside his bunker. Correspondents from UP and the AP had learned of this first and flew to Paris to file, as there were no direct communications out of Berlin. But Hooper found a British dispatch rider preparing to fly to Lubeck, the nearest communications head, 150 miles away. He hastily scribbled a brief dispatch and gave it to the rider, promising him a bottle of Scotch if the message were safely delivered. Four hours later, the Reuters story was being broadcast on the BBC while Hooper's competitors were still airborne.[10]

Alan Moorehead and Alex Clifford decided not to go into Berlin. "We could not bear to see another ruined city," Moorehead wrote. "We no longer possessed the necessary emotions for a victory parade." Arthur Christiansen, Moorehead's editor, wrote that he kept raising Moorehead's salary in an attempt to keep him and, by the time of the German surrender, he was earning more than Field Marshal Montgomery. "But I lost him just the same." Moorehead wanted to be a full-time author and revolted against the politics of Lord Beaverbrook, proprietor of the *Daily Express*. Christiansen called him "the greatest of the war correspondents."

Clifford remained with the *Daily Mail* as Berlin correspondent while Moorehead produced a 1946 biography of Montgomery, then wrote a series of popular histories, the most famous of which were books on the nineteenth-century search for the sources of the Nile, *The White Nile* (1960) and *The Blue Nile* (1962). Clifford's last book, *Enter Citizens*, was published in 1950 and examined the political prospects of Europe in a new "Dark Ages" of materialistic, mass-produced man. That same year, Clifford learned he had Hodgkin's disease and was given two years to live. He was 42. He died in London in 1952, with Moorehead at his side.

Moorehead suffered a stroke in 1966 and, at age 56, could neither speak, read nor write. Four years later his journalist wife Lucy put together a collection of his writing, mostly about his friendship with Clifford, and published it under the title *A Late Education*. Moorehead died, aged 73, in London in September 1983. An Australian historian of war correspondents, Pat Burgess, wrote of him: "Despite his success as a journalist and author, he remained diffident, not quite completely confident." Arthur Christiansen thought that he, Clifford and a few other correspondents should have been given knighthoods.[11]

Joseph C. Harsch of the *Christian Science Monitor* produced a significant exclusive report when he was the only correspondent present for the British arrest of Albert Speer, Hitler's architect and armaments minister, in Glücksburg Castle near Flensburg on May 23, 1945. British officers and Harsch burst in on Speer in his bathroom to find him "seated on the throne," then quickly closed the door and waited outside. Speer told Harsch that he had known since the defeat at Stalingrad that the war was lost and had tried to countermand Hitler's orders to destroy everything in any retreat.

While continuing to write a column for the *Monitor*, Harsch joined NBC in 1953 and, four years later, became NBC's senior European correspondent in London. He returned to the U.S. as diplomatic correspondent in 1965. Two years later, he became a commentator for ABC, holding that job for four years. He remained a *Monitor* columnist, rounding out more than sixty years with the paper. A year after his wife of sixty-five years, Anne, died in 1997, he married his long-time editorial assistant, Edna Raemer, on the eve of his 93rd birthday. He died a few months later.[12]

George Weller, in Guam after the war, tried but failed to get carbon copies of his Nagasaki dispatches through Navy censorship. But there he also uncovered the story of a major Japanese war crime, involving a prison ship that brought 1,600 American soldiers from the Philippines to Japan. The prisoners were stuffed into a nearly airless hold below decks where men soon began dying in 130-degree Fahrenheit heat. Some went insane, and some murdered fellow prisoners. Just 435 survived the trip, and 161 died soon after. Weller filed a 25,000-word dispatch and the *Chicago Daily News* began running it as an eleven-part series on November 9, 1945. But references to murder among the prisoners were minimized or eliminated.

Weller returned to Athens to cover the 1946 Greek war against partisan guerrillas. He was later based in Rome, remaining there until his retirement in 1975. He also continued his prewar career as novelist and playwright and published several non-fiction works. He died at his home in San Felice Circeo, Italy, in December 2002 at age 95. Six months later his novelist son Anthony found the long-missing carbon copies of his Nagasaki dispatches and his articles on Japanese POW camps. They were in Weller's house, lodged in a mildewed crate that had remained unopened for more than a half-century. In 2006 Anthony used these dispatches to produce a book, *First into Nagasaki*, and three years later assembled his father's other wartime articles for a much longer book, *Weller's War*.[13]

Robert J. Casey returned to Chicago and retired from the *Daily News* in 1947. Resuming his career as an author—he wrote thirty-five books—and writer of freelance newspaper articles, he died in December 1962, aged 72.[14]

Don Whitehead had a wartime romance with Lee Carson of INS but when Carson returned to New York she was visited by Whitehead's wife Marie, pistol in hand, and she relinquished any claims on him. Whitehead went on to cover the Korean War and in 1951 won the first of two Pulitzer Prizes—the second for national reporting a year later. In 1956 he became Washington bureau chief of the *New York Herald-Tribune*, but later returned to his native South as a columnist for the *Knoxville* [Tennessee] *News-Sentinel*. He wrote five books, including *The FBI Story* in 1956, which was made into a film. He died in January 1981, aged 72.[15]

Hal Boyle covered the Korean and Vietnam Wars and was a widely read AP columnist—producing 7,680 in a long career. He died in April 1974 of a heart attack, just four months after learning he had motor neuron disease. He was 63.[16]

Ann Stringer remained with UP in Europe. On August 22, 1946, she married Dan De Luce, the AP manager for Germany, after he had divorced his first wife. "I quickly discovered I'd make a mistake," Stringer wrote. After a few months she had the marriage annulled. In 1949 she married Henry Ries, a German-born U.S. citizen who was on the staff of the director of U.S. intelligence for Germany and later became a photographer for the *New York Times*. She filed for divorce in 1979 and wrote: "Why or how I stayed married for more than 30 years I don't know . . . What hurts me more than anything else is the realization that I threw so much of my life away. Just threw it away." She died in November 1990, a month shy of her 72nd birthday.[17]

De Luce remarried his first wife Alma. The winner of a 1944 Pulitzer Prize for a series on Tito's partisan movement in Yugoslavia, he reported from Jordan during the 1948 Arab–Israeli war, then was AP bureau chief in Frankfurt. He returned to AP headquarters in New York and retired as deputy general manager in 1976. In 2002, aged 90, he died at his home in San Diego.[18]

Soon after Lee Miller returned to England, still haunted by images of the concentration camps, she fell into clinical depression, suffered post-traumatic stress syndrome and began drinking heavily. In 1946, discovering she was pregnant with her only child, Antony, she divorced the husband from whom she had long been separated, Egyptian businessman Aziz Eloui Bey. The following year, she married author and artist Roland Penrose, the father of her child. She gave up photography and became a gourmet cook. But her depression may have owed something to Penrose's long affair with trapeze artist Diane Deriaz. Her son Antony Penrose later wrote that "her iron will rallied and she clawed her way back up out of the pit" of depression and alcohol abuse before dying in 1977, aged 70.[19]

In 1949 Martha Gellhorn adopted an Italian orphan, whom she named Sandy, but her travels kept her away from him much of the time and he grew to disappoint her. She covered the Vietnam War, the 1967 Six-Day War in the Middle East and civil wars in Central Africa. Already an accomplished author, she published novels, travel books and collections of journalism. She had affairs with Laurence Rockefeller, journalist William Walton and Dr. David Gurewitsch, but admitted she never enjoyed sex. "I daresay I was the worst bed partner in five continents." In 1954 she married the former managing editor of *Time*, Tom Matthews, and settled down in London, but they were divorced in 1963. After a long battle with cancer and almost total blindness, she committed suicide by drug overdose in 1998, aged 89.[20]

Virginia Cowles took a break from war reporting in 1943 to serve as special assistant to American Ambassador Gil Winant in London. A year later she rejoined the *Sunday Times* and covered the Italian campaign, the liberation of Paris and the Allied drive into Germany. She married Aidan Crawley, who had been shot down over Libya and spent four years in a German prison camp. He was a Member of Parliament and the first editor-in-chief of Independent Television News. Cowles and Gellhorn collaborated in writing a play about two women correspondents on the Italian front. It got rave reviews in London but lasted four nights on Broadway. Then Cowles turned her hand to biography, writing of Winston Churchill (she was godmother to his grandson of the same name), the Rothschild family, Kaiser Wilhelm and King Edward VII. In 1983, suffering from emphysema and given weeks to live, she went with Crawley on a last trip to Spain. Just after they drove out of Spain into France, their car overturned and she was killed, aged 73. He was injured but recovered.[21]

Toward the end of the war, Marguerite Higgins met George Reid Millar, a *Daily Express* correspondent who was estranged from his wife. They began a relationship, but it didn't help that he regarded Americans as vulgar. He wanted to return to an English village to write fiction, which did not appeal to Higgins, and they parted. She remained in Germany to cover the Nuremberg trials and the Soviet blockade of Berlin, going on to cover the wars in Korea and Vietnam. Gen. Walton Walker ordered her out of Korea, arguing that women did not belong at the front, but Higgins appealed to MacArthur, who ruled she could stay. In 1951 she became the first woman to win a Pulitzer Prize for international reporting. The following year, she married Air Force Maj. Gen. William Hall. In 1965 she contracted leishmaniasis, a tropical disease, and she died in January 1966 when she was just 45 years old.[22]

Homer Bigart won a Pulitzer Prize for his war coverage, then another for the Korean War. *Newsweek* described him as "the best war correspondent of an embattled generation." In 1955 he joined the *New York Times* staff. Sent to Vietnam in 1962, he was expelled by President Ngo Dinh Diem for persistent criticism of him and members of his family. Later Bigart remembered the life of a war correspondent "as being either grimly exciting or painfully boring . . . and I don't want to relive a minute of it." Thrice married, he died of cancer in 1991, aged 83.[23]

Reynolds Packard went to Peking (Beijing) for UP after the war but was fired in 1947. *Time* magazine reported he had claimed a number of scoops that proved to be phony. In 1948 Packard and his wife Eleanor returned to Rome for the *New York Daily News*. She died there in May 1972, aged 67, and he died in October 1976, aged 72. Packard is best remembered among correspondents as the author of a 1950 novel, *The Kansas City Milkman*, a classic fictional account of news agency reporting.[24]

Russell J. Hill remained in Europe after the war and wrote a book about the emerging Cold War, *Struggle for Germany*. In 1952 he joined Radio Free Europe and spent thirty years based in various European capitals and Washington, retiring in 1983. A member of the American Contract Bridge League, he reached the level of life master. In July 2007 he died of prostate cancer in Medford, New Jersey, aged 88.[25]

Quentin Reynolds left *Collier's* to devote himself to writing books full time. He had produced seven books during the conflict, then eighteen more. He filed a libel suit against the right-wing columnist Westbrook Pegler, who had called him "yellow" and an "absentee war correspondent." Reynolds won a $175,001 judgment, at the time the largest American libel award ever. A Broadway play, *A Case of Libel*, was based on the suit and the story was twice adapted for TV movies. Reynolds died in San Francisco in 1965, aged 64.[26]

Chester Wilmot wrote a highly regarded history, *The Struggle for Europe*, in 1952. He became military correspondent of the *Observer*, and BBC Television commissioned him to write and present a series of films on Communism in Asia. Returning to London from Rangoon on January 9, 1954, he took a flight that exploded off the island of Elba, killing all thirty-five people on board. He was 42. The British broadcaster and war historian Trevor Royle called Wilmot the outstanding correspondent of World War II.[27]

Osmar White was one of the best correspondents of the war but outside his country is a forgotten man today and even at the time never achieved great fame. But he was an excellent reporter and writer, a perceptive student of military tactics and strategy, and a man of keen sensitivity toward victims of war. At the end of the conflict, he reported on the expulsion of Sudeten Germans from Czechoslovakia, then went to Berlin in July 1945, reporting a "stench of quenched fire and stale death" on its shattered streets. "Uncounted corpses lay rotting under the wreckage . . . Yet this macabre burial ground still teemed with life. Four million human beings were existing in it like vermin in a garbage tip." He was assigned to cover the Nuremberg trials but was repelled by "an unpleasant caricature of the processes of civilized justice. The 'trials' could have no more moral or judicial status than any trial by kangaroo court in the backwoods of Tennessee . . ." He applied for reassignment and did not see the trials through. For nearly two decades, he was in Papua New Guinea as the *Herald*'s special correspondent. He retired in 1963 and devoted himself to writing books, radio and TV scripts, and newspaper and magazine pieces. He died in Melbourne in May 1991, aged 82.[28]

Wilfred Burchett was one of the most controversial journalists of his generation because of his Communist sympathies. He spent three years in Greece and Berlin for the *Daily Express*, then joined *The Times* of London to cover Eastern Europe. In 1951 he traveled to China for the French Communist newspaper *L'Humanité* and, six months later, to North Korea to cover talks to end the Korean War. He visited several prisoner-of-war camps, stirring the anger of POWs when he compared one to a "holiday resort in Switzerland."

In 1956 Burchett became Moscow correspondent of an American left-wing newspaper, the *National Guardian*, and wrote admiringly of the Soviet system. During the Vietnam War, although 60 years old, he traveled hundreds of miles through rough terrain with North Vietnamese and Viet Cong troops. He praised the Cambodian government of Pol Pot despite that regime's record of mass murder. But after visiting refugee camps in 1978 he condemned the Khmer Rouge and was placed on its death list. Burchett moved in 1982 to Bulgaria, where he died of cancer the following year, aged 72.[29]

George H. Johnston wrote several books and afterward was appointed first editor of the *Australasian Post*. But his relationship with a staff member, Charmian Clift, caused a scandal and forced his resignation in 1946. Thereafter he and Clift began writing fiction. Divorced from his first wife in 1947, he married Clift. In 1954 he moved his family to the Greek islands to devote himself to writing fiction full time. In 1964 Johnston wrote an autobiographical novel, *My Brother Jack*, that propelled him from literary mediocrity to fame in Australia. Five years later, as he was working on a sequel, his wife committed suicide. The third volume in what was to have been a trilogy was incomplete when he died of pulmonary tuberculosis in July 1970, two days after his 58th birthday.[30]

Noel Monks became a roving correspondent of the *Daily Mail*, and later covered the Korean War and the Malayan insurgency. The author of four books, he was the *Mail*'s royal correspondent in London at the time of his death in 1960.[31]

Edward Ward went to India in 1947 as a special correspondent. Afterward he retired from the BBC, becoming a freelance and working for the network's features department until 1960. The author of nine books, he succeeded his father as the seventh Viscount Bangor in 1950. His first three marriages ended in divorce and his fourth wife, BBC producer Marjorie Banks, died two years before his own death in May 1993, aged 88.[32]

Patrick Maitland became the 17th Earl of Lauderdale on the death of his father, an Anglican priest. He went to Washington for *The Times*, then joined the Foreign Office. In 1951 he was elected a Conservative Member of Parliament, but lost his seat in 1959. Lord Lauderdale died in December 2008, aged 87.[33]

Darrell Berrigan was murdered in Bangkok in 1965, aged 51. During the war he began working for U.S. intelligence services, helping funnel information and money to Free Thai insurgents fighting the Japanese. In the 1950s he became editor of the *Bangkok World* and, in the estimation of *Time*, turned it into "one of the genuinely cultured pearls of the East." Berrigan was a well-known figure in the Bangkok gay community. At 6:45 a.m. on October 3, 1965, he was found dead in the back seat of his Volkswagen, killed by a shot from a .38 revolver fired into the base of his skull. Police later arrested a 22-year-old Thai man, a member of an urban street gang, who was charged with murder and who confessed to the killing. The source of this information, a book about gay life in Thailand, does not reveal the fate of the killer.[34]

Jack Belden, after being wounded in Italy, returned to Europe in April 1944 in time for D-Day, but was fired nine months later after clashes with his editors. *Harper's* magazine gave him press credentials but never used anything from him. After the war he married a French woman, had a son by her and tried to freelance from Paris. He and his wife separated in 1946. A year later, he returned to China to cover the civil war and in 1949 published *China Shakes the World*. One of the major books on the Communist revolution, it was largely ignored until it was reprinted in the 1960s. Belden married again and fathered a second son, but deserted his family and moved to Summit, New Jersey, to live with his mother. He held a series of jobs, including school bus driver, before moving to Paris, where he spent his last twenty years. He died of lung cancer in June 1989, aged 79.[35]

Robert Sherrod covered the Korean and Vietnam wars. From 1955 to 1962, he was managing editor of the *Saturday Evening Post*, then editor for three years. He wrote five books on World War II and worked with NASA on a book about the Apollo mission. He was married three times but two of his wives preceded him in death. Suffering from emphysema, he died in Washington in February 1994, aged 85.[36]

Vasily Grossman returned to Moscow from Berlin in June 1945 and collapsed with nervous exhaustion, but soon recovered. In 1943 he and Ilya Ehrenburg had begun work on a "Black Book" intended to document German atrocities against Jews, but it was suppressed after the war. The Jewish Anti-Fascist Committee on which Grossman and Ehrenburg served was closed down in 1947. Grossman published a novel about Stalingrad, *For a Just Cause*, in 1952 but was furiously denounced for not having mentioned Stalin. Throughout the 1950s he worked on a sequel, *Life and Fate*, a modern *War and Peace,* which was to be his masterpiece. But parallels between Nazism and Stalinism caused the KGB to seize every copy of the manuscript in 1961. The Communist Party's chief ideologue, Mikhail Suslov, ruled that the book could not be published for more than 200 years. Grossman's previous books were withdrawn from circulation. He was reduced to penury, had few friends prepared to stand by him and developed cancer of the stomach. He died in September 1964, just short of his 59th birthday. A copy of the manuscript of *Life and Fate* was later discovered, smuggled out to Switzerland and published in 1980 to great acclaim. *The Black Book* was published in English in 1981 by Yad Vashem, the Holocaust memorial center in Jerusalem.[37]

Ilya Ehrenburg published a controversial anti-Stalin novel in 1954, after the dictator's death, entitled *The Thaw*. He was one of Russia's most prolific writers, having published around a hundred titles. In 1967 he died of cancer and his gravestone in Moscow's Novodevichy Cemetery is adorned with a reproduction of his portrait, drawn by his friend Pablo Picasso.[38]

Henry T. "Hank" Gorrell wrote a memoir after the war but never succeeded in getting it published. He left UP to establish and edit a publication he called *Veterans' Report*. In January 1958 he died at age 47, leaving a wife and three young children. Years later a distant relation, Kenneth Gorrell, found his manuscript in an attic and it was published in 2009 as *Soldier of the Press*.[39]

Helen Kirkpatrick went to Hitler's Eagle's Nest retreat at the end of the war and stole a frying pan from the Führer's kitchen to cook field rations. She remained in Germany to cover the Nuremberg trials, then joined the *New York Post* as a roving correspondent. Later she became information officer for the Marshall Plan mission in Paris, then public affairs officer for the State Department's West European division. Later she became secretary to the president of Smith College, her alma mater, and in 1954 she married Robbins Milbank, a Smith trustee and member of a prominent New England family. After his death in 1985 she moved to Williamsburg, Virginia, where she died on December 29, 1997, aged 88.[40]

Iris Carpenter married Col. Russell F. Akers, the First Army's operations officer, on January 20, 1946, having divorced her first husband, a wealthy real estate operator. She continued reporting from Washington and later joined Voice of America. She died in 1997, aged 93.[41]

Eve Curie returned to Europe in 1943 as a volunteer in the women's medical corps of the Free French during the Italian campaign. After the liberation of France, she served as co-editor of *Paris-Presse* and remained active in women's affairs for the de Gaulle government. In 1952–4 she was a special adviser to Lord Ismay, first secretary general of NATO, then married American diplomat Henry Richardson Labouisse Jr. and worked with him when he was made executive director of UNICEF. After his death in 1987, she lived in New York and died in October 2007, aged 102. She once joked that she brought shame on her family. "There were five Nobel Prizes in my family, two for my mother, one for my father, one for sister and brother-in-law and one for my husband. Only I was not successful . . ."[42]

Leland Stowe became foreign editor of *Reporter* magazine, then director of Radio Free Europe's news and information service. In 1955 he was appointed a professor of journalism at the University of Michigan, alternating between teaching and working as an editor and writer for *Reader's Digest*. Over a fifty-year period, he wrote eight books. Retiring in 1970, he remained in Ann Arbor, Michigan, until his death in January 1994 at age 94.[43]

Robert St. John wrote a best-selling memoir, *From the Land of Silent People*. Afterward he joined NBC Radio and moved to London as bureau chief in 1942, then a year later returned to the U.S. to broadcast general war news. In 1950 he was one of 151 writers, performers, directors and others listed in *Red Channels*, an American Business Consultants' report of alleged Communist influence in broadcasting. NBC fired him.[44] St. John spent the next fifteen years in Switzerland, writing books and magazine articles and broadcasting. He covered the 1948 Israeli war of independence and five more Middle

Eastern wars—the last the 1982 Israeli invasion of Lebanon when he was 80. Deeply touched by the Jewish pogrom in Romania he had witnessed, St. John became a spokesman for Jewish causes and produced biographies of Israeli leaders. He wrote twenty-three books, the last in 2002 when he turned 100. Married twice, he died in February 2003 just a month shy of his 101st birthday.

Clark Lee became a witness in 1949 at the treason trial of Iva Togiuri D'Aquino, known as "Tokyo Rose." He testified she had admitted to propaganda broadcasts for Japan, but her husband claimed Lee and other correspondents framed her. She was convicted, sentenced to ten years in prison and fined $10,000. Lee became a freelance writer but in 1952 died at his home in Pebble Beach, California, of a heart attack at age 46. A native Californian, he was the son of Clayton D. Lee, a founder and first president of UP.[45]

Carl Mydans headed the *Time-Life* bureau in Tokyo and his wife, Shelley Smith, became a radio broadcaster and novelist. He covered the Korean War and traveled the globe for two decades for *Life* before it folded in 1972. Widowed in 2002, after sixty-four years of marriage, he died at his home in Larchmont, New York, in August 2004, aged 97. Their son Seth became a foreign correspondent for the *New York Times*.[46]

Cyrus L. "Cy" Sulzberger II was a foreign correspondent of the newspaper owned by his family, the *New York Times*, for forty years and the author of two dozen books. In his postwar career, he established friendships with a number of world leaders, including de Gaulle, and in 1961 conveyed a note from President Kennedy to Nikita Khrushchev. He died at his Paris home in September 1993, aged 80.[47]

Drew Middleton covered peace conferences, the Nuremberg trials and the Soviet blockade of Berlin. From 1953 to 1963 he became chief correspondent of the *New York Times* in London, afterward serving as bureau chief in Paris, the UN and Brussels. The newspaper's military correspondent from 1970 until his retirement in 1984, he wrote more than a dozen books and, after stepping down as military correspondent, wrote a twice-weekly column until his death at age 76 in January 1990. He wrote that his career enabled him to meet "in all stages of sobriety and sanity, presidents and prime ministers, monarchs and mountebanks, heroes and rogues."[48]

Otto Tolischus was a member of the *New York Times* editorial board after the war. He retired in 1964 and died of cancer three years later, aged 76.[49]

Raymond Daniell and his journalist wife Tania Long reopened the *New York Times* bureau in Berlin and covered the Nuremberg trials. Later they moved to London and New York, then Ottawa for eleven years before he became UN correspondent. After his retirement, they returned to Canada and he died in April 1969, aged 67. Tania became public relations director for music at the National Arts Centre of Canada. In September 1998, after suffering a series of illnesses, she took her own life, aged 85.[50]

Wes Gallagher headed AP operations in Germany and covered the Nuremberg trials, scoring a notable news beat on the verdicts when he dashed a hundred yards to a phone line being held open by his wife Betty. Recalled to New York in 1951, he was appointed assistant general manager of the AP three years later, then from 1962 to 1976 was general manager and chief executive. A native Californian, he died in October 1997 at age 86.[51]

Ross Munro covered the Korean War. After retiring as a war correspondent, he became publisher of the *Vancouver Daily Province*, then the *Winnipeg Tribune* and *Edmonton Journal*. The Ross Munro Awards for Canadian military writing were instituted in 2002 by the Conference of Defence Associations, in concert with the Canadian Defence and Foreign Affairs Institute. He died in June 1990, aged 76.[52]

Godfrey Talbot devoted his postwar career to radio—disdaining television as a medium that pandered to the lowest tastes. He was the BBC's first royal court correspondent, a position he held for twenty-one years. His last important broadcast was his commentary in 1965 on the funeral of Winston Churchill. Four years later he retired, but in 1973 returned to radio to describe Princess Anne's wedding for the new London Broadcasting Company. A stickler for the correct use of English, he became president of the Queen's English Society in 1982. Talbot died in September 2000, aged 91.[53]

John MacVane went to New York as NBC's UN correspondent. In 1953 he joined ABC in the same post and remained there until retirement in 1977. A resident of South Portland, Maine, he died of a heart attack in January 1984, aged 71.[54]

Frank Tremaine died in 2006, aged 92, on the sixty-fifth anniversary of the Japanese attack on Pearl Harbor that he had covered. In 1945, he reopened UP's Tokyo bureau and was later posted to Mexico and Los Angeles before returning to Tokyo during the Korean War. Recalled to UP's New York headquarters in 1952, Tremaine retired as a senior vice-president in 1980 after forty-four years with the agency, which had now become United Press International.[55]

John H. "Jack" Thompson of the *Chicago Tribune* spent two years in Europe after the war, chronicling the continent's recovery, and covered two food mission tours with former President Herbert Hoover. In 1947 he returned to Chicago as the *Tribune*'s military editor and covered the Korean

War. He wrote a weekly column called "Friend of the Yanks" and launched a "Christmas Cash for Yanks" program for hospitalized veterans. In 1959–60 he covered the Cuban Revolution and reported on the 1963 Cuban missile crisis. He also reported from Vietnam while serving as an editorial writer. He died in December 1995, aged 87.[56]

Frank Gervasi left *Collier's* to become a correspondent for the *Washington Post* and a syndicated columnist. From 1950 to 1954, he served as information director for the Marshall Plan in Italy. He died in New York in January 1990, aged 81.[57]

William Walton rates few mentions in this book, but had one of the most distinguished postwar careers of any correspondent. Moving to the *Time* Washington bureau in 1946, he briefly joined the *New Republic* two years later, then abandoned journalism and became a well-known abstract expressionist painter. He was a neighbor and close friend of Senator John F. Kennedy and played an active role in Kennedy's presidential campaign in 1960. Frequently he escorted Jacqueline Kennedy to social functions when the president's duties kept him away, and he helped her redecorate the Oval Office with sculptures and paintings. In June 1963 Kennedy appointed him to the Commission on Fine Arts, and he later became its chairman. President Johnson reappointed him in 1967. Walton was named a trustee of the John F. Kennedy Presidential Library and Museum in the 1970s. He left government service in 1975 and resumed his career as a painter. In December 1994 he died, aged 84.[58]

This book ends almost as it began—with Clare Hollingworth, who covered the German invasion of Poland as her first journalistic assignment. In 1946, she was across the street from the King David Hotel in Jerusalem when Jewish terrorists blew it up, killing ninety-one people. While living in Cairo, she met Donald Maclean, a diplomat and long-time Soviet spy, who later defected to Moscow. Through the Macleans, Hollingworth met Kim Philby, another spy who defected in 1951, and, as a *Guardian* correspondent in 1963, she uncovered his role as the "third man" in a Soviet spy ring. In the decades to come she reported on conflicts in Algeria, China, Aden and Vietnam. Her husband Geoffrey Hoare died in 1965 and, since the early 1980s, she has lived in Hong Kong. Now blind, she celebrated turning 105 on October 10, 2016, and for a long time was a frequent visitor to the Foreign Correspondents' Club of Hong Kong.[59]

NOTES

Introduction

1. Max Hastings, *All Hell Let Loose*, pp. xv, xvi.
2. John Maxwell Hamilton, *Journalism's Roving Eye*, p. 337.
3. Robert W. Desmond, *Tides of War*, p. 461.
4. Ibid., p. 453.
5. Hamilton, *Journalism's Roving Eye*, p. 310; Desmond, *Tides of War*, pp. 176, 454.
6. The Pulitzer Prize winners were Louis Lochner, Otto Tolischus, Hanson Baldwin, Ira Wolfert, George Weller, Lawrence E. Allen, Ernie Pyle, Daniel De Luce, Hal Boyle, Mark S. Watson, Homer Bigart and William L. Laurence.
7. Noel Monks, *Eyewitness*, p. 233.
8. Susan Wiant, *Between the Bylines*, p. ix.
9. Samuel Hynes et al., *Reporting World War II*, Part 1, pp. 300–1.
10. James Tobin, *Ernie Pyle's War*, pp. 141–2.
11. John Steinbeck, *Once There Was a War*, pp. xii–xv.
12. Col. Barney Oldfield, *Never a Shot in Anger*, p. x.
13. Cyrus Sulzberger, *A Long Row of Candles*, p. 94.
14. John Hohenberg, *Foreign Correspondence*, p. 93.
15. Phillip Knightley, *The First Casualty*, pp. 363–4.
16. Desmond, *Tides of War*, p. 462.
17. Joseph J. Matthews, *Reporting the Wars*, p. 177.
18. *Binghamton Press*, "Real War Reporters Who Do All the Work Miss Out on the Glory," Jan. 25, 1943.

1 Hitler Unleashes the War

1. Associated Press, *Breaking News*, p. 219; Richard Collier, *The Warcos*, p. 3.
2. Clare Hollingworth, Front Line, pp. 11–24, 33–41; *Daily Telegraph*, "Second World War Anniversary: The Scoop," Aug. 30, 2009; Cedric Salter, *Flight from Poland*, p. 190.
3. Joe Alex Morris, *Deadline Every Minute*, pp. 221–2.
4. Edward R. Murrow, *This Is London*, pp. 6–7, 14.
5. Patrick Maitland, *European Dateline*, pp. 40, 43–8.
6. Salter, *Flight from Poland*, pp. 39, 41–3, 46–9, 55–6, 64.
7. Edward W. Beattie, *Passport to War*, pp. 125–6.
8. Robert St. John, *Foreign Correspondent*, pp. 22, 12, 17–18, 26, 36–7.

9. Denis Sefton Delmer, *Trail Sinister*, pp. 394, 397–8.
10. William Shirer, *Berlin Diary*, pp. 198, 201.
11. Virginia Cowles, *Looking for Trouble*, pp. 268–9.
12. Salter, *Flight from Poland*, pp. 68–9, 77–9.
13. Ibid., p. 77; Cecil Brown, *From Suez to Singapore*, p. 26.
14. Otto Tolischus, *They Wanted War*, pp. 293, 297.
15. Frederick Oeschner, *This Is the Enemy*, pp. 120, 124–5.
16. Tolischus, *They Wanted War*, pp. 293, 297.
17. James Reston, *Deadline: A Memoir*, pp. 77, 86.
18. Henry T. Gorrell, *Soldier of the Press*, pp. 63, 65.
19. Murrow, *This is London*, p. 25.
20. Frank Gervasi, *The Violent Decade*, pp. 203–5.
21. Helen P. Kirkpatrick, *Under the British Umbrella*, pp. 345–8; Lilya Wagner, *Women War Correspondents of World War II*, pp. 75, 77.
22. Raymond Daniell, *Civilians Must Fight*, pp. 17, 118.
23. Reston, *Deadline: A Memoir*, pp. 81–2; Daniell, *Civilians Must Fight*, pp. 119–33.
24. Hohenberg, *Foreign Correspondence*, p. 200.
25. Tim Crook, *International Radio Journalism*, pp. 183–4; Stanley Cloud and Lynn Olson, *The Murrow Boys*, pp. 77–8.
26. Salter, *Flight from Poland*, pp. 95–100; Collier, *The Warcos*, p. 53.
27. Ibid., p.55.
28. Leigh White, *The Long Balkan Night*, pp. 1–2, 51.
29. Gorrell, *Soldier of the Press*, pp. 71, 78–9.
30. St. John, *Foreign Correspondent*, pp. 85, 144–5.
31. Leigh White, *The Long Balkan Night*, p. 156.
32. Patrick Garrett, *Of Fortunes and War*, pp. 150–1.
33. Maitland, *European Dateline*, pp. 136–40.
34. David Walker, *Death at My Heels*, pp. 90–2.
35. St. John, *Foreign Correspondent*, pp. 178, 180; Walker, *Death at My Heels*, p. 156.
36. Leigh White, *The Long Balkan Night*, pp. 149–50.
37. St. John, *Foreign Correspondent*, p. 185; Walker, *Death at My Heels*, p. 66.
38. St. John, *Foreign Correspondent*, p. 186.
39. Pierre J. Huss, *Heil! And Farewell*, p. 185.

2 War in Finland, Norway and Denmark

1. Morris, *Deadline Every Minute*, pp. 225–6.
2. *Milwaukee Journal*, "Dodging Bullets to Get the News," Feb. 2, 1940.
3. Karl Eskelund, *My Chinese Wife*, pp. 121–2.
4. Cowles, *Looking for Trouble*, pp. 295, 301, 304.
5. *Milwaukee Journal*, "Dodging Bullets to Get the News," Feb. 2, 1940.
6. Martha Gellhorn, *The Face of War*, pp. 56, 60, 68, 70, 44.
7. Richard Busvine, *Gullible Travels*, pp. 1, 2, 4, 78–81, 98–9.
8. Cheryl Heckler, *An Accidental Journalist*, pp. x, 1, 11, 78–9, 81–3.
9. Leland Stowe, *No Other Road to Freedom*, pp. 47–8, 51.
10. Beattie, *Passport to War*, p. 200.
11. Carl Mydans, *More Than Meets the Eye*, p. 24.
12. Edward Ward, *Dispatches from Finland*, pp. 9, 29–31, 54–5, 138–40.
13. Stowe, *No Other Road to Freedom*, p. 57.
14. Gellhorn, *The Face of War*, pp. 73–4.
15. Hugh Baillie, *High Tension*, pp. 142–3; Webb Miller, *I Found No Peace*, pp. 9–10; Collier, *The Warcos*, pp. 17, 20; Harrison Salisbury, *A Journey for Our Times*, p. 156; Shirer, *Berlin Diary*, pp. 329–30; Gordon Young, *Outposts of War*, pp. 39–40.
16. Heckler, *An Accidental Journalist*, pp. 87–8.

17. Stowe, *No Other Road to Freedom*, pp. 67–8.
18. Young, *Outposts of War*, pp. 60–72.
19. Stowe, *No Other Road to Freedom*, pp. 73–4, 83–4, 88, 90–1, 93–4, 85–7.
20. Heckler, *An Accidental Journalist*, p. 92; Stowe, *No Other Road to Freedom*, p. 117.
21. Crook, *International Radio Journalism*, pp. 183–4.
22. Stowe, *No Other Road to Freedom*, pp. 102–4, 108–13.
23. Desmond, *Tides of War*, p. 116.
24. Stowe, *No Other Road to Freedom*, pp. 115–16, 118–19; Nancy Caldwell Sorel, *The Women Who Wrote the War*, pp. 74–6.
25. Eskelund, *My Chinese Wife*, pp. 145–7.
26. David Woodward, *Front Line and Front Page*, p. 19; Desmond, *Tides of War*, p. 116.
27. Oechsner, *This Is the Enemy*, 277.
28. Louis Lochner, *What about Germany?*, pp. 98–9.

3 The Fall of France and the Low Countries

1. Knightley, *The First Casualty*, p. 239.
2. Alexander Werth, *The Last Days of Paris*, p. 29.
3. Joseph R. L. Sterne, *Combat Correspondents*, p. 3.
4. Gellhorn, *The Face of War*, p. 75.
5. Clare Boothe, *European Spring*, pp. 168, 176–7.
6. Drew Middleton, *Where Has Last July Gone?*, p. 18.
7. Lochner, *What about Germany?*, pp. 119–20; Shirer, *Berlin Diary*, pp. 322–3.
8. Woodward, *Front Line and Front Page*, pp. 19–21.
9. Busvine, *Gullible Travels*, pp. 126, 130, 134; Woodward, *Front Line and Front Page*, pp. 23, 25.
10. Oechsner, *This Is the Enemy*, p. 278.
11. Shirer, *Berlin Diary*, p. 367.
12. Bernard Gray, *War Reporter*, pp. 72, 81, 83, 89–92, 118.
13. Eric Sevareid, *Not So Wild a Dream*, pp. 76, 82, 85, 106–7, 134, 136, 138, 140–2.
14. Gordon Waterfield, *What Happened to France*, pp. 46–51, 74, 77, 86–7.
15. Robert J. Casey, *I Can't Forget!*, pp. 166, 175–8, 222–4, 259–60, 264, 306; Joseph J. Matthews, *Reporting the Wars*, p. 180.
16. Quentin Reynolds, *By Quentin Reynolds*, pp. 138–42.
17. A. J. Liebling, *The Road Back to Paris*, pp. 84–5.
18. *Daily Telegraph*, Aug. 15, 2011.
19. Reynolds, *By Quentin Reynolds*, pp. 156–7, 161, 163, 166–7; Joseph J. Matthews, *Reporting the Wars*, p. 214.
20. Werth, *The Last Days of Paris*, pp. 149–50, 155.
21. Liebling, *The Road Back to Paris*, pp. 85–6.
22. Sevareid, *Not So Wild a Dream*, pp. 150, 152–3, 156, 159, 163.
23. Delmer, *Trail Sinister*, p. 401.
24. Waterfield, *What Happened to France*, p. 134.
25. Delmer, *Trail Sinister*, p. 402.
26. Waterfield, *What Happened to France*, p. 134.
27. Monks, *Eyewitness*, pp. 125–8; Mary Welsh, *How It Was*, pp. 50–3; Caldwell Sorel, *The Women Who Wrote the War*, p. 35.
28. Cowles, *Looking for Trouble*, pp. 378, 381–4, 386, 389–92, 394–5, 417.
29. Joseph C. Harsch, *Pattern of Conquest*, p. 49.
30. Shirer, *Berlin Diary*, pp. 409–10, 428, 444–6.
31. Desmond, *Tides of War*, p. 129.
32. Collier, *The Warcos*, pp. 42–3.
33. Harsch, *Pattern of Conquest*, pp. 21–2.
34. Oechsner, *This Is the Enemy*, p. 263.

35. Harsch, *Pattern of Conquest*, pp. 87, 104–6, 126–7.
36. Howard K. Smith, *Last Train from Berlin*, p. 42.
37. Shirer, *Berlin Diary*, pp. 450, 461, 511–12, 542–3, 569–75, 591–2, 599; Cloud and Olson, *The Murrow Boys*, pp. 269–70.
38. Reston, *Deadline: A Memoir*, p. 94.
39. Caldwell Sorel, *The Women Who Wrote the War*, p. 111; William Shirer, *The Nightmare Years*, p. 259; Wagner, *Women War Correspondents*, pp. 100–1.
40. Harsch, *Pattern of Conquest*, pp. 249–50; Desmond, *Tides of War*, p. 155.
41. Howard K. Smith, *Last Train from Berlin*, pp. 66–7, 187–206, 297, 300, 302; Morris, *Deadline Every Minute*, pp. 235–7.

4 The Battle of Britain and the Air War on Germany

1. Welsh, *How It Was*, pp. 54–5.
2. Molly Panter-Downes, *London War Notes 1939–1945*, pp. 82–3.
3. Shirer, *The Nightmare Years*, p. 579.
4. Frederick Oechsner, *This Is the Enemy*, p. 172.
5. Shirer, *Berlin Diary*, pp. 486, 490.
6. Oechsner, *This Is the Enemy*, pp. 173–4.
7. Edward R. Murrow, *This Is London*, p. 164.
8. Cloud and and Olson, *The Murrow Boys*, pp. 18, 20, 90; R. J. Brown, *Manipulating the Ether*, p. 188.
9. Murrow, *In Search of Light*, p. 31.
10. Ben Robertson, *I Saw England*, pp. 106–8.
11. John MacVane, *On the Air in World War II*, p. 24.
12. Casey, *I Can't Forget!*, pp. 328, 333, 335–6.
13. Robertson, *I Saw England*, pp. 84, 87–9, 98, 79–80, 85; Desmond, *Tides of War*, p. 134; Casey, *I Can't Forget!*, p. 375.
14. Sevareid, *Not So Wild a Dream*, pp. 179–80.
15. Cloud and Olson, *The Murrow Boys*, p. 96; MacVane, *On the Air in World War II*, p. 38; R. J. Brown, *Manipulating the Ether*, p. 187.
16. Robertson, *I Saw England*, p. 112.
17. Daniell, *Civilians Must Fight*, pp. 255–60, 268, 289–90; Collier, *The Warcos*, p. 57; Wagner, *Women War Correspondents*, p. 46.
18. Robertson, *I Saw England*, p. 170.
19. Panter-Downes, *London War Notes*, pp. 89, 97–8.
20. Reynolds, *By Quentin Reynolds*, pp. 184–7.
21. Middleton, *Where Has Last July Gone?*, p. 49.
22. Reston, *Deadline: A Memoir*, pp. 89–91.
23. Murrow, *This Is London*, pp. 175–6.
24. Drew Middleton, *The Sky Suspended*, pp. 147, 154–7; Middleton, *Where Has Last July Gone?*, p. 54.
25. Robertson, *I Saw England*, p. 134.
26. Daniell, *Civilians Must Fight*, p. 219; Murrow, *This Is London*, p. 191–4.
27. Casey, *I Can't Forget!*, pp. 362–7; Robert J. Casey, *This Is Where I Came In*, pp. 23–4.
28. Morris, *Deadline Every Minute*, p. 235.
29. Panter-Downes, *London War Notes*, pp. 106, 111.
30. Beattie, *Passport to War*, pp. 279, 322–3, 255–6, 274–8.
31. Lee G. Miller, *The Story of Ernie Pyle*, pp. 145–7.
32. MacVane, *On the Air in World War II*, p. 54.
33. Cowles, *Looking for Trouble*, p. 1.
34. Gellhorn, *The Face of War*, pp. 108, 123–4.
35. Donald Read, *The Power of News*, pp. 218–19.
36. Jim Hamilton, *The Writing 69th*, p. 31.

37. Andy Rooney, *My War*, pp. 98–10.
38. Walter Cronkite, *A Reporter's Life*, p. 96; Salisbury, *A Journey for Our Times*, p. 193.
39. Hamilton, *The Writing 69th*, pp. 37, 39–43, 53–4.
40. Ibid., pp. 13, 51.
41. Cronkite, *A Reporter's Life*, p. 98; Hamilton, *The Writing 69th*, pp. 45, 67.
42. Rooney, *My War*, pp. 125–6, 130–1.
43. Cronkite, *A Reporter's Life*, p. 99.
44. Hamilton, *The Writing 69th*, pp. 71–2.
45. Ibid., pp. 121, 125.
46. Salisbury, *A Journey for Our Times*, p. 198; Hamilton, *The Writing 69th*, p. 108.
47. Rooney, *My War*, p. 133.
48. Hohenberg, *Foreign Correspondence*, p. 225; Betsy Wade, *Forward Positions*, p. 9.
49. Salisbury, *A Journey for Our Times*, p. 198.
50. Wade, *Forward Positions*, p. 13.
51. Hamilton, *The Writing 69th*, pp. 111–12.
52. Jonathan Dimbleby, *Richard Dimbleby*, pp. 168–70.
53. Murrow, *In Search of Light*, pp. 67–75.
54. Lowell Bennett, *Parachute to Berlin*, pp. 3, 4, 13, 23, 27–9, 32, 34–5, 42, 46, 50, 57, 81–2, 84, 113, 121–2, 131–2, 141–2, 155–6, 160–1, 165–6, 168, 186, 226–7, 252.

5 The German Conquest of Greece and Yugoslavia

1. Maitland, *European Dateline*, pp. 154–5.
2. Reynolds Packard and Eleanor Packard, *Balcony Empire*, pp. 109–10, 112–16, 118–20.
3. Heckler, *An Accidental Journalist*, pp. 111, 113.
4. Stowe, *No Other Road to Freedom*, pp. 181, 192–3, 198–206, 321–2, 185.
5. Heckler, *An Accidental Journalist*, p. 114; Hill, *Desert Conquest*, p. 71.
6. Woodward, *Front Line and Front Page*, p. 65.
7. Sulzberger, *A Long Row of Candles*, p. 125.
8. Woodward, *Front Line and Front Page*, pp. 67–71.
9. Betty Wason, *Miracle in Hellas*, pp. 10–11; Caldwell Sorel, *The Women Who Wrote the War*, p. 114.
10. Gorrell, *Soldier of the Press*, pp. 82–91.
11. Richard Dimbleby, *The Frontiers are Green*, pp. 88, 90–1.
12. Walker, *Death at My Heels*, pp. 115, 121, 125, 132–3, 146, 143–6; Maitland, *European Dateline*, p. 168.
13. Heckler, *An Accidental Journalist*, p. 118.
14. Stowe, *No Other Road to Freedom*, pp. 219–21, 224, 240.
15. Heckler, *An Accidental Journalist*, p. 120.
16. Walker, *Death at My Heels*, p. 109.
17. Sulzberger, *A Long Row of Candles*, p. 121.
18. George Weller, *Weller's War*, pp. 36–7, 45.
19. Wason, *Miracle in Hellas*, pp. 70, 73–5, 88–92, 102–6.
20. Weller, *Weller's War*, p. 58.
21. en.wikipedia.org/wiki/Betty_Wason.
22. Lochner, *What about Germany?*, p. 107.
23. Richard Massock, *Italy from Within*, p. 236.
24. Oechsner, *This Is the Enemy*, pp. 142–3.
25. Maitland, *European Dateline*, pp. 111–12.
26. Ray Brock, *Nor Any Victory*, pp. 3–4, 22–3, 30–1, 46–7, 53–4, 100–1, 103–6, 119.
27. Ibid., p. 149–50.
28. Walker, *Death at My Heels*, pp. 176–7, 179–80.
29. Robert St. John, *From the Land of Silent People*, pp. 13, 17–19, 26, 31, 36, 40–2, 44, 47–8, 50; St. John, *Foreign Correspondent*, pp. 76–7; Brock, *Nor Any Victory*, pp. 193–4.

30. Walker, *Death at My Heels*, p. 196.
31. Maitland, *European Dateline*, pp. 192, 194–5.
32. Woodward, *Front Line and Front Page*, p. 106.
33. St. John, *From the Land of Silent People*, pp. 62, 64.
34. Maitland, *European Dateline*, p. 198; Walker, *Death at My Heels*, pp. 204–9.
35. Brock, *Nor Any Victory*, pp. 242, 284–5, 289–90, 294–5, 302–3, 305, 349; *New York Times*, "Ray Brock Dead; Newsman Author," Feb. 19, 1968.
36. Walker, *Death at My Heels*, p. 211.
37. St. John, *From the Land of Silent People*, pp. 146–7, 154, 165, 177.
38. Leigh White, *The Long Balkan Night*, pp. 314, 316–17, 324, 326–7, 329.
39. St. John, *From the Land of Silent People*, pp. 191, 194, 196; Leigh White, *The Long Balkan Night*, pp. 334, 336.
40. St. John, *From the Land of Silent People*, pp. 198, 200–2, 204, 209–10; Leigh White, *The Long Balkan Night*, p. 338.
41. St. John, *From the Land of Silent People*, pp. 212–15; Leigh White, *The Long Balkan Night*, pp. 346–8.
42. St. John, *From the Land of Silent People*, pp. 226–7, 247, 255, 259.
43. Leigh White, *The Long Balkan Night*, p. 350; en.wikipedia.org/wiki/Operation_Hydra.
44. Leigh White, *The Long Balkan Night*, pp. 358–60, 367, 421–2, 434, 442.
45. Walker, *Death at My Heels*, pp. 219–20, 223–4, 226, 229, 231–2, 234, 237, 239, 245, 248–50.
46. Woodward, *Front Line and Front Page*, p. 106.

6 Germany Invades the Soviet Union

1. Collier, *The Warcos*, pp. 77–8.
2. Morris, *Deadline Every Minute*, pp. 256–7.
3. Howard K. Smith, *Last Train from Berlin*, pp. 54–9.
4. Oechsner, *This Is the Enemy*, pp. 147–8.
5. Hohenberg, *Foreign Correspondence*, p. 207.
6. Knightley, *The First Casualty*, p. 278.
7. Curzio Malaparte, *Il Volga Nasce in Europa*, p. 93; Curzio Malaparte, *Kaputt*, pp. 221–2, 432; Knightley, *The First Casualty*, p. 279.
8. Malaparte, *Il Volga Nasce in Europa*, pp. 137, 139, 141–3.
9. Knightley, *The First Casualty*, p. 279; Malaparte, *Il Volga Nasce in Europa*, p. 175.
10. Morris, *Deadline Every Minute*, p. 239.
11. Antony Beevor and Luba Vinogradova, eds, *A Writer at War*, pp. 3–6, 8, 11.
12. Ilya Ehrenburg, *Russia at War*, pp. 206–8.
13. Erskine Caldwell, *Russia Under Fire*, pp. 11, 20, 26, 29, 32.
14. Oechsner, *This Is the Enemy*, pp. 282–4, 196.
15. Caldwell, *Moscow Under Fire*, pp. 90–1.
16. Whitman Bassow, *The Moscow Correspondents*, p. 100.
17. Wallace Carroll, *We're in This with Russia*, pp. 104–5, 126–7, 135.
18. Philip Jordan, *Russian Glory*, pp. 53, 38.
19. Beevor and Vinogradova, *A Writer at War*, pp. 48–9.
20. Caldwell, *Moscow Under Fire*, p. 107.
21. Heckler, *An Accidental Journalist*, pp. 193, 211.
22. Reynolds, *By Quentin Reynolds*, pp. 210, 219–21, 225–6, 265–6.
23. Larry LeSueur, *Twelve Months that Changed the World*, pp. 7, 13, 49, 52–4.
24. Sulzberger, *A Long Row of Candles*, p. 180.
25. Jordan, *Russian Glory*, p. 120.
26. LeSueur, *Twelve Months that Changed the World*, pp. 71–2, 76, 83–4.
27. Henry C. Cassidy, *Moscow Dateline 1941–1943*, pp. 141–2.
28. Beevor and Vinogradova, *A Writer at War*, pp. 52, 64.

29. Konstantin Simonov, *Always a Journalist*, pp. 23, 255.
30. Beevor and Vinogradova, *A Writer at War*, pp. 86, 110–11, 114.
31. Eve Curie, *Journey Among Warriors*, pp. 158, 171, 174–5, 180–2, 201, 203, 218, 246, 248, 257–8.
32. Eddy Gilmore, *Me and My Russian Wife*, pp. 57–8, 60–1.
33. Ehrenburg, *Russia at War*, pp. 245–7.
34. Jordan, *Russian Glory*, pp. 69, 73, 78, 83–4, 106.
35. LeSueur, *Twelve Months that Changed the World*, pp. 157–8.
36. Alexander Werth, *Moscow '41*, p. 9; Alexander Werth, *The Year of Stalingrad*, pp. 72–3, 86, 256–8.
37. LeSueur, *Twelve Months that Changed the World*, pp. 168, 206, 221–2, 273.
38. Bassow, *The Moscow Correspondents*, pp. 104–5.
39. Walter Graebner, *Round Trip to Russia*, pp. 71, 76–7.
40. Leland Stowe, *They Shall Not Sleep*, pp. 212, 232, 239, 253–4, 273–5, 282–3, 288, 295–7.
41. Cassidy, *Moscow Dateline 1941–1943*, pp. 182–92, 201, 204–5; Associated Press, *Breaking News*, p. 221.

7 Pearl Harbor

1. Caldwell Sorel, *The Women Who Wrote the War*, p. 129.
2. Clark Lee, *They Call It Pacific*, pp. 7, 8, 10, 11.
3. Packard and Packard, *Balcony Empire*, pp. 237–8.
4. Morris, *Deadline Every Minute*, p. 243.
5. Frank Tremaine and Kay Tremaine, *The Attack on Pearl Harbor*, pp. 4–5, 7, 9–12, 21–5.
6. Associated Press, *Breaking News*, pp. 222, 224; Tremaine and Tremaine, *The Attack on Pearl Harbor*, pp. 132–3.
7. Gordon Carroll, *History in the Writing*, p. 38.
8. Harsch, *At the Hinge of History*, pp. 73–4; Erwin D. Canham, *Commitment to Freedom*, p. 306.
9. en.wikipedia.org/wiki/Edgar_Rice_Burroughs.
10. Associated Press, *Breaking News*, pp. 223–4.
11. Morris, *Deadline Every Minute*, pp. 243–4.
12. R. J. Brown, *Manipulating the Ether*, pp. 190–1.
13. Reston, *Deadline: A Memoir*, p. 106.
14. Eskelund, *My Chinese Wife*, pp. 185, 187–8, 194, 197; Hohenberg, *Foreign Correspondence*, p. 218; Morris, *Deadline Every Minute*, pp. 245–6.
15. Robert J. Casey, *Torpedo Junction*, pp. 16, 28.
16. Keith Wheeler, *The Pacific Is My Beat*, pp. 15–16.
17. Morris, *Deadline Every Minute*, p. 245.
18. Packard and Packard, *Balcony Empire*, pp. 179–80.
19. Caldwell Sorel, *The Women Who Wrote the War*, pp. 26–7; Reynolds Packard, *Rome Was My Beat*, p. 56.
20. Packard and Packard, *Balcony Empire*, pp. 220, 237, 242–7.
21. Massock, *Italy from Within*, pp. 210–11; Herbert Matthews, *The Education of a Correspondent*, p. 210.
22. Massock, *Italy from Within*, pp. 311–12.
23. Packard and Packard, *Balcony Empire*, pp. 249–51, 255–6, 260.
24. Lochner, *What about Germany?*, pp. 262–70.
25. Hohenberg, *Foreign Correspondence*, p. 218; en.wikipedia.org/wiki/Robert_Henry_Best.
26. *Orlando Sentinel*, "Frederick Oeschner, Writer and Diplomat," Apr. 20, 1992.
27. en.wikipedia.org/wiki/Louis_P._Lochner.
28. Otto Tolischus, *Tokyo Record*, pp. 9, 223–6, 228–32, 236–9, 241–50, 254, 258, 260–9, 271–2, 274–6, 279.

29. Gwen Dew, *Prisoner of the Japs*, pp. 20, 92, 104, 110, 117, 128–30, 136–7, 152–3, 163, 198, 243, 245–6, 265– 6, 279, 283–4, 298–9; Harold Guard, *The Pacific War*, pp. 185, 188–9.

8 Japan Invades: The Philippines, Singapore, Burma

1. Lee, *They Call It Pacific*, pp. 15, 21, 24–6, 29, 142.
2. Royal Arch Gunnison, *So Sorry No Peace*, pp. 35–7.
3. Lee, *They Call It Pacific*, pp. 29, 52, 62–3, 69–76, 78–9; Russell Brines, *Until They Eat Stones*, p. 23.
4. R. J. Brown, *Manipulating the Ether*, p. 192; Gunnison, *So Sorry No Peace*, p. 48.
5. Caldwell Sorel, *The Women Who Wrote the War*, pp. 140–2, 146.
6. Lee, *They Call It Pacific*, pp. 80, 86, 94, 99.
7. Morris, *Deadline Every Minute*, pp. 248–9.
8. Lee, *They Call It Pacific*, pp. 80, 86, 94, 99, 100, 110, 123, 136, 138–9, 141–2, 149, 151, 155–8, 162, 174–5.
9. Pat Burgess, *Warco*, p. 95.
10. Brines, *Until They Eat Stones*, pp. 13, 23, 28–9, 58, 104.
11. Gunnison, *So Sorry No Peace*, pp. 110–11.
12. Mydans, *More than Meets the Eye*, pp. 73–4; Burgess, *Warco*, p. 96; Gunnison, *So Sorry No Peace*, pp. 97, 110–11.
13. Mydans, *More than Meets the Eye*, pp. 76–7, 79–80.
14. Brines, *Until They Eat Stones*, pp. 134–5; Burgess, *Warco*, p. 96.
15. Gunnison, *So Sorry No Peace*, pp. 132–3, 138–9, 141, 150, 152–3, 173, 225, 232, 236; Mydans, *More than Meets the Eye*, pp. 115–16.
16. Cecil Brown, *From Suez to Singapore*, pp. 234–6, 240; Knightley, *The First Casualty*, p. 312.
17. Guard, *The Pacific War Uncensored*, pp. 47, 49, 54.
18. O'D. Gallagher, *Retreat in the East*, p. 66; Brown, *From Suez to Singapore*, pp. 276–7.
19. Guard, *The Pacific War Uncensored*, pp. 59–61, 63, 66, 67.
20. Brown, *From Suez to Singapore*, pp. 293–6.
21. Lee, *They Call It Pacific*, p. 42.
22. Brown, *From Suez to Singapore*, pp. 306, 309; O'D. Gallagher, *Retreat in the East*, p. 49.
23. O'D. Gallagher, *Retreat in the East*, p. 50.
24. Brown, *From Suez to Singapore*, pp. 318–19, 322, 324–5, 327–8, 330–3, 337.
25. O'D. Gallagher, *Retreat in the East*, pp. 52–5, 74.
26. Brown, *From Suez to Singapore*, pp. 344, 397–8.
27. Weller, *Weller's War*, pp. 196–7; en. wikipedia.org/wiki/Cecil_Brown.
28. Ibid.
29. Collier, *The Warcos*, p. 207.
30. Weller, *Weller's War*, pp. 173, 194–5, 200, 206, 217, 219, 224, 231.
31. Guard, *The Pacific War Uncensored*, pp. 8–10, 73–5, 77, 82–3, 86, 90.
32. Associated Press, *Breaking News*, p. 225.
33. Guard, *The Pacific War Uncensored*, pp. 92–7, 99, 100.
34. William J. Dunn, *Pacific Microphone*, pp. 119–23, 125, 127–9; Weller, *Weller's War*, pp. 240, 242–3, 246–7; Graham Storey, *Reuters' Century*, p. 224.
35. Dunn, *Pacific Microphone*, pp. 134–6.
36. O'D. Gallagher, *Retreat in the East*, pp. 74, 76–7; Stowe, *They Shall Not Sleep*, pp. 86–7.
37. Gordon Young, *Outposts of Victory*, pp. 55–6.
38. Stowe, *They Shall Not Sleep*, pp. 87–9.
39. Young, *Outposts of Victory*, pp. 59, 66, 68–70.
40. Tom Treanor, *One Damn Thing after Another*, p. 124.
41. Curie, *Journey Among Warriors*, pp. 319, 328.
42. O'D. Gallagher, *Retreat in the East*, pp. 163–4; Stowe, *They Shall Not Sleep*, p. 110–11.
43. Stowe, *They Shall Not Sleep*, pp. 111, 129, 130, 132.

44. Wilfred Burchett, *At the Barricades*, pp. 66–7, 70, 74–5, 77, 86; en.wikipedia.org/wiki/Wilfred_Burchett.
45. Morris, *Deadline Every Minute*, pp. 246–7.
46. Jack Belden, *Retreat with Stilwell*, pp. 28–9, 49, 50, 53, 126, 130, 147, 161–2, 165, 167, 188, 191, 193, 197, 216, 218.
47. Associated Press, *Breaking News*, p. 233.
48. Belden, *Retreat with Stilwell*, pp. 254, 260, 263.
49. Knightley, *The First Casualty*, pp. 317–18.
50. George Johnston, *Journey through Tomorrow*, pp. 368–9, 371–80.
51. Theodore White, *In Search of History*, pp. 66, 76–7, 84, 102.
52. Gellhorn, *The Face of War*, pp. 75–7.
53. Stowe, *They Shall Not Sleep*, pp. 35–9, 41, 44–5, 50, 53–5, 57–9, 63–9, 71, 74, 76–7.
54. Curie, *Journey Among Warriors*, pp. 341, 344, 383–4, 399, 402, 407–9.
55. Gordon Carroll, *History in the Writing*, pp. 115–17.
56. Eskelund, *My Chinese Wife*, p. 205.
57. Gordon Carroll, *History in the Writing*, pp. 113–14.
58. Stowe, *They Shall Not Sleep*, pp. 36, 143–7.
59. Theodore White, *In Search of History*, pp. 134, 153–4; Theodore White and Annalee Jacoby, *Thunder Out of China*, pp. 143, 145–7, 159, 162–4, 168–9; Knightley, *The First Casualty*, pp. 302–3.
60. Sevareid, *Not So Wild a Dream*, pp. 228–9, 250–6, 258–9, 264–5, 269, 282–3, 294–5, 343–4, 351–2.
61. George Johnston, *Journey through Tomorrow*, pp. 96–8, 189.
62. Knightley, *The First Casualty*, p. 303.
63. White and Jacoby, *Thunder Out of China*, pp. 171, 173, 209, 211–12; Morris, *Deadline Every Minute*, p. 271.
64. Knightley, *The First Casualty*, p. 303.
65. White and Jacoby, *Thunder Out of China*, pp. 233–40; *New York Times*, "Annalee Whitmore Fadiman, 85, Screenwriter and War Journalist," Feb. 6, 2002.

9 Pacific Island Campaigns

1. Osmar White, *Green Armour*, pp. 40, 48, 51.
2. Frank Legg, *War Correspondent*, p. 58.
3. George Johnston, *The Toughest Fighting in the World*, pp. 15–18.
4. Osmar White, *Green Armour*, pp. 83, 89, 91, 94, 121–2, 128, 141, 169, 175, 178, 183–4, 188–9, 191, 195–8, 200–4, 206, 209.
5. Trevor Royle, *War Report*, pp. 146–7, 157–9.
6. Osmar White, *Conquerors' Road*, p. ix.
7. George Johnston, *The Toughest Fighting in the World*, pp. 48–9.
8. Collier, *The Warcos*, p. 126; Hohenberg, *Foreign Correspondence*, p. 217; M. L. Stein, *Under Fire*, pp. 107–8.
9. Weller, *Weller's War*, p. 359.
10. George Johnston, *The Toughest Fighting in the World*, p. 50.
11. Weller, *Weller's War*, pp. 364–5.
12. George Johnston, *The Toughest Fighting in the World*, pp. 132, 138–40, 141, 167, 193.
13. John Darnton, *Almost a Family*, pp. 10, 11, 13, 15–18, 201; Weller, *Weller's War*, pp. 343–5; Guard, *The Pacific War Uncensored*, p. 179.
14. Weller, *Weller's War*, pp. 320–7, 376–7, 380, 409.
15. George Johnston, *The Toughest Fighting in the World*, p. 167.
16. Stenbuck, *Typewriter Battalion*, pp. 70–3.
17. Collier, *The Warcos*, pp. 174–5.
18. George Johnston, *The Toughest Fighting in the World*, pp. 226–7, 232–3.
19. Weller, *Weller's War*, pp. 356–8.

20. Burgess, *Warco*, pp. 27–8.
21. Stenbuck, *Typewriter Battalion*, pp. 100–3.
22. Stanley Johnston, *Queen of the Flattops*, pp. 138, 140, 154, 160–2, 166–7, 169–70, 180, 183–5, 187, 190, 201, 207, 211–13, 215, 219, 223–5; Hohenberg, *Foreign Correspondence*, pp. 216–17.
23. Guard, *The Pacific War Uncensored*, p. 109.
24. Casey, *Torpedo Junction*, pp. 223–38.
25. Foster Hailey, *Pacific Battle Line*, pp. 163–7, 170–7.
26. Casey, *Torpedo Junction*, pp. 223–38.
27. Hailey, *Pacific Battle Line*, pp. 178, 181; *New York Times*, "Foster Hailey, Times Reporter and Editorial Writer, Dies at 67," Aug. 14, 1966.
28. Casey, *Torpedo Junction*, pp. 242, 247, 254.
29. Hohenberg, *Foreign Correspondence*, p. 217.
30. Keith Wheeler, *The Pacific Is My Beat*, pp. 61–2, 69, 141–3, 157–9, 179–83, unnumbered Foreword.
31. Gordon Carroll, *History in the Writing*, p. 191.
32. en.wikipedia.org/wiki/Dashiell_Hammett.
33. Richard Tregaskis, *Guadalcanal Diary*, p. 41.
34. Lee, *They Call It Pacific*, pp. 196–8.
35. Tregaskis, *Guadalcanal Diary*, pp. 48, 50, 56.
36. Hailey, *Pacific Battle Line*, pp. 202–5.
37. Morris, *Deadline Every Minute*, pp. 254–5.
38. Gordon Carroll, *History in the Writing*, pp. 268–72.
39. Lee, *They Call It Pacific*, pp. 200–5, 208–11.
40. Osmar White, *Conquerors' Road*, p. 243.
41. Hailey, *Pacific Battle Line*, p. 217.
42. Tregaskis, *Guadalcanal Diary*, pp. 165–6, 168–71.
43. Stein, *Under Fire*, pp. 110–11; Hynes et al., *Reporting World War II*, Part 1, pp. 414–18.
44. Ira Wolfert, *Battle for the Solomons*, pp. 66, 69; Stein, *Under Fire*, p. 111.
45. Hailey, *Pacific Battle Line*, pp. 310–12.
46. Tregaskis, *Guadalcanal Diary*, p. 173.
47. Osmar White, *Conquerors' Road*, pp. 246, 254–6, 258, 263, 277–9, 281, 286–7.
48. Hohenberg, *Foreign Correspondence*, p. 233.
49. Robert Sherrod, *Tarawa: The Story of a Battle*, pp. 14, 61–2, 64–5, 67–9, 72, 74.
50. Associated Press, *Breaking News*, p. 238.
51. Hohenberg, *Foreign Correspondence*, p. 235.
52. Sherrod, *Tarawa: The Story of a Battle*, pp. 82–4, 86–7, 99; Morris, *Deadline Every Minute*, pp. 266–7.
53. Sherrod, *Tarawa: The Story of a Battle*, p. 123.
54. Dunn, *Pacific Microphone*, p. 337.

10 The Desert War

1. Jonathan Dimbleby, *Richard Dimbleby*, pp. 107, 109.
2. Alan Moorehead, *A Late Education*, pp. 14, 18, 40–1, 132.
3. Moorehead, *African Trilogy*, pp. 74–5, 78.
4. Ed Kennedy, *Ed Kennedy's War*, p. 67.
5. Alexander Clifford, *Three Against Rommel*, pp. 36–7, 52.
6. Moorehead, *African Trilogy*, pp. 90–1, 98.
7. Moorehead, *A Late Education*, pp. 66, 67.
8. Moorehead, *African Trilogy*, p. 104.
9. Clifford, *Three Against Rommel*, pp. 64–6; Moorehead, *African Trilogy*, p. 105; Moorehead, *A Late Education*, p. 139.
10. Clifford, *Three Against Rommel*, pp. 64–6, 18–22; Moorehead, *A Late Education*, p. 139.

11. Cecil Brown, *From Suez to Singapore*, p. 32.
12. Woodward, *Front Line and Front Page*, pp. 92–3.
13. Gervasi, *The Violent Decade*, pp. 311, 313.
14. *Pittsburgh Post-Gazette*, "Writers Duck Bombs Near Cleopatra's Bath," June 17, 1940.
15. Moorehead, *African Trilogy*, p. 113.
16. Curie, *Journey Among Warriors*, pp. 33, 41; Moorehead, *African Trilogy*, p. 267.
17. Jonathan Dimbleby, *Richard Dimbleby*, p. 119.
18. Gordon Carroll, *History in the Writing*, p. 140.
19. Moorehead, *African Trilogy*, pp. 221, 223, 226–7.
20. Edward Ward, *Number One Boy*, p. 158.
21. Chester Wilmot, *Tobruk 1941*, pp. 55–6.
22. Harold Denny, *Behind Both Lines*, pp. 15, 16, 19, 21, 23, 25, 27–9, 33–4, 37, 47, 49–51, 54–5, 65, 86, 133–4; Ward, *Number One Boy*, pp. 179–80, 197–8, 200–2, 205, 211, 215, 224–5.
23. Moorehead, *African Trilogy*, pp. 231–3.
24. Clifford, *Three Against Rommel*, pp. 175–6, 190, 270–1.
25. Wilmot, *Tobruk 1941*, p. 54.
26. Russell Hill, *Desert War*, p. 126.
27. Associated Press, *Breaking News*, pp. 219–21; Kent Cooper, *Kent Cooper and the Associated Press*, pp. 45–6.
28. Reynolds, *By Quentin Reynolds*, pp. 235–6, 242.
29. Richard McMillan, *Rendezvous with Rommel*, pp. 31–3.
30. Jonathan Dimbleby, *Richard Dimbleby*, pp. 158–9.
31. Gervasi, *The Violent Decade*, pp. 397, 421, 442–3.
32. Hill, *Desert Conquest*, pp. 9–16.
33. Moorehead, *African Trilogy*, pp. 353, 356; Clifford, *Three Against Rommel*, pp. 280, 297–9.
34. Allan A. Michie, *Retreat to Victory*, pp. 249, 251.
35. Arthur Christensen, *Headlines All My Life*, pp. 206–7.
36. Gorrell, *Soldier of the Press*, pp. 154–5, 158, 160–1, 168, 193, 198.
37. Ibid., pp. 199–200, 204, 220, 227, 230–1.
38. Treanor, *One Damn Thing after Another*, pp. 8, 10, 29.
39. Godfrey Talbot, *Speaking from the Desert*, p. 71.
40. Gorrell, *Soldier of the Press*, pp. 244–5, 259.
41. Hill, *Desert Conquest*, pp. 86–9.
42. Don Whitehead, *Combat Reporter*, pp. 3, 11, 47, 98; John B. Romeiser, *Beachhead Don*, p. xxvi.
43. Heckler, *An Accidental Journalist*, pp. 221–2, 225–6.
44. Kennedy, *Ed Kennedy's War*, p. 99.
45. Whitehead, *Combat Reporter*, p. 114; Hollingworth, *Front Line*, pp. 134–6.
46. Clifford, *Three Against Rommel*, pp. 297–9, 302, 329–30, 340–1.
47. Morris, *Deadline Every Minute*, pp. 259–60.
48. John MacVane, *War and Diplomacy in North Africa*, pp. 63, 73, 81–2.
49. Cloud and Olson, *The Murrow Boys*, p. 162.
50. Royle, *War Report*, p. 148.
51. Miller, *The Story of Ernie Pyle*, pp. 219–21, 252–3, 263, 293; David Nichols, *Ernie's War*, pp. 178–81.
52. MacVane, *War and Diplomacy*, pp. 98–100.
53. Ibid., p. 154; Cloud and Olson, *The Murrow Boys*, p. 160.
54. Associated Press, *Breaking News*, p. 221; Kennedy, *Ed Kennedy's War*, pp. 106–7; Wagner, *Women War Correspondents*, p. 33.
55. Kennedy, *Ed Kennedy's War*, pp. 105–6; Boyle, *Help, Help! Another Day!*, unnumbered photo page.
56. Moorehead, *African Trilogy*, pp. 434, 493–4; John D'Arcy Dawson, *Tunisian Battle*, pp. 90–1.

57. Whitehead, *Combat Reporter*, pp. 130, 139–42, 144.
58. Associated Press, *Breaking News*, p. 226.
59. Boyle, *Help, Help! Another Day!*, pp. 54–5.
60. *Scottish Daily Express*, "How the Desert Armies Met," Mar. 5, 1943.
61. Gordon Carroll, *History in the Writing*, p. 207.
62. John D'Arcy Dawson, *European Victory*, pp. 27, 199–200, 205.
63. Middleton, *Where Has Last July Gone?*, pp. 95–8, 110.
64. Nichols, *Ernie's War*, p. 27.
65. Hill, *Desert Conquest*, pp. 153–4.
66. Wes Gallagher, *Back Door to Berlin*, p. 236.
67. MacVane, *On the Air in World War II*, pp. 185–7; Gordon Carroll, *History in the Writing*, p. 213; Collier, *The Warcos*, p. 144.
68. Clifford, *Three Against Rommel*, pp. 400–2.
69. Cloud and Olson, *The Murrow Boys*, pp. 157, 166.

11 Stalingrad and Leningrad

1. Beevor and Vinogradova, *A Writer at War*, pp. 119, 125, 156, 180.
2. Werth, *The Year of Stalingrad*, pp. 278, 281.
3. Ibid., p. 282.
4. Beevor and Vinogradova, *A Writer at War*, pp. 190–2, 195, 198, 200, 205, 211; Werth, *The Year of Stalingrad*, p. 428.
5. Graebner, *Round Trip to Russia*, p. 138.
6. Ilya Ehrenburg, *The War 1941–5*, p. 131; Beevor and Vinogradova, *A Writer at War*, pp. 242–3; Werth, *The Year of Stalingrad*, pp. 354–8; Bassow, *The Moscow Correspondents*, pp. 108–9.
7. Gilmore, *Me and My Russian Wife*, pp. 124, 129–30.
8. Cloud and Olson, *The Murrow Boys*, pp. 156, 196.
9. Werth, *The Year of Stalingrad*, pp. 441, 444–6, 451, 466–7; Knightley, *The First Casualty*, p. 285.
10. Gordon Carroll, *History in the Writing*, pp. 265–7.
11. Alexander Werth, *Russia at War 1941–1945*, pp. 612, 615.
12. Ehrenburg, *The War 1941–5*, pp. 95, 111–13.
13. Heckler, *An Accidental Journalist*, pp. 248–50, 252–3.
14. Gilmore, *Me and My Russian Wife*, pp. 143–6; Salisbury, *A Journey for Our Times*, pp. 251, 256–7; Ehrenburg, *The War 1941–5*, p. 131; Bassow, *The Moscow Correspondents*, p. 107.
15. Read, *The Power of News*, p. 222.
16. *New York Times*, "Edmund Stevens, 81, a Reporter in Moscow for 40 Years, Is Dead," May 27, 1992.
17. en.wikipedia.org/wiki/Alexander_Werth.
18. Knightley, *The First Casualty*, p. 280; Malaparte, *Il Volga Nasce in Europa*, p. 221, 226, 263–4, 272–3, 317–18.
19. Hastings, *All Hell Let Loose*, p. 170.
20. Alexander Werth, *Leningrad*, pp. 9, 27, 30.
21. Werth, *Russia at War 1941–1945*, p. 338.
22. Werth, *Leningrad*, pp. 33, 37, 38, 43–5, 49, 67, 73, 131–2, 185–6, 188–9; Werth, *Russia at War 1941–1945*, p. 353.
23. Arvid Fredborg, *Behind the Steel Wall*, pp. 60–3, 67, 91, 180, 195–6, 209–13, 255–6.

12 The Battle for Italy

1. Ross Munro, *Gauntlet to Overlord*, pp. 359, 364, 376–7, 431–2.
2. Sterne, *Combat Correspondents*, pp. 46–7.
3. Whitehead, *Combat Reporter*, pp. 160–3, 168; Collier, *The Warcos*, p. 145.

4. Collier, *The Warcos*, p. 163.
5. Whitehead, *Combat Reporter*, pp. 173–4, 179.
6. Miller, *The Story of Ernie Pyle*, p. 274; Nichols, *Ernie's War*, pp. 29, 30; Pyle, *Brave Men*, pp. 77–8, 84–6; James Tobin, *Ernie Pyle's War*, p. 112.
7. Monks, *Eyewitness*, p. 194.
8. Herbert Matthews, *The Education of a Correspondent*, pp. 415–16, 418.
9. Peter Stursberg, *The Sound of War*, p. 119.
10. Whitehead, *Combat Reporter*, p. 206.
11. See: www.armchairgeneral.com, Carlo D'Este, "The Triumph and Tragedy of George S. Patton Jr.: The Slapping Incidents in Sicily," May 4, 2005; Monks, *Eyewitness*, pp. 195–8; James Tobin, *Ernie Pyle's War*, p. 110.
12. Kennedy, *Ed Kennedy's War*, pp. 110–11.
13. Reynolds, *By Quentin Reynolds*, p. 272.
14. Kennedy, *Ed Kennedy's War*, p. 111.
15. Lionel S. B. Shapiro, *They Left the Back Door Open*, pp. 36, 40, 43, 48, 51.
16. Gordon Carroll, *History in the Writing*, pp. 231–2, 234–5, 237.
17. Christopher Buckley, *The Road to Rome*, pp. 38, 47, 66–7, 131, 136–7; Hollingworth, *Front Line*, p. 131.
18. Reynolds, *By Quentin Reynolds*, p. 275.
19. Shapiro, *They Left the Back Door Open*, pp. 72–3, 75, 77–8, 81, 85–6, 91.
20. Monks, *Eyewitness*, pp. 200–7, 219–21.
21. Romeiser, *Beachhead Don*, p. xxvii.
22. Belden, *Still Time to Die*, pp. 262–71.
23. Herbert Matthews, *The Education of a Correspondent*, pp. 419, 435–6.
24. Monks, *Eyewitness*, pp. 209, 211–12, 214–15; Reynolds Packard, *Rome Was My Beat*, p. 109.
25. Sterne, *Combat Correspondents*, pp. 47, 51.
26. Miller, *The Story of Ernie Pyle*, pp. 289–90; Pyle, *Brave Men*, pp. 95–6, 117.
27. Herbert Mitgang, *Newsmen in Khaki*, pp. 100–1; Pyle, *Brave Men*, pp. 126–7.
28. Alan Moorehead, *Eclipse*, pp. 61, 64–5.
29. Packard, *Rome Was My Beat*, p. 110.
30. Richard Tregaskis, *Invasion Diary*, pp. 116–17, 201, 208–12, 214–16, 291–20, 225, 229, 233, 241; Pyle, *Brave Men*, pp. 120–2.
31. Pyle, *Brave Men*, pp. 143, 154–6; Miller, *The Story of Ernie Pyle*, p. 297; Romeiser, *Beachhead Don*, p. xxiv.
32. Pyle, *Brave Men*, pp. 162, 192–3.
33. Gervasi, *The Violent Decade*, pp. 544–5.
34. Treanor, *One Damn Thing after Another*, pp. 231, 238–47, 249, 256, 269–71.
35. Romeiser, *Beachhead Don*, p. xxvii.
36. Gervasi, *The Violent Decade*, p. 531.
37. Treanor, *One Damn Thing after Another*, pp. 281–3; Wade, *Forward Positions*, pp. 35–6, 40–2.
38. Pyle, *Brave Men*, pp. 232–3, 246–50.
39. Sterne, *Combat Correspondents*, p. 66.
40. Wade, *Forward Positions*, p. 50.
41. Collier, *The Warcos*, p. 196.
42. Buckley, *The Road to Rome*, pp. 256–7, 261–2, 286–8, 296–305, 309, 311, 313, 320.
43. Pyle, *Brave Men*, pp. 300–1; *Sydney Morning Herald*, May 19, 1943.
44. Wade, *Forward Positions*, pp. 42–3.
45. Sterne, *Combat Correspondents*, p. 74.
46. Stursberg, *The Sound of War*, p. 167.
47. Stenbuck, *Typewriter Battalion*, pp. 83–6.
48. Sevareid, *Not So Wild a Dream*, p. 409.
49. Denis Johnston, *Nine Rivers from Jordan*, pp. 238–40.
50. Sterne, *Combat Correspondents*, p. 69.

51. Wade, *Forward Positions*, pp. 47–9.
52. Denis Johnston, *Nine Rivers from Jordan*, pp. 245, 252; Sterne, *Combat Correspondents*, 69.
53. Sevareid, *Not So Wild a Dream*, pp. 411–12.
54. Herbert Matthews, *The Education of a Correspondent*, pp. 473–5.
55. Mitgang, *Newsmen in Khaki*, pp. 129–30.
56. Sevareid, *Not So Wild a Dream*, pp. 424–5.
57. Mitgang, *Newsmen in Khaki*, pp. 136–7.
58. Gellhorn, *The Face of War*, pp. 156, 158, 160–1.
59. Caroline Moorehead, *The Letters of Martha Gellhorn*, pp. 169–70.

13 D-Day Landings in Normandy

1. Pyle, *Brave Men*, pp. 298–9; Associated Press, *Breaking News*, p. 228; A. J. Liebling, *Normandy Revisited*, pp. 2, 3.
2. Oldfield, *Never a Shot in Anger*, pp. 67–9; Hohenberg, *Foreign Correspondence*, p. 226.
3. Oldfield, *Never a Shot in Anger*, pp. 106–7.
4. Pyle, *Brave Men*, pp. 353, 358–60, 364–5, 372.
5. *Chicago Tribune*, "D-Day's Cauldron," May 29, 1994.
6. Nichols, *Ernie's War*, p. 440.
7. MacVane, *On the Air in World War II*, pp. 232–5, 241–7, 252–3.
8. Collier, *The Warcos*, p. 160.
9. Huddle, *Roi Ottley's World War II*, pp. 56–8.
10. Oldfield, *Never a Shot in Anger*, p. 82.
11. Holbrook Bradley, *War Correspondent*, pp. xx, 1, 2, 10, 21.
12. www.freerepublic.com/focus/f-news/3165139/posts.
13. www.history.net/covering_d-day_an_allied_journalists_perspective.htm.
14. Jonathan Dimbleby, *Richard Dimbleby*, pp. 181–2.
15. Leonard Miall, *Richard Dimbleby, Broadcaster*, p. 36.
16. Rooney, *My War*, pp. 157, 159, 161.
17. Cronkite, *A Reporter's Life*, pp. 103–4, 106–7.
18. Richard Tobin, *Invasion Journal*, pp. 83–5, 92–5.
19. Munro, *Gauntlet to Overlord*, pp. 61, 65, 67–8, 81–2, 108.
20. Collier, *The Warcos*, p. 164.
21. Dawson, *European Victory*, pp. 66, 72–4.
22. Read, *The Power of News*, pp. 223–5.
23. Monks, *Eyewitness*, pp. 226–8.
24. Moorehead, *Eclipse*, pp. 102–3, 110–12.
25. Casey, *This Is Where I Came In*, pp. 110, 114–15, 159, 161.
26. Oldfield, *Never a Shot in Anger*, pp. 78–80.
27. Ibid., p. 84.
28. Cloud and Olson, *The Murrow Boys*, p. 206.
29. Oldfield, *Never a Shot in Anger*, p. 80; www.54warcorrespondents-kia.30-ww2.com/government_file.html.
30. *Manchester Guardian*, "Airborne Troops Landed behind Enemy Lines," June 9, 1944.
31. Murrow, *In Search of Light*, p. 80.
32. Panter-Downes, *London War Notes*, pp. 327–9.
33. Desmond Hawkins, *War Report*, p. 76.
34. Carlos Baker, *Ernest Hemingway*, p. 391.
35. Welsh, *How It Was*, pp. 85, 94–5.
36. Stephen E. Ambrose, *D-Day: June 6, 1944*, pp. 478–9.
37. Gellhorn, *The Face of War*, pp. 108, 122–4, 134–6, 140, 143–6, 148, 151–2; *Guardian*, "There Is a Point Where You Feel So Small and Helpless in an Enormous, Insane Nightmare of a World that You Cease to Give a Hoot and Start Laughing," May 28, 2004; Caroline Moorehead, *The Letters of Martha Gellhorn*, pp. 166–7.

38. Antony Penrose, *Lee Miller's War*, pp. 15–17, 24.
39. Iris Carpenter, *No Woman's World*, pp. 29, 33, 40–4.
40. Monks, *Eyewitness*, p. 231.
41. Dawson, *European Victory*, p. 35; Crook, *International Radio Journalism*, p. 217.
42. Alan Moorehead, *Eclipse*, pp. 135–7, 139–40.
43. Miller, *The Story of Ernie Pyle*, pp. 338–9.
44. Richard McMillan, *Miracle before Berlin*, p. 36.
45. Dawson, *European Victory*, pp. 53–6.
46. Sterne, *Combat Correspondents*, pp. 93, 96.
47. Oldfield, *Never a Shot in Anger*, pp. 87–8; Rooney, *My War*, p. 209.
48. www.bbc.co.uk.broadcastinghouse/memorial.html.
49. Huddle, *Roi Ottley's World War II*, pp. 60, 62–4, 88.

14 The Battle for France

1. Cloud and Olson, *The Murrow Boys*, p. 228.
2. Moorehead, *Eclipse*, pp. 145–6.
3. Sterne, *Combat Correspondents*, p. 101.
4. Dawson, *European Victory*, p. 87; Sterne, *Combat Correspondents*, p. 102.
5. McMillan, *Miracle before Berlin*, pp. 37–8, 48–9.
6. Dawson, *European Victory*, pp. 163–4; Carpenter, *No Woman's World*, pp. 39–40, 46–8.
7. Pyle, *Brave Men*, pp. 436–7, 459, 444–5, 453; James Tobin, *Ernie Pyle's War*, p. 201.
8. Huddle, *Roi Ottley's World War II*, p. 75.
9. Associated Press, *Breaking News*, p. 230.
10. Munro, *Gauntlet to Overlord*, pp. 173–4.
11. Carpenter, *No Woman's World*, pp. 64–5.
12. Stenbuck, *Typewriter Battalion*, pp. 187–91.
13. Bradley, *War Correspondent*, pp. 36–7, 40, 44, 46–51, 53–6, 59, 68, 71–4.
14. Penrose, *Lee Miller's War*, pp. 36–7, 41–2, 48, 50–1, 58.
15. Casey, *This Is Where I Came In*, p. 221.
16. Baker, *Ernest Hemingway*, pp. 403–5.
17. Alan Wood, *The Falaise Road*, pp. 27, 43–7.
18. Munro, *Gauntlet to Overlord*, pp. 187–9.
19. Dawson, *European Victory*, p. 157.
20. Moorehead, *Eclipse*, p. 155.
21. Desmond, *Tides of War*, p. 372.
22. Stenbuck, *Typewriter Battalion*, pp. 226–9.
23. Ann Stringer, *"Bravo, Amerikanski!"*, pp. 16–21.
24. Whitehead, *Combat Reporter*, p. 203.
25. Gervasi, *The Violent Decade*, pp. 606–7, 610–12; Mydans, *More than Meets the Eye*, p. 175.
26. Sevareid, *Not So Wild a Dream*, pp. 457–9.
27. Sterne, *Combat Correspondents*, p. 118.
28. Sevareid, *Not So Wild a Dream*, pp. 458–9.
29. Gervasi, *The Violent Decade*, pp. 612–15, 617.
30. Sevareid, *Not So Wild a Dream*, p. 461.
31. Cloud and Olson, *The Murrow Boys*, pp. 226–7.
32. Kennedy, *Ed Kennedy's War*, pp. 136–7.
33. Baker, *Ernest Hemingway*, pp. 409–10.
34. MacVane, *On the Air in World War II*, p. 279.
35. Baker, *Ernest Hemingway*, p. 407.

15 The Liberation of Paris

1. Romeiser, *Beachhead Don*, pp. 208–9.
2. Rooney, *My War*, pp. 204–5, 208.

3. Romeiser, *Beachhead Don*, pp. xxi, 211–12.

4. Ibid., pp. xxiv, xxv.

5. Rooney, *My War*, pp. 212–13, 216.

6. Ibid., p. 210.

7. McMillan, *Miracle before Berlin*, p. 59.

8. Stenbuck, *Typewriter Battalion*, p. 280.

9. Pyle, *Brave Men*, pp. 456–7, 465; Miller, *The Story of Ernie Pyle*, pp. 361–3; James Tobin, *Ernie Pyle's War*, p. 201; Nichols, *Ernie's War*, pp. 41, 46; Collier, *The Warcos*, p. 196.

10. Monks, *Eyewitness*, pp. 234–5.

11. Moorehead, *Eclipse*, pp. 160–1, 163.

12. Oldfield, *Never a Shot in Anger*, p. 110.

13. Casey, *This Is Where I Came In*, pp. 264–6; Sterne, *Combat Correspondents*, p. 114.

14. Casey, *This Is Where I Came In*, pp. 270–1.

15. MacVane, *On the Air in World War II*, pp. 282, 288–9, 291–5.

16. Wood, *The Falaise Road*, p. 58.

17. *San Francisco Chronicle*, "Liberating France Hemingway's Way," Aug. 22, 2004; Liebling, *Normandy Revisited*, pp. 235–7; Moorehead, *Eclipse*, p. 170.

18. Caldwell Sorel, *The Women Who Wrote the War*, p. 260; *San Francisco Chronicle*, "Liberating France Hemingway's Way," Aug. 22, 2004.

19. Hawkins, *War Report*, pp. 160–1.

20. Moorehead, *Eclipse*, pp. 174–5.

21. Dawson, *European Victory*, pp. 176–8.

22. Carpenter, *No Woman's World*, pp. 109–10, 112.

23. *San Francisco Chronicle*, "Liberating France Hemingway's Way," Aug. 22, 2004.

24. Welsh, *How It Was*, pp. 145–6, 171.

25. Gellhorn, *The Face of War*, pp. 176–82.

26. Antoinette May, *Witness to War*, pp. 74, 76–7.

27. Penrose, *Lee Miller's War*, pp. 65, 69, 70, 73, 77–8, 105.

28. Edward W. Beattie, *Diary of a Kriegie*, pp. 1, 3, 75–6, 81–2, 102–3, 180, 198, 204, 279, 281, 291, 293, 296, 309–11; *Saturday Evening Post*, "The Nervy Exploit of Lt. Sam Magill," Nov. 11, 1944; triggertimeforum.yuku.com.

16 The Western Allies Drive Toward Germany

1. Dawson, *European Victory*, pp. 194–5.

2. Cloud and Olson, *The Murrow Boys*, p. 228.

3. Moorehead, *Eclipse*, pp. 193–4.

4. Cronkite, *A Reporter's Life*, pp. 109–14.

5. Dawson, *European Victory*, pp. 212–13.

6. Hawkins, *War Report*, pp. 186–7, 201, 205–8.

7. Moorehead, *Eclipse*, p. 212.

8. Arthur Christiansen, *Headlines All My Life*, pp. 204–5.

9. See: www.market-garden.info.html-books/five-days-in-hell.html.

10. *Daily Mail*, "24 Hours of Hell," Sept. 28, 1944.

11. Caroline Moorehead, *The Letters of Martha Gellhorn*, p. 166.

12. Hawkins, *War Report*, pp. 227–9, 212.

13. Penrose, *Lee Miller's War*, p. 169.

14. Rooney, *My War*, p. 237; www.tridget.com/rwljr.html; en.wikipedia.org/wiki/Richard_Tregaskis.

15. Carpenter, *No Woman's World*, pp. 189–90.

16. Sterne, *Combat Correspondents*, pp. 178–9.

17. Associated Press, *Breaking News*, pp. 233–4.

18. Sterne, *Combat Correspondents*, pp. 134, 146, 148, 153–4, 158–60.

19. Caldwell Sorel, *The Women Who Wrote the War*, pp. 286–7.

20. Carpenter, *No Woman's World*, pp. 218–19.

21. Cronkite, *A Reporter's Life*, pp. 119–21.
22. McMillan, *Miracle before Berlin*, p. 124.
23. Rooney, *My War*, pp. 238–9.
24. Baker, *Ernest Hemingway*, pp. 425, 428–9, 432–3, 436, 441–5; Frederick S. Voss, *Reporting the War*, p. 190.
25. Collier, *The Warcos*, p. 167.
26. Knightley, *The First Casualty*, p. 289; Werth, *Russia at War 1941–1945*, p. 663.
27. Gordon Carroll, *History in the Writing*, pp. 366–9.
28. Beevor and Vinogradova, *A Writer at War*, pp. 250–1, 255.
29. Werth, *Russia at War 1941–1945*, pp. 688–9, 691, 693–4, 698, 702, 784–5, 787, 793, 800, 802, 813–14, 822.
30. Salisbury, *A Journey for Our Times*, p. 263.
31. Beevor and Vinogradova, *A Writer at War*, pp. 270–1, 273.
32. Ehrenburg, *The War 1941–5*, pp. 137–8.
33. Gilmore, *Me and My Russian Wife*, pp. 167–72; Bassow, *The Moscow Correspondents*, p. 111.
34. Stenbuck, *Typewriter Battalion*, pp. 147–52.
35. Beevor and Vinogradova, *A Writer at War*, pp. 279–81.
36. Simonov, *Always a Journalist*, pp. 42–50, 52, 56–9.
37. Hynes et al., *Reporting World War II*, Part Two, p. 267.
38. Werth, *Russia at War 1941–1945*, pp. 890, 892, 894–8.
39. Beevor and Vinogradova, *A Writer at War*, pp. 280–2, 306, 311–12, 314, 316–17, 320–1, 327.

17　Germany Invaded

1. Stringer, *"Bravo, Amerikanski!"*, pp. 24–37, 161.
2. Oldfield, *Never a Shot in Anger*, pp. 92–3.
3. See: www.bbc.co.uk/broadcastinghouse/memorial.html.
4. Stenbuck, *Typewriter Battalion*, pp. 302–5.
5. McMillan, *Miracle before Berlin*, pp. 128, 133.
6. Stringer, *"Bravo, Amerikanski!"*, pp. 23, 42–3.
7. Moorehead, *Eclipse*, pp. 233–4.
8. Penrose, *Lee Miller's War*, p. 166.
9. Rooney, *My War*, p. 250.
10. Gellhorn, *The Face of War*, p. 213; Stringer, *"Bravo, Amerikanski!"*, pp. 43–7.
11. Carpenter, *No Woman's World*, pp. 275, 278–9.
12. Hawkins, *War Report*, p. 265; Oldfield, *Never a Shot in Anger*, p. 217.
13. Jonathan Dimbleby, *Richard Dimbleby*, p. 187.
14. Oldfield, *Never a Shot in Anger*, p. 217.
15. Read, *The Power of News*, p. 226.
16. Cloud and Olson, *The Murrow Boys*, p. 231.
17. Dawson, *European Victory*, pp. 256, 279–80, 285, 289–90.
18. Osmar White, *Conquerors' Road*, pp. 33–8, 42–3, 47–8, 50, 63, 65–6, 68–9, 70, 72–4.
19. Carpenter, *No Woman's World*, pp. 291–2
20. Stringer, *"Bravo, Amerikanski!"*, pp. 54–6.
21. Carpenter, *No Woman's World*, pp. 293–5, 299–301.
22. Hawkins, *War Report*, pp. 284, 287–8.
23. Sevareid, *Not So Wild a Dream*, pp. 504–5.
24. Osmar White, *Conquerors' Road*, pp. 99–104, 96–8.
25. MacVane, *On the Air in World War II*, p. 311.
26. Ward, *Number One Boy*, pp. 231, 233–4; Hawkins, *War Report*, pp. 304–5.
27. Carpenter, *No Woman's World*, pp. 310–12.
28. Caldwell Sorel, *The Women Who Wrote the War*, pp. 351–3.

29. MacVane, *On the Air in World War II*, pp. 314–15.
30. Caldwell Sorel, *The Women Who Wrote the War*, p. 353.
31. Carpenter, *No Woman's World*, pp. 316–17.
32. Penrose, *Lee Miller's War*, p. 177.
33. *New Orleans Times-Picayune*, "Yanks Bitter at Nazi Brutality," Apr. 21, 1945.
34. Knightley, *The First Casualty*, p. 360.
35. Moorehead, *A Late Education*, pp. 151–3.
36. Knightley, *The First Casualty*, p. 346.
37. Bradley, *War Correspondent*, pp. 131, 133–5, 143, 175–7, 180.
38. Wiant, *Between the Bylines*, pp. 258, 263–6, 274–5, 281–2, 290, 302, 319–20, 324.

18 The Camps Inside Germany

1. Hynes et al., *Reporting World War II*, Part 1, pp. 355–6; Murrow, *In Search of Light*, pp. 54–5.
2. Sterne, *Combat Correspondents*, pp. 178–80.
3. Osmar White, *Conquerors' Road*, pp. 90–2.
4. Sterne, *Combat Correspondents*, pp. 186–8.
5. Stenbuck, *Typewriter Battalion*, pp. 319–22.
6. Murrow, *In Search of Light*, pp. 90–4.
7. Collier, *The Warcos*, p. 189.
8. Romeiser, *Beachhead Don*, p. 350.
9. May, *Witness to War*, pp. 66, 82–91, 17, 20.
10. Osmar White, *Conquerors' Road*, pp. 78, 80–3, 87–9.
11. Stringer, *"Bravo, Amerikanski!"*, pp. 58–9.
12. Penrose, *Lee Miller's War*, pp. 161, 163, 165.
13. Ward, *Number One Boy*, pp. 227–8.
14. Hawkins, *War Report*, pp. 316–17.
15. Denis Johnston, *Nine Rivers from Jordan*, pp. 393–5.
16. Miall, *Richard Dimbleby, Broadcaster*, pp. 42–3, 47–8; Crook, *International Radio Journalism*, p. 202.
17. Dawson, *European Victory*, pp. 291–4, 296, 298–9.
18. Moorehead, *Eclipse*, pp. 262–4, 266–7.
19. Richard McMillan, *Miracle before Berlin*, pp. 141–6.
20. Knightley, *The First Casualty*, p. 346.
21. R. W. Thompson, *Men Under Fire*, pp. vii, 135, 139–40, 144.
22. May, *Witness to War*, pp. 87–91.
23. Sam Dann, *29 Dachau 1945*, pp. 14–16, 18, 22.
24. Stringer, *"Bravo, Amerikanski!"*, pp. 58–9, 61–2.
25. Collier, *The Warcos*, pp. 189–90.
26. Gellhorn, *The Face of War*, pp. 235–40; Stenbuck, *Typewriter Battalion*, pp. 334–44.
27. Penrose, *Lee Miller's War*, pp. 181–2, 187, 189.
28. Hawkins, *War Report*, pp. 319–20.
29. Crook, *International Radio Journalism*, p. 207.

19 The End of the War in Europe

1. Stringer, *"Bravo, Amerikanski!"*, pp. 63–6, 68–70, 72.
2. Hawkins, *War Report*, pp. 330–1.
3. Cloud and Olson, *The Murrow Boys*, pp. 235–6.
4. Caldwell Sorel, *The Women Who Wrote the War*, pp. 365–9.
5. Stenbuck, *Typewriter Battalion*, pp. 306–14, 323–9.
6. MacVane, *On the Air in World War II*, pp. 335, 338–9, 342, 345, 371, 374.
7. Sterne, *Combat Correspondents*, pp. 190–1.

8. Louis L. Snyder and Richard B. Morris, *A Treasury of Great Reporting*, pp. 687–8; Hohenberg, *Foreign Correspondence*, p. 230.
9. Hawkins, *War Report*, p. 329.
10. Monks, *Eyewitness*, pp. 242–3.
11. May, *Witness to War*, pp. 86–7.
12. Penrose, *Lee Miller's War*, pp. 191, 193, 197–9.
13. Royle, *War Report*, pp. 167–8.
14. Moorehead, *Eclipse*, pp. 284, 287, 289, 291–3, 296.
15. Read, *The Power of News*, p. 226.
16. Beevor and Vinogradova, *A Writer at War*, pp. 331–2, 338, 342.
17. Kennedy, *Ed Kennedy's War*, pp. 155–68, 170–6, 180–2, 185, 188–9, 192, 194, 200–1; Oldfield, *Never a Shot in Anger*, pp. 243–4, 246–54, 257; Associated Press, *Breaking News*, p. 236; Osmar White, *Conquerors' Road*, pp. 114–15.
18. *Daily Telegraph*, "Stop the Press! Apology for Reporter Sacked Over War Scoop," May 5, 2012.
19. Voss, *Reporting the War*, p. 196.

20 Final Battles in the Pacific

1. Sherrod, *On to Westward*, pp. 45, 47, 52.
2. Sterne, *Combat Correspondents*, p. 234.
3. Sherrod, *On to Westward*, pp. 56, 59, 61–2, 68, 78, 80.
4. Ibid., pp. 88–92; Harold J. Goldberg, *D-Day in the Pacific*, pp. 225–7; Holland M. Smith, *Coral and Brass*, pp. 179–80.
5. Sherrod, *On to Westward*, p. xii.
6. Ibid., pp. 143–8.
7. Sterne, *Combat Correspondents*, pp. 239–41.
8. Burchett, *At the Barricades*, pp. 94–100.
9. Legg, *War Correspondent*, pp. 91, 95–6, 98–9, 103.
10. Morris, *Deadline Every Minute*, p. 279; Dunn, *Pacific Microphone*, pp. 255–6.
11. Burchett, *At the Barricades*, pp. 104–5.
12. Morris, *Deadline Every Minute*, pp. 280–2; Hohenberg, *Foreign Correspondence*, pp. 235–6.
13. Stenbuck, *Typewriter Battalion*, pp. 253–63.
14. Wade, *Forward Positions*, pp. 59–61.
15. www.54warcorrespondents-kia-30-ww2.com.chapter15.html.
16. Mydans, *More than Meets the Eye*, pp. 183, 186, 188–95.
17. Burgess, *Warco*, pp. 100, 105.
18. Mydans, *More than Meets the Eye*, pp. 206, 208, 209.
19. Morris, *Deadline Every Minute*, pp. 282–3.
20. Wade, *Forward Positions*, p. 62; Stenbuck, *Typewriter Battalion*, pp. 281–4.
21. Sterne, *Combat Correspondents*, pp. 244–5.
22. Sherrod, *On to Westward*, pp. 156, 169, xii, 174–5.
23. Miller, *The Story of Ernie Pyle*, pp. 412–13.
24. Sherrod, *On to Westward*, pp. 176, 178, 180, 182–4, 189, 293.
25. Sterne, *Combat Correspondents*, p. 248.
26. Sherrod, *On to Westward*, pp. 199–200.
27. Sterne, *Combat Correspondents*, pp. 250–1, 253.
28. Sherrod, *On to Westward*, p. 270.
29. Nichols, *Ernie's War*, p. 668; journalism.indiana.edu (Ernie Pyle) Wartime Columns.
30. Sherrod, *On to Westward*, pp. 281, 296; James Tobin, *Ernie Pyle's War*, p. 239.
31. Desmond, *Tides of War*, p. 435.
32. Miller, *The Story of Ernie Pyle*, p. 427; Nichols, *Ernie's War*, pp. 53–4, 58–9; James Tobin, *Ernie Pyle's War*, pp. 2, 4.

21 Victory over Japan

1. Wade, *Forward Positions*, pp. 73, 75.
2. William L. Laurence, *Dawn Over Zero*, pp. 171, 173–9, 181–3, 185, 187, 189–94, 196–201, 203.
3. Wade, *Forward Positions*, p. 76.
4. Legg, *War Correspondent*, pp. 233, 256.
5. Canham, *Commitment to Freedom*, p. 307; Burgess, *Warco*, p. 102.
6. George Johnston, *Journey through Tomorrow*, pp. 388–90.
7. Wade, *Forward Positions*, pp. 81–3.
8. Weller, *Weller's War*, pp. 608–9.
9. Wade, *Forward Positions*, p. 84.
10. Burchett, *At the Barricades*, pp. 107–10, 112–16; Christiansen, *Headlines All My Life*, p. 216.
11. Nuclear Age Peace Foundation article by Amy Goodman and David Goodman, "Hiroshima Cover-up: How the War Department's Timesman Won a Pulitzer," Aug. 10, 2004; Wade, *Forward Positions*, pp. 86, 89.
12. Weller, *Weller's War*, pp. 602–3; George Weller, *First into Nagasaki*, pp. 3–5, 8, 11, 15–20, 22, 30, 43, 50, 56, 58.
13. Clark Lee, *One Last Look Around*, pp. 125–6; en.wikipedia.org/wiki/Joseph_Meisinger.
14. Lee, *One Last Look Around*, pp. 94, 96, 99–102, 104–7, 110–13.
15. Cooper, *Kent Cooper and the Associated Press*, p. 251.
16. Stein, *Under Fire*, pp. 147–8; *Guardian*, "Revealed: How Associated Press Cooperated with the Nazis," Mar. 30, 2016; Harsch, *At the Hinge of History*, p. 45; Shirer, *The Nightmare Years*, p. 579.

22 After the War

1. Murrow, *In Search of Light*, p. 97.
2. *New York Times*, "Edward R. Murrow, Broadcaster and Ex-Chief of U.S.I.A., Dies," Apr. 28, 1965.
3. *New York Times*, "Walter Cronkite, 92, Dies; Trusted Voice of TV News," July 18, 2009.
4. *New York Times*, "Winston Burdett Is Dead at 79; Covered World and War for CBS," May 21, 1993.
5. *New York Times*, "Eric Sevareid, 79, Is Dead; Commentator and Reporter," July 10, 1992.
6. *New York Times*, "William L. Shirer, Author, Is Dead at 89," Dec. 29, 1993.
7. *New York Times*, "Larry LeSueur, Pioneering War Correspondent, Dies at 93," Feb. 7, 2003.
8. *New York Times*, "Charles Collingwood Is Dead; CBS Correspondent was 68," Oct. 4, 1985.
9. Jonathan Dimbleby, *Richard Dimbleby*, pp. 194–5; Miall, *Richard Dimbleby, Broadcaster*, pp. 49, 53–6.
10. Read, *The Power of News*, pp. 226, 228.
11. Moorehead, *A Late Education*, pp. 143, 145–6, 165–6, 170–1; en.wikipedia.org/wiki/Alan_Moorehead; Christiansen, *Headlines All My Life*, pp. 207, 246.
12. Harsch, *At the Hinge of History*, pp. 128–9; en.wikipedia.org/wiki/Joseph_C._Harsch.
13. Weller, *First into Nagasaki*, pp. 177, 179, 182, 185, 238, 297, 301, 305–6.
14. *New York Times*, "Robert J. Casey Is Dead at 72," Dec. 5, 1962.
15. Whitehead, *Combat Reporter*, p. 7; Caldwell Sorel, *The Women Who Wrote the War*, p. 395.
16. en.wikipedia.org/wiki/Hal_Boyle.
17. Stringer, *"Bravo, Amerikanski!"*, pp. 127–8, 143–5, 149.
18. *Los Angeles Times*, "Daniel De Luce, 90; '44 Pulitzer Winner," Jan. 31, 2002.
19. en.wikipedia.org/wiki/Lee_Miller.

20. Caldwell Sorel, *The Women Who Wrote the War*, p. 394; en.wikipedia.org/wiki/Martha_Gellhorn.

21. Caldwell Sorel, *The Women Who Wrote the War*, pp. 393–4; en.wikipedia.org/wiki/Virginia_Cowles.

22. May, *Witness to War*, pp. 93–4, 98–9; Caldwell Sorel, *The Women Who Wrote the War*, pp. 396–7; Sevareid, *Not So Wild a Dream*, p. 169.

23. Wade, *Forward Positions*, pp. 221–2, 226; Stenbuck, *Typewriter Battalion*, p. 263.

24. *New York Times*, "Eleanor Packard, War Reporter and Rome Correspondent, Dies," May 5, 1972; *New York Times*, "Reynolds Packard Dies; Covered Wars on 4 Continents Since '30s," Oct. 16, 1976.

25. *Washington Post*, "Correspondent Russell J. Hill; Covered WWII and Postwar Europe," Aug. 20, 2007.

26. en.wikipedia.org/wiki/Quentin_Reynolds.

27. Royle, *War Report*, pp. 149, 173.

28. Osmar White, *Conquerors' Road*, pp. 117, 199, 130, 179–80, 195; en.wikipedia.org/wiki/Osmar_White.

29. en.wikipedia.org/wiki/Wilfred_Burchett.

30. en.wikipedia.org/wiki/George_Johnston.

31. en.wikipedia.org/wiki/Noel_Monks.

32. *Independent*, "Edward Ward," May 10, 1993.

33. *Southern Reporter*, "Patrick Francis Maitland," Dec. 9, 2008.

34. Gary L. Atkins, *Imagining Gay Paradise*, pp. 146, 149–51.

35. John Maxwell Hamilton, *Journalism's Roving Eye*, pp. 327–8, 330.

36. en.wikipedia.org/wiki/Robert_Sherrod.

37. Beevor and Vinogradova, *A Writer at War*, pp. 344–5, 347–60.

38. en.wikipedia.org/wiki/Ilya_Ehrenburg.

39. Gorrell, *Soldier of the Press*, pp. ix, x.

40. en.wikipedia.org/wiki/Helen_Kirkpatrick.

41. www.findagrave.com/cgi-bin/fg.cgi?page=psr&GScid=81071; Wagner, *Women War Correspondents*, p. 28.

42. en.wikipedia.org/wiki/Eve_Curie.

43. en.wikipedia.org/Leland_Stowe.

44. en.wikipedia.org/wiki/Robert_St._John.

45. *New York Times*, "Clark Lee Is Dead; War Reporter, 46," Feb. 16, 1953.

46. en.wikipedia.org/wiki/Carl_Mydans.

47. *New York Times*, "Cyrus L. Sulzberger, Columnist, Dies at 80," Sept. 21, 1993.

48. *New York Times*, "Drew Middleton of The Times Dies at 76," Jan. 12, 1990.

49. *New York Times*, "Otto D. Tolischus of Times, 76, Dies," Feb. 25, 1967.

50. Caldwell Sorel, *The Women Who Wrote the War*, pp. 385, 392–3; en.wikipedia.org/wiki/Raymond_Daniell.

51. *New York Times*, "Wes Gallagher, 86, President and General Manager of A.P.," Oct. 23, 1997.

52. en.wikipedia.org/wiki/Ross_Munro.

53. *Daily Telegraph*, "Godfrey Talbot," Sept. 5, 2000.

54. *New York Times*, "John MacVane Dies; Radio Correspondent," Feb. 24, 1984.

55. *Los Angeles Times*, "Frank Tremaine, 92; Wire Reporter Sent Pearl Harbor News Flash," Dec. 24, 2006.

56. *Chicago Tribune*, "Tribune Writer John Thompson," Dec. 15, 1995.

57. *New York Times*, "Frank Gervasi, Author and Correspondent, 82," Jan. 22, 1990.

58. *New York Times*, "William Walton Dead at 84," Dec. 20, 1994.

59. *Daily Telegraph*, "Clare Hollingworth: I Saw the Tanks Lined Up Ready to Invade Poland," Oct. 8, 2011.

BIBLIOGRAPHY

Ambrose, Stephen E., *D-Day, June 6, 1944*, Simon & Schuster, New York, 1994.
Associated Press (eds), *Breaking News*, Princeton Architectural Press, Princeton, 2007.
Atkins, Gary L., *Imagining Gay Paradise*, Hong Kong University Press, Hong Kong, 2012.
Baillie, Hugh, *High Tension*, Harper & Brothers, New York, 1959.
Baker, Carlos, *Ernest Hemingway*, Charles Scribner's Sons, New York, 1969.
Bassow, Whitman, *The Moscow Correspondents*, William Morris, New York, 1988.
Beattie, Edward W., *Diary of a Kriegie*, Thomas Y. Crowell, New York, 1946.
—— *Passport to War*, Peter Davies, London, 1943.
Beevor, Antony, and Vinogradova, Luba (eds), *A Writer at War*, Pimlico, London, 2006.
Belden, Jack, *Retreat with Stilwell*, Cassell, London, 1943.
—— *Still Time to Die*, Victor Gollancz, London, 1945.
Bennett, Lowell, *Parachute to Berlin*, Vanguard Press, New York, 1945.
Boothe, Clare, *European Spring*, Hamish Hamilton, London, 1940.
Boyle, Hal, *Help, Help! Another Day!*, Associated Press, New York, 1969.
Bradley, Holbrook, *War Correspondent*, iUniverse Inc., New York, 2007.
Brines, Russell, *Until They Eat Stones*, J.B. Lippincott, Philadelphia, 1944.
Brock, Ray, *Nor Any Victory*, Reynal & Hitchcock, New York, 1942.
Brown, Cecil, *From Suez to Singapore*, Random House, New York, 1942.
Brown, Robert J., *Manipulating the Ether*, McFarland & Co., Jefferson, NC, 1998.
Buckley, Christopher, *The Road to Rome*, Hodder & Stoughton, London, 1945.
Burchett, Wilfred, *At the Barricades*, Quartet Books, London, 1980.
Burgess, Pat, *Warco*, William Heinemann Australia, Melbourne, 1986.
Busvine, Richard, *Gullible Travels*, Constable, London, 1945.
Caldwell, Erskine, *Moscow Under Fire*, Hutchinson, London, 1941.
Caldwell Sorel, Nancy, *The Women Who Wrote the War*, Arcade Publishing, New York, 1999.
Canham, Erwin D., *Commitment to Freedom*, Houghton Mifflin, Boston, 1958.
Carroll, Gordon, editor, *History in the Writing*, Duell, Sloan & Pearce, New York, 1945.
Carroll, Wallace, *We're in This with Russia*, Houghton Mifflin, Boston, 1942.
Carpenter, Iris, *No Woman's World*, Houghton Mifflin, Boston, 1946.
Casey, Robert J., *I Can't Forget!*, Bobbs-Merrill, New York, 1941.
—— *This Is Where I Came In*, Bobbs-Merrill, New York, 1945.
—— *Torpedo Junction*, Jarrold's, London, 1944.
Cassidy, Henry C., *Moscow Dateline 1941–1943*, Cassell, London, 1943.
Christiansen, Arthur, *Headlines All My Life*, Heinemann, London, 1961.
Clifford, Alexander, *Three Against Rommel*, George G. Harrap, London, 1943.

Cloud, Stanley, and Olson, Lynn, *The Murrow Boys*, Houghton Mifflin Co., Boston, 1996.

Collier, Richard, *The Warcos*, Weidenfeld and Nicolson, London, 1989.

Cooper, Kent, *Kent Cooper and the Associated Press*, Random House, New York, 1959.

Cowles, Virginia, *Looking for Trouble*, Hamish Hamilton, London, 1941.

Cronkite, Walter, *A Reporter's Life*, Alfred A. Knopf, 1996.

Crook, Tim, *International Radio Journalism*, Routledge, London, 1998.

Curie, Eve, *Journey Among Warriors*, William Heinemann Ltd., London, 1943.

Daniell, Raymond, *Civilians Must Fight*, Doubleday, Doran & Co., Garden City, NY, 1941.

Dann, Sam, editor, *Dachau 29 April 1945*, Texas Tech University Press, Lubbock, TX, 1998.

Darnton, John, *Almost a Family*, Alfred A. Knopf, New York, 2011.

Dawson, John D'Arcy, *European Victory*, MacDonald & Co., London, 1945.

—— *Tunisian Battle,* MacDonald & Co., London, 1943.

Delmer, Sefton, *Trail Sinister*, Secker & Warburg, London, 1961.

Denny, Harold, *Behind Both Lines*, Michael Joseph, London, 1943.

Desmond, Robert W., *Tides of War*, University of Iowa Press, Iowa City, 1984.

Dew, Gwen, *Prisoner of the Japs*, Alfred A. Knopf, New York, 1943.

Dimbleby, Jonathan, *Richard Dimbleby*, Hodder & Stoughton, London, 1975.

Dimbleby, Richard, *The Frontiers Are Green*, Hodder & Stoughton, 1943.

Dunn, William J., *Pacific Microphone*, Texas A&M University Press, College Station, 1988.

Ehrenburg, Ilya, *Russia at War*, Hamish Hamilton, London, 1943.

—— *The War 1941–5*, MacGibbon & Kee, London, 1964.

Eskelund, Karl, *My Chinese Wife*, George G. Harrap, London, 1946.

Fredborg, Arvid, *Behind the Steel Wall*, George G. Harrap, London, 1944.

Gallagher, O'D., *Retreat in the East*, George G. Harrap, London, 1942.

Gallagher, Wes, *Back Door to Berlin*, Doubleday, Doran and Co., Garden City, New York, 1943.

Garrett, Patrick, *Of Fortunes and War*, Thistle Publishing, London, 2015.

Gellhorn, Martha, *The Face of War*, Rupert Hart-Davis, London, 1959.

Gervasi, Frank, *The Violent Decade*, W. W. Norton, New York, 1989.

Gilmore, Eddy, *Me and My Russian Wife*, W. Foulsham, London, undated.

Goldberg, Harold J., *D-Day in the Pacific*, Indiana University Press, Bloomington and Indiapanolis, 2007.

Gorrell, Henry, *Soldier of the Press*, University of Missouri Press, Columbia, 2009.

Graebner, Walter, *Round Trip to Russia*, J. B. Lippincott, New York, 1943.

Gray, Bernard, *War Reporter*, Robert Hale, London, 1942.

Guard, Harold, *The Pacific War Uncensored*, Casemate, Philadelphia and Newbury, 2011.

Gunnison, Royal Arch, *So Sorry No Peace*, Viking Press, New York, 1944.

Hailey, Foster, *Pacific Battle Line*, Macmillan, New York, 1944.

Hamilton, Jim, *The Writing 69th*, Green Harbor Publications, Marshfield, MA, 1999.

Hamilton, John Maxwell, *Journalism's Roving Eye*, LSU Press, Baton Rouge, LA, 2009.

Harsch, Joseph C., *At the Hinge of History*, University of Georgia Press, Athens, GA, 1993.

—— *Pattern of Conquest*, William Heinemann, London, 1942.

Hastings, Max, *All Hell Let Loose*, Harper Press, London, 2011.

Hawkins, Desmond, *War Report*, Ariel Books, London, 1946.

Heckler, Cheryl, *An Accidental Journalist*, University of Missouri Press, Columbia, 2007.

Hill, Russell, *Desert Conquest*, Jarrolds, London, 1943.

—— *Desert War*, Jarrolds, London, 1942.

Hohenberg, John, *Foreign Correspondence*, Syracuse University Press, Syracuse, NY, 1995.

Hollingworth, Clare, *Front Line*, Jonathan Cape, London, 1990.

Huddle, Mark, *Roi Ottley's World War II*, University Press of Kansas, Lawrence, 2011.

Huss, Pierre J., *Heil! And Farewell*, Herbert Jenkins Ltd., London, 1943.

Hynes, Samuel; Matthews, Anne; Caldwell Sorel, Nancy; Spiller, Roger J., *Reporting World War II, Parts One and Two*, Library of America, New York, 1995.

Johnston, Denis, *Nine Rivers from Jordan*, Derek Verschoyle, London, 1953.

Johnston, George H., *Journey through Tomorrow*, F. W. Cheshire, Melbourne, 1947.

—— *The Toughest Fighting in the World*, Westholme, Yardley, Pennsylvania, 2011.

Johnston, Stanley, *Queen of the Flat-tops*, Bantam Books, New York, 1984.

Jordan, Philip, *Russian Glory*, Cresset Press, London, 1942.

Kennedy, Ed, *Ed Kennedy's War*, Louisiana State University Press, Baton Rouge, 2012.

Kirkpatrick, Helen P., *Under the British Umbrella*, Charles Scribner's Sons, New York, 1939.

Knightley, Phillip, *The First Casualty*, Johns Hopkins University Press, Baltimore, MD, 2004.

Laurence, William L., *Dawn Over Zero*, Museum Press, London, 1947.

Lee, Clark, *One Last Look Around*, Duell, Sloan and Pearce, New York, 1947.

—— *They Call It Pacific*, John Long Ltd., London, 1943.

Legg, Frank, *War Correspondent*, Angus & Robertson, London, 1965.

LeSueur, Larry, *Twelve Months that Changed the World*, George G. Harrap & Co., London, 1944.

Liebling, A. J., *Normandy Revisited*, Victor Gollancz, London, 1959.

—— *The Road Back to Paris*, Michael Joseph, London, 1944.

Lochner, Louis, *What about Germany?*, Hodder & Stoughton, London, 1943.

MacVane, John, *On the Air in World War II*, William Morrow, New York, 1979.

—— *War and Diplomacy in North Africa*, Robert Hale Ltd., London, 1944.

Maitland, Patrick, *European Dateline*, Quality Press, London, 1946.

Malaparte, Curzio, *Kaputt*, New York Review Books, New York, 2005.

—— *Il Volga Nasce in Europa*, Bompiani, Milan, 1943.

Massock, Richard G., *Italy from Within*, Macmillan & Co., London, 1943.

Matthews, Herbert, *The Education of a Correspondent*, Harcourt, Brace, New York, 1946.

Matthews, Joseph J., *Reporting the Wars*, University of Minnesota Press, Minneapolis, 1957.

May, Antoinette, *Witness to War*, Beaufort Books, New York, 1983.

McMillan, Richard, *Miracle before Berlin*, Jarrolds, London, 1946.

—— *Rendezvous with Rommel*, Jarrolds, London, 1943.

Miall, Leonard, *Richard Dimbleby, Broadcaster*, BBC, London, 1966.

Michie, Allan A., *Retreat to Victory*, George Allen & Unwin, London, 1942.

Middleton, Drew, *The Sky Suspended*, Secker & Warburg, London, 1960.

—— *Where Has Last July Gone?*, Quadrangle, New York Times Books, New York, 1973.

Miller, Lee G., *The Story of Ernie Pyle*, The Viking Press, New York, 1950.

Miller, Webb, *I Found No Peace*, Victor Gollancz, London, 1937.

Mitgang, Herbert, *Newsmen in Khaki*, Lanham, MD, Taylor Trade Publishing, 2004.

Monks, Noel, *Eyewitness*, Frederick Muller, London, 1955.

Moorehead, Alan, *African Trilogy*, Hamish Hamilton, London, 1944.

—— *Eclipse*, Hamish Hamilton, London, 1945.

—— *A Late Education*, Penguin Books, London, 1976.

Moorehead, Caroline, *The Letters of Martha Gellhorn*, Chatto & Windus, London, 2006.

Morris, Joe Alex, *Deadline Every Minute*, Greenwood Press, New York, 1968.

Munro, Ross, *Gauntlet to Overlord*, Macmillan, Toronto, 1946.

Murrow, Edward R., *In Search of Light*, Macmillan, London, 1967.

—— *This Is London*, Cassell, London, 1941.

Mydans, Carl, *More than Meets the Eye*, Hutchinson, London, 1961.

Nichols, David, *Ernie's War*, G. K. Hall & Co., Boston, 1986.

Oechsner, Frederick, *This Is the Enemy*, William Heinemann Ltd., London, 1943.

Oldfield, Colonel Barney, *Never a Shot in Anger*, Capra Press, Santa Barbara, 1956.

Packard, Reynolds, *Rome Was My Beat*, Lyle Stuart, Secaucus, NJ, 1975.

Packard, Reynolds and Packard, Eleanor, *Balcony Empire*, Chatto & Windus, London, 1943.

Panter-Downes, Mollie, *London War Notes 1939–1945*, Longman, London, 1971.

Penrose, Antony, *Lee Miller's War*, Condé Nast Books, London, 1992.

Pyle, Ernie, *Brave Men*, Greenwood Press, Westport, CT, 1974.

Read, Donald, *The Power of News*, Oxford University Press, Oxford, 1992.

Reston, James, *Deadline: A Memoir*, Random House, New York, 1991.

Reynolds, Quentin, *By Quentin Reynolds*, Heinemann, London, 1964.

Robertson, Ben, *I Saw England*, Jarrolds, London, 1941.

Romeiser, John B., *Beachhead Don*, Fordham University Press, New York, 2004.

Rooney, Andy, *My War*, Public Affairs, New York, 1995.
Royle, Trevor, *War Report*, Mainstream Publishing, London, 1987.
Salisbury, Harrison, *A Journey for Our Times*, Harper & Row, New York, 1983.
Salter, Cedric, *Flight from Poland*, Faber & Faber, London, 1940.
Sevareid, Eric, *Not So Wild a Dream*, University of Missouri Press, Columbia, 1946.
Shapiro, Lionel S. B., *They Left the Back Door Open*, Jarrolds, London, 1944.
Sherrod, Robert, *On to Westward*, Duell, Sloan and Pearce, New York, 1945.
—— *Tarawa: The Story of a Battle*, Admiral Nimitz Foundation, Fredericksburg, TX, 1973.
Shirer, William, *Berlin Diary*, Book of the Month Club, New York, 1987.
—— *The Nightmare Years, 1930–1940*, Little, Brown & Co., Boston, MA, 1984.
Simonov, Konstantin, *Always a Journalist*, Progress Publishers, Moscow, 1989.
Smith, Holland M., *Coral and Brass*, Zenger Publishing Co., Washington, DC, 1948.
Smith, Howard K., *Last Train from Berlin*, The Book Club, London, 1943.
Snyder, Louis L. and Morris, Richard B., *A Treasury of Great Reporting*, Simon & Schuster, New York, 1949.
St. John, Robert, *Foreign Correspondent*, Hutchinson, London, 1960.
—— *From the Land of Silent People*, George G. Harrap, London, 1942.
Stein, M. L., *Under Fire*, Julian Messner, New York, 1968.
Steinbeck, John, *Once There Was a War*, Penguin Books, London, 1994.
Stenbuck, Jack, *Typewriter Battalion*, William Morrow, New York, 1995.
Sterne, Joseph R. L., *Combat Correspondents*, Maryland Historical Society, Baltimore, 2009.
Storey, Graham, *Reuters' Century*, Max Parrish, London, 1951.
Stowe, Leland, *No Other Road to Freedom*, Faber & Faber Ltd, London, 1942.
—— *They Shall Not Sleep*, Alfred A. Knopf, New York, 1945.
Stringer, Ann, *"Bravo, Amerikanski!"*, as told to Mark Scott, 1st Books Library, 2000.
Stursberg, Peter, *The Sound of War*, University of Toronto Press, Toronto, 1993.
Sulzberger, Cyrus, *A Long Row of Candles*, MacDonald, London, 1969.
Talbot, Godfrey, *Speaking from the Desert*, Hutchinson, London, undated.
Thompson, R. W., *Men Under Fire*, MacDonald, London, undated.
Tobin, James, *Ernie Pyle's War*, The Free Press, New York, 1997.
Tobin, Richard, *Invasion Journal*, E. P. Dutton, New York, 1944.
Tolischus, Otto D., *They Wanted War*, Hamish Hamilton, London, 1940.
—— *Tokyo Record*, Hamish Hamilton, London, 1943.
Treanor, Tom, *One Damn Thing after Another*, The Country Life Press, Garden City, NY, 1944.
Tregaskis, Richard, *Guadalcanal Diary*, Random House, New York, 1943.
—— *Invasion Diary*, Random House, New York, 1944.
Tremaine, Frank and Tremaine, Kay, *The Attack on Pearl Harbor*, Admiral Nimitz Foundation, Fredericksburg, TX, 1997.
Voss, Frederick S., *Reporting the War*, Smithsonian Institution Press, Washington, DC, 1994.
Wade, Betsy, *Forward Positions*, University of Arkansas Press, Fayetteville, 1992.
Wagner, Lilya, *Women War Correspondents of World War II*, Greenwood Press, New York, 1989.
Walker, David, *Death at My Heels*, Chapman & Hall, London, 1942.
Ward, Edward, *Dispatches from Finland*, John Lane, London, 1940.
—— *Number One Boy*, Michael Joseph, London, 1969.
Wason, Betty, *Miracle in Hellas*, Museum Press Ltd., London, 1943.
Waterfield, Gordon, *What Happened to France*, John Murray, London, 1940.
Weller, George, *First into Nagasaki*, Crown Publishers, New York, 2006.
—— *Weller's War*, Crown Publishers, New York, 2009.
Welsh, Mary, *How It Was*, Alfred A. Knopf, New York, 1976.
Werth, Alexander, *The Last Days of Paris*, Hamish Hamilton, London, 1940.
—— *Leningrad*, Hamish Hamilton, London, 1944.
—— *Moscow '41*, Hamish Hamilton, London, 1942.
—— *Russia at War 1941–1945*, Carroll & Graf, New York, 1964.
—— *The Year of Stalingrad*, Hamish Hamilton, London, 1946.
Wheeler, Keith, *The Pacific Is My Beat*, F. E. Robinson & Co., London, 1945.

White, Leigh, *The Long Balkan Night*, Charles Scribner's Sons, New York, 1944.

White, Osmar, *Conquerors' Road*, Cambridge University Press, 1996.

—— *Green Armour*, Corgi Books, London, 1945.

White, Theodore, *In Search of History*, Jonathan Cape, London, 1979.

White, Theodore and Jacoby, Annalee, *Thunder Out of China*, Victor Gollancz, London, 1947.

Whitehead, Don, *Combat Reporter*, Fordham University Press, New York, 2006.

Wiant, Susan, *Between the Bylines*, Fordham University Press, New York, 2011.

Wilmot, Chester, *Tobruk 1941*, Angus & Robertson, London, 1945.

Wolfert, Ira, *Battle for the Solomons*, Jarrolds, London, 1943.

Wood, Alan, *The Falaise Road*, W. H. Allen, London, 1944.

Woodward, David, *Front Line and Front Page*, Eyre & Spottiswoode, London, 1943.

Young, Gordon, *Outposts of Victory*, Hodder & Stoughton, London, 1943.

—— *Outposts of War*, Hodder & Stoughton, London, 1941.

INDEX

ILLUSTRATION CREDITS